Beyond Disney®

THE *unofficial* **GUIDE**®
ᵀᴼUniversal®, SeaWorld®,
and the Best of
Central Florida

STH EDITION

Typhoon Lagoon - Disney

Beyond Disney®

THE *unofficial* GUIDE® to Universal®, SeaWorld®, and the Best of Central Florida

5TH EDITION

BOB SEHLINGER *and* GRANT RAFTER
with
KATIE BRANDON

WILEY

Please note that prices fluctuate in the course of time and that travel information changes under the impact of many factors that influence the travel industry. We therefore suggest that you write or call ahead for confirmation when making your travel plans. Every effort has been made to ensure the accuracy of information throughout this book, and the contents of this publication are believed to be correct at the time of printing. Nevertheless, the publishers cannot accept responsibility for errors or omissions, for changes in details given in this guide, or for the consequences of any reliance on the information provided by the same. Assessments of attractions and so forth are based upon the authors' own experiences; therefore, descriptions given in this guide necessarily contain an element of subjective opinion, which may not reflect the publisher's opinion or dictate a reader's own experience on another occasion. Readers are invited to write the publisher with ideas, comments, and suggestions for future editions.

Published by:
John Wiley & Sons, Inc.
111 River Street
Hoboken, NJ 07030-5774

Produced by Menasha Ridge Press

Cover design by Michael J. Freeland

Interior design by Vertigo Design

For information on our other products and services or to obtain technical support, please contact our Customer Care Department within the United States at 800-762-2974, outside the United States at 317-572-3993, or by fax at 317-572-4002.

John Wiley & Sons, Inc., also publishes its books in a variety of electronic formats. Some content that appears in print may not be available in electronic formats.

ISBN 978-0-470-09843-1

Manufactured in the United States of America

5 4 3 2 1

CONTENTS

LIST *of* MAPS

ABOUT *the* AUTHORS

BOB SEHLINGER is the author of *The Unofficial Guide to Walt Disney World* and the executive publisher of the *Unofficial Guide* series.

GRANT RAFTER is a graduate of Dartmouth College and a veteran *Unofficial Guide* hotel inspector and researcher. He makes his home in Maine.

KATIE BRANDON is a 2004 graduate of the University of Florida College of Journalism.

Beyond Disney®

THE *unofficial* GUIDE®
TO Universal®, SeaWorld®, and the Best of Central Florida

5TH EDITION

INTRODUCTION

WHY *"Unofficial"*?

THE AUTHORS AND RESEARCHERS OF THIS GUIDE specifically and categorically declare that they are and always have been totally independent. The material in this guide originated with the authors and has not been reviewed, edited, or in any way approved by the companies whose travel products are discussed. The purpose of this guide is to provide you with the information necessary to tour central Florida with the greatest efficiency and economy and with the least hassle and stress. In this guide we represent and serve you, the consumer. If a restaurant serves bad food, or a gift item is overpriced, or a certain ride isn't worth the wait, we can say so, and in the process we hope to make your visit more fun, efficient, and economical.

THERE'S *another* WORLD *out* THERE

IF YOU THINK THAT CENTRAL FLORIDA consists only of Walt Disney World, you're wrong. What's more, you're passing up some great fun and amazing sights. Admittedly, it's taken a while, but Walt Disney World now has plenty of competition that measures up toe-to-toe. And though it may sound blasphemous to suggest a whole vacation in central Florida without setting foot on Disney property, it's not only possible but also in many ways a fresh and appealing idea.

The big four non-Disney theme parks are Universal Studios Florida, Universal Islands of Adventure, SeaWorld, and Busch Gardens. Each is unique. Universal Studios Florida, a longtime rival of the Disney-MGM Studios, draws its inspiration from movies and television and is every bit the equal of the Disney movie-themed park. Universal Islands of Adventure is arguably the most modern, high-tech theme park in the United States, featuring an all-star lineup of thrill rides that make it the best park in Florida for older kids and young-at-heart adults. SeaWorld provides an incomparable glimpse into the world of marine mammals and fish, served up in a way that (for the most part) eliminates those never-ending lines. Finally, Busch Gardens, with its shows, zoological exhibits, and knockout coasters, offers the most eclectic entertainment mix of any theme park we know. All four parks approximate, equal, or exceed the Disney standard without imitating Disney, successfully blending distinctive presentations and personalities into every attraction.

In addition to the big four, there are several specialty parks that are also worthy of your attention. The Kennedy Space Center Visitor Complex at Cape Canaveral provides an inside look at the past, present, and future of America's space program, and Gatorland showcases the alligator, one of the most ancient creatures on Earth. After closing for several years, Cypress Gardens is newly resurgent with its signature landscaping supplemented by a new lineup of rides and attractions. SeaWorld's Discovery Cove offers central Florida's first-ever dolphin swim, and the Holy Land Experience is the first Christian theme park in the state and quite likely the most elaborate one in the world. All of these places offer an experience that is different from a day at one of the big theme parks, including a respite from standing in line, all of the walking, and the frenetic pace.

But these are just for starters. In central Florida, you'll also find a vibrant dinner-theater scene, two excellent non-Disney water parks, nightlife, and great shopping, all surrounded by some of the best hiking, biking, fishing, and canoeing available anywhere.

The **ATTRACTION** that **ATE FLORIDA**

BEFORE WALT DISNEY WORLD, Florida was a happy peninsula of many more or less equal tourist attractions. Distributed around the state in great profusion, these attractions constituted the nation's most perennially appealing vacation opportunity. There were the Monkey Jungle, the Orchid Jungle, venerable Marineland, the St. Augustine Alligator Farm, Silver Springs, the Miami Wax Museum, the Sunken Gardens, the Coral Castle, and the Conch Train Tour. These, along with Cypress Gardens, Busch Gardens, and others, were the attractions that ruled Florida. Now, like so many dinosaurs, those remaining survive precariously on the leavings of the greatest beast of them all, Walt Disney World. Old standbys continue to welcome tourists, but when was the last time you planned your vacation around a visit to Jungle Larry's Safari Park?

When Walt Disney World arrived on the scene, Florida tourism changed forever. Before Disney (BD), southern Florida was the state's and the nation's foremost tourist destination. Throngs sunned on the beaches of Miami, Hollywood, and Fort Lauderdale and patronized such nearby attractions as the Miami Serpentarium and the Parrot Jungle. Attractions in the Ocala and St. Augustine areas upstate hosted road travelers in great waves as they journeyed to and from southern Florida. At the time, Orlando was a sleepy central Florida town an hour's drive from Cypress Gardens, with practically no tourist appeal whatsoever.

Then came Disney, snapping up acres of farm- and swampland before anyone even knew who the purchaser was. Bargaining hard, Walt demanded improved highways, tax concessions, bargain financing, and community support. So successful had been his California Disneyland that whatever he requested, he received.

Generally approving, and hoping for a larger aggregate market, the existing Florida attractions failed to discern the cloud on the horizon. Walt had tipped his hand early, however, and all the cards were on the table. When Disney bought 27,500 central Florida acres, it was evident he didn't intend to raise cattle.

The Magic Kingdom opened on October 1, 1971, and was immediately successful. Hotel construction boomed in Orlando, Kissimmee, and around Walt Disney World. Major new attractions popped up along recently completed Interstate 4 to cash in on the tide of tourists arriving at Disney's latest wonder. Walt Disney World became a destination, and suddenly nobody cared as much about going to the beach. The Magic Kingdom was good for two days, and then you could enjoy the rest of the week at SeaWorld, Cypress Gardens, Circus World, Gatorland, Busch Gardens, the Stars Hall of Fame Wax Museum, and the Kennedy Space Center.

These attractions, all practically new and stretching from Florida's east to west coasts, formed what would come to be called the Orlando Wall. Tourists no longer poured into Miami and Fort Lauderdale. Instead they stopped at the Orlando Wall and exhausted themselves and their dollars in the shiny attractions arrayed between Cape Canaveral and Tampa. In southern Florida, venerable attractions held on by a parrot feather, and more than a few closed their doors. Flagship hotels on the fabled Gold Coast went bust or were converted into condominiums.

When Walt Disney World opened, the very definition of a tourist attraction changed. Setting new standards for cleanliness, size, scope, grandeur, variety, and attention to detail, Walt Disney World relegated the majority of Florida's headliner attractions to comparative insignificance almost overnight. Newer attractions such as SeaWorld and the vastly enlarged Busch Gardens successfully matched the standard Disney set. Cypress Gardens, Weeki Wachi, and Silver Springs expanded and modernized. Most other attractions, however, slipped into a limbo of diminished status. Far from being headliners or tourist destinations, they plugged along as local diversions, pulling in the curious, the bored, and the sunburned for mere two-hour excursions.

Many of the affected attractions were and are wonderful places to spend a day, but even collectively they don't command sufficient appeal to lure many tourists beyond the Orlando Wall. We recommend them, however, not only for a variety of high-quality offerings but also as a glimpse of Florida's golden age, a time of less sophisticated, less plastic pleasures before the Mouse. Take a day or two and drive three-and-a-half hours south of Orlando. Visit the Miami Seaquarium, Vizcaya Museum and Gardens, Fairchild Tropical Garden, and Lion Country Safari. Drive Collins Avenue along the Gold Coast. You'll be glad you did.

When Epcot opened in Walt Disney World on October 1, 1982, another seismic shock reverberated throughout the Florida attractions industry. This time it wasn't only the smaller and more vulnerable attractions that were affected but the newer large-scale attractions along the Orlando Wall. Suddenly, Disney World swallowed up another one or two days of each tourist's vacation week. When the Magic Kingdom stood alone, most visitors had three or four days remaining to sample other attractions. With the addition of Epcot, that time was cut to one or two days.

Disney ensured its market share by creating multiday admission passes, which allowed unlimited access to both the Magic Kingdom and Epcot. More cost-efficient than a one-day pass to a single park, these passes kept the guest on Disney turf for three to five days.

Kennedy Space Center and SeaWorld, by virtue of their very specialized products, continued to prosper after Epcot opened. Most other attractions were forced to focus on local markets. Some, like Busch Gardens, did very well, with increased local support replacing the decreased numbers of Walt Disney World tourists coming over for the day. Others, like Cypress Gardens, suffered badly but worked diligently to improve their product. Some, like Circus World and the Hall of Fame Wax Museum, passed into history.

Though long an innovator, Disney turned in the mid-1980s to copying existing successful competitors. Except *copying* is not exactly the right word. What Disney did was to take a competitor's concept, improve it, and reproduce it in Disney style and on a grand scale.

The first competitor to feel the heat was SeaWorld, when Disney added the Living Seas Pavilion to the Future World section of Epcot. SeaWorld, however, had killer whales, the Shark Encounter, and sufficient corporate resources to remain preeminent among marine exhibits. Still, many Disney patrons willingly substituted a visit to the Living Seas for a visit to SeaWorld.

One of Disney's own products was threatened when the Wet 'n Wild water park took aim at the older and smaller but more aesthetically pleasing River Country. Never one to take a challenge sitting down,

Disney responded in 1989 with the opening of Typhoon Lagoon, then the world's largest swimming theme park.

Also in 1989, Disney opened Pleasure Island, a single-cover multi-nightclub entertainment complex patterned on Orlando's successful Church Street Station. Tourist traffic around the theme parks starting gravitating to Pleasure Island for nightlife rather than traveling to Church Street.

The third big Disney opening of 1989 was Disney-MGM Studios, a combination working motion picture and television production complex and theme park. Copying the long-lauded Universal Studios tour in Southern California, Disney-MGM Studios was speeded into operation after Universal announced its plans for a central Florida park.

Disney-MGM Studios, however, affected much more than Universal's plans. With the opening of Disney-MGM, the Three-Day World Passport was discontinued. Instead, Disney patrons were offered a single-day pass or the more economical multiday passports, good for either four or five days. With three theme parks on a multiday pass, plus two swimming parks, several golf courses, various lakes, and a nighttime entertainment complex, Disney effectively swallowed up the average family's entire vacation. Break away to SeaWorld or the Kennedy Space Center for the day? How about a day at the ocean (remember the ocean)? Fat chance.

In 1995, Disney opened Blizzard Beach, a third swimming theme park, and began plans for a fourth major theme park, the Animal Kingdom, designed to compete directly with Busch Gardens. During the same year, the first phase of Disney's All-Star resorts came online, featuring (by Disney standards) budget accommodations. The location and rates of the All-Star resorts were intended to capture the market of the smaller independent and chain hotels along US 192. Disney even discussed constructing a monorail to the airport so that visitors wouldn't have to set foot in Orlando.

As time passed, Disney continued to consolidate its hold. With the openings in 1996 of Disney's BoardWalk, Fantasia Gardens miniature golf, and the Walt Disney World Speedway; in 1997 of Disney's Wide World of Sports, Disney's West Side shopping and entertainment district, and a new convention center; and in 1998 of the Animal Kingdom, Disney attracted armies of central Floridians to compensate for decreased tourist traffic during off-season. For people who can never get enough, there is the town of Celebration, a Disney residential land-development project where home buyers can live in Disney-designed houses in Disney-designed neighborhoods, protected by Disney-designed security.

In 1999, however, for the first time in many years, the initiative passed to Disney's competitors. Universal Studios Florida became a *bona fide* destination with the opening of its second major theme park (Islands of Adventure), on-property hotels, and the CityWalk dining and entertainment complex that directly competed with Pleasure Island (and Church Street Station, which was promptly forced out of business). SeaWorld announced the 2000 debut of its Discovery Cove park, and Busch Gardens turned up the heat with the addition of new roller coasters. The latest additions bring Busch Gardens' total to seven coasters, making them the roller-coaster capital of Florida. Cypress Gardens briefly closed, then had a face-lift and reopened will all-new rides and attractions. Giving Disney some of its own medicine, Busch Gardens, SeaWorld, and Universal combined with Wet 'n Wild to offer multiday passes good at any of the parks. Although it may be too early to say that Disney's hegemony is at an end, one thing's for sure: Disney's not the only 800-pound gorilla on the block anymore.

The tourism slump that began during the collapse of the Internet bubble economy peaked during post-9/11 paranoia, affected the big players in central Florida, but has gotten incrementally better as of this writing. While the big boys tightened their belts and cut corners where they could, some had to call it quits. The classic Ocean World in Fort Lauderdale was shut down for good shortly after the turn of the millennium. Splendid China, a vast landscaped garden filled with miniature recreations of Chinese buildings, monuments, palaces, cities, temples, and landmarks, closed its doors in 2003, and Water Mania, a swimming park, followed in 2006.

Even with these recent bad patches, most attractions and theme parks in central Florida are just learning how to become more adaptive and creative. Those that survive will be leaner, cleaner, and even more competitive than ever before. All this competition, of course, is good for central Florida, and it's good for you. The time, money, and energy invested in developing ever-better parks and attractions boggle the mind. Nobody, including Disney, can rest on their laurels in this market. And as for you, you're certain to find something new and amazing on every visit.

TRYING TO REASON WITH THE TOURIST SEASON

CENTRAL FLORIDA THEME PARKS AND ATTRACTIONS are busiest Christmas Day through New Year's Day. Thanksgiving weekend, the week of Washington's birthday, Martin Luther King Jr. holiday weekend, and spring break for colleges, plus the two weeks around Easter are also extremely busy. What does "busy" mean? More than 90,000 people can tour one of the larger theme parks on a single day during these peak times! Although this level of attendance isn't typical, it is possible, and only the ignorant or foolish challenge the major Florida theme parks at their peak periods.

The least busy time extends from after the Thanksgiving weekend until the week before Christmas. The next slowest times are November up to the weekend preceding Thanksgiving, January 4 through the first week of February, and the week after Easter through early

June. Late February, March, and early April are dicey. Crowds ebb and flow according to spring break schedules and the timing of Presidents' Day weekend. Though crowds have grown markedly in September and October as a result of special promotions aimed at locals and the international market, these months continue to be good for weekday touring.

It **TAKES MORE** *than* **ONE BOOK** *to* **DO** *the* **JOB RIGHT**

WE'VE BEEN COVERING CENTRAL FLORIDA tourism for over 25 years. We began by lumping everything into one guidebook, but that was when the Magic Kingdom was the only theme park at Walt Disney World, at the very beginning of the boom that has made central Florida the most visited tourist destination on Earth. As central Florida grew, so did our guide, until eventually we needed to split the tome into smaller, more in-depth (and more portable) volumes. The result is a small library of six titles, designed to work both individually and together. All six provide specialized information tailored to very specific central Florida and Walt Disney World visitors. Although some tips (like arriving at the theme parks early) are echoed or elaborated in all the guides, most of the information in each book is unique.

The Unofficial Guide to Walt Disney World is the centerpiece of our central Florida coverage because, well, Walt Disney World is the centerpiece of most central Florida vacations. *The Unofficial Guide to Walt Disney World* is evaluative, comprehensive, and instructive— the ultimate planning tool for a successful Walt Disney World vacation. *The Unofficial Guide to Walt Disney World* is supplemented by four additional titles, including this guide:

Mini-Mickey: The Pocket-Sized Unofficial Guide to Walt Disney World, by Bob Sehlinger

The Unofficial Guide to Walt Disney World with Kids, by Bob Sehlinger and Liliane Opsomer

The Unofficial Guide to Walt Disney World for Grown-Ups, by Eve Zibart

Mini-Mickey is a nifty, portable, *Cliffs Notes* version of *The Unofficial Guide to Walt Disney World.* Updated semiannually, it distills information from this comprehensive guide to help short-stay or last-minute visitors decide quickly how to plan their limited hours at Disney World. *The Unofficial Guide to Walt Disney World for Grown-Ups* helps adults traveling without children make the most of their Disney vacation, and *The Unofficial Guide to Walt Disney World with Kids* presents a wealth of planning and touring tips for a successful Disney family vacation. Finally, this guide, *Beyond Disney,* is a complete consumer guide to the non-Disney attractions, hotels, restaurants, and nightlife in Orlando and central Florida. All of the guides are available from Wiley Publishing and at most bookstores.

LETTERS AND COMMENTS FROM READERS

Many of those who use *The Unofficial Guides* write us to make comments or share their own strategies for visiting central Florida. We appreciate all such input, both positive and critical, and encourage our readers to continue writing. Readers' comments and observations are frequently incorporated into revised editions of *The Unofficial Guides* and have contributed immeasurably to their improvement. If you write us, you can rest assured that we won't release your name and address to any mailing lists, direct-mail advertisers, or other third party.

How to Write the Authors

Bob Sehlinger and Grant Rafter
The Unofficial Guides
P.O. Box 43673
Birmingham, AL 35243
UnofficialGuides@menasharidge.com

When you write by mail, put your address on both your letter and envelope, as sometimes the two get separated. It is also a good idea to include your phone number. And remember, as travel writers, we're often out of the office for long periods of time, so forgive us if our response is slow.

PART ONE

ACCOMMODATIONS

ORLANDO LODGING OPTIONS

SELECTING AND BOOKING A HOTEL

LODGING COSTS IN ORLANDO VARY INCREDIBLY. If you shop around, you can find a clean motel with a pool for as low as $35 a night. You also can find luxurious, expensive hotels with all the extras. Because of hot competition, discounts abound, particularly for AAA and AARP members.

There are three primary areas to consider:

1. INTERNATIONAL DRIVE AREA This area, about 5 minutes from Universal Orlando, parallels Interstate 4 on its eastern side and offers a wide selection of hotels and restaurants. Prices range from $56 to $400 per night. The chief drawbacks of this area are its terribly congested roads, countless traffic signals, and inadequate access to westbound I-4. While International's biggest bottleneck is its intersection with Sand Lake Road, the mile between Kirkman and Sand Lake roads is almost always gridlocked.

Regarding traffic on International Drive (known locally as I-Drive), these comments are representative. From a Seattle mom:

After spending half our trip sitting in traffic on International Drive, those Disney hotels didn't sound so expensive after all.

A convention-goer from Islip, New York, weighed in with this:

When I visited with my family last summer, we wasted huge chunks of time in traffic on International Drive. Our hotel was in the section between the big McDonald's [at Sand Lake Drive] and Wet 'n Wild [at Universal Boulevard]. There are practically no left-turn lanes in this section, so anyone turning left can hold up traffic for a long time. Recently, I returned to Orlando for a trade show and stayed at a hotel on International Drive near the convention center. This section was much saner and far less congested.

south orlando and walt disney world area

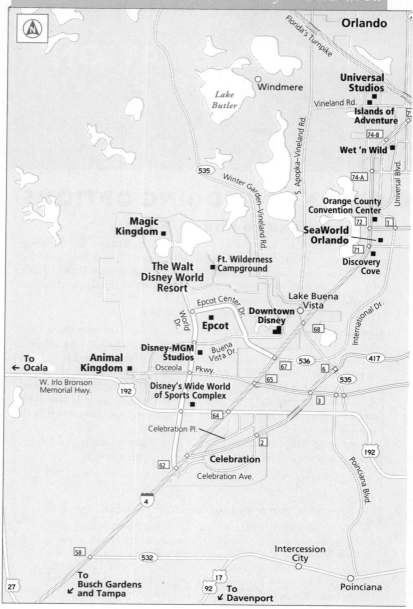

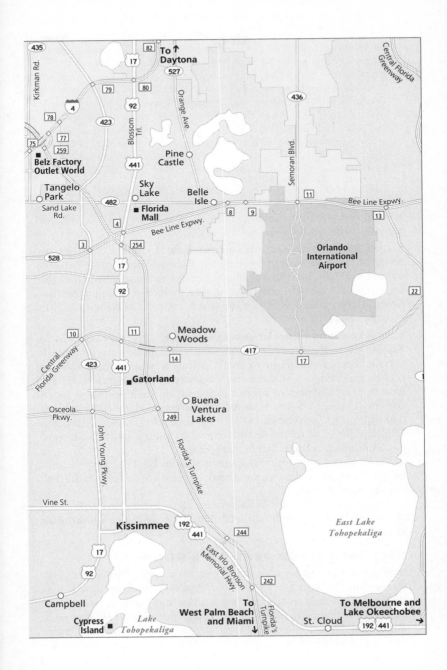

Traffic aside, a man from Ottawa, Canada, sings the praises of his I-Drive experience:

> *International Drive is the place to stay when going to [Orlando]. Your single-paragraph description of this location failed to point out that [there are] several discount stores, boutiques, restaurants, mini-putts, and other entertainment facilities, all within walking distance of remarkably inexpensive accommodations and a short drive away from [the attractions]. Many of the chain motels and hotels are located in this area, and the local merchants have created a mini-resort to cater to the tourists. It is the ideal place to unwind after a hard day visiting [the theme park]. I have recommended this location for years and have never heard anything but raves about the wisdom of this advice.*

I-Drive hotels are listed in the *Orlando Official Accommodations Guide* published by the Orlando–Orange County Convention and Visitors Bureau. For a copy, call ☎ 800-255-5786 or 407-363-5872, or see **www.orlandoinfo.com.**

2. LAKE BUENA VISTA AND THE I-4 CORRIDOR A number of hotels are along FL 535 and west of I-4 between Disney World and I-4's intersection with the Florida Turnpike. They're easily reached from the interstate and are near many restaurants, including those on International Drive. The *Orlando Official Accommodations Guide* lists most of them.

3. US 192/IRLO BRONSON MEMORIAL HIGHWAY This is the highway to Kissimmee to the south of Disney World. In addition to large, full-service hotels, there are many small, privately owned motels that are often a good value. The number and variety of restaurants on US 192 have increased markedly, compensating for the area's primary shortcoming. Locally, US 192 is called Irlo Bronson Memorial Highway. The section to the west of I-4 is designated Irlo Bronson Memorial Highway West, while the section from I-4 running southeast toward Kissimmee is Irlo Bronson Highway East.

We're happy to report that construction on US 192 has been completed. The highway has been widened and medians added. Traffic flow has improved considerably.

Hotels on US 192 and in Kissimmee are listed in the *Kissimmee–St. Cloud Visitor's Guide*. Call ☎ 800-327-9159 or see **www.florida kiss.com.**

GETTING A GOOD DEAL ON A ROOM

HOTEL DEVELOPMENT HAS SHARPENED competition among lodgings throughout the Walt Disney World–Orlando–Kissimmee area. Hotels struggle to fill their rooms and lure patrons with bargain rates. These deals vary with season, day of the week, and area events. In high-season, during holiday periods, and during large conventions at the Orange County Convention Center, even the most modest property is sold out.

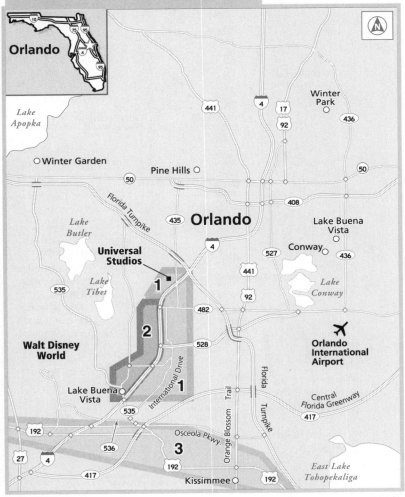

hotel concentrations around orlando area attractions

Here are strategies for getting a good deal on a room. The list may refer to travel-market players unfamiliar to you, but many tips we provide for deals work equally well almost any place you need a hotel. Once you understand these strategies, you'll be able to routinely obtain rooms for the lowest possible rates.

international drive area

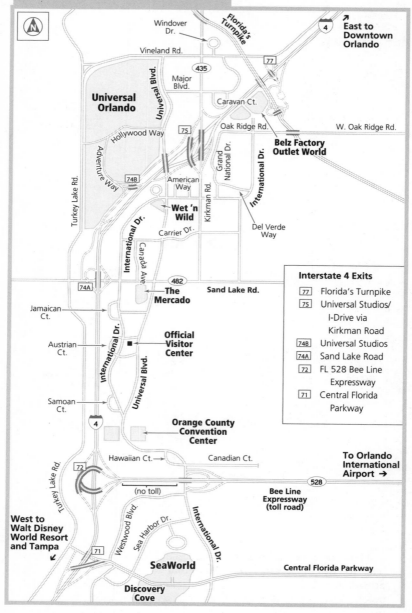

Interstate 4 Exits

77 Florida's Turnpike

75 Universal Studios/
I-Drive via
Kirkman Road

74B Universal Studios

74A Sand Lake Road

72 FL 528 Bee Line
Expressway

71 Central Florida
Parkway

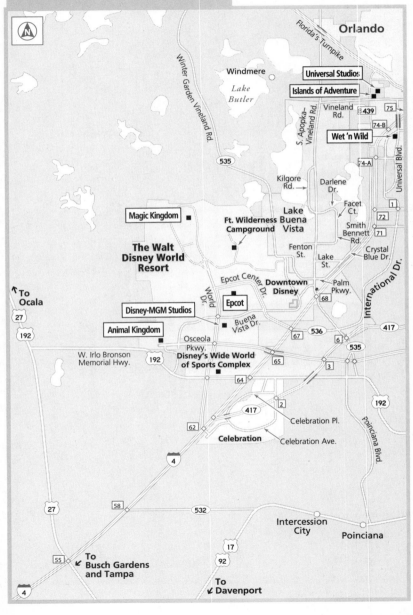

lake buena vista resort area and the I-4 corridor

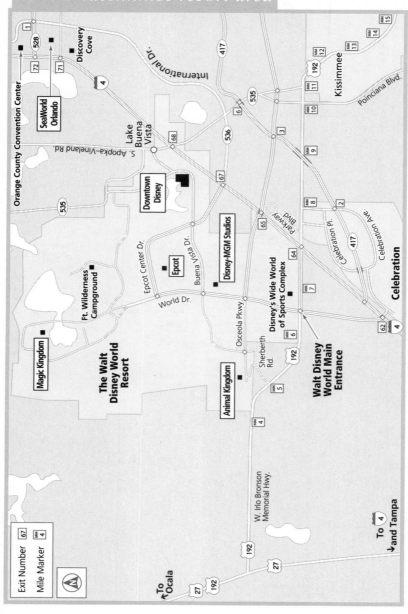

I. ORLANDO MAGICARD Orlando Magicard is a discount program sponsored by the Orlando–Orange County Convention and Visitors Bureau. Cardholders are eligible for discounts of 20% to 50% at about 50 hotels. The Magicard is also good for discounts at area attractions, including SeaWorld, the Universal parks, several dinner theaters, and Disney's Pleasure Island. Valid for up to six persons, the card isn't available for larger groups or conventions.

To obtain a free Magicard and a list of participating hotels and attractions, call ☎ 800-643-9492 or 407-363-5872. On the Internet, go to **www.orlandoinfo.com/magicard;** the Magicard and accompanying brochure can be printed from a personal computer. Anyone ages 18 or older is eligible. If you miss getting one before you leave home, obtain one at the Convention and Visitors Bureau Information Center at 8723 International Drive. When you call for a Magicard, also request the *Orlando Official Accommodations Guide* and the *Orlando Vacation Planner.*

2. EXIT INFORMATION GUIDE Exit Information Guide (EIG) publishes a book of coupons for discounts at hotels statewide. It's free in many restaurants and motels on main highways leading to Florida. Because most travelers make reservations before leaving home, picking up the book en route doesn't help much. If you call and use a credit card, EIG will send the guide first class for $3 ($5 U.S. for Canadian delivery). Contact Exit Information Guide at 4205 NW Sixth Street, Gainesville, FL 32609; ☎ 352-371-3948 or 800-332-3948; **www.travelersdiscount guide.com.**

3. HOTEL SHOPPING ON THE INTERNET Hotels use the Internet to fill rooms during slow periods and to advertise limited-time specials. Hotels also use more traditional communication avenues such as promoting specials through travel agents. If you enjoy cybershopping, have at it, but hotel shopping on the Internet isn't as quick or convenient as handing the task to your travel agent. When we bump into a great deal on the Web, we call our agent. Often she can beat the deal or improve on it (perhaps with an upgrade). Although a good agent working alone can achieve great things, the same agent working with a savvy, helpful client can work wonders.

See the chart on the following page for Web sites we've found most dependable for discounts on Orlando-area hotels.

The secret to shopping on the Internet is . . . shopping. When we're really looking for a deal, we check all the sites described below. Flexibility on dates and location are helpful, and we always give our travel agent the opportunity to beat any deal we find.

We recommend choosing a hotel based on location, room quality, price, commuting time to the attractions, plus any features important to you. Next, check each of the applicable sites on the next page. You'll be able to ferret out the best Internet deal in about 30 minutes. Then call the hotel to see if you can save more by booking directly. Start by

www.mousesavers.com Best site for hotels in Disney World

www.dreamsunlimitedtravel.com Excellent for both Disney and non-Disney hotels

www.2000orlando-florida.com Comprehensive hotel site

www.valuetrips.com Specializes in budget accommodations

www.travelocity.com Multidestination travel superstore

www.roomsaver.com Provides discount coupons for hotels

www.floridakiss.com Primarily US 192–Kissimmee area hotels

www.orlandoinfo.com Good info; not user-friendly for booking

www.orlandovacation.com Great rates for a small number of properties, including condos and home rentals

www.expedia.com Largest of the multidestination travel sites

www.hotels.com Largest Internet hotel-booking service; many other sites link to hotels.com and their subsidiary, **www.hoteldiscounts.com**

asking the hotel for specials. If their response doesn't beat the Internet deal, tell them what you've found and ask if they can do better.

SO WHO OFFERS THE BEST DEALS ON THE NET? *Unofficial Guide* statistician Fred Hazelton analyzed more than 4.5 million rate quotes from Internet sellers, individual and chain-hotel Web sites, and hotel reservations departments for 350 Disney and Orlando-area hotels. The idea was to determine which sellers had the best deals most (or a high percentage) of the time.

The ranking of the sellers in the chart on page 20 is based on how often a seller's rate was lower than all its competitors. Thus, a success rate of 70% means that the seller beat all competitors who market the same hotels 70% of the time. The numbers can be tricky, though. A seller who offers hotels not sold by others is obviously going to have the best deals on those properties most (if not all) of the time, and consequently score high. Conversely, a seller that lists a large number of hotels also sold by many competitors will offer the best price a lower percentage of the time.

We collected rates from most of the Web sites that offer rates for hotels in and around the Orlando-Kissimmee area. Then we also obtained rates from the hotel front desk and from the hotel's Web site. When we compared all the rates from all sellers, we found that **www.octopustravel.com** and **www.floridakiss.com** had the best bang for your Internet buck. The rates offered by these Web sites beat out all others about 81% of the time. These sites, however, offer a much smaller selection of hotels than biggies like Expedia and Travelocity. The best of the large Web sites was **www.hotelkingdom.com,** with an impressive 75% success rate. Also note that the hotel front desk and the hotel Web site offered the lowest rate about two-thirds of the time (65% and 60%, respectively). The Web site **www.mousesavers.com,** which specializes in discount codes for hotels, is not listed because the site doesn't actually sell rooms. To use the codes, you quote the relevant code to an actual seller.

One thing we noticed when getting rates from all the different sellers is that no one seller offered the best rate all the time. Rankings are ordered from top to bottom, best to worst.

During our research on hotel rates we noticed that there is a period where the rates are almost always at their lowest. It happens between 45 and 60 days before the date of arrival. We collected more than 4.5 million rate quotes, covering all possible dates of arrival and starting at 300 days before the date of arrival. As the date gets closer we record the changes in the price and see that the lowest available price for a hotel room occurs in that 45- to 60-day window about 80% of the time. This means that no matter when you book your hotel room always check to see if a lower rate is available about 60 days before your date of arrival. We checked this result with experts in the hotel industry and discovered that hotel companies typically discuss their occupancy rates about 45 to 60 days in the future. So if a hotel is experiencing lower-than-expected occupancy rates, they are most likely to adjust their prices around the 60-day mark.

While Expedia is often able to offer better deals on some larger properties (for example, Hilton and DoubleTree), some Disney-centric travel sites, such as **www.dreamsunlimitedtravel.com** and **www.mouse savers.com,** form special relationships with specific hotels that result in unusually juicy discounts. Because the megasites like Orbitz, Expedia, and **www.hotels.com** have neither the time nor inclination to nurture such relationships, they can't obtain these sweetheart deals. At the boutique Celebration Hotel, for example, Dreams Unlimited's rate was more than 35% lower than Expedia's.

The following chart (page 20) summarizes how much you can expect to save on average from each of the Internet sellers listed below (only those for which we have a minimum of 1,000 observations are included).

Method 1: Average percentage by which the seller beats its nearest competitor.

Method 2: Average percentage by which the seller beats the highest rate advertised.

Another option is to book hotel rooms through the travel site **Price-line** (**www.priceline.com**). What makes Priceline different from other travel sites is that you don't get to pick the specific hotel where you'll be staying. Rather, you tell Priceline how much you're willing to spend on a general class of lodging (for example, a two-and-a-half star hotel in the Universal Studios vicinity for less than $40 per night), and Priceline will try to find a hotel that meets or exceeds those specifications and

SELLER	NUMBER OF OBSERVATIONS	AVERAGE SAVINGS (METHOD 1)	AVERAGE SAVINGS (METHOD 2)
www.octopustravel.com	4,408	22%	32%
www.aanhotels.com	10,252	12%	19%
www.onetravel.com	8,100	11%	20%
www.placestostay.com	13,983	9%	15%
www.hotelkingdom.com	984,504	8%	10%
www.hotels.com	37,850	7%	13%
www.orbitz.com	38,541	7%	13%
www.travelocity.com	521,820	5%	5%
www.inntopia.com	1,874	4%	8%
www.travelworm.com	243,111	4%	4%
www.expedia.com	632,104	3%	4%

stays within your budget. There's no canceling a bid once Priceline has found a hotel that matches your criteria—you have to agree before bidding to pay the full cost up front, with no refunds, transfers, or changes whatsoever.

Another tool in the hotel-hunting arsenal is **www.travelaxe.com.** Travelaxe offers free software you can download to your PC (won't run on Macs) that will scan an assortment of hotel-discount sites and find the cheapest rate for each of over 200 Disney-area hotels. The site offers filters such as price, quality rating, and proximity to a specific location (Universal Orlando, SeaWorld, the convention center, airport, and so on) to allow you to narrow your search. The same software also scans for the best rates in cities throughout the United States and the world.

4. IF YOU MAKE YOUR OWN RESERVATION Always call the hotel in question, not the chain's national toll-free number. Often, reservationists at the toll-free number are unaware of local specials. Always ask about specials before you inquire about corporate rates. Don't hesitate to bargain, but do it before you check in. If you're buying a hotel's weekend package and want to extend your stay, for example, you can often obtain at least the corporate rate for the extra days.

CONDOMINIUMS AND VACATION HOMES

VACATION HOMES ARE FREE-STANDING, while condominiums are essentially one- to three-bedroom accommodations in a larger building housing a number of similar units. Because condos tend to be part of large developments (frequently time-shares), amenities such as swimming pools, playgrounds, game arcades, and fitness centers often rival those found in the best hotels. Generally speaking, condo developments do not have restaurants, lounges, or spas. In a condo, if something goes wrong, there will be someone on hand to fix the problem. Vacation homes rented from a property-management company likewise will have someone to come to the rescue, though responsiveness tends to vary vastly from company to company. If you rent directly from an owner, correcting problems is often more difficult, particularly when the owner doesn't live in the same area as the rental home.

In a vacation home, all the amenities are contained in the home (though in planned developments there may be community amenities available as well). Depending on the specific home, you might find a small swimming pool, hot tub, two-car garage, family room, game room, and even a home theater. Features found in both condos and vacation homes include full kitchens, laundry rooms, TVs, DVD players/VCRs, and frequently stereos. Interestingly, though almost all free-standing vacation homes have private pools, very few have backyards. This means that, except for swimming, the kids are pretty much relegated to playing in the house.

Time-share condos are clones when it comes to furniture and decor, but single-owner condos and vacation homes are furnished and decorated in a style that reflects the taste of the owner. Vacation homes, usually one- to two-story houses located in a subdivision, very rarely afford interesting views (though some overlook lakes or natural areas), while condos, especially the high-rise variety, sometimes offer exceptional ones.

The Price Is Nice

The best deals in lodging are vacation homes and single-owner condos. Prices range from about $65 a night for two-bedroom condos and townhomes to $200 to $500 a night for three- to seven-bedroom vacation homes. Forgetting about taxes to keep the comparison simple, let's compare renting a vacation home to staying at one of Disney's Value Resorts. A family of two parents, two teens, and two grandparents would need three hotel rooms at Disney's Pop Century Resort. At the lowest rate obtainable, that would run you $79 per night per room or $237 total. Rooms are 260 square feet each, so you'd have a total of 780 square feet. Each room has a private bath and a television.

Renting at the same time of year from **All Star Vacation Homes** (no relation to Disney's All-Star Resorts), you can rent a 2,053-square-foot, four-bedroom, three-bath vacation home with a private pool for $219—a savings of $18 per night over the Disney Value Resort rate. With four bedrooms, each of the teens can have his or her own room. Further, for the dates we checked, All Star Vacation Homes was running a special in which they threw in a free rental car with a one-week home rental.

But that's not all—the home comes with the following features and amenities: a big-screen TV with PlayStation, DVD player, and VCR (assorted games and DVDs available for complimentary checkout at the rental office); a CD player; a heatable private pool; five additional TVs (one in each bedroom and one in the family room); a fully equipped kitchen; a two-car garage; a hot tub; a laundry room with full-size washer and dryer; a fully furnished private patio; and a child-safety fence.

The home is in a community with a 24-hour gated entrance. Available at the community center are a large swimming pool; a whirlpool; tennis, volleyball, and half-court basketball courts; a children's playground; a gym and exercise room; a convenience store; and a 58-seat cinema.

One thing we like about All Star Vacation Homes is that its Web site (**www.allstarvacationhomes.com**) offers detailed information, including a dozen or more photos of each specific home. When you book, the home you've been looking at is the actual one you're reserving. (If you want to see how the home described is furnished, for instance, go to the site and click on "Resort Homes" in the middle right of the screen; when the Resort Homes page loads, scroll down until you see the home with Property Code 2-8144 SP-WP. Click on that for lots of photos and a floor plan.) On the other hand, some vacation-home companies, like rental-car agencies, don't assign you a specific home until the day you arrive. These companies provide photos of a "typical home" instead of making information available on each of the individual homes in their inventory. In this case, you have to take the company's word that the typical home pictured is representative and that the home you'll be assigned will be just as nice.

How the Vacation-home Market Works

In the Orlando–Walt Disney World area, there are almost 19,000 rental homes, including stand-alone homes, single-owner condos (that is, not time-shares), and townhomes. The same area has about 112,000 hotel rooms. Almost all the rental homes are owned by individuals who occupy them for at least a week or two each year; the rest of the year, the owners make the homes available for rent. Some owners deal directly with renters, while others enlist the assistance of a property-management company.

Incredibly, about 700 property-management companies operate in the Orlando–Walt Disney World market. Most of these are mom-and-pop outfits that manage an inventory of ten homes or less (probably fewer than 70 companies oversee more than 100 rental homes).

Homeowners pay these companies to maintain and promote their properties and handle all rental transactions. Some homes are made available to wholesalers, vacation packagers, and travel agents in deals negotiated either directly by the owners or by property-management companies on the owners' behalf. A wholesaler or vacation packager will occasionally drop its rates to sell slow-moving inventory, but more commonly the cost to renters is higher than when dealing directly with owners or management companies: because most wholesalers and packagers sell their inventory through travel agents, both the wholesaler/packager's markup and the travel agent's commission are passed along to the renter. These costs are in addition to the owner's cut and/or the fee for the property manager.

Along similar lines, logic may suggest that the lowest rate of all can be obtained by dealing directly with owners, thus eliminating middlemen. Although this is sometimes true, it's more often the case that property-management companies offer the best rates. With their marketing expertise and larger customer base, these companies can produce a higher occupancy rate than can the owners themselves. What's more, management companies, or at least the larger ones, can achieve economies of scale not available to owners in regard to maintenance, cleaning, linens, even acquiring furniture and appliances (if a house is not already furnished). The combination of higher occupancy rates and economies of scale adds up to a win–win situation for owners, management companies, and renters alike.

Location, Location, Location

The best vacation home is one that is within easy commuting distance of the theme parks. If you plan to spend some time at SeaWorld and the Universal parks, you'll want something just to the northeast of Walt Disney World (between the World and Orlando). If you plan to spend some of your time in the World or Cypress Gardens, the best selection of vacation homes is along US 192 to the south of the park.

A small southern tip of Orange County that dips into Osceola County, which, along with Polk County to the west of Walt Disney World, is where most vacation homes and single-owner condos and town houses are located. For many years, zoning laws in Orange County (which also includes most of Orlando, Universal Studios, Sea-World, Lake Buena Vista, and the International Drive area) have prohibited short-term rentals of homes and single-owner condos. However, in light of the economic boom fueled by such rentals in Osceola and Polk counties, Orange County has loosened its zoning restrictions in a few predominantly tourist-oriented areas. So far, practically all of the vacation-rental homes in Orange County are located in a new development called **Vista Cay.**

By our reckoning, about half the rental homes in Osceola County and all the rental homes in Polk County are too far away from the attractions for commuting to be practical. You might be able to save a few bucks by staying farther out, but the most desirable homes to be found are in Vista Cay and in developments no more than four miles from I-4 access.

To get the most from a vacation home, you need to be close enough to commute in 20 minutes or less to your destination. This will allow for naps, quiet time, swimming, and dollar-saving meals you prepare yourself.

Shopping for a Vacation Home

The only practical way to shop for a rental home is on the Web. This makes it relatively easy to compare different properties and rental companies; on the downside, there are so many owners, rental companies, and individual homes to choose from that you could research yourself into a stupor. There are three main types of Web sites in the home-rental game: those for property-management companies, which showcase a given company's homes and are set up for direct bookings; individual owner sites; and third-party listings sites, which advertise properties available through different owners and sometimes management companies as well. Sites in the last category will usually refer prospective renters to an owner's or management company's site for reservations.

We've found that most property-management sites are not very well designed and will test your patience to the max. You can practically click yourself into old age trying to see all the homes available or figure out where on earth they're located. Nearly all claim to be "just minutes from Disney or Universal." (By that reasoning, we should list our homes; they're also just minutes from Universal . . . 570 minutes, to be exact!)

Many Web sites list homes according to towns (such as Auburndale, Clermont, Davenport, Haines City, and Winter Garden) or real estate developments (including Eagle Point, Formosa Gardens, Indian Ridge, and Wyndham Palms) in the general Disney–Universal area, none of which you're likely to be familiar with. If you visit a site that lists homes by towns or real estate developments, begin by looking at our map on the following pages that shows where all these places are.

The best Web sites provide the following:

- Numerous photos and in-depth descriptions of individual homes to make comparisons quick and easy

- Overview maps or text descriptions that reflect how distant specific homes or developments are from the attractions

- The ability to book the specific individual rental home of your choice on the site

- A prominently displayed phone number for non-Internet bookings and questions.

The best sites are also easy to navigate, let you see what you're interested in without logging in or giving personal information, and list memberships in such organizations as the Better Business Bureau and the Central Florida Property Management Association (log on to **www .cfpma.org** for the association's code of ethics and a list of members).

Recommended Web Sites

After checking out dozens upon dozens of sites, here are the ones we recommend. All of them meet the criteria listed above. If you're stunned that there are so few of them, well, so were we. (For the record, we elected not to list some sites that met our criteria but whose homes are too far away from Orlando area attractions.)

All Star Vacation Homes (**www.allstarvacationhomes.com**) is easily the best of the management-company sites, with easily accessible photos and plenty of details about featured homes. All the company's rental properties are within either four miles of Walt Disney World or three miles of Universal Studios.

Disney Rents (**www.disneyrents.com**) is the Web site of Orlando's Finest Vacation Homes, a rental agency representing both home owners and vacation-home–management companies. Offering a broad inventory, the site features photos and information on individual homes. Although the info is not as detailed as the one offered by the All Star Vacation Homes site, friendly sales agents can fill in the blanks.

The Web site for the **Orlando–Orange County Convention and Visitors Bureau** (**www.orlandoinfo.com**) is the place to go if you're interested in a condo at one of the many time-share developments (click on "Accommodations" at the home page). You can call the developments directly, but going through this site allows you to bypass sales departments and escape their high-pressure invitations to sit through sales presentations. The site also lists hotels and vacation homes.

Vacation Rental by Owner (**www.vrbo.com**) is a nationwide listings service that puts prospective renters in direct contact with owners. The site is straightforward and always lists a large number of rental properties near the attractions. Two similar listings services with good Web sites are **Vacation Rentals 411** (**www.vacationrentals 411.com**) and **Last Minute Villas** (**www.lastminutevillas.net**).

VillaDirect Florida (**www.villadirect.com**) manages more than 600 rental homes and condos in the greater Walt Disney World/Universal area. Though some of the properties are too far from area attractions for our taste, the site offers a lot to choose from and is a snap to navigate.

Making Contact

Once you've found a vacation home you like, check around the Web site for a Frequently Asked Questions (FAQ) page. If there's not a FAQ page, here are some of the things you'll want to check out on the phone with the owner or rental company.

1. How close is the property to your touring destination?
2. Is the home or condo I see on the Internet the one I get?
3. Is the property part of a time-share development?
4. Are there any specials or discounts available?
5. Is everything included in the rental price, or are there additional charges? What about taxes?
6. How old is the home or condo I'm interested in? Has it been refurbished recently?

rental-home developments

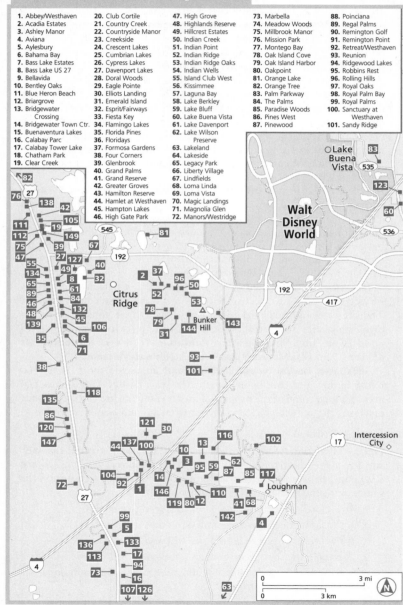

1. Abbey/Westhaven
2. Acadia Estates
3. Ashley Manor
4. Aviana
5. Aylesbury
6. Bahama Bay
7. Bass Lake Estates
8. Bass Lake US 27
9. Bellavida
10. Bentley Oaks
11. Blue Heron Beach
12. Briargrove
13. Bridgewater Crossing
14. Bridgewater Town Ctr.
15. Buenaventura Lakes
16. Calabay Parc
17. Calabay Tower Lake
18. Chatham Park
19. Clear Creek

20. Club Cortile
21. Country Creek
22. Countryside Manor
23. Creekside
24. Crescent Lakes
25. Cumbrian Lakes
26. Cypress Lakes
27. Davenport Lakes
28. Doral Woods
29. Eagle Pointe
30. Elliots Landing
31. Emerald Island
32. Esprit/Fairways
33. Fiesta Key
34. Flamingo Lakes
35. Florida Pines
36. Floridays
37. Formosa Gardens
38. Four Corners
39. Glenbrook
40. Grand Palms
41. Grand Reserve
42. Greater Groves
43. Hamilton Reserve
44. Hamlet at Westhaven
45. Hampton Lakes
46. High Gate Park

47. High Grove
48. Highlands Reserve
49. Hillcrest Estates
50. Indian Creek
51. Indian Point
52. Indian Ridge
53. Indian Ridge Oaks
54. Indian Wells
55. Island Club West
56. Kissimmee
57. Laguna Bay
58. Lake Berkley
59. Lake Bluff
60. Lake Buena Vista
61. Lake Davenport
62. Lake Wilson Preserve
63. Lakeland
64. Lakeside
65. Legacy Park
66. Liberty Village
67. Lindfields
68. Loma Linda
69. Loma Vista
70. Magic Landings
71. Magnolia Glen
72. Manors/Westridge

73. Marbella
74. Meadow Woods
75. Millbrook Manor
76. Mission Park
77. Montego Bay
78. Oak Island Cove
79. Oak Island Harbor
80. Oakpoint
81. Orange Lake
82. Orange Tree
83. Palm Parkway
84. The Palms
85. Paradise Woods
86. Pines West
87. Pinewood

88. Poinciana
89. Regal Palms
90. Remington Golf
91. Remington Point
92. Retreat/Westhaven
93. Reunion
94. Ridgewood Lakes
95. Robbins Rest
96. Rolling Hills
97. Royal Oaks
98. Royal Palm Bay
99. Royal Palms
100. Sanctuary at Westhaven
101. Sandy Ridge

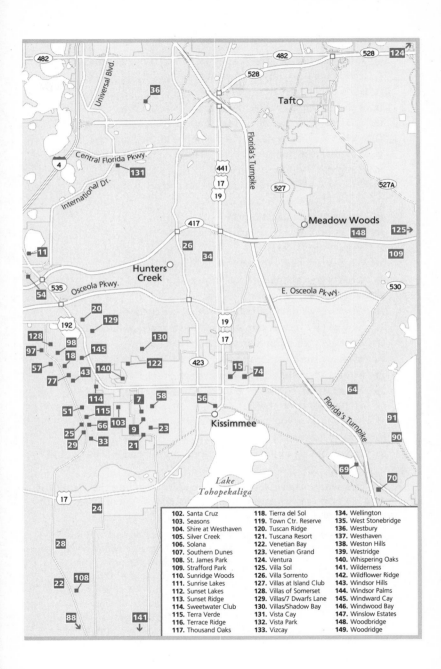

102. Santa Cruz	118. Tierra del Sol	134. Wellington
103. Seasons	119. Town Ctr. Reserve	135. West Stonebridge
104. Shire at Westhaven	120. Tuscan Ridge	136. Westbury
105. Silver Creek	121. Tuscana Resort	137. Westhaven
106. Solana	122. Venetian Bay	138. Weston Hills
107. Southern Dunes	123. Venetian Grand	139. Westridge
108. St. James Park	124. Ventura	140. Whispering Oaks
109. Strafford Park	125. Villa Sol	141. Wilderness
110. Sunridge Woods	126. Villa Sorrento	142. Wildflower Ridge
111. Sunrise Lakes	127. Villas at Island Club	143. Windsor Hills
112. Sunset Lakes	128. Villas of Somerset	144. Windsor Palms
113. Sunset Ridge	129. Villas/7 Dwarfs Lane	145. Windward Cay
114. Sweetwater Club	130. Villas/Shadow Bay	146. Windwood Bay
115. Terra Verde	131. Vista Cay	147. Winslow Estates
116. Terrace Ridge	132. Vista Park	148. Woodbridge
117. Thousand Oaks	133. Vizcay	149. Woodridge

7. What is the view from the property?
8. Is the property near any noisy roads?
9. What is your smoking policy?
10. Are pets allowed? [This is as important to those who want to avoid pets as to those who want to bring pets.]
11. Is the pool heated?
12. Is there a fenced backyard where children can play?
13. How many people can be seated at the main dining table?
14. Is there a separate dedicated telephone at the property?
15. Is high-speed Internet access available?
16. Are linens and towels provided?
17. How far are the nearest supermarket and drugstore?
18. Are child-care services available?
19. Are there restaurants nearby?
20. Is transportation to the parks provided?
21. Will we need a car?
22. What is required to make a reservation?
23. What is your change/cancellation policy?
24. When is checkout time?
25. What will we be responsible for when we check out?
26. How will we receive our confirmation and arrival instructions?
27. What are your office hours?
28. What are the directions to your office?
29. What if we arrive after your office has closed?
30. Whom do we contact if something breaks or otherwise goes wrong during our stay?
31. How long have you been in business?
32. Are you licensed by the state of Florida?
33. Do you belong to the Better Business Bureau and/or the Central Florida Property Managers Association?

We frequently receive letters from readers extolling the virtues of renting a condo or vacation home. This endorsement by a family from Ellington, Connecticut, is typical:

Our choice to stay [in a vacation home] was based on cost and sanity. We've found over the last couple of years that our children can't share the same bed. We have also gotten tired of having to turn off the lights at 8 p.m. and lie quietly in the dark waiting for our children to fall asleep. With this in mind, we needed a condo/suite layout. We decided on the Sheraton Vistana Resort. We had a two-bedroom villa with full kitchen, living room, three TVs, and washer/dryer. I packed for half the trip and did laundry almost every night. The facilities offered a daily children's program and several pools, kiddie pools, and "playscapes." Located on FL 535, we had a five- to ten-minute drive to most attractions, including SeaWorld, Disney, and Universal.

A St. Joe, Indiana, family also had a good experience, writing:

We rented a home in Kissimmee this time, and we'll never stay in a hotel again. It was by far the nicest, most relaxing time we've ever had down there. Our rental home was within 10 to 15 minutes of all the Disney parks, and 25 minutes from SeaWorld. We had three bed-rooms, two baths, and an in-ground pool in a screened enclosure out back. We paid $90 per night for the whole shootin' match. We did spring for the pool heating, $25 per night extra [in February]. We used AAA Dream Homes Rental Company and they did a great job by us. They provided us with detailed info before we went down so we would know what we needed to bring.

AAA Dream Homes (**www.dreamhomes.com**) has a good reputation for customer service but does not have photos of or information about the homes in its inventory online, citing lack of room.

ORLANDO'S BEST HOTELS *for* FAMILIES

WHAT MAKES A SUPER FAMILY HOTEL? Roomy accommodations, in-room fridge, great pool, complimentary breakfast, child-care options, and programs for kids are a few of the things the *Unofficial Guide* hotel team researched in selecting the top hotels for families from among hundreds of properties in the attractions area. Some of our picks are expensive, others are more reasonable, and some are a bargain. Regardless of price, be assured that these hotels understand a family's needs.

Though all hotels listed below offer some type of shuttle to the theme parks, some offer very limited service. Call the hotel before you book and ask what the shuttle schedule will be when you visit. Since families, like individuals, have different wants and needs, we haven't ranked the following properties here; they're listed by zone and alphabetically.

International Drive Area

DoubleTree Castle Hotel

Rate per night $150+. **Pool** ★★★. **Fridge in room** Yes. **Shuttle to parks** Yes (Disney, Universal, and SeaWorld). **Maximum number of occupants per room** 4. **Special comments** Add $20 to room rate, and up to 4 people receive continental breakfast; 2 signature chocolate-chip cookies come with every room.

YOU CAN'T MISS THIS ONE; it's the only castle on I-Drive. Inside you'll find royal colors (purple dominates), opulent fixtures, European art,

8629 International Drive
Orlando
☎ 407-345-1511 or
800-952-2785
www.doubletreecastle.com

Renaissance music, and a mystical Castle Creature at the door. The 216 guest rooms also receive the royal treatment in decor, though some guests may find them gaudy. All, however, are fairly large and well equipped with TV with PlayStation, fridge, three phones, coffeemaker, iron and board, hair dryer, and safe. The Castle Café off the lobby serves full or continental breakfast. For lunch or dinner, you might walk next door to Vito's Chop House (dinner only) or Café Tu Tu Tango (an *Unofficial* favorite). The heated circular pool is five feet deep and features a fountain in the center, a poolside bar, and a whirlpool. There's no separate kiddie pool. Other amenities include a fitness center, arcade, gift shop, lounge, valet laundry service and facilities, and guest services desk with park passes for sale and babysitting recommendations. Security feature: elevators require an electronic key card.

Hard Rock Hotel

Rate per night $300+. **Pool** ★★★★. **Fridge in room** Available, $15 per day. **Shuttle to parks** Yes (Universal, SeaWorld, and Wet 'n Wild). **Maximum number of occupants per room** 4. **Special comments** Microwaves available for $15 per day.

5800 Universal Boulevard
Orlando
☎ 407-503-ROCK or
888-273-1311
www.hardrock.com

LOCATED ON UNIVERSAL PROPERTY, the 650-room Hard Rock Hotel is nirvana for any kid older than eight, especially those interested in music. Architecture is California Mission–style, and rock memorabilia is displayed throughout. If you plan to spend at least a few days at Universal parks, this is an excellent upscale option. Guests get theme-park privileges such as early admission on select days and all-day access to the Universal Express line-breaking program, plus delivery of packages to their room and priority seating at select Universal restaurants. The music-filled pool area has a white-sand beach, a 260-foot waterslide, a 12,000-square-foot pool, an underwater audio system, and an ultrahip pool bar. You'll also find five restaurants and lounges, including the Palm Restaurant, a chic lounge, fitness center, and Hard Rock merchandise store. Guest rooms are ultrahip too, with cutting-edge contemporary decor, a CD sound system, TV with pay-per-view movies and video games, coffeemaker, iron and board, robes, hair dryer, and two phones. A supervised activity center, Camp Lil' Rock, serves kids ages 4 to 14. Pet-friendly rooms are available.

Nickelodeon Family Suites by Holiday Inn

Rate per night $180–$370. **Pools** ★★★★. **Fridge in room** Yes. **Shuttle to parks** Yes (Disney only). **Maximum number of occupants per room** 7. **Special comments** Daily character breakfast.

SPONGEBOB SQUAREPANTS, EAT YOUR HEART OUT. This revamped resort is as kid-friendly as they come. Decked out in all themes Nickelodeon, the hotel is sure to please any fan of TV shows the likes of *Rugrats, Jimmy Neutron: Boy Genius,* and *The Fairly Odd-Parents,* to name a few. Nickelodeon characters from the channel's many shows hang out in the resort's lobby and mall area, greeting kids while parents check

14500 Continental Gateway
Orlando
☎ 407-387-5437 or
866-GO2-NICK
www.nickhotel.com

in. Guests can choose from among 777 one-, two-, and three-bedroom Kid Suites executed in a number of different themes—all very brightly and creatively decorated. All suites include a kitchenette with microwave, fridge, coffeemaker, TV and DVD player, iron and board, two hair dryers, and a safe. Kid Suites feature a semiprivate kids' bedroom with bunk beds, pull-out sleeper bed, 36-inch TV and DVD player, Nintendo 64 (you can rent games for a small fee at the hotel's video arcade), CD/cassette player, and activity table. The master bedroom offers ample storage space that the kids' bedroom lacks. Additional amenities include high-tech video arcade, Studio Nick—a game-show studio that will host six game shows a night for the entertainment of a live studio audience, a buffet (kids 12 and younger eat free with a paying adult), food court offering Pizza Hut and A&W Root Beer, the Nicktoons Cafe coffeehouse, convenience store, lounge, gift shop, fitness center, washer and dryer in each courtyard, and guest-activities desk (buy Disney tickets and get recommendations on babysitting). Not to be missed—don't worry, your kids won't let you—are the resort's two pools, Oasis and Lagoon. Oasis features a water park complete with water cannons, rope ladders, geysers, and dump buckets, as well as two hot tubs for adults (with a view of the rest of the pool to keep an eye on little ones) and a smaller play area for younger kids. Kids will love the huge, zero-depth-entry Lagoon pool, replete with a 400-gallon dump bucket, plus nearby basketball court and nine-hole minigolf course. Pool activities for kids are scheduled several times a day, seasonally; some games feature the infamous green slime. "Dive-in" movies, family-friendly films shown on a giant screen on the deck, are in the works. Whatever you do, avoid letting your kids catch you saying the phrase "I don't know" while you're here—trust us.

Portofino Bay Hotel

Rate per night $329. **Pools** ★★★★. **Fridge in room** Minibar; fridge available for $15 per day. **Shuttle to parks** Yes (Universal, SeaWorld, Discovery Cove, and Wet 'n Wild). **Maximum number of occupants per room** 4. **Special comments** Character dinner on Friday.

LOCATED IN UNIVERSAL ORLANDO, the 750-room Portofino Bay Hotel is themed like an Italian Riviera village. Guests receive theme-park privileges such as early admission on select days and all-day access to the Universal Express line-breaking program, plus delivery of packages to their room and priority seating at select Univer-

5601 Universal Boulevard
Orlando
☎ 407-503-1000 or
888-273-1311
www.loewshotels.com/
hotels/orlando_portofino_bay

sal restaurants. Rooms are ultraluxurious, with Italian furnishings, opulent baths, and soothing neutral hues. Standard guest-room amenities include minibar, coffeemaker, iron and board, hair dryer, safe, umbrella, and TV with pay-per-view movies. Microwaves are available ($15 one-time fee for length of stay). Camp Portofino offers supervised activities (movies, video games, crafts, and such) for children ages 4 to 14. The cost is $12 per hour, per child; hours vary. Trattoria del Porto restaurant offers a character dinner from 6 until 9 p.m. on Friday, with characters such as Scooby Doo and Woody Woodpecker in attendance. The cost is $16.50 for adults, $1.50 for children ages 12 and younger. Portofino has four other Italian restaurants (each with a children's menu), an Italian bakery (also serves gelato), and two bars. Three elaborate pools, gardens, jogging trails, pet-friendly rooms, and a spa and fitness center round out major amenities. If you have the bank account to pay for it and plan to spend time at Universal, you can't go wrong here.

Rosen Shingle Creek

Rate per night $375–$425. **Pools** ★ ★ ★ ★. **Fridge in room** Yes. **Maximum persons per room** 4. **Shuttle to parks** Yes (Universal, Wet 'n Wild, and SeaWorld only).

9939 Universal Boulevard
Orlando
☎ 407-996-9939 or
866-996-9939
www.rosenshinglecreek.com

BEAUTIFUL ROOMS (those facing east have great views) and excellent restaurants distinguish this mostly meeting-and-convention resort. Swimming options include a lap pool, a family pool, and a kiddie wading pool. There's an 18-hole golf course on-site, as well as a superior spa, a decent fitness center, and even a horseshoe pitch. The Kids Swamp Club provides both activities and child care. Though a state-of-the-art video arcade will gobble up your kids' pocket change, the real kicker, especially for the 8-years-and-up-crowd, is a natural area encompassing lily ponds, grassy wetlands, Shingle Creek, and an adjacent cypress swamp. Running through the area is a nature trail complete with signs to help you identify wildlife. Blue herons, wood storks, coots, egrets, mallards, anhingas, and ospreys are common, as are sliders (turtles), chameleons, and skinks (lizards). Oh yeah, there are alligators and snakes, too—real ones, but that's part of the fun. If you stay at Shingle Creek and plan to visit the theme parks, you'll want to take a car: shuttle service is limited, departing and picking up at rather inconvenient times and stopping at three other hotels before delivering you to your destination.

Sheraton World Resort

Rate per night $130–$160. **Pools** ★ ★ ★ ½. **Fridge in room** Yes. **Shuttle to parks** Yes (Disney only). **Maximum number of occupants per room** 4. **Special comments** A good option if you're visiting SeaWorld.

SET ON 28 ACRES, the Sheraton World Resort offers plenty of room for kids to roam. And with three heated pools, two kiddie pools, a small playground, an arcade, and a free minigolf course (very mini), this resort offers ample kid-friendly diversions. The main pool is especially pleasant, with fountains, lush landscaping, and a poolside bar. Other amenities and services include a fitness center, spa, gift shop, guest services desk, and lounge. Book a room in the tower if possible, even though it's away from the kiddie pools and playground. Tower rooms are a bit larger and more upscale than low-rise rooms, some of which could use renovation. All 1,102 rooms include a fridge, coffeemaker, TV with Nintendo, iron and board, hair dryer, and safe. The Sheraton has one restaurant and a deli with a Pizza Hut. If your family loves SeaWorld, you're in luck: Shamu and friends are within walking distance.

10100 International Drive
Orlando
☎ 407-352-1100 or
800-327-0363
www.sheratonworld.com

Lake Buena Vista and I-4 Corridor

Buena Vista Palace

Rate per night $200. **Pools** ★★★½. **Fridge in room** Minibar. **Shuttle to parks** Yes (Disney only). **Maximum number of occupants per room** 4. **Special comments** Sunday character breakfast available.

IN THE DOWNTOWN DISNEY RESORT AREA, the Buena Vista Palace is upscale and convenient. Surrounded by a man-made lake and plenty of palms, the spacious pool area contains three heated pools, the largest of which is partially covered (nice for

1900 Buena Vista Drive
Lake Buena Vista
☎ 407-827-2727
www.buenavistapalace.com

when you need a little shade); a whirlpool and sauna; a basketball court; and a sand volleyball court. Plus, a pool concierge will fetch your favorite magazine or fruity drink. On Sunday, the Watercress Café hosts a character breakfast ($24 for adults and $13 for children). The 1,014 guest rooms are posh and spacious; each comes with a desk, coffeemaker, hair dryer, cable TV with pay-per-view movies, iron and board, and minibar. There are also 112 suites. In-room babysitting is available through the All about Kids and Sitters Solutions services. Three lighted tennis courts, a European-style spa offering 60 services, a fitness center, an arcade, a playground, and a beauty salon round out amenities. Three restaurants and a mini-market are on site. And if you aren't wiped out after time in the parks, consider dropping by the Lobby Lounge or Top of the Palace Lounge for a nightcap. *Note:* All these amenities and services come at a price; a $13 per night resort fee will be added to your bill.

Hilton Walt Disney World

Rate per night $189. **Pools** ★★★½. **Fridge in room** Minibar. **Shuttle to parks** Yes (Disney theme and water parks only). **Maximum number of occupants per room** 4. **Special comments** Sunday character breakfast and Disney early-entry program.

THE HILTON OCCUPIES 23 ACRES in the Downtown Disney Resort Area. Since it's an official Walt Disney World hotel, guests can take advantage of the Disney Extra Magic Hours program, which allows entry to a selected Disney park one hour before official opening and late stays to a selected park up to

1751 Hotel Plaza Boulevard
Lake Buena Vista
☎ 407-827-4000 or
800-782-4414
www.hilton-wdwv.com

three hours after official close. The Hilton's 814 guest rooms and suites are spacious, luxurious, and tasteful. Decorated in earth tones, all standard rooms have marble baths, iron and board, hair dryer, two phones, desk, minibar, coffeemaker, and cable TV with pay-per-view movies and video games. One big plus family amenity is the character breakfast, offered from 8:30 to 11 a.m. on Sunday. (Reservations aren't accepted.) Food is served buffet-style, and four characters attend (only two are present at a time). Other important family amenities include the Hilton Vacation Station, where kids ages 4 to 12 can join supervised activities; babysitting services; an arcade and pool table; and two beautifully landscaped heated swimming pools, as well as a kiddie pool. Adults and older children can relax in the fitness center after a long day touring. Three restaurants, including Benihana, add to the hotel's convenience.

Holiday Inn SunSpree Resort

Rate per night $124. **Pool** ★★★. **Fridge in room** Yes. **Shuttle to parks** Yes (Disney only). **Maximum number of occupants per room** 4–6. **Special comments** The first hotel in the world to offer KidSuites.

13351 FL 535
Lake Buena Vista
☎ 407-239-4500 or
800-366-6299
www.kidsuites.com

PUT ON YOUR SUNGLASSES. You'll know you're here when the hot pink, bright blue, green, and yellow exterior comes into view. Inside, kids have their own check-in counter, where they'll receive a free goody bag. Character mascots Max, Maxine, and the KidSuite Gang come out to play at scheduled times. But the big lure is KidSuites, 405-square-foot rooms with a separate children's area. Themes include a tree house, jail, space capsule, and fort, among others. The kids' area sleeps three to four children in two sets of bunk beds or one bunk bed and a twin; it has a cable TV and VCR, Nintendo, radio/cassette or CD player, fun phone, and game table. The separate adult area has its own TV and VCR, safe, hair dryer, and mini-kitchenette with fridge, microwave, sink, and coffeemaker. Standard guest rooms offer these adult amenities. Other kid-friendly amenities include free bedtime tuck-in by a member of the KidSuite Gang (reservations required); the tiny Castle Movie Theater, which shows movies all day every day and presents clown and magic shows and karaoke nightly; a playground; an arcade with Sega games and air hockey, among its many games; a basketball court; and Camp Holiday, a supervised program for ages 4 to 12 ($5 per hour, per child). Held every day in Max's Magic Castle, Camp Holiday might include movies and cartoons, bingo, face painting, and karaoke. Also offered are a large, free-form pool complete with kiddie pool and two whirlpools, and a fitness center ($6 per hour per child, 10 a.m. to 10 p.m.). Maxine's Kitchen serves breakfast and dinner buffets and offers an à la carte menu for dinner. There's also a mini-mart. Another perk: kids 12 and younger eat free from a special menu when dining with one paying adult (maximum four kids per adult). Finally, pets weighing 30 pounds or less are welcome (for an additional $40 nonrefundable fee).

Hyatt Regency Grand Cypress

Rate per night $269. **Pool** ★★★★★. **Fridge in room** Minibar; fridge available on request. **Shuttle to parks** Yes (Disney only). **Maximum number of occupants per room** 4. **Special comments** Wow, what a pool!

THERE ARE MYRIAD REASONS to stay at this 1,500-acre resort, but the pool ranks as number one. The 800,000-gallon tropical paradise has a 125-foot waterslide, waterfalls, caves and grottos, and a suspension bridge. Your kids may never want to leave the pool to visit the theme parks. The Hyatt also is a golfer's paradise. With a 45-hole championship Jack Nicklaus–designed course, an 18-hole course, a 9-hole pitch-and-putt course, and a golf academy, there's something for golfers of all abilities. Other recreational perks include a racquet facility with hard and clay courts, a private lake with beach, a fitness center, and miles of trails for biking, walking, jogging, and horseback riding. The 750 standard guest rooms are 360 square feet and have a Florida ambience, with green and reddish hues, touches of rattan, and private balconies. Amenities include minibar, iron and board, safe, hair dryer, ceiling fan, and cable TV with pay-per-view movies and video games. Suite and villa accommodations offer even more amenities. Camp Hyatt (also Camp Gator) provides supervised programs for kids 5 to 12; in-room babysitting is available. Five restaurants offer dining options. Four lounges provide nighttime entertainment. If outdoor recreation is high on your family's list, Hyatt is an excellent high-end choice.

One Grand Cypress Boulevard
Lake Buena Vista
☎ 407-239-1234 or
888-591-1234
www.hyattgrandcypress.com

Marriott Village at Lake Buena Vista

Rate per night $129–$149. **Pools** ★★★. **Fridge in room** Yes. **Shuttle to parks** Yes (Disney, Universal, SeaWorld, and Wet 'n Wild). **Maximum number of occupants per room** 4. **Special comments** Free continental breakfast at Fairfield Inn and Spring Hill Suites.

THIS GATED COMMUNITY INCLUDES a 388-room Fairfield Inn, a 400-suite Spring Hill Suites, and a 312-room Courtyard. Whatever your budget, you'll find a room here to fit it. For a bit more space, book Spring Hill Suites; if you're looking for value, try the Fairfield Inn; if you need limited business amenities, reserve at the Courtyard. Amenities at all three properties include fridge, cable TV with PlayStation (for an additional fee), iron and board, and hair dryer. Additionally, all Spring Hill suites have microwaves, and all Courtyard rooms feature Web TV. Cribs and rollaway beds are available free at all locations. Pools at all three hotels are attractive and medium-sized, with children's interactive splash zones and whirlpools. Each property has a fitness center. The incredibly convenient Village Marketplace food court includes Pizza Hut, TCBY, Oscar Mayer Hot Dog Construction Company, Oscar Mayer 1883 Deli, Village Grill, Gourmet Bean Coffee and Pastry Shop, and a 24-hour convenience store. The Bahama Breeze, Fish Bones, and Golden Corral

8623 Vineland Avenue
Lake Buena Vista
☎ 407-938-9001 or
877-682-8552
www.marriottvillage.com

full-service restaurants are within walking distance. Each hotel has a Kids Club (no extra charge) for ages 4 to 8. Kids Clubs are themed (backyard, tree house, and library) and feature a big-screen TV, computer stations, and three educational centers (math and science, reading, and creative activities). They operate about six hours daily; a staff member is on duty at all times. Marriott Village also offers a supervised Kids Night Out program (ages 4 to 10) from 6 to 10 p.m. on select nights. The cost is $35 per child, which includes activities and dinner. Other services and amenities include an attraction planning station and ticket sales, an arcade, and a Hertz car-rental desk. Shoppers will find the Orlando Premium Outlets adjacently located. You'll get a lot of bang for your buck at Marriott Village.

Sheraton Safari Hotel & Suites

Rate per night $159. **Pool** ★★★. **Fridge in room** Safari suites only. **Shuttle to parks** Yes (Disney free; other parks for a fee). **Maximum number of occupants per room** 4–6. **Special comments** Cool python waterslide.

12205 South Apopka–
Vineland Road
Orlando
☎ 407-239-0444 or
800-423-3297
www.sheratonsafari.com

THE SAFARI THEME IS NICELY EXECUTED throughout the property—from the lobby dotted with African artifacts and native decor to the 79-foot python waterslide dominating the pool. The 400 guest rooms and 90 safari suites sport African-inspired art and tasteful animal-print soft goods in brown, beige, and jewel tones. Amenities include cable TV with PlayStation, coffeemaker, iron and board, hair dryer, and safe. Suites are a good option for families since they provide added space with a separate sitting room and a kitchenette with a fridge, microwave, and sink. The first thing your kids will probably want to do is take a turn on the python waterslide. It's pretty impressive, but as one *Unofficial Guide* researcher pointed out, it's somewhat of a letdown: the python doesn't actually spit you out of its mouth. Instead you're deposited below its chin. Other on-site amenities include a restaurant (children's menu available), deli, lounge, arcade, and fitness center. Babysitting is available.

Sheraton Vistana Resort

Rate per night $189. **Pools** ★★★½. **Fridge in room** Minibar. **Shuttle to parks** Yes (Disney). **Maximum number of occupants per room** 6. **Special comments** Though time-shares, the villas are rented nightly as well.

8800 Vistana Centre Drive
Orlando
☎ 866-208-0003 or
407-239-3100
www.starwoodvo.com

SHERATON VISTANA IS DECEPTIVELY LARGE, stretching across both sides of Vistana Center Drive. Since Sheraton's emphasis is on selling the time-shares, the rental angle is little known. But families should consider it; the Vistana is one of Orlando's best off-Disney properties. If you want a serene retreat from your days in the theme parks, this is an excellent base. The spacious villas come in one-bedroom, two-bedroom, and two-bedroom-with-lock-off models. All are decorated in beachy pastels, but the emphasis is on the pro-fusion of amenities. Each villa has a full kitchen (including fridge/freezer, microwave, oven/range, dishwasher, toaster, and coffeemaker, with an option to prestock with groceries), clothes washer and dryer, TVs in the living room and each bedroom (one with VCR), stereo with CD player, separate dining area, and private patio or balcony in most. Grounds offer seven swimming pools (four with bars), four playgrounds, three restaurants, game rooms, fitness centers, a minigolf course, sports equipment rental (including bikes), and courts for basketball, volleyball, tennis, and shuffleboard. A mind-boggling array of activities for kids (and adults) ranges from crafts to games and sports tournaments. Of special note: Vistana is highly secure, with locked gates bordering all guest areas, so children can have the run of the place without parents worrying about them wandering off.

US 192 Area
Comfort Suites Maingate Resort
Rate per night $159. **Pool** ★★★. **Fridge in room** Yes. **Shuttle to parks** Yes (Disney, Universal, SeaWorld, and Wet 'n Wild). **Maximum number of occupants per room** 6. **Special comments** Complimentary continental breakfast daily.

THIS PROPERTY HAS 150 SPACIOUS one-room suites with double sofa bed, microwave, fridge, coffeemaker, TV, hair dryer, and safe. The suites aren't lavish but are clean and contemporary, with muted deep-purple and beige tones. Extra bathroom counter space is especially convenient for larger families. The heated pool is large and has plenty of lounge chairs and moderate landscaping. A kiddie pool, whirlpool, and poolside bar complete the courtyard. Other amenities include Carrabas Italian restaurant, an arcade, and a gift shop. But Maingate's big plus is its location next door to a shopping center with about everything a family could need. There, you'll find seven dining options, including Outback Steakhouse, Dairy Queen, Subway, T.G.I. Friday's, and Chinese, Japanese, and Italian eateries; a Goodings supermarket; one-hour film developing; a hair salon; a bank; a dry cleaner; a tourist information center with park passes for sale; and a Centra Care walk-in clinic, among other services. All this a short walk from your room.

7888 West Irlo Bronson Memorial Highway
Kissimmee
☎ 407-390-9888 or 888-390-9888
www.comfortsuites
kissimmee.com

Gaylord Palms Resort
Rate per night $200. **Pool** ★★★★. **Fridge in room** Yes. **Shuttle to parks** Yes (Disney). **Maximum number of occupants per room** 4. **Special comments** Probably the closest you'll get off World to Disney-level extravagance.

THIS DECIDEDLY UPSCALE RESORT has a colossal convention facility and strongly caters to business clientele but still is a nice (if pricey) family resort. Hotel wings are defined by the three themed, glass-roofed atriums they overlook. Key West's design is reminiscent of island life in the Florida Keys; Everglades is an overgrown spectacle of shabby swamp chic, complete with

6000 West Osceola Parkway
Kissimmee
☎ 407-586-0000
www.gaylordpalms.com

piped-in cricket noise and a robotic alligator; and the immense, central St. Augustine harks back to Spanish Colonial Florida. Lagoons, streams, and waterfalls cut through and connect all three, and walkways and bridges abound. Rooms reflect the colors of their respective areas, though there's no particular connection in decor (St. Augustine atrium-view rooms are the most opulent, but they're not Spanish). A fourth wing, Emerald Tower, overlooks the Emerald Bay shopping and dining area of the St. Augustine atrium. These rooms are the nicest and the most expensive, and they're mostly used by convention-goers. Though rooms have fridges and stereos with CD (as well as other high-end perks, like high-speed Internet access), the rooms themselves really work better as retreats for adults rather than kids. However, children will enjoy wandering the themed areas, playing in the family pool (with water-squirting octopus), or participating in La Petite Academy Kids Station, which organizes games and activities for ages 3 to 14.

Orange Lake Resort & Country Club

Rate per night $220 (2-bedroom summer rate). **Pools** ★★★★. **Fridge in room** Yes. **Shuttle to parks** Yes (fee varies depending on destination). **Maximum number of occupants per room** Varies. **Special comments** This is a time-share property, but if you rent directly through the resort (as opposed to the sales office), you can avoid time-share sales pitches.

8505 West Irlo Bronson
Memorial Highway
Kissimmee
☎ 800-877-6522 or
407-239-0000
www.orangelake.com

YOU COULD SPEND YOUR ENTIRE VACATION never leaving this property, located about 10 to 15 minutes from the Disney theme parks. From its eight pools and mini–water park, Splash Lagoon, to its 40-plus holes of golf, Orange Lake offers an extensive menu of amenities and recreational opportunities. If you tire of lazing by the pool, try waterskiing, wakeboarding, tubing, fishing, or other activities on the 80-acre lake. There's also a live alligator show, exercise programs, organized competitive sports and games, arts-and-crafts sessions, and miniature golf. Activities don't end when the sun goes down. Karaoke, live music, a Hawaiian luau, and movies at the resort cinema are some of the evening options.

The more than 2,000 units are tastefully decorated and comfortably furnished, ranging from suites and studios to three-bedroom villas, all containing fully equipped kitchens. If you'd rather not cook on vacation, try one of the seven restaurants scattered across the resort: two cafes, three grilles, one pizzeria, and a buffet-style eatery. If you need help with (or a break from) the kids, babysitters are available to come to your villa, accompany your family on excursions, or take your children to attractions for you.

Radisson Resort Parkway

Rate per night $177. **Pool** ★★★★½. **Fridge in room** Minibar. **Shuttle to parks** Yes (Disney, Universal, and SeaWorld). **Maximum number of occupants per**

room 4. **Special comments** Kids 10 and younger eat free with a paying adult at any hotel restaurant.

THE POOL ALONE IS WORTH A STAY HERE, but the Radisson Resort gets high marks in all areas. The free-form pool is huge, with a waterfall and waterslide surrounded by palms and flowering plants, plus a smaller heated pool, two whirlpools, and a kiddie pool. Other outdoor amenities include two lighted tennis courts,

2900 Parkway Boulevard
Kissimmee
☎ 407-396-7000 or
800-634-4774
www.radisson.com

sand volleyball, a playground, and jogging areas. Kids can also blow off steam at the arcade, while adults might visit the fitness center. Rooms are elegant, featuring Italian furnishings and marble baths. They're of above-average size and include a minibar, coffeemaker, color TV, iron and board, hair dryer, and safe. Dining options include Mandolin's for breakfast and dinner buffets, and a 1950s-style diner serving burgers, sandwiches, shakes, and Pizza Hut pizza, among other fare. A sports lounge with an 11- by 6-foot TV offers nighttime entertainment. Guest services can help with tours, park passes, car rental, and babysitting. The only downside: no children's programs.

HOTELS *and* MOTELS:
Rated and Ranked

IN THIS SECTION, WE COMPARE HOTELS in three main areas outside Walt Disney World (see pages 9–12) with those inside the World.

In addition to Disney properties, we rate hotels in the three lodging areas defined earlier in this chapter. There are additional hotels at the intersection of US 27 and Interstate 4, on US 441 (Orange Blossom Trail), and in downtown Orlando. Most of these require more than 30 minutes of commuting to Disney World and thus are not rated. We also haven't rated lodging east of Siesta Lago Road on US 192.

WHAT'S IN A ROOM?

EXCEPT FOR CLEANLINESS, state of repair, and decor, travelers pay little attention to hotel rooms. There is, of course, a clear standard of quality and luxury that differentiates Motel 6 from Holiday Inn, Holiday Inn from Marriott, and so on. Many guests, however, fail to appreciate that some rooms are better engineered than others. Making the room usable to its occupants is an art that combines both form and function.

Decor and taste are important. No one wants to stay in a room that's dated, garish, or ugly. But beyond decor, how "livable" is the room? In Orlando, for example, we have seen some beautifully appointed rooms that aren't well designed for human habitation. The next time you stay in a hotel,

unofficial **TIP**
The key to avoiding disappointment is to snoop in advance. Ask how old the hotel is and when its guest rooms were last renovated.

note your room's details and design elements. Even more than decor, these are the things that will make you feel comfortable and at home.

ROOM RATINGS

TO EVALUATE PROPERTIES FOR THEIR QUALITY, tastefulness, state of repair, cleanliness, and size of their standard rooms, we have grouped the hotels and motels into classifications denoted by stars— the overall star rating. Star ratings in this guide apply only to Orlando-area properties and don't necessarily correspond to ratings awarded by Frommer's, Mobil, AAA, or other travel critics. Because stars have little relevance when awarded in the absence of recognized standards of comparison, we have tied our ratings to expected levels of quality established by specific American hotel corporations.

Overall star ratings apply only to room quality and describe the property's standard accommodations. For most hotels, a standard accommodation is a room with one king bed or two queen beds. In an all-suite property, the standard accommodation is either a studio or one-bedroom suite. In addition to standard accommodations, many hotels offer luxury rooms and special suites, which aren't rated in this guide. Star ratings for rooms are assigned without regard to whether a property has restaurant(s), recreational facilities, entertainment, or other extras.

OVERALL STAR RATINGS		
★★★★★	Superior rooms	Tasteful and luxurious by any standard
★★★★	Extremely nice rooms	What you would expect at a Hyatt Regency or Marriott
★★★	Nice rooms	Holiday Inn or comparable quality
★★	Adequate rooms	Clean, comfortable, and functional without frills—like a Motel 6
★	Super-budget	These exist but are not included in our coverage

In addition to stars (which delineate broad categories), we use a numerical rating system—the room-quality rating. Our scale is 0 to 100, with 100 being the best possible rating and zero (0) the worst. Numerical ratings show the difference we perceive between one property and another. Rooms at both the Hawthorn Suites Universal and Grosvenor Resort are rated three-and-a-half stars (★★★½). In the supplemental numerical ratings, Hawthorn Suites Universal is an 82 and Grosvenor a 76. This means that within the three-and-a-half-star category, Hawthorn Suites Universal has slightly nicer rooms than Grosvenor.

The location column identifies the area around Walt Disney World where you'll find a particular property. The designation "WDW" means the property is inside Walt Disney World. A "1" means it's on

LODGING AREAS	
WDW	Walt Disney World
1	International Drive
2	I-4 Corridor
3	US 192 (Irlo Bronson Memorial Highway)

or near International Drive. Properties on or near US 192 (aka Irlo Bronson Memorial Highway, Vine Street, and Space Coast Parkway) are indicated by a "3." All other properties are marked with a "2" and for the most part are along the FL 535 and the I-4 corridor, though some are in nearby locations that don't meet any other criteria.

Names of properties along US 192 also designate location; for example, Holiday Inn Maingate West. The consensus in Orlando seems to be that the main entrance to Disney World is the broad interstate-type road that runs off US 192. This is called Maingate. Properties along US 192 call themselves Maingate East or West to differentiate their positions along the highway. So, driving southeast from Clermont or the Florida Turnpike, the properties before you reach the Maingate turnoff are called Maingate West, while the properties after you pass the Maingate turnoff are called Maingate East.

Cost estimates are based on the hotel's published rack rates for standard rooms. Each "$" represents $50. Thus a cost symbol of "$$$" means that a room (or suite) at that hotel will be about $150 a night.

We've focused on room quality and excluded consideration of location, services, recreation, or amenities. In some instances, a one- or two-room suite is available for the same price or less than that of a single standard hotel room.

If you've used an earlier edition of this guide, you'll notice that new properties have been added and many ratings and rankings have changed, some because of room renovation or improved maintenance or housekeeping. Failure to maintain rooms or lax housekeeping can bring down ratings.

Before you shop for a hotel, consider this letter from a man in Hot Springs, Arkansas:

> We canceled our room reservations to follow the advice in your book and reserved a hotel highly ranked by the Unofficial Guide. We wanted inexpensive, but clean and cheerful. We got inexpensive, but [also] dirty, grim, and depressing. I really felt disappointed in your advice and the room. It was the pits. That was the one real piece of information I needed from your book! The room spoiled the holiday for me aside from our touring.

This letter was as unsettling to us as the bad room was to our reader. Our integrity as travel journalists is based on the quality of the information we provide. When rechecking the hotel our reader disliked, we found our rating was representative, but he had been assigned one of a small number of threadbare rooms scheduled for renovation.

Note that some chains use the same guest-room photo in promotional literature for all its hotels and that the room in a specific property may not resemble the photo. When you or your travel agent call, ask how old the property is and when the guest room you're being assigned was last renovated. If you are assigned a room inferior to expectations, demand to be moved.

A WORD ABOUT TOLL-FREE TELEPHONE NUMBERS

AS WE'VE REPEATED SEVERAL TIMES IN THIS CHAPTER, it's essential to communicate with the hotel directly when shopping for deals and stating your room preferences. Most 800 and other toll-free numbers are routed directly to a hotel chain's central reservations office, usually located hundreds of miles from the hotel. Reservation agents at the central office typically have little or no knowledge of the individual hotels in the chain or of any specials those hotels may be offering. In the following charts, therefore, we list the toll-free number only if it connects directly to the hotel in question; otherwise, we provide the hotel's local phone number. Notable exceptions are the Disney hotels that must be booked through Disney Central Reservations (DCR).

THE TOP 30 BEST DEALS

LET'S LOOK AT THE BEST COMBINATIONS of quality and value in a room. Rankings are made without consideration for location or the availability of restaurant(s), recreational facilities, entertainment, and/or amenities.

A reader recently wrote to complain that he had booked one of our top-ranked rooms in terms of value and had been very disappointed in the room. We noticed that the room the reader occupied had a quality rating of ★★½. Remember that the list of top deals is intended to give you some sense of value received for dollars spent. A ★★½ room at $40 may have the same value as a ★★★★ room at $115, but that doesn't mean the rooms will be of comparable quality. Regardless of whether it's a good deal, a ★★½ room is still a ★★½ room.

The Top 30 Best Deals

HOTEL	LOCATION	OVERALL QUALITY RATING	ROOM-QUALITY RATING	COST ($=$50)
1. Westgate Lakes	2	★★★★½	92	$$–
2. HomeSuiteHome Eastgate*	3	★★½	57	$–
3. Shades of Green	WDW	★★★★½	91	$$
4. Vacation Village at Parkway	3	★★★★½	91	$$
5. Hawthorn Suites Lake Buena Vista	2	★★★★	87	$$–
6. Extended Stay Deluxe Lake Buena Vista	2	★★★★	83	$$–
7. Quality Suites Maingate East	3	★★★½	80	$$–
8. Cypress Pointe Resort	2	★★★★	83	$$
9. Magic Castle Inn & Suites	3	★★½	59	$
10. Westgate Resorts (town center)	3	★★★★½	93	$$$–
11. Palms Hotel & Villas Maingate	3	★★★★	85	$$
12. Crowne Plaza Resort	1	★★★★½	94	$$$–
13. Econo Lodge Polynesian Resort	3	★★½	62	$–
14. Hampton Inn Maingate	3	★★★½	76	$$–
15. Travelodge Suites Eastgate	3	★★★	67	$+
16. Hilton Grand Vacations Club SeaWorld	1	★★★★	89	$$$–
17. Best Western Lake Buena Vista Resort Hotel	WDW	★★★★	85	$$+
18. Palms Hotel & Villas Kissimmee	3	★★★★	85	$$+
19. Holiday Inn Lake Buena Vista	2	★★★½	80	$$
20. Suburban Extended Stay Universal	1	★★★	65	$+
21. Inn at Summer Bay Resort	3	★★½	63	$
22. Monte Carlo	3	★★	48	$–
23. Extended Stay Deluxe Convention Center	1	★★★	73	$$–
24. Radisson Barcelo Inn I-Drive (tower)	1	★★★★	85	$$$–
25. HomeSuiteHome Maingate	3	★★★½	81	$$
26. I-Drive Inn	1	★★½	63	$
27. Motel 6 I-Drive	1	★★½	61	$
28. Rosen Plaza Hotel	1	★★★★½	90	$$$
29. Hilton Grand Vacations Club	1	★★★★	88	$$$–
30. Motel 6 Maingate West	3	★★	52	$–

* requires 3-night minimum stay

How the Hotels Compare

HOTEL	LOCATION	OVERALL QUALITY RATING	ROOM-QUALITY RATING	COST ($=$50)
Omni Orlando Resort at ChampionsGate	3	★★★★★	96	$$$$$
Crowne Plaza Resort	1	★★★★½	94	$$$–
Ritz-Carlton Orlando Grande Lakes	1	★★★★½	94	$$$$$$
Contemporary Resort	WDW	★★★★½	93	$$$$$$$–
Grand Floridian Resort & Spa	WDW	★★★★½	93	$$$$$$$$$+
Hard Rock Hotel	1	★★★★½	93	$$$$$$
Orange Lake Country Club	3	★★★★½	93	$$$+
Westgate Resorts (town center)	3	★★★★½	93	$$$–
Marriott Orlando World Center	2	★★★★½	92	$$$$$–
Marriott Vista Grande Villas	1	★★★★½	92	$$$+
Polynesian Resort	WDW	★★★★½	92	$$$$$$$$$–
Portofino Bay Hotel	1	★★★★½	92	$$$$$$$–
Westgate Lakes	2	★★★★½	92	$$–
Shades of Green	WDW	★★★★½	91	$$
Swan	WDW	★★★★½	91	$$$$$$$
Vacation Village at Parkway	3	★★★★½	91	$$
Beach Club Resort	WDW	★★★★½	90	$$$$$$$$+
Beach Club Villas	WDW	★★★★½	90	$$$$$$$$+
BoardWalk Villas	WDW	★★★★½	90	$$$$$$$$+
Rosen Shingle Creek	1	★★★★½	90	$$$$$$$$–
Celebration Hotel	WDW	★★★★½	90	$$$$$
Celebrity Resorts Orlando	3	★★★★½	90	$$$
Gaylord Palms Resort	3	★★★★½	90	$$$$
Hyatt Regency Grand Cypress	2	★★★★½	90	$$$$$+
Old Key West Resort	WDW	★★★★½	90	$$$$$$
Peabody Orlando	1	★★★★½	90	$$$$$$$
Rosen Plaza Hotel	1	★★★★½	90	$$$
Royal Pacific Resort	1	★★★★½	90	$$$$$$
Saratoga Springs Resort & Spa	WDW	★★★★½	90	$$$$$$
Westgate Resorts (villas)	3	★★★★½	90	$$$$
Wilderness Lodge Villas	WDW	★★★★½	90	$$$$$$$
Animal Kingdom Lodge	WDW	★★★★	89	$$$$$$

HOTEL	LOCATION	OVERALL QUALITY RATING	ROOM-QUALITY RATING	COST ($=$50)
BoardWalk Inn	WDW	★★★★	89	$$$$$$$$+
DoubleTree Universal	1	★★★★	89	$$$−
Hilton Grand Vacations Club SeaWorld	1	★★★★	89	$$$−
Yacht Club Resort	WDW	★★★★	89	$$$$$$$$+
Buena Vista Palace	WDW	★★★★	88	$$$$+
Hilton Grand Vacations Club	1	★★★★	88	$$$−
Hilton Walt Disney World	WDW	★★★★	88	$$$$−
Caribe Royale Resort Suites	3	★★★★	87	$$$$
Dolphin	WDW	★★★★	87	$$$$$$$
Hawthorn Suites Lake Buena Vista	2	★★★★	87	$$−
Hotel Royal Plaza (tower)	WDW	★★★★	87	$$$$$−
Wyndham Palms	3	★★★★	87	$$$$+
Crowne Plaza Universal	1	★★★★	86	$$$$−
Fairfield Orlando Cypress Palms	3	★★★★	86	$$$−
Fort Wilderness Resort (cabins)	WDW	★★★★	86	$$$$$$+
Marriott Cypress Harbour Villas	1	★★★★	86	$$$$$
Marriott Imperial Palm Villas	1	★★★★	86	$$$$$$
Wilderness Lodge	WDW	★★★★	86	$$$$$$
Best Western Lake Buena Vista Resort Hotel	WDW	★★★★	85	$$+
Celebrity Resorts Lake Buena Vista	2	★★★★	85	$$$
Palms Hotel & Villas Kissimmee	3	★★★★	85	$$+
Palms Hotel & Villas Maingate	3	★★★★	85	$$
Radisson Barcelo Inn I-Drive (tower)	1	★★★★	85	$$$−
Residence Inn SeaWorld	1	★★★★	85	$$$+
Embassy Suites Orlando I-Drive	1	★★★★	84	$$$
Port Orleans Resort (French Quarter)	WDW	★★★★	84	$$$$−
Radisson Resort Orlando Celebration	3	★★★★	84	$$$$−
Sheraton Vistana Resort	2	★★★★	84	$$$$−
Star Island Resort	3	★★★★	84	$$$$−
Buena Vista Suites	3	★★★★	83	$$$+
Coronado Springs Resort	WDW	★★★★	83	$$$$−

How the Hotels Compare (continued)

HOTEL	LOCATION	OVERALL QUALITY RATING	ROOM-QUALITY RATING	COST ($=$50)
Cypress Pointe Resort	2	★★★★	83	$$
Extended Stay Deluxe Lake Buena Vista	2	★★★★	83	$$−
Polynesian Isles Resort	3	★★★★	83	$$$−
Port Orleans Resort (Riverside)	WDW	★★★★	83	$$$$−
Sheraton Safari Hotel & Suites	2	★★★★	83	$$$
Wyndham Orlando	1	★★★★	83	$$$
AmeriSuites Lake Buena Vista South	3	★★★½	82	$$$
Country Inn & Suites Calypso Cay	3	★★★½	82	$$$
DoubleTree Castle Hotel	1	★★★½	82	$$$
DoubleTree Guest Suites	WDW	★★★½	82	$$$$−
Hawthorn Suites Universal	1	★★★½	82	$$$−
Hilton Garden Inn Orlando	3	★★★½	82	$$$
Liki Tiki Village	3	★★★½	82	$$$
Nickelodeon Family Suites by Holiday Inn	1	★★★½	82	$$$$−
Sheraton Studio City	1	★★★½	82	$$$−
Staybridge Suites Hotel	1	★★★½	82	$$$$−
Club Hotel by DoubleTree	2	★★★½	81	$$$+
Embassy Suites Resort Lake Buena Vista	2	★★★½	81	$$$$−
HomeSuiteHome Maingate	3	★★★½	81	$$
Westgate Resorts (tower)	3	★★★½	81	$$+
Caribbean Beach Resort	WDW	★★★½	80	$$$$−
Embassy Suites Plaza I-Drive	1	★★★½	80	$$$−
Holiday Inn Lake Buena Vista	2	★★★½	80	$$
Quality Suites Maingate East	3	★★★½	80	$$−
Renaissance Orlando Resort	1	★★★½	80	$$$$
Residence Inn Convention Center	1	★★★½	80	$$$
Rosen Centre Hotel	1	★★★½	80	$$$$$$$
Saratoga Resort Villas	3	★★★½	80	$$$−
Spring Hill Suites by Marriott	1	★★★½	80	$$$
Homewood Suites I-Drive	1	★★★½	79	$$$$−
Sheraton World Resort (tower)	1	★★★½	79	$$$+
Country Inn & Suites Lake Buena Vista (suites)	2	★★★½	78	$$$−

HOTEL	LOCATION	OVERALL QUALITY RATING	ROOM-QUALITY RATING	COST ($=$50)
Hilton Garden Inn	1	★★★½	77	$$$+
Radisson Worldgate Resort	3	★★★½	77	$$
AmeriSuites Universal	1	★★★½	76	$$$$+
Courtyard by Marriott I-Drive	1	★★★½	76	$$$+
Grand Lake Resort	3	★★★½	76	$$$$–
Grosvenor Resort	WDW	★★★½	76	$$$–
Hampton Inn Maingate	3	★★★½	76	$$–
Radisson Barcelo Inn I-Drive(garden)	1	★★★½	76	$$$–
Residence Inn Lake Buena Vista	2	★★★½	76	$$$–
Holiday Inn WDW Resort	WDW	★★★½	75	$$$$–
Parkway International Resort	3	★★★½	75	$$
Quality Suites Universal	1	★★★½	75	$$+
Residence Inn Orlando	1	★★★½	75	$$$
Hampton Inn Convention Center	1	★★★	74	$$$–
Hawthorn Suites Orlando at SeaWorld	1	★★★	74	$$+
Holiday Inn Hotel & Suites Convention Center	1	★★★	74	$$
Marriott Village Spring Hill Suites	2	★★★	74	$$$
Palomino Suites Lake Buena Vista	2	★★★	74	$$$–
RIU Orlando	2	★★★	74	$$–
All-Star Resort	WDW	★★★	73	$$+
Comfort Suites Maingate	3	★★★	73	$$$
Extended Stay Deluxe Universal	1	★★★	73	$$
Fairfield Inn & Suites Universal	1	★★★	73	$$+
Holiday Inn International Resort	1	★★★	73	$$$–
La Quinta Inn I-Drive	1	★★★	73	$$+
Country Inn & Suites Lake Buena Vista(rooms)	2	★★★	72	$$+
Extended Stay Convention Center	1	★★★	72	$$–
Extended Stay Universal	1	★★★	72	$$–
Ramada Inn I-Drive Orlando	1	★★★	72	$$
Staybridge Suites Lake Buena Vista	2	★★★	72	$$$$
Clarion Maingate	3	★★★	71	$$+
Hotel Royal Plaza(garden)	WDW	★★★	71	$$$$

How the Hotels Compare *(continued)*

HOTEL	LOCATION	OVERALL QUALITY RATING	ROOM-QUALITY RATING	COST ($=$50)
Marriott Village at Lake Buena Vista	2	★★★	71	$$$–
Pop Century Resort	WDW	★★★	71	$$+
Ramada Plaza & Inn Gateway **(tower)**	3	★★★	71	$$–
Seralago Hotel	3	★★★	71	$$–
Comfort Suites Orlando	2	★★★	69	$$
Hampton Inn Maingate West	3	★★★	69	$$$–
Holiday Inn Sun Spree Resort	2	★★★	69	$$+
Holiday Inn Universal Studios	1	★★★	69	$$+
Best Western Movieland	1	★★★	68	$$–
Holiday Inn Maingate West	3	★★★	68	$$+
Sheraton World Resort **(garden)**	1	★★★	68	$$$–
Westgate Palace	1	★★★	68	$$$$–
Best Western Lakeside	3	★★★	67	$$$–
Clarion Universal	1	★★★	67	$$$
Courtyard by Marriott Lake Buena Vista	2	★★★	67	$$$$–
Enclave Suites	1	★★★	67	$$$
Hampton Inn Universal	1	★★★	67	$$
Quality Inn & Suites Universal	1	★★★	67	$$–
Travelodge Suites Eastgate	3	★★★	67	$+
Comfort Inn Sandlake	1	★★★	66	$$
Comfort Suites Universal	1	★★★	66	$$$
Howard Johnson Inn Maingate West	3	★★★	66	$$$–
Quality Inn & Suites Eastgate	3	★★★	66	$$–
Ramada Eastgate Fountain Park	3	★★★	66	$$
Days Inn Lake Buena Vista	2	★★★	65	$$–
Hampton Inn Lake Buena Vista	2	★★★	65	$$
Quality Inn I-Drive	1	★★★	65	$$$–
Extended Stay Deluxe Convention Center	1	★★★	73	$$–
Suburban Extended Stay Universal	1	★★★	65	$+
Travelodge Maingate East	3	★★★	65	$$
AmeriHost Resort	3	★★½	64	$$$$$$–
Comfort Inn Lake Buena Vista	2	★★½	64	$$–

HOTEL	LOCATION	OVERALL QUALITY RATING	ROOM- QUALITY RATING	COST ($=$50)
Comfort Inn Maingate West	3	★★½	64	$+
Days Inn Eastgate	3	★★½	64	$+
Hampton Inn Kirkman	1	★★½	64	$$$
Marriott Village Fairfield Inn	2	★★½	64	$$$–
Meridian Hotel	3	★★½	64	$$+
Orlando Grand Plaza	1	★★½	64	$+
Ramada Plaza & Inn Gateway **(garden)**	3	★★½	64	$$–
Silver Lake Resort	3	★★½	64	$$$$–
Best Western Universal Inn	1	★★½	63	$$
Country Inn & Suites I-Drive	1	★★½	63	$$
Howard Johnson Plaza Hotel & Suites at Orlando Convention Center	1	★★½	63	$$
I-Drive Inn	1	★★½	63	$
Inn at Summer Bay Resort	3	★★½	63	$
La Quinta Universal	1	★★½	63	$$
Microtel Inn & Suites	1	★★½	63	$$–
Baymont Inn Kissimmee	3	★★½	62	$$+
Best Western Plaza I-Drive	1	★★½	62	$$
Days Inn West Kissimmee	3	★★½	62	$+
Econo Lodge Polynesian Resort	3	★★½	62	$–
Holiday Inn Express Summer Bay Resort	3	★★½	62	$$–
Howard Johnson Express Inn & Suites **(suites)**	3	★★½	62	$$–
Quality Inn Plaza	1	★★½	62	$$–
Reedy Creek Inn	3	★★½	62	$+
Days Inn I-Drive	1	★★½	61	$+
Days Inn Suites Old Town	3	★★½	61	$+
Imperial Swan Hotel	1	★★½	61	$+
Motel 6 I-Drive	1	★★½	61	$
Wellesley Inn Kissimmee/Lake Cecile	3	★★½	61	$$–
Comfort Inn I-Drive	1	★★½	60	$$+
Days Inn SeaWorld/Convention Center	1	★★½	60	$+
Days Inn Universal Studios	1	★★½	60	$+

How the Hotels Compare (continued)

HOTEL	LOCATION	OVERALL QUALITY RATING	ROOM-QUALITY RATING	COST ($=$50)
Quality Inn Maingate West	3	★★½	60	$$–
Super 8 Kissimmee	3	★★½	60	$$–
Travelodge I-Drive	1	★★½	60	$+
Econo Lodge Hawaiian Resort	3	★★½	59	$$–
Howard Johnson Inn Orlando	1	★★½	59	$$
Magic Castle Inn & Suites	3	★★½	59	$
Rodeway Inn Maingate	3	★★½	59	$+
Travelodge Convention Center	1	★★½	59	$+
Westgate Inn	3	★★½	59	$$–
Extended Stay Deluxe Convention Center/ Pointe Orlando	1	★★½	58	$$–
Howard Johnson Inn Maingate East	3	★★½	58	$$–
Park Inn & Suites Maingate East	3	★★½	58	$$$–
Red Roof Inn Convention Center	1	★★½	58	$$
Rodeway Inn Carrier	1	★★½	58	$
Super 8 Lakeside	3	★★½	58	$+
HomeSuiteHome Eastgate	3	★★½	57	$–
Howard Johnson's Lake Front Park	3	★★½	57	$$–
Super 8 East	3	★★½	57	$$–
Travelodge Suites Maingate	3	★★½	56	$+
Buena Vista Motel	3	★★	55	$
Knights Inn Kissimmee	3	★★	55	$+
Masters Inn Kissimmee	3	★★	55	$

HOTEL	LOCATION	OVERALL QUALITY RATING	ROOM- QUALITY RATING	COST ($=$50)
Masters Inn Maingate	3	★★	55	$
Baymont Inn & Suites	1	★★	54	$
Golden Link Motel	3	★★	54	$+
Sleep Inn Convention Center	1	★★	54	$$−
Sun Inn & Suites	3	★★	53	$
Knights Inn Maingate East	3	★★	52	$
Motel 6 Maingate East	3	★★	52	$
Motel 6 Maingate West	3	★★	52	$−
Central Motel	3	★★	51	$
Key Motel	3	★★	51	$
Rodeway Inn I-Drive	1	★★	51	$+
Super 8 Universal	1	★★	51	$$−
La Quinta Inn I-Drive North	1	★★	50	$$−
Masters Inn I-Drive	1	★★	50	$+
Red Carpet Inn East	3	★★	50	$
Monte Carlo	3	★★	48	$−
Condolodge	3	★★	47	$$$$−
Riande Continental Plaza	1	★★	47	$+
Red Roof Inn Kissimmee	3	★½	42	$
Howard Johnson Enchantedland Resort Hotel	3	★½	41	$+
Palm Lakefront Resort & Hostel	3	★½	38	$−

Hotel Information Chart

All-Star Resorts ★★★
Walt Disney World
1701–1901 W. Buena Vista Drive
Orlando 32830
☎ 407-934-7639
www.waltdisneyworld.com

LOCATION	WDW
ROOM RATING	73
COST ($ = $50)	$$+

AmeriHost Resort ★★½
7491 W. Irlo Bronson Mem. Hwy.
Kissimmee 34747
☎ 407-396-6000
FAX 407-396-7393
www.amerihostinn.com

LOCATION	3
ROOM RATING	64
COST ($ = $50)	$$$$$$–

AmeriSuites Lake Buena Vista South ★★★½
4991 Calypso Cay Way
Kissimmee 34746
☎ 407-997-1300
FAX 407-997-1301
www.amerisuites.com

LOCATION	3
ROOM RATING	82
COST ($ = $50)	$$$

Baymont Inn Kissimmee ★★½
5196 W. Irlo Bronson Mem. Hwy.
Kissimmee 34746
☎ 407-787-3555
FAX 407-787-0700
www.baymontinns.com

LOCATION	3
ROOM RATING	62
COST ($ = $50)	$$+

Beach Club Resort ★★★★½
Walt Disney World
1800 Epcot Resort Blvd.
Lake Buena Vista 32830
☎ 407-934-8000
FAX 407-934-3850
www.waltdisneyworld.com

LOCATION	WDW
ROOM RATING	90
COST ($ = $50)	$$$$$$$$+

Beach Club Villas ★★★★½
Walt Disney World
1900 Epcot Resort Blvd.
Lake Buena Vista 32830
☎ 407-934-2175
FAX 407-934-3850
www.waltdisneyworld.com

LOCATION	WDW
ROOM RATING	90
COST ($ = $50)	$$$$$$$$+

Best Western Plaza I-Drive ★★½
8738 International Drive
Orlando 32819
☎ 407-345-8195
FAX 407-352-819
www.bestwestern.com

LOCATION	1
ROOM RATING	62
COST ($ = $50)	$$

Best Western Universal Inn ★★½
5618 Vineland Road
Orlando 32819
☎ 407-226-9119
FAX 407-770-2448
www.bestwestern.com

LOCATION	1
ROOM RATING	63
COST ($ = $50)	$$

BoardWalk Inn ★★★★
Walt Disney World
2101 Epcot Resort Blvd.
Orlando 32830
☎ 407-939-5100
FAX 407-939-5150
www.waltdisneyworld.com

LOCATION	WDW
ROOM RATING	89
COST ($ = $50)	$$$$$$$$+

Buena Vista Suites ★★★★
8203 World Center Drive
Orlando 32821
☎ 407-239-8588
FAX 407-239-1401
www.bvsuites.com

LOCATION	3
ROOM RATING	83
COST ($ = $50)	$$$+

Caribbean Beach Resort ★★★½
Walt Disney World
900 Cayman Way
Orlando 32830
☎ 407-934-3400
FAX 407-934-3288
www.waltdisneyworld.com

LOCATION	WDW
ROOM RATING	80
COST ($ = $50)	$$$$–

Caribe Royale Resort Suites ★★★★
8101 World Center Drive
Orlando 32821
☎ 407-238-8000
FAX 407-238-8050
www.cariberesorts.com

LOCATION	3
ROOM RATING	87
COST ($ = $50)	$$$$

Central Motel ★★
4698 W. Irlo Bronson Mem. Hwy.
Kissimmee 34747
☎ 407-396-2333
FAX 407-396-0739

LOCATION	3
ROOM RATING	51
COST ($ = $50)	$

Clarion Maingate ★★★
7675 W. Irlo Bronson Mem. Hwy.
Kissimmee 34747
☎ 407-396-4000
FAX 407-396-0714
www.choicehotels.com

LOCATION	3
ROOM RATING	71
COST ($ = $50)	$$+

Clarion Universal ★★★
7299 Republic Drive
Orlando 32819
☎ 407-351-5009
FAX 407-352-7277
www.choicehotels.com

LOCATION	1
ROOM RATING	67
COST ($ = $50)	$$$

AmeriSuites Universal ★★★½
5895 Caravan Court
Orlando 32819
☎ 407-351-0627
FAX 407-351-3317
www.amerisuites.com

LOCATION	1
ROOM RATING	76
COST ($ = $50)	$$$$+

Animal Kingdom Lodge ★★★★
Walt Disney World
2901 Osceola Parkway
Bay Lake 32830
☎ 407-938-3000
FAX 407-938-4799
www.waltdisneyworld.com

LOCATION	WDW
ROOM RATING	89
COST ($ = $50)	$$$$$$

Baymont Inn & Suites ★★
8342 Jamaican Court
Orlando 32819
☎ 407-363-1944
FAX 407-363-4844
www.baymontinns.com

LOCATION	1
ROOM RATING	54
COST ($ = $50)	$

Best Western Lake Buena Vista Resort Hotel ★★★★
2000 Hotel Plaza Blvd.
Lake Buena Vista 32830
☎ 407-828-2424
FAX 407-828-8933
www.orlandoresorthotel.com

LOCATION	WDW
ROOM RATING	85
COST ($ = $50)	$$+

Best Western Lakeside ★★★
7769 W. Irlo Bronson Mem. Hwy.
Kissimmee 34747
☎ 407-396-2222
FAX 407-396-7087
www.bestwesternflorida.com

LOCATION	3
ROOM RATING	67
COST ($ = $50)	$$$–

Best Western Movieland ★★★
6233 International Drive
Orlando 32819
☎ 407-351-3900
FAX 407-363-5119
www.bestwestern.com

LOCATION	1
ROOM RATING	68
COST ($ = $50)	$$-

BoardWalk Villas ★★★★½
Walt Disney World
2101 Epcot Resort Blvd.
Orlando 32830
☎ 407-939-5100
FAX 407-939-5150
www.waltdisneyworld.com

LOCATION	WDW
ROOM RATING	90
COST ($ = $50)	$$$$$$$$+

Buena Vista Motel ★★
5200 W. Irlo Bronson Mem. Hwy.
Kissimmee 34746
☎ 407-396-2100
FAX 407-396-4359
www.buenavistamotel192.com

LOCATION	3
ROOM RATING	55
COST ($ = $50)	$

Buena Vista Palace ★★★★
Walt Disney World
1900 Buena Vista Drive
Lake Buena Vista 32830
☎ 407-827-2727
FAX 407-827-3136
www.buenavistapalace.com

LOCATION	WDW
ROOM RATING	88
COST ($ = $50)	$$$$+

Celebration Hotel ★★★★½
700 Bloom St.
Celebration 34747
☎ 407-566-6000
FAX 407-566-1844
www.celebrationhotel.com

LOCATION	WDW
ROOM RATING	90
COST ($ = $50)	$$$$$

Celebrity Resorts Lake Buena Vista ★★★★
8451 Palm Parkway
Lake Buena Vista 32836
☎ 407-238-1700
FAX 407-238-0255
www.celebrityresorts.com/lbv

LOCATION	2
ROOM RATING	85
COST ($ = $50)	$$$

Celebrity Resorts Orlando ★★★★½
2800 N. Poinciana Blvd.
Orlando 34746
☎ 407-396-8300
FAX 407-997-5222
www.orlando-celebrityresort.com

LOCATION	3
ROOM RATING	90
COST ($ = $50)	$$$

Club Hotel by DoubleTree ★★★½
12490 Apopka–Vineland Road
Orlando 32836
☎ 407-239-4646
FAX 407-239-8469
www.doubletree.com

LOCATION	2
ROOM RATING	81
COST ($ = $50)	$$$+

Comfort Inn I-Drive ★★½
8134 International Drive
Orlando 32819
☎ 407-313-4000
FAX 407-313-4001
www.choicehotels.com

LOCATION	1
ROOM RATING	60
COST ($ = $50)	$$+

Comfort Inn Lake Buena Vista ★★½
8442 Palm Parkway
Lake Buena Vista 32836
☎ 407-239-7300
FAX 407-996-7301
www.choicehotels.com

LOCATION	2
ROOM RATING	64
COST ($ = $50)	$$-

Hotel Information Chart (continued)

Comfort Inn Maingate West ★★½
9330 W. Irlo Bronson Mem. Hwy.
Kissimmee 34711
☎ 863-424-8420
FAX 863-424-9670
www.choicehotels.com

LOCATION	3
ROOM RATING	64
COST ($ = $50)	$+

Comfort Inn Sandlake ★★★
6101 Sandlake Road
Orlando 32919
☎ 407-363-7886
FAX 407-345-0670
www.choicehotels.com

LOCATION	1
ROOM RATING	66
COST ($ = $50)	$$

Comfort Suites Maingate ★★★
7888 W. Irlo Bronson Mem. Hwy.
Kissimmee 34747
☎ 407-390-9888
FAX 407-390-0981
www.comfortsuiteskissimmee.com

LOCATION	3
ROOM RATING	73
COST ($ = $50)	$$$

Contemporary Resort ★★★★½
Walt Disney World
4600 N. World Drive
Orlando 32830
☎ 407-934-7639
FAX 407-824-3539
www.waltdisneyworld.com

LOCATION	WDW
ROOM RATING	93
COST ($ = $50)	$$$$$$$–

Coronado Springs Resort ★★★★
Walt Disney World
1000 W. Buena Vista Drive
Orlando 32830
☎ 407-939-1000
FAX 407-939-1001
www.waltdisneyworld.com

LOCATION	WDW
ROOM RATING	83
COST ($ = $50)	$$$$–

**Country Inn & Suites
Calypso Cay** ★★★½
5001 Calypso Cay Way
Kissimmee 34746
☎ 407-997-1400
FAX 407-997-1401
www.countryinns.com

LOCATION	3
ROOM RATING	82
COST ($ = $50)	$$$

**Courtyard by Marriott
Lake Buena Vista** ★★★
8501 Palm Parkway
Lake Buena Vista 32836
☎ 407-938-9001
FAX 407-239-1287
www.marriott.com

LOCATION	2
ROOM RATING	67
COST ($ = $50)	$$$$–

Crowne Plaza Resort ★★★★½
12000 International Drive
Orlando 32821
☎ 407-239-1222
FAX 407-239-1190
www.crowneplaza.com

LOCATION	1
ROOM RATING	94
COST ($ = $50)	$$$–

Crowne Plaza Universal ★★★★
7800 Universal Blvd.
Orlando 32819
☎ 407-355-0550
FAX 407-355-0504
www.crowneplaza.com

LOCATION	1
ROOM RATING	86
COST ($ = $50)	$$$$–

Days Inn Lake Buena Vista ★★★
12799 Apopka–Vineland Road
Lake Buena Vista 32836
☎ 407-239-4441
FAX 407-239-0325
www.daysinn.com

LOCATION	2
ROOM RATING	65
COST ($ = $50)	$$-

**Days Inn SeaWorld/
Convention Center** ★★½
9990 International Drive
Orlando 32819
☎ 407-352-8700
FAX 407-363-3965
www.daysinn.com

LOCATION	1
ROOM RATING	60
COST ($ = $50)	$+

Days Inn Suites Old Town ★★½
5820 W. Irlo Bronson Mem. Hwy.
Kissimmee 34746
☎ 407-396-7900
FAX 407-396-1789
www.daysinn.com

LOCATION	3
ROOM RATING	61
COST ($ = $50)	$+

DoubleTree Castle Hotel ★★★½
8629 International Drive
Orlando 32819
☎ 407-345-1511
FAX 407-248-8181
www.doubletreecastle.com

LOCATION	1
ROOM RATING	82
COST ($ = $50)	$$$

DoubleTree Guest Suites ★★★½
2305 Hotel Plaza Blvd.
Lake Buena Vista 32830
☎ 407-934-1000
FAX 407-934-1015
www.doubletree.com

LOCATION	WDW
ROOM RATING	82
COST ($ = $50)	$$$$–

DoubleTree Universal ★★★★
5780 Major Blvd.
Orlando 32819
☎ 407-351-1000
FAX 407-353-0106
www.doubletree.com

LOCATION	1
ROOM RATING	89
COST ($ = $50)	$$$–

Comfort Suites Orlando ★★★
9350 Turkey Lake Road
Orlando 32819
☎ 407-351-5050
FAX 407-363-7953
www.comfortsuitesorlando.com

LOCATION	2
ROOM RATING	69
COST ($ = $50)	$$

Comfort Suites Universal ★★★
5617 Major Blvd.
Orlando 32819
☎ 407-363-1967
FAX 407-363-6873
www.choicehotels.com

LOCATION	1
ROOM RATING	66
COST ($ = $50)	$$$

Condolodge ★★
3147 Hempstead Ave.
Kissimmee 34741
☎ 407-931-2383
FAX 407-931-2385
www.condolodge.com

LOCATION	3
ROOM RATING	47
COST ($ = $50)	$$$$–

Country Inn & Suites I-Drive
★★½
7701 Universal Blvd.
Orlando 32819
☎ 407-313-4200
FAX 407-313-4201
www.countryinns.com

LOCATION	1
ROOM RATING	63
COST ($ = $50)	$$

Country Inn & Suites Lake Buena Vista ★★½/★★★*
12191 S. Apopka–Vineland Road
Lake Buena Vista 32836
☎ 407-239-1115; FAX 407-239-8882
www.countryinns.com

LOCATION	2
ROOM RATING	78/72*
COST ($ = $50)	$$$–/$$+*

* suites/rooms

Courtyard by Marriott I-Drive ★★★½
8600 Austrian Court
Orlando 32819
☎ 407-351-2244
FAX 407-351-3306
www.marriott.com

LOCATION	1
ROOM RATING	76
COST ($ = $50)	$$$+

Cypress Pointe Resort ★★★★
8651 Treasure Cay Lane
Orlando 32836
☎ 407-597-2700
www.cypresspointe.net

LOCATION	2
ROOM RATING	83
COST ($ = $50)	$$

Days Inn Eastgate ★★½
5245 W. Irlo Bronson Mem. Hwy.
Kissimmee 34746
☎ 407-396-7700
FAX 407-396-0293
www.daysinn.com

LOCATION	3
ROOM RATING	64
COST ($ = $50)	$+

Days Inn I-Drive ★★½
5858 International Drive
Orlando 32819
☎ 407-351-4410
FAX 407-351-2481
www.daysinn.com

LOCATION	1
ROOM RATING	61
COST ($ = $50)	$+

Days Inn Universal Studios ★★½
5827 Caravan Court
Orlando 32819
☎ 407-351-3800
FAX 407-363-0907
www.daysinn.com

LOCATION	1
ROOM RATING	60
COST ($ = $50)	$+

Days Inn West Kissimmee ★★½
9240 W. Irlo Bronson Mem. Hwy.
Kissimmee 34711
☎ 863-424-6099
FAX 863-424-5779
www.daysinn.com

LOCATION	3
ROOM RATING	62
COST ($ = $50)	$+

Dolphin ★★★★
Walt Disney World
1500 Epcot Resort Blvd.
Lake Buena Vista 32830
☎ 407-934-7639
FAX 407-934-4884
www.swandolphin.com

LOCATION	WDW
ROOM RATING	87
COST ($ = $50)	$$$$$$$

Econo Lodge Hawaiian Resort ★★½
7514 W. Irlo Bronson Mem. Hwy.
Kissimmee 34747
☎ 407-396-1890
FAX 407-396-1295
www.econolodge.com

LOCATION	3
ROOM RATING	59
COST ($ = $50)	$$–

Econo Lodge Polynesian Resort ★★½
2934 Polynesian Isle Blvd.
Kissimmee 34746
☎ 407-396-2121
FAX 407-396-2191
www.econolodge.com

LOCATION	3
ROOM RATING	62
COST ($ = $50)	$–

Embassy Suites Orlando I-Drive ★★★★
8978 International Drive
Orlando 32819
☎ 407-352-1400
FAX 407-363-1120
www.embassysuitesorlando.com

LOCATION	1
ROOM RATING	84
COST ($ = $50)	$$$

Hotel Information Chart (continued)

**Embassy Suites Plaza
I-Drive** ★★★½
8250 Jamaican Court
Orlando 32819
☎ 407-345-8250
FAX 407-352-1463
www.embassysuites.com

LOCATION	1
ROOM RATING	80
COST ($ = $50)	$$$–

**Embassy Suites Resort
Lake Buena Vista** ★★★½
8100 Lake Ave.
Orlando 32836
☎ 407-239-1144
FAX 407-238-0230
www.embassysuitesorlando.com

LOCATION	2
ROOM RATING	81
COST ($ = $50)	$$$$–

Enclave Suites ★★★
6165 Carrier Drive
Orlando 32819
☎ 407-351-1155
FAX 407-351-2001
www.enclavesuites.com

LOCATION	1
ROOM RATING	67
COST ($ = $50)	$$$

**Extended Stay Deluxe
Lake Buena Vista** ★★★★
8100 Palm Parkway
Orlando 32836
☎ 407-239-4300
FAX 407-239-4446
www.extendedstaydeluxe.com

LOCATION	2
ROOM RATING	83
COST ($ = $50)	$$–

**Extended Stay Deluxe
Universal** ★★★
5610 Vineland Road
Orlando 32821
☎ 407-370-4428
FAX 407-370-9456
www.extendedstaydeluxe.com

LOCATION	1
ROOM RATING	73
COST ($ = $50)	$$

Extended Stay Universal ★★★
5620 Major Blvd.
Orlando 32819
☎ 407-351-1788
FAX 407-351-7899
www.extendedstayamerica.com

LOCATION	1
ROOM RATING	72
COST ($ = $50)	$$–

Gaylord Palms Resort ★★★★½
6000 W. Osceola Parkway
Kissimmee 34746
☎ 407-586-0000
FAX 407-586-1999
www.gaylordpalms.com

LOCATION	3
ROOM RATING	90
COST ($ = $50)	$$$$

Golden Link Motel ★★
4914 W. Irlo Bronson Mem. Hwy.
Kissimmee 34746
☎ 407-396-0555
FAX 407-396-6531
www.goldenlinkmotel.com

LOCATION	3
ROOM RATING	54
COST ($ = $50)	$+

Grand Floridian Resort & Spa
★★★★½
Walt Disney World
4401 Grand Floridian
Orlando 32830
☎ 407-824-3000
www.waltdisneyworld.com

LOCATION	WDW
ROOM RATING	93
COST ($ = $50)	$$$$$$$$$+

Hampton Inn Kirkman ★★½
7110 S. Kirkman Road
Orlando 32819
☎ 407-345-1112
FAX 407-352-6591
hamptoninn.hilton.com

LOCATION	1
ROOM RATING	64
COST ($ = $50)	$$$

**Hampton Inn
Lake Buena Vista** ★★★
8150 Palm Parkway
Orlando 32836
☎ 407-465-8150
FAX 407-465-0150
hamptoninn.hilton.com

LOCATION	2
ROOM RATING	65
COST ($ = $50)	$$

Hampton Inn Maingate ★★★½
3104 Parkway Blvd.
Kissimmee 34747
☎ 407-396-8484
FAX 407-396-7344
hamptoninn.hilton.com

LOCATION	3
ROOM RATING	76
COST ($ = $50)	$$–

**Hawthorn Suites
Lake Buena Vista** ★★★★
8303 Palm Parkway
Orlando 32836
☎ 407-597-5000
FAX 407-597-6000
www.hawthorn.com

LOCATION	2
ROOM RATING	87
COST ($ = $50)	$$–

**Hawthorn Suites Orlando
at SeaWorld** ★★★
6435 Westwood Blvd.
Orlando 32821
☎ 407-351-6600
FAX 407-351-1977
www.hawthornsuitesorlando.com

LOCATION	1
ROOM RATING	74
COST ($ = $50)	$$+

Hawthorn Suites Universal ★★★½
7601 Canada Ave.
Orlando 32819
☎ 407-581-2151
FAX 407-581-2152
www.hawthornsuitesuniversal.com

LOCATION	1
ROOM RATING	82
COST ($ = $50)	$$$–

**Extended Stay
Convention Center** ★★★
6451 Westwood Blvd.
Orlando 32821
☎ 407-352-3454
FAX 407-352-1708
www.extendedstayamerica.com

LOCATION	1
ROOM RATING	72
COST ($ = $50)	$$–

**Extended Stay Deluxe
Convention Center** ★★★
6443 Westwood Blvd.
Orlando 32821
☎ 407-351-1982
FAX 407-351-1719
www.extendedstayamerica.com

LOCATION	1
ROOM RATING	73
COST ($ = $50)	$$–

**Extended Stay Deluxe Convention
Center/Pointe Orlando** ★★½
8750 Universal Blvd.
Orlando 32819
☎ 407-903-1500
FAX 407-903-1555
www.extendedstaydeluxe.com

LOCATION	1
ROOM RATING	58
COST ($ = $50)	$$–

**Fairfield Inn & Suites
Universal** ★★★
5614 Vineland Road
Orlando 32819
☎ 407-581-5600
FAX 407-581-5601
www.marriott.com

LOCATION	1
ROOM RATING	73
COST ($ = $50)	$$+

**Fairfield Orlando
Cypress Palms** ★★★★
5300 Fairfield Lake Drive
Kissimmee 34746
☎ 800-438-6493
www.fairfieldresorts.com

LOCATION	3
ROOM RATING	86
COST ($ = $50)	$$$–

Fort Wilderness Resort
(cabins) ★★★★
Walt Disney World
4510 N. Fort Wilderness Trail
Orlando 32830
☎ 407-824-2900
FAX 407-824-3508
www.waltdisneyworld.com

LOCATION	WDW
ROOM RATING	86
COST ($ = $50)	$$$$$$+

Grand Lake Resort ★★★½
7770 W. Irlo Bronson Mem. Hwy.
Kissimmee 34747
☎ 407-396-3000
FAX 407-396-1822
www.dailymanagementresorts.
com/grandlake.htm

LOCATION	3
ROOM RATING	76
COST ($ = $50)	$$$$–

Grosvenor Resort ★★★½
1850 Hotel Plaza Blvd.
Lake Buena Vista 32830
☎ 407-828-4444
FAX 407-828-8192
www.grosvenorresort.com

LOCATION	WDW
ROOM RATING	76
COST ($ = $50)	$$$–

**Hampton Inn
Convention Center** ★★★
8900 Universal Blvd.
Orlando 32819
☎ 407-354-4447
FAX 407-354-3031
hamptoninn.hilton.com

LOCATION	1
ROOM RATING	74
COST ($ = $50)	$$$–

**Hampton Inn
Maingate West** ★★★
3000 Maingate Lane
Kissimmee 34747
☎ 407-396-6300
FAX 407-396-8989
hamptoninn.hilton.com

LOCATION	3
ROOM RATING	69
COST ($ = $50)	$$$–

Hampton Inn Universal ★★★
5621 Windhover Drive
Orlando 32819
☎ 407-351-6716
FAX 407-363-1711
hamptoninn.hilton.com

LOCATION	1
ROOM RATING	67
COST ($ = $50)	$$

Hard Rock Hotel ★★★★½
5800 Universal Blvd.
Orlando 32819
☎ 407-503-rock
FAX 407-503-9655
www.hardrock.com

LOCATION	1
ROOM RATING	93
COST ($ = $50)	$$$$$

Hilton Garden Inn ★★★½
6850 Westwood Blvd.
Orlando 32821
☎ 407-354-1500
FAX 407-354-1528
www.hiltongardeninn.com

LOCATION	1
ROOM RATING	77
COST ($ = $50)	$$$+

**Hilton Garden Inn
Orlando** ★★★½
5877 American Way
Orlando 32819
☎ 407-363-9332
FAX 407-363-9335
www.hiltongardenorlando.com

LOCATION	3
ROOM RATING	82
COST ($ = $50)	$$$

**Hilton Grand
Vacations Club** ★★★★
6355 Metrowest Blvd., Suite 180
Orlando 32835
☎ 800-448-2736
FAX 407-521-3112
www.hiltongrandvacations.com

LOCATION	1
ROOM RATING	88
COST ($ = $50)	$$$–

Hotel Information Chart (continued)

**Hilton Grand Vacations Club
SeaWorld** ★★★★
6924 Grand Vacations Way
Orlando 32821
☎ 407-239-0100
FAX 407-239-0200
www.hilton.com

LOCATION	1
ROOM RATING	89
COST ($ = $50)	$$$-

Hilton Walt Disney World ★★★★
1751 Hotel Plaza Blvd.
Lake Buena Vista 32830
☎ 407-827-4000
FAX 407-827-3890
www.hilton-wdwv.com

LOCATION	WDW
ROOM RATING	88
COST ($ = $50)	$$$$-

**Holiday Inn Express
Summer Bay Resort** ★★½
105 Summer Bay Blvd.
Clermont 34711
☎ 407-239-8315
FAX 407-239-8297
www.hiexpress.com

LOCATION	3
ROOM RATING	62
COST ($ = $50)	$$-

Holiday Inn Maingate West ★★★
7601 Black Lake Road
Kissimmee 34747
☎ 407-396-1100
FAX 407-396-0689
www.ichotelsgroup.com

LOCATION	3
ROOM RATING	68
COST ($ = $50)	$$+

Holiday Inn SunSpree Resort
★★★
13351 FL 535
Lake Buena Vista 32821
☎ 407-239-4500
FAX 407-239-8463
www.kidsuites.com

LOCATION	2
ROOM RATING	69
COST ($ = $50)	$$+

**Holiday Inn
Universal Studios** ★★★
5905 Kirkman Road
Orlando 32819
☎ 407-351-3333
FAX 407-351-3577
www.ichotelsgroup.com

LOCATION	1
ROOM RATING	69
COST ($ = $50)	$$+

Homewood Suites I-Drive ★★★½
8745 International Drive
Orlando 32819
☎ 407-248-2232
FAX 407-248-6552
www.homewoodsuitesorlando.com

LOCATION	1
ROOM RATING	79
COST ($ = $50)	$$$$-

Hotel Royal Plaza ★★★★/★★★
1905 Hotel Plaza Blvd.
Orlando 32830
☎ 407-828-2828
FAX 407-827-6338
www.royalplaza.com

LOCATION	WDW
ROOM RATING	87/71*
COST ($ = $50)	$$$$$-/$$$$*

* tower/garden

**Howard Johnson Enchantedland
Resort Hotel** ★½
4985 W. Irlo Bronson Mem. Hwy.
Kissimmee 34746
☎ 407-396-4343
FAX 407-396-8998
www.hojo.com

LOCATION	3
ROOM RATING	41
COST ($ = $50)	$+

**Howard Johnson Inn
Orlando** ★★½
6603 International Drive
Orlando 32819
☎ 407-351-2900
FAX 407-351-1327
www.hojo.com

LOCATION	1
ROOM RATING	59
COST ($ = $50)	$$

**Howard Johnson Plaza Hotel
& Suites at Orlando
Convention Center** ★★½
9956 Hawaiian Court
Orlando 32819
☎ 407-351-5100; FAX 407-352-7188
www.hojo.com

LOCATION	1
ROOM RATING	63
COST ($ = $50)	$$

**Howard Johnson's
Lake Front Park** ★★½
4836 W. Irlo Bronson Mem. Hwy.
Kissimmee 34746
☎ 407-396-4762
FAX 407-396-4866
www.hojo.com

LOCATION	3
ROOM RATING	57
COST ($ = $50)	$$-

Inn at Summer Bay Resort ★★½
9400 US Hwy. 192
Clermont 34711
☎ 800-654-6102
www.summerbayresort.com

LOCATION	3
ROOM RATING	63
COST ($ = $50)	$

Key Motel ★★
4810 W. Irlo Bronson Mem. Hwy.
Kissimmee 34747
☎ 407-396-6200
FAX 407-396-6200

LOCATION	3
ROOM RATING	51
COST ($ = $50)	$

Knights Inn Kissimmee ★★
7475 W. Irlo Bronson Mem. Hwy.
Kissimmee 34747
☎ 407-396-4200
FAX 407-396-8838
www.knightsinn.com

LOCATION	3
ROOM RATING	55
COST ($ = $50)	$+

**Holiday Inn Hotel & Suites
Convention Center** ★★★
8214 Universal Blvd.
Orlando 32819
☎ 407-581-9001
FAX 407-581-9002
www.ichotelsgroup.com

LOCATION	1
ROOM RATING	74
COST ($ = $50)	$$

**Holiday Inn International
Resort** ★★★
6515 International Drive
Orlando 32819
☎ 407-351-3500
FAX 407-351-5727
www.ichotelsgroup.com

LOCATION	1
ROOM RATING	73
COST ($ = $50)	$$$–

**Holiday Inn
Lake Buena Vista** ★★★½
8686 Palm Parkway
Orlando 32836
☎ 407-239-8400
FAX 407-239-8025
www.ichotelsgroup.com

LOCATION	2
ROOM RATING	80
COST ($ = $50)	$$

Holiday Inn WDW Resort ★★★½
1805 Hotel Plaza Blvd.
Lake Buena Vista 32830
☎ 407-828-8888
FAX 407-827-4623
www.hiorlando.com

LOCATION	WDW
ROOM RATING	75
COST ($ = $50)	$$$$–

HomeSuiteHome Eastgate ★★½
5565 W. Irlo Bronson Mem. Hwy.
Kissimmee 34746
☎ 407-396-0707
FAX 407-396-6644
www.homesuitehome.com

LOCATION	3
ROOM RATING	57
COST ($ = $50)	$–

HomeSuiteHome Maingate
★★★½
7300 W. Irlo Bronson Mem. Hwy.
Kissimmee 34747
☎ 407-396-7300
FAX 407-646-5600
www.homesuitehome.com

LOCATION	3
ROOM RATING	81
COST ($ = $50)	$$

**Howard Johnson Express Inn
& Suites** (suites) ★★½
4836 W. Irlo Bronson Mem. Hwy.
Kissimmee 34747
☎ 407-396-4762
FAX 407-396-4866
www.hojo.com

LOCATION	3
ROOM RATING	62
COST ($ = $50)	$$–

**Howard Johnson Inn
Maingate East** ★★½
6051 W. Irlo Bronson Mem. Hwy.
Kissimmee 34747
☎ 407-396-1748
FAX 407-396-1394
www.hojo.com

LOCATION	3
ROOM RATING	58
COST ($ = $50)	$$–

**Howard Johnson Inn
Maingate West** ★★★
8660 W. Irlo Bronson Mem. Hwy.
Kissimmee 34747
☎ 407-396-9300
FAX 407-396-0305
www.hojo.com

LOCATION	3
ROOM RATING	66
COST ($ = $50)	$$$–

**Hyatt Regency
Grand Cypress** ★★★★½
1 Grand Cypress Blvd.
Lake Buena Vista 32836
☎ 407-239-1234
FAX 407-239-3800
www.hyattgrandcypress.com

LOCATION	2
ROOM RATING	90
COST ($ = $50)	$$$$$+

I-Drive Inn ★★½
6323 International Drive
Orlando 32819
☎ 407-351-4430
FAX 407-345-0742

LOCATION	1
ROOM RATING	63
COST ($ = $50)	$

Imperial Swan Hotel ★★½
7050 S. Kirkman Road
Orlando 32819
☎ 407-351-2000
FAX 407-363-1835
www.imperialswanhotel.com

LOCATION	1
ROOM RATING	61
COST ($ = $50)	$+

Knights Inn Maingate East ★★
2880 Poinciana Blvd.
Kissimmee 34747
☎ 407-396-8186
FAX 407-396-8569
www.knightsinn.com

LOCATION	3
ROOM RATING	52
COST ($ = $50)	$

La Quinta Inn I-Drive ★★★
8300 Jamaican Court
Orlando 32819
☎ 407-351-1660
FAX 407-351-9264
www.lq.com

LOCATION	1
ROOM RATING	73
COST ($ = $50)	$$+

La Quinta Inn I-Drive North ★★
5825 International Drive
Orlando 32819
☎ 407-351-4100
FAX 407-996-4599
www.lq.com

LOCATION	1
ROOM RATING	50
COST ($ = $50)	$$–

Hotel Information Chart (continued)

La Quinta Universal ★★½
5621 Major Blvd.
Orlando 32819
☎ 407-313-3100
FAX 407-313-2131
www.lq.com

LOCATION	1
ROOM RATING	63
COST ($ = $50)	$$

Liki Tiki Village ★★★½
17777 Bali Blvd.
Winter Garden 34787
☎ 800-634-3119
FAX 407-239-5092
www.islandone.com/ior/likitiki
village.html

LOCATION	3
ROOM RATING	82
COST ($ = $50)	$$$

Magic Castle Inn & Suites ★★½
5055 W. Irlo Bronson Mem. Hwy.
Kissimmee 34746
☎ 407-396-2212
FAX 407-396-0253
www.magicorlando.com

LOCATION	3
ROOM RATING	59
COST ($ = $50)	$

**Marriott Village
Fairfield Inn** ★★½
8623 Vineland Ave.
Orlando 32821
☎ 407-938-9001
FAX 407-938-9002
www.marriottvillage.com

LOCATION	2
ROOM RATING	64
COST ($ = $50)	$$$–

**Marriott Village at
Lake Buena Vista** ★★★
8623 Vineland Ave.
Orlando 32821
☎ 407-938-9001
FAX 407-938-9002
www.marriottvillage.com

LOCATION	2
ROOM RATING	71
COST ($ = $50)	$$$–

**Marriott Village Spring Hill
Suites** ★★★
8623 Vineland Ave.
Orlando 32821
☎ 407-938-9001
FAX 407-938-9002
www.marriottvillage.com

LOCATION	2
ROOM RATING	74
COST ($ = $50)	$$$

Masters Inn Maingate ★★
2945 Entry Point Blvd.
Kissimmee 34747
☎ 407-396-7743
FAX 407-396-6307
www.mastersinn.com

LOCATION	3
ROOM RATING	55
COST ($ = $50)	$

Meridian Hotel ★★½
8536 W. Irlo Bronson Mem. Hwy.
Kissimmee 34747
☎ 407-396-1600
FAX 407-396-1971
www.meridianorlando.com

LOCATION	3
ROOM RATING	64
COST ($ = $50)	$$+

Microtel Inn & Suites ★★½
7531 Canada Ave.
Orlando 32819
☎ 407-226-9887
FAX 407-226-9877
www.microtelinn.com

LOCATION	1
ROOM RATING	63
COST ($ = $50)	$$–

Motel 6 Maingate West ★★
7455 W. Irlo Bronson Mem. Hwy.
Kissimmee 34747
☎ 407-396-6422
FAX 407-396-0720
www.motel6.com

LOCATION	3
ROOM RATING	52
COST ($ = $50)	$–

**Nickelodeon Family Suites
by Holiday Inn** ★★★½
14500 Continental Gateway
Orlando 32821
☎ 407-387-5437
FAX 407-387-1490
www.nickhotel.com

LOCATION	1
ROOM RATING	82
COST ($ = $50)	$$$$–

Old Key West Resort ★★★★½
Walt Disney World
1510 N. Cove Road
Orlando 32830
☎ 407-827-7700
FAX 407-827-7710
www.waltdisneyworld.com

LOCATION	WDW
ROOM RATING	90
COST ($ = $50)	$$$$$$

**Palm Lakefront Resort
& Hostel** ★½
4840 W. Irlo Bronson Mem. Hwy.
Kissimmee 34741
☎ 407-396-1759
FAX 407-396-1598
www.orlandohostels.com

LOCATION	3
ROOM RATING	38
COST ($ = $50)	$–

**Palms Hotel & Villas
Kissimmee** ★★★★
4786 W. Irlo Bronson Mem. Hwy.
Kissimmee 34746
☎ 407-396-2056
FAX 407-396-2909

LOCATION	3
ROOM RATING	85
COST ($ = $50)	$$+

**Palms Hotel & Villas
Maingate** ★★★★
3100 Parkway Blvd.
Kissimmee 34747
☎ 407-396-2229
FAX 407-396-4833
www.palmshotelandvillas.com

LOCATION	3
ROOM RATING	85
COST ($ = $50)	$$

Marriott Cypress Harbour Villas ★★★★
11251 Harbour Villa Road
Orlando 32821
☎ 407-238-1300
FAX 407-238-1083
www.marriott.com/property/propertypage/MCOCY

LOCATION	1
ROOM RATING	86
COST ($ = $50)	$$$$$

Marriott Imperial Palm Villas ★★★★
8404 Vacation Way
Orlando 32821
☎ 407-238-6200
FAX 407-238-6247
www.marriott.com/property/propertypage/MCOIP

LOCATION	1
ROOM RATING	86
COST ($ = $50)	$$$$$$

Marriott Orlando World Center ★★★★½
8701 World Center Drive
Orlando 32821
☎ 407-239-4200
FAX 407-238-8777
www.marriottworldcenter.com

LOCATION	2
ROOM RATING	92
COST ($ = $50)	$$$$$–

Marriott Vista Grande Villas ★★★★½
5925 Avenida Vista
Orlando 32821
☎ 407-238-7676
FAX 407-238-0900
www.marriott.com/property/propertypage/MCOGV

LOCATION	1
ROOM RATING	92
COST ($ = $50)	$$$+

Masters Inn I-Drive ★★
8222 Jamaican Court
Orlando 32819
☎ 407-345-1172
FAX 407-352-2081
www.mastersinn.com

LOCATION	1
ROOM RATING	50
COST ($ = $50)	$+

Masters Inn Kissimmee ★★
5367 W. Irlo Bronson Mem. Hwy.
Kissimmee 34746
☎ 407-396-4020
FAX 407-396-5450
www.mastersinn.com

LOCATION	3
ROOM RATING	55
COST ($ = $50)	$

Monte Carlo ★★
192 Blossom Hwy.
Kissimmee 34746
☎ 407-396-4700

LOCATION	3
ROOM RATING	48
COST ($ = $50)	$–

Motel 6 I-Drive ★★½
5909 American Way
Orlando 32819
☎ 407-351-6500
FAX 407-352-5481
www.motel6.com

LOCATION	1
ROOM RATING	61
COST ($ = $50)	$

Motel 6 Maingate East ★★
5731 W. Irlo Bronson Mem. Hwy.
Kissimmee 34747
☎ 407-396-6333
FAX 407-396-7715
www.motel6.com

LOCATION	3
ROOM RATING	52
COST ($ = $50)	$

Omni Orlando Resort at ChampionsGate ★★★★★
1500 Masters Blvd.
ChampionsGate 33896
☎ 407-390-6664
FAX 407-390-0600
www.omnihotels.com

LOCATION	3
ROOM RATING	96
COST ($ = $50)	$$$$$

Orange Lake Resort & Country Club ★★★★½
8505 W. Irlo Bronson Mem. Hwy.
Kissimmee 34747
☎ 407-239-0000
FAX 407-239-1039
www.orangelake.com

LOCATION	3
ROOM RATING	93
COST ($ = $50)	$$$+

Orlando Grand Plaza ★★½
7400 International Drive
Orlando 32819
☎ 407-351-4600
FAX 407-996-7453
www.orlandograndplaza.com

LOCATION	1
ROOM RATING	64
COST ($ = $50)	$+

Palomino Suites Lake Buena Vista ★★★
8200 Palm Parkway
Orlando 32836
☎ 407-465-8200
FAX 407-465-0200
www.palominosuites.com

LOCATION	2
ROOM RATING	74
COST ($ = $50)	$$$–

Park Inn & Suites Maingate East ★★½
6075 W. Irlo Bronson Mem. Hwy.
Kissimmee 34747
☎ 407-396-6100
FAX 407-396-6965

LOCATION	3
ROOM RATING	58
COST ($ = $50)	$$$–

Parkway International Resort ★★★½
6200 Safari Trail
Kissimmee 34746
☎ 407-396-6600
FAX 407-396-6165
www.islandone.com

LOCATION	3
ROOM RATING	75
COST ($ = $50)	$$

Hotel Information Chart (continued)

Peabody Orlando ★★★★½
9801 International Drive
Orlando 32819
☎ 407-352-4000
FAX 407-321-3501
www.peabodyorlando.com

LOCATION	1
ROOM RATING	90
COST ($ = $50)	$$$$$$$

Polynesian Isles Resort ★★★★
3045 Polynesian Isles Blvd.
Kissimmee 34746
☎ 407-396-1622
FAX 407-396-1744
www.polynesianisle.com

LOCATION	3
ROOM RATING	83
COST ($ = $50)	$$$–

Polynesian Resort ★★★★½
Walt Disney World
1600 Seven Seas Drive
Orlando 32830
☎ 407-824-2000
FAX 407-824-3174
www.waltdisneyworld.com

LOCATION	WDW
ROOM RATING	92
COST ($ = $50)	$$$$$$$$$–

Portofino Bay Hotel ★★★★½
5601 Universal Blvd.
Orlando 32819
☎ 407-503-1000
FAX 407-224-7118
www.loewshotels.com/hotels/
orlando_portofino_bay

LOCATION	1
ROOM RATING	92
COST ($ = $50)	$$$$$$$–

**Quality Inn & Suites
Eastgate** ★★★
4960 W. Irlo Bronson Mem. Hwy.
Kissimmee 34746
☎ 407-396-1376
FAX 407-396-0716
www.qualityinn.com

LOCATION	3
ROOM RATING	66
COST ($ = $50)	$$–

**Quality Inn & Suites
Universal** ★★★
5635 Windhover Drive
Orlando 32819
☎ 407-370-5100
FAX 407-370-2026
www.qualityinn.com

LOCATION	1
ROOM RATING	67
COST ($ = $50)	$$–

**Quality Suites
Maingate East** ★★★½
5876 W. Irlo Bronson Mem. Hwy.
Kissimmee 34746
☎ 407-396-8040
FAX 407-396-6766
www.qualityinn.com

LOCATION	3
ROOM RATING	80
COST ($ = $50)	$$–

Quality Suites Universal ★★★½
7400 Canada Ave.
Orlando 32819
☎ 407-363-0332
FAX 407-352-2598
www.qualityinn.com

LOCATION	1
ROOM RATING	75
COST ($ = $50)	$$+

**Radisson Barcelo Inn
I-Drive** ★★★★/★★★½*
8444 International Drive
Orlando 32819
☎ 407-345-0505
FAX 407-581-2022
www.radisson.com

LOCATION	1
ROOM RATING	85/76*
COST ($ = $50)	$$$–

* tower/garden

**Ramada Inn I-Drive
Orlando** ★★★
6500 International Drive
Orlando 32819
☎ 407-345-5340
FAX 407-345-0976
www.ramada.com

LOCATION	1
ROOM RATING	72
COST ($ = $50)	$$

**Ramada Plaza & Inn
Gateway** ★★★/★★★½*
7470 W. Irlo Bronson Mem. Hwy
Kissimmee 34747
☎ 407-396-4400
FAX 407-396-4320
www.ramada.com

LOCATION	3
ROOM RATING	71/64*
COST ($ = $50)	$$–

* tower/garden

Red Carpet Inn East ★★
4700 W. Irlo Bronson Mem. Hwy.
Kissimmee 34746
☎ 407-396-1133
FAX 407-396-0224

LOCATION	3
ROOM RATING	50
COST ($ = $50)	$

**Renaissance Orlando
Resort** ★★★½
6677 Sea Harbor Drive
Orlando 32819
☎ 407-351-5555
FAX 407-351-9994
www.marriott.com/property/
propertypage/MCOSR

LOCATION	1
ROOM RATING	80
COST ($ = $50)	$$$$

**Residence Inn
Convention Center** ★★★½
8800 Universal Blvd.
Orlando 32819
☎ 407-226-0288
FAX 407-226-9979
www.marriott.com/property/
propertypage/MCOCV

LOCATION	1
ROOM RATING	80
COST ($ = $50)	$$$

**Residence Inn
Lake Buena Vista** ★★★½
11450 Marbella Palms Court
Orlando 32836
☎ 407-465-0075
FAX 407-465-0050
www.marriott.com/property/
propertypage/MCORL

LOCATION	2
ROOM RATING	76
COST ($ = $50)	$$$–

Pop Century Resort ★★★
Walt Disney World
1050 Century Drive
Orlando 32830
☎ 407-938-4000
FAX 407-938-4040
www.waltdisneyworld.com

LOCATION	WDW
ROOM RATING	71
COST ($ = $50)	$$+

Port Orleans Resort
(French Quarter) ★★★★
Walt Disney World
2201 Orleans Drive
Lake Buena Vista 32830
☎ 407-934-5000
FAX 407-934-5353
www.waltdisneyworld.com

LOCATION	WDW
ROOM RATING	84
COST ($ = $50)	$$$$−

Port Orleans Resort
(Riverside) ★★★★
Walt Disney World
1251 Riverside Drive
Lake Buena Vista 32830
☎ 407-934-6000
FAX 407-934-5777
www.waltdisneyworld.com

LOCATION	WDW
ROOM RATING	83
COST ($ = $50)	$$$$−

Quality Inn I-Drive ★★★
7600 International Drive
Orlando 32819
☎ 407-351-1600
FAX 407-996-5328
www.qualityinn.com

LOCATION	1
ROOM RATING	65
COST ($ = $50)	$$$−

Quality Inn Maingate West ★★½
7785 W. Irlo Bronson Mem. Hwy.
Kissimmee 34747
☎ 407-396-1828
FAX 407-396-1305
www.qualityinn.com

LOCATION	3
ROOM RATING	60
COST ($ = $50)	$$−

Quality Inn Plaza ★★½
9000 International Drive
Orlando 32819
☎ 407-345-8585
FAX 407-996-6839
www.qualityinn.com

LOCATION	1
ROOM RATING	62
COST ($ = $50)	$$−

Radisson Resort Parkway ★★★★
2900 Parkway Blvd.
Kissimmee 34747
☎ 407-396-7000
FAX 407-396-8770
www.radissonparkway.com

LOCATION	3
ROOM RATING	84
COST ($ = $50)	$$$$−

**Radisson Worldgate
Resort** ★★★½
3011 Maingate Lane
Kissimmee 34747
☎ 407-396-1400
FAX 407-396-0660
www.radisson.com

LOCATION	3
ROOM RATING	77
COST ($ = $50)	$$

**Ramada Eastgate
Fountain Park** ★★★
5150 W. Irlo Bronson Mem. Hwy.
Kissimmee 34746
☎ 407-396-1111
FAX 407-396-1607
www.ramadaeastgate.com

LOCATION	3
ROOM RATING	66
COST ($ = $50)	$$

**Red Roof Inn
Convention Center** ★★½
9922 Hawaiian Court
Orlando 32801
☎ 407-352-1507
www.redroof.com

LOCATION	1
ROOM RATING	58
COST ($ = $50)	$$

Red Roof Inn Kissimmee ★½
4970 Kyng's Heath Road
Kissimmee 34746
☎ 407-396-0065
FAX 407-396-0245
www.redroof.com

LOCATION	3
ROOM RATING	42
COST ($ = $50)	$

Reedy Creek Inn ★★½
2950 Reedy Creek Blvd.
Kissimmee 34747
☎ 407-396-4466
FAX 407-396-6418
www.reedycreekinn.com

LOCATION	3
ROOM RATING	62
COST ($ = $50)	$+

Residence Inn Orlando ★★★½
7975 Canada Ave.
Orlando 32819
☎ 407-345-0117
FAX 407-352-2689
www.marriott.com/property/
propertypage/MCOIC

LOCATION	1
ROOM RATING	75
COST ($ = $50)	$$$

Residence Inn SeaWorld ★★★★
11000 Westwood Blvd.
Orlando 32821
☎ 407-313-3600
FAX 407-313-3611
www.marriott.com/property/
propertypage/MCOSW

LOCATION	1
ROOM RATING	85
COST ($ = $50)	$$$+

Riande Continental Plaza ★★
6825 Visitors Circle
Orlando 32819
☎ 407-352-8211
FAX 407-370-3485
www.hotelsriande.com

LOCATION	1
ROOM RATING	47
COST ($ = $50)	$+

Hotel Information Chart (continued)

Ritz-Carlton Orlando Grande Lakes ★★★★½
4012 Central Florida Parkway
Orlando 32837
☎ 407-206-2400
FAX 407-206-2401
www.ritzcarlton.com/resorts/
orlando_grande_lakes

LOCATION	1
ROOM RATING	94
COST ($ = $50)	$$$$$$

RIU Orlando ★★★
8688 Palm Parkway
Orlando 32836
☎ 407-239-8500
FAX 407-239-8591
www.riuorlando.com

LOCATION	2
ROOM RATING	74
COST ($ = $50)	$$–

Rodeway Inn Carrier ★★½
7200 International Drive
Orlando 32801
☎ 407-351-1200
FAX 407-363-1182
www.rodewayinn.com

LOCATION	1
ROOM RATING	58
COST ($ = $50)	$

Rosen Shingle Creek ★★★★½
9939 Universal Boulevard
Orlando 32819
☎ 407-996-9939
FAX 407-996-9935
www.rosenshinglecreek.com

LOCATION	1
ROOM RATING	90
COST ($ = $50)	$$$$$$$$$–

Rosen Plaza Hotel ★★★★½
9700 International Drive
Orlando 32819
☎ 407-352-9700
FAX 407-354-5774
www.rosenplaza.com

LOCATION	1
ROOM RATING	90
COST ($ = $50)	$$$

Royal Pacific Resort ★★★★½
6300 Hollywood Way
Orlando 32819
☎ 407-503-3000
FAX 407-503-3010
www.loewshotels.com

LOCATION	1
ROOM RATING	90
COST ($ = $50)	$$$$$$

Shades of Green ★★★★½
Walt Disney World
1950 W. Magnolia Palm Drive
Lake Buena Vista 32830
☎ 407-824-3400
FAX 407-824-3665
www.shadesofgreen.org

LOCATION	WDW
ROOM RATING	91
COST ($ = $50)	$$

Sheraton Safari Hotel & Suites ★★★★
12205 S. Apopka–Vineland Road
Orlando 32836
☎ 407-239-0444
FAX 407-239-4566
www.sheratonsafari.com

LOCATION	2
ROOM RATING	83
COST ($ = $50)	$$$

Sheraton Studio City ★★★½
5905 International Drive
Orlando 32819
☎ 407-351-2100
FAX 407-352-8028
www.sheraton.com

LOCATION	1
ROOM RATING	82
COST ($ = $50)	$$$–

Sleep Inn Convention Center ★★
6301 Westwood Blvd
Orlando 32821
☎ 407-313-4100
FAX 407-313-4101
www.orlandosleepinn.com

LOCATION	1
ROOM RATING	54
COST ($ = $50)	$$–

Spring Hill Suites by Marriott ★★★½
8840 Universal Blvd.
Orlando 32819
☎ 407-345-9073
FAX 407-345-9075
www.marriott.com

LOCATION	1
ROOM RATING	80
COST ($ = $50)	$$$

Star Island Resort ★★★★
5000 Avenue of the Stars
Kissimmee 34746
☎ 407-997-8000
FAX 407-997-5252
www.star-island.com

LOCATION	3
ROOM RATING	84
COST ($ = $50)	$$$$–

Sun Inn & Suites ★★
5020 W. Irlo Bronson Mem. Hwy.
Kissimmee 34746
☎ 407-396-2673
FAX 407-396-0878

LOCATION	3
ROOM RATING	53
COST ($ = $50)	$

Super 8 East ★★½
5875 W. Irlo Bronson Mem. Hwy.
Kissimmee 34746
☎ 407-396-8883
FAX 407-396-8907
www.super8.com

LOCATION	3
ROOM RATING	57
COST ($ = $50)	$$–

Super 8 Kissimmee ★★½
1815 W. Vine St.
Kissimmee 34741
☎ 407-847-6121
FAX 407-847-0728
www.super8.com

LOCATION	3
ROOM RATING	60
COST ($ = $50)	$$–

Rodeway Inn I-Drive ★★
6327 International Drive
Orlando 32819
☎ 407-351-4444
FAX 407-996-5806
www.rodewayinnorlando.com

LOCATION	1
ROOM RATING	51
COST ($ = $50)	$+

Rodeway Inn Maingate ★★½
5995 W. Irlo Bronson Mem. Hwy.
Kissimmee 34747
☎ 407-396-4300
FAX 407-589-1240
www.choicehotels.com

LOCATION	3
ROOM RATING	59
COST ($ = $50)	$+

Rosen Centre Hotel ★★★½
9840 International Drive
Orlando 32819
☎ 407-354-9840
FAX 407-996-2659
www.rosencentre.com

LOCATION	1
ROOM RATING	80
COST ($ = $50)	$$$$$$

Saratoga Resort Villas ★★★½
4787 W. Irlo Bronson Mem. Hwy.
Kissimmee 34746
☎ 407-397-0555
FAX 407-397-0553
www.saratogaresortvillas.com

LOCATION	3
ROOM RATING	80
COST ($ = $50)	$$$–

Saratoga Springs Resort & Spa
★★★★½
Walt Disney World
1901 E. Buena Vista Drive
Lake Buena Vista 32830
☎ 407-827-1100
www.waltdisneyworld.com

LOCATION	WDW
ROOM RATING	90
COST ($ = $50)	$$$$$$$

Seralago Hotel ★★★
5678 W. Irlo Bronson Mem. Hwy.
Kissimmee 34746
☎ 407-396-4488
FAX 407-396-8915
www.seralagohotel.com

LOCATION	3
ROOM RATING	71
COST ($ = $50)	$$–

Sheraton Vistana Resort ★★★★
8800 Vistana Centre Drive
Orlando 32821
☎ 407-239-3100
FAX 407-239-3111
www.starwoodvo.com

LOCATION	2
ROOM RATING	84
COST ($ = $50)	$$$$–

**Sheraton World
Resort** ★★★½/★★★*
10100 International Drive
Orlando 32821
☎ 407-352-1100
FAX 407-354-4700
www.sheratonworld.com

LOCATION	1
ROOM RATING	79/68*
COST ($ = $50)	$$$+/$$$–*

* tower/garden

Silver Lake Resort ★★½
7751 Black Lake Road
Kissimmee 34747
☎ 407-397-2828
FAX 407-589-8410
www.silverlake.net

LOCATION	3
ROOM RATING	64
COST ($ = $50)	$$$$–

Staybridge Suites Hotel ★★★½
8480 International Drive
Orlando 32819
☎ 407-352-2400
FAX 407-352-4631
www.staybridge.com

LOCATION	1
ROOM RATING	82
COST ($ = $50)	$$$$–

**Staybridge Suites
Lake Buena Vista** ★★★
8751 Suite Side Drive
Orlando 32836
☎ 407-238-0777
FAX 407-238-2640
www.staybridge.com

LOCATION	2
ROOM RATING	72
COST ($ = $50)	$$$$

**Suburban Extended Stay
Universal** ★★★
5615 Major Blvd.
Orlando 32819
☎ 407-313-2000
FAX 407-313-2010
www.suburbanlodge.com

LOCATION	1
ROOM RATING	65
COST ($ = $50)	$+

Super 8 Lakeside ★★½
4880 W. Irlo Bronson Mem. Hwy.
Kissimmee 34746
☎ 407-396-1144
FAX 407-396-4389
www.super8.com

LOCATION	3
ROOM RATING	58
COST ($ = $50)	$+

Super 8 Universal ★★
5900 American Way
Orlando 32819
☎ 407-352-8383
FAX 407-352-3496
www.super8.com

LOCATION	1
ROOM RATING	51
COST ($ = $50)	$$–

Swan ★★★★½
Walt Disney World
1500 Epcot Resort Blvd.
Lake Buena Vista 32830
☎ 407-934-3000
FAX 407-934-4499
www.swandolphin.com

LOCATION	WDW
ROOM RATING	91
COST ($ = $50)	$$$$$$$

Hotel Information Chart (continued)

**Travelodge
Convention Center** ★★½
6263 Westwood Blvd.
Orlando 32821
☎ 800-346-1551
FAX 407-345-1508
www.travelodge.com

LOCATION	1
ROOM RATING	59
COST ($ = $50)	$+

Travelodge I-Drive ★★½
5859 American Way
Orlando 32819
☎ 407-345-5880
FAX 407-363-9366
www.travelodge.com

LOCATION	1
ROOM RATING	60
COST ($ = $50)	$+

Travelodge Maingate East ★★★
5711 W. Irlo Bronson Mem. Hwy.
Kissimmee 34746
☎ 407-396-4222
FAX 407-396-0570
www.travelodge.com

LOCATION	3
ROOM RATING	65
COST ($ = $50)	$$

**Wellesley Inn Kissimmee/
Lake Cecile** ★★½
4944 W. Irlo Bronson Mem. Hwy.
Kissimmee 34746
☎ 407-396-4455
FAX 407-997-2435
www.wellesleyinnandsuites.com

LOCATION	3
ROOM RATING	61
COST ($ = $50)	$$–

Westgate Inn ★★½
9200 US Hwy. 192
Kissimmee 34714
☎ 863-424-2621
FAX 863-424-4630
www.westgateinnorlando.com

LOCATION	3
ROOM RATING	59
COST ($ = $50)	$$–

Westgate Lakes ★★★★½
10000 Turkey Lake Road
Orlando 32819
☎ 407-345-0000
www.westgateresorts.com

LOCATION	2
ROOM RATING	92
COST ($ = $50)	$$–

Wilderness Lodge Villas ★★★★½
Walt Disney World
901 Timberline Drive
Orlando 32830
☎ 407-824-3200
FAX 407-824-3232
www.waltdisneyworld.com

LOCATION	WDW
ROOM RATING	90
COST ($ = $50)	$$$$$$$$

Wyndham Orlando ★★★★
8001 International Drive
Orlando 32819
☎ 407-351-2420
FAX 407-345-5611
www.wyndhamorlandohotels.com

LOCATION	1
ROOM RATING	83
COST ($ = $50)	$$$

Wyndham Palms ★★★★
7900 Palms Parkway
Kissimmee 34747
☎ 407-390-1991
www.wyndhamorlandohotels.com

LOCATION	3
ROOM RATING	87
COST ($ = $50)	$$$$+

Travelodge Suites Eastgate ★★★
5399 W. Irlo Bronson Mem. Hwy.
Kissimmee 34746
☎ 407-396-7666
FAX 407-396-0696
www.travelodge.com

LOCATION	3
ROOM RATING	67
COST ($ = $50)	$+

Travelodge Suites Maingate ★★½
4694 W. Irlo Bronson Mem. Hwy.
Kissimmee 34746
☎ 407-396-1780
FAX 407-396-1448
www.travelodge.com

LOCATION	3
ROOM RATING	56
COST ($ = $50)	$+

**Vacation Village
at Parkway** ★★★★½
2949 Arabian Nights Blvd.
Kissimmee 34747
☎ 407-396-9086
FAX 407-390-7247
www.worldhotels.com/usa/
orlando/hotel_orlpar.html

LOCATION	3
ROOM RATING	91
COST ($ = $50)	$$

Westgate Palace ★★★
6145 Carrier Drive
Orlando 32819
☎ 407-996-6000
www.westgateresorts.com

LOCATION	1
ROOM RATING	68
COST ($ = $50)	$$$$–

Westgate Resorts
★★★★½/★★★★½/★★★½*
2770 Old Lake Wilson Road
Kissimmee 34747
☎ 800-925-9999
www.westgateresorts.com

LOCATION	3
ROOM RATING	93/90/81*
COST ($ = $50)	$$$–/$$$$/$$+

* town center/villas/tower

Wilderness Lodge ★★★★
Walt Disney World
901 Timberline Drive
Orlando 32830
☎ 407-824-3200
FAX 407-824-3232
www.waltdisneyworld.com

LOCATION	WDW
ROOM RATING	86
COST ($ = $50)	$$$$$$

Yacht Club Resort ★★★★
Walt Disney World
1700 Epcot Resort Blvd.
Orlando 32830
☎ 407-934-7000
FAX 407-934-3450
www.waltdisneyworld.com

LOCATION	WDW
ROOM RATING	89
COST ($ = $50)	$$$$$$$$+

PART TWO

BUSCH GARDENS TAMPA BAY

SPANNING 335 ACRES, BUSCH GARDENS combines elements of a zoo and a theme park. The park is divided into eight African-themed regions (as you encounter them moving counterclockwise through the park): Morocco, Crown Colony, Egypt, Nairobi, Timbuktu, Congo, Stanleyville, and Bird Gardens. A haven for thrill-ride fanatics, several of the park's eight roller coasters are consistently rated among the top five in the country. Busch Gardens is more than thrill fare, however, with beautiful landscaping, excellent shows, and a really wonderful children's play area.

With the wildlife of Disney's Animal Kingdom and the thrills of Universal Studios Islands of Adventure, some may wonder, why leave Orlando for a day at Busch Gardens in Tampa? For those who love roller coasters, Busch Gardens boasts eight, four in the super-coaster category. No other area attraction can top that in terms of thrills. Nor can Busch Gardens be matched in its ability to offer a balanced day of fun for all ages. Those who shy away from roller coasters will find plenty to do at the park, with its abundance of animal exhibits, children's rides, gardens, shows, and shops.

In addition, the drive is easy and only about 90 minutes from Orlando. With Florida's fickle weather, it could be raining in Orlando but bright and sunny in Tampa, so it's a good idea to check the weather if you're rained out of O-town. Of course, this holds true in reverse, and, unlike at Disney, where most of the rides are indoors, any rain will cause the closing of most of the rides at Busch Gardens.

unofficial **TIP**
Busch Gardens offers proximity to Tampa, including the city's beaches and other attractions.

The park is only minutes away from the white-sand beaches of St. Petersburg and Tampa Bay, an often-overlooked advantage. A Busch Gardens weekend visit can also be combined with a trip to Adventure Island, the Anheuser-Busch water park across the street from Busch Gardens in Tampa Bay.

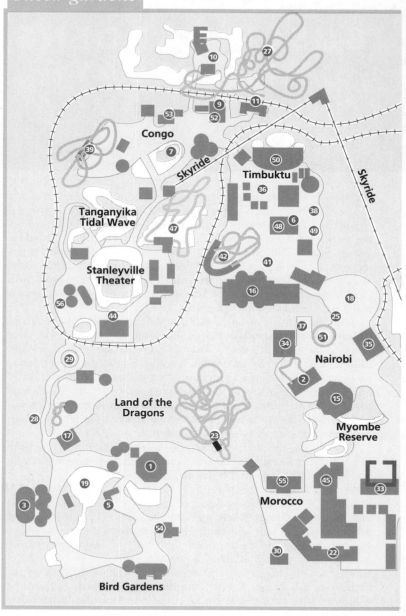

busch gardens

Congo

Skyride

Timbuktu

Tanganyika
Tidal Wave

Stanleyville
Theater

Skyride

Nairobi

Land of the
Dragons

Myombe
Reserve

Morocco

Bird Gardens

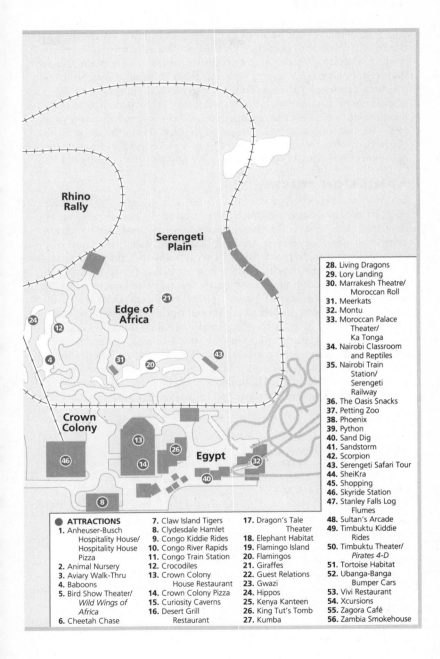

Rhino
Rally

Serengeti
Plain

Edge of
Africa

Crown
Colony

Egypt

28. Living Dragons
29. Lory Landing
30. Marrakesh Theatre/
Moroccan Roll
31. Meerkats
32. Montu
33. Moroccan Palace
Theater/
Ka Tonga
34. Nairobi Classroom
and Reptiles
35. Nairobi Train
Station/
Serengeti
Railway
36. The Oasis Snacks
37. Petting Zoo
38. Phoenix
39. Python
40. Sand Dig
41. Sandstorm
42. Scorpion
43. Serengeti Safari Tour
44. SheiKra
45. Shopping
46. Skyride Station
47. Stanley Falls Log
Flumes
48. Sultan's Arcade
49. Timbuktu Kiddie
Rides
50. Timbuktu Theater/
Pirates 4-D
51. Tortoise Habitat
52. Ubanga-Banga
Bumper Cars
53. Vivi Restaurant
54. Xcursions
55. Zagora Café
56. Zambia Smokehouse

● **ATTRACTIONS**
1. Anheuser-Busch
Hospitality House/
Hospitality House
Pizza
2. Animal Nursery
3. Aviary Walk-Thru
4. Baboons
5. Bird Show Theater/
*Wild Wings of
Africa*
6. Cheetah Chase

7. Claw Island Tigers
8. Clydesdale Hamlet
9. Congo Kiddie Rides
10. Congo River Rapids
11. Congo Train Station
12. Crocodiles
13. Crown Colony
House Restaurant
14. Crown Colony Pizza
15. Curiosity Caverns
16. Desert Grill
Restaurant

17. Dragon's Tale
Theater
18. Elephant Habitat
19. Flamingo Island
20. Flamingos
21. Giraffes
22. Guest Relations
23. Gwazi
24. Hippos
25. Kenya Kanteen
26. King Tut's Tomb
27. Kumba

GETTING THERE

BUSCH GARDENS IS ABOUT 70 miles from Walt Disney World. The trip should take about an hour and a half, depending on traffic and the construction that plagues Interstate 4. The best way to get there is via Interstate 275. Driving west on I-4, there are signs for Busch Gardens, but we recommend ignoring them to avoid a long journey through Tampa city streets. Proceed instead to the junction of I-275 and go north. Exit at Busch Boulevard (Exit 50), turn right, and drive a little over two miles; the entrance to Busch Gardens will be on your left. Car and motorcycle parking is $9 in a lot across the street from the park (trams are provided) and $14 in a preferred lot closer to the main entrance, which fills up quickly. RV and camper parking is $10.

ADMISSION PRICES

BEFORE PURCHASING TICKETS TO BUSCH GARDENS, consider some of the choices below, which are similar to the options offered by its sister park, SeaWorld (both Busch Gardens and SeaWorld are owned by Anheuser-Busch Brewing Company, which explains why both parks feature beer schools). As with SeaWorld, the best option for most visitors to Busch Gardens is a one-day pass. In fact, Busch Gardens has discontinued most of its multiday tickets in favor of package deals and annual passes. However, Busch Gardens really wants your business, and there are several options that will get you a lot more time in the park for slightly more money than the cost of a one-day ticket. If you're planning to spend time at other Orlando theme parks, however, consider the FlexTicket, which includes admission to SeaWorld, Wet 'n Wild, Universal Studios, and Universal's Islands of Adventure. Discounts are available for AAA members, disabled visitors, senior citizens, and military personnel.

One-day Pass
Adults $57.95 + tax
Children ages 3–9 $47.95
Children under age 3 Free

Busch Gardens Fun Card

This pass is by far the best deal for admission to Busch Gardens. For $4 more than general admission, you can return to the park an unlimited amount of times for an entire calendar year. Fun Cards aren't valid on Memorial Day weekend or weekends between June 4th and August 7th, the park's most popular times of year.
BUSCH GARDENS $61.95
BUSCH GARDENS AND SEAWORLD ORLANDO $99.95

FUN CARD PLUS BUSCH GARDENS
Adults $119.95 + tax
Children ages 3–9 $99.95 + tax

Two-park Unlimited Admission Ticket

This pass is a 7-day admission ticket good for both SeaWorld and Busch Gardens and includes a free shuttle between Orlando and Tampa.
All Ages $85 + tax

Annual Passports

These allow unlimited admission to either Busch Gardens alone or Busch Gardens and SeaWorld for one or two years and include free general parking and 10% off merchandise and food purchases in the park(s). The Platinum is offered only for a two-year period and includes free preferred parking, no blackout dates, and ride-again privileges at all Anheuser-Busch parks.

BUSCH GARDENS SILVER PASSPORT (ONE YEAR)
Adults $94.95 | *Children ages 3–9 and seniors ages 50+* $84.95

BUSCH GARDENS GOLD PASSPORT (TWO YEARS)
Adults $144.95 | *Children ages 3–9 and seniors ages 50+* $134.95

BUSCH GARDENS/SEAWORLD SILVER PASSPORT (ONE YEAR)
Adults $144.95 | *Children ages 3–9 and seniors ages 50+* $134.95

BUSCH GARDENS/SEAWORLD GOLD PASSPORT (TWO YEARS)
Adults $219.95 | *Children ages 3–9 and seniors ages 50+* $209.95

BUSCH GARDENS/ADVENTURE ISLAND/
SEAWORLD SILVER PASSPORT (ONE YEAR)
Adults $184.95 | *Children ages 3–9 and seniors ages 50+* $174.95

BUSCH GARDENS/ADVENTURE ISLAND/
SEAWORLD GOLD PASSPORT (TWO YEARS)
Adults $269.95 | *Children ages 3–9 and seniors ages 50+* $259.95

ANHEUSER-BUSCH PLATINUM PASSPORT (TWO YEARS)
Adults $299.95 + tax | *Children ages 3–9 and seniors ages 50+*
$280.95 + tax

Orlando FlexTicket

This pass is good for up to 14 consecutive days at five parks: Busch Gardens, Universal Studios Florida, Universal's Islands of Adventure, SeaWorld, and Wet 'n Wild. There's a version that excludes Busch Gardens, so be sure to get the one you want.

FLEXTICKET
Adults $251 + tax | *Children ages 3–9 and seniors ages 50+* $214 + tax

FLEXTICKET WITHOUT BUSCH GARDENS
Adults $203 + tax | *Children ages 3–9 and seniors ages 50+* $167 + tax

ARRIVING

NORMAL PARK HOURS VARY MONTH to month and sometimes day to day but are always between 9 a.m. and 8 p.m. The park stays open until 10 p.m. mid-June through the end of July. Unlike other local attractions, Busch Gardens does not allow you through the turnstiles before the scheduled opening time. We recommend checking the Web site (**www.buschgardens.com**) for exact hours of operation. Visiting during peak season equals waiting in long lines. Busch Gardens also draws crowds of locals, so avoid visiting on weekends or holidays.

Even when crowds are low, it requires a lot of planning and hustling to see Busch Gardens in one day. In particular, expect to spend a lot of time getting oriented and consulting park maps and signage. With no central hub and few connecting walkways, it's very easy to get lost. Go slow until you have a feel for where you are in the park, or you could spend some frustrating time retracing your steps. Of course, group ages and personal tastes will eliminate some rides and exhibits. Groups without children, for instance, don't need to budget time for kiddie rides. However, even selective touring may not afford enough time to enjoy the park fully. Following are a few tips that may help:

unofficial **TIP**
As with all the theme parks, get to the entrance at or before opening time.

PLAN AHEAD The Busch Gardens map is crammed full of rides and exhibits; the first time many visitors see it, they develop a glazed look in their eyes and begin a crazed tour. Somehow, we doubt these folks see even half of what the park offers. Instead, determine in advance what you really want to see. For many groups this involves compromise: parents may not want to spend as much time as children on rides, whereas older kids may want to steer clear of many of the zoological exhibits. If children are old enough, we recommend splitting up after determining a few meeting times and locations for checking in throughout the day. Alternately, parents may want to plan kids' rides around the live entertainment schedule, placing children safely in line and then attending a performance of a nearby show while the youngsters wait and ride. Note that bags, cameras, and other belongings are not permitted on most of the thrill rides; for $0.50, you can temporarily stow such items in lockers near the ride entrances. Thrill-ride enthusiasts should bring a roll of quarters to pay for the lockers.

ARRIVE EARLY As with other central Florida attractions, this is the single most effective strategy for efficient touring and avoiding long line waits. Leave Orlando around 7 a.m. to arrive a little before 8:30 a.m. during peak season. Give yourself an extra half hour during other times, when the park doesn't open until 9:30 a.m. Have a quick breakfast before leaving, or eat in the car to save time. Park, purchase tickets (either at windows or through the self-service kiosks), and be at the turnstile ready to roll when the gate opens at either 9 or 9:30 a.m. First thing in the morning, there should be no lines and relatively few people. Rides that require up to an hour (or more) wait later in the day can be experienced in less than 15 minutes first thing in the morning.

There are three ways to hit the four major coasters at prime times for as little waiting as possible:

Route 1: Ride Gwazi (located at the front of the park) first thing, then head to Montu, followed by Kumba, and save SheiKra for mid- to late afternoon.

Route 2: After riding Gwazi first, continue onto Stanleyville to ride SheiKra, followed by Kumba; hit Montu late in the day.

Route 3: Head to Montu first, then backtrack to Gwazi, followed by SheiKra. Since Kumba is located in the rear of the park it will not be as crowded in the morning, and you should be able to ride all four major coasters within an hour and a half of the park's opening. This route is only practical with very small groups on off-peak days, when the park isn't packed. Even on slower days, you will find a slight line at both Gwazi and SheiKra with this route, but you should still be able to check the coasters off your list first thing in the morning and free up the rest of your day for other attractions.

BE READY TO WALK AND WALK AND WALK Busch Gardens is huge and requires lots of walking. Bring strollers for little ones and consider wheelchairs for others who tire quickly. Both stroller and wheelchair rentals are available at the rentals desk, located in the fourth gift shop on the right as you enter the main gate. Single strollers cost $10 plus tax, while double strollers cost $15 plus tax and wheelchairs are available for $10 plus tax. Motorized scooters (EVCs) are available for $35 plus tax. Guests renting motorized scooters must be at least 18 years old. One reader suggests that you save money and bring your own stroller:

> *[Rental] strollers at Busch Gardens really are strollers; there is very little space for bags and no cup holder. They are not like the big plastic ones they have at SeaWorld and Magic Kingdom.*

Once you've secured transportation, you'll need to find your way around the park. Make sure to have all the members in your group grab a park map; show schedules are printed on the reverse side. Due to the park's confusing layout, you'll appreciate having the navigational assistance of your entire group. With all of the calories burned walking around this large park, be aware of keeping everyone fed. You might want to stop for group meals, as eateries are widely spaced and roving snack vendors are sometimes scarce.

AVOID BOTTLENECKS An early arrival will help you avoid the bottlenecks at most of the major attractions. As for smaller rides, if there's a line, don't wait. Go see a show or visit the animal exhibits that usually have no wait. Then return to the rides later in the day, when lines should subside.

CONTACTING BUSCH GARDENS

FOR MORE INFORMATION, call ☎ 888-800-5447. In addition to park information, the Busch Gardens Web site (**www.buschgardens.com**) also contains an animal information database.

ATTRACTIONS

MOROCCO

Marrakesh Theatre/Moroccan Roll ★★★

APPEAL BY AGE	PRESCHOOL ★★½	GRADE SCHOOL ★★½	TEENS ★★½
YOUNG ADULTS ★★		OVER 30 ★★	SENIORS ★½

What it is Song-and-dance show. **Scope and scale** Major attraction. **When to go** Check daily entertainment schedule. **Authors' rating** Dorky but amusing; ★★★. **Duration of show** 30 minutes.

DESCRIPTION AND COMMENTS Dancers and singers in vaguely Middle Eastern garb fling themselves around to the beats of pop and rock songs. All of the songs contain a Middle Eastern bent, but Christina Aguilera's "Genie in a Bottle," the Bangles' "Walk Like an Egyptian," and The Clash's "Rock the Casbah" are far from indigenous fare. Still, the performers don't take themselves or their routines too seriously, and neither does the audience.

TOURING TIPS Rows of wrought-iron patio seats fill this outdoor theater. They are not on an incline, and it is difficult to see the stage from the back. Arrive ten minutes early to get the best seats near the front of the house. Also, rows to the right or left of the stage don't fill up as quickly and offer great views.

Moroccan Palace Theater/KaTonga ★★★★

APPEAL BY AGE	PRESCHOOL ★★½	GRADE SCHOOL ★★★½	TEENS ★★★
YOUNG ADULTS ★★★★		OVER 30 ★★★★	SENIORS ★★★★

What it is Musical stage show. **Scope and scale** Headliner. **When to go** Check daily entertainment schedule. **Authors' rating** Great music, beautiful puppets, and interesting history; ★★★★. **Duration of show** 30 minutes.

DESCRIPTION AND COMMENTS A day in the lives of masterly African storytellers called griots, who weave involved and interesting historical tales using music, dance, and impressive colorful puppets akin to those found in Julie Taymor's Broadway production of *The Lion King*. African folklore, traditional music, and dance are all beautiful and well presented.

TOURING TIPS The best time to see this show is either as a first or last stop, depending on the show schedule for the day. Try to sit as close to the stage as possible for the best view.

CROWN COLONY

Adventure Tours ★★★½

APPEAL BY AGE	PRESCHOOL ★★★	GRADE SCHOOL ★★★★	TEENS ★★★
YOUNG ADULTS ★★★★		OVER 30 ★★★½	SENIORS ★★★½

What it is Guided tours on the plain and behind the scenes. **Scope and scale** Major attraction. **When to go** Call reservation number for a schedule. **Special comments** Must be at least 5 years old. **Authors' rating** Worthwhile for animal enthusiasts or the affluent, but can be too expensive for the average visitor; ★★★½. **Duration of tour** Varies.

DESCRIPTION AND COMMENTS   Busch Gardens offers a wide variety of Adventure Tours, but many of them contain overlapping locations, so pick the one that is right for you. Although you can book all the tours listed below the day of your visit at the Adventure Touring Center near the main gate, the limited capacity of the tours makes them sell out early most of the year. During peak seasons, you should call weeks in advance. The number for reservations is ☎ 888-800-5447.

None of the tour prices include park admission, and the prices vary due to the length and capacity of each tour. Prices are the same for all participants, regardless of age. Although the tours are worthwhile for animal enthusiasts, many—if not all—are too expensive for the average visitor. All prices below are listed without tax.

SERENGETI SAFARI TOUR $34 per person, 30 minutes. Riding in an open-backed truck, guides drive you out into the Serengeti plain for up-close encounters with some of the tamer animals. A zoologist accompanies the trip and doles out information on all of the animals you encounter. The highlight of the trip is feeding the antelope and giraffes. It's a treat to watch the long tongue of a giraffe remove the leaves from a prickly branch while adeptly avoiding thorns. Bring your camera!

SAVING A SPECIES TOUR $45 per person, 45 minutes. A tour very similar to the Serengeti Safari, Saving a Species is 15 minutes longer and visits the white and black rhinos. Due to their turbulent nature, you cannot feed the rhinos, only the aforementioned antelope and giraffes. The park donates a portion of the proceeds from this tour to the World Wildlife Fund. The tour leaves at 12:45 daily, and the tickets for this tour are nonrefundable, unless the park cancels the tour.

SUNSET SERENGETI TOUR $40 per person, 1 hour. The same sights as the Saving a Species Tour, except with beer. Guests are given a beer sample and then taken out on safari, where they are each allowed two more beers. This tour is offered only in the late afternoon for guests ages 21 and older.

ANIMAL ADVENTURE TOUR $120 per person, 2 hours. If you're willing to drop the loot, you can add a bit of walking to your truck ride. This tour consists of an open-backed truck outing on the Serengeti Plains that includes all the animals you see on the Saving a Species Tour. The walking portion makes a brief stop at the Clydesdale Hamlet, but the real showpiece of the walking portion is a visit inside the Nairobi Field Station, where the baby animals are being cared for. Of course, you can see almost all of the animals from outside the station without handing over $120, but you won't receive a fully guided narration or a chance to meet the caretakers.

TOURING TIPS   Four different half- and full-day guided tours of the park are also available, and their prices range from $95 to $250 plus tax and park admission. The selling point for all of these tours is one-time front-of-the-line access to all of the major rides and/or front seats at all of the shows and/or an Adventure Tour. Of course, if you're following the Touring Plans in the book, front-of-the-line access should not be an issue; we're here to save you those hundred bucks. If you're in the mood for the VIP treatment, call ☎ 888-800-5447 for more information.

Edge of Africa ★★★½

APPEAL BY AGE	PRESCHOOL ★★★½		GRADE SCHOOL ★★★★		TEENS ★★★
YOUNG ADULTS ★★★		OVER 30 ★★★½		SENIORS ★★★½	

What it is Walking tour of animal habitats. **Scope and scale** Headliner. **When to go** Crowds are minuscule in the afternoon, and the animals are fairly active. **Authors' rating** Good presentation; ★★★½.

DESCRIPTION AND COMMENTS This walking safari features hippopotamuses, giraffes, lions, baboons, meerkats, hyenas, and vultures in naturalistic habitats. The area was designed for up-close viewing, many times with just a pane of glass between you and the animals. Exhibits of note are the hippopotamus habitat and the hyena area. The hippopotamuses wade in five-foot-deep water filled with colorful fish, all visible through the glass wall. In the hyena habitat, open safari vehicles are built into the glass, offering a great photo opportunity if you climb in when the animals come near.

TOURING TIPS Animals are most active during feedings, but these are not regularly scheduled, so the animals don't fall into a pattern that would not exist in the wild. Employees are usually willing to tell you feeding times for the day. It might be a hike to return to this area, but seeing the lions chomp into raw meat is definitely worth it.

There is a hidden entrance to this area between Tut's Tomb and the restrooms near Montu. This is useful if you ride the roller coaster before seeing the animals.

kids Rhino Rally ★★★★½

APPEAL BY AGE	PRESCHOOL ★★★½		GRADE SCHOOL ★★★★★		TEENS ★★★★½
YOUNG ADULTS ★★★★½		OVER 30 ★★★★½		SENIORS ★★★★	

What it is Off-road adventure through African-themed terrain. **Scope and scale** Headliner. **When to go** Before 10 a.m. or after 3:30 p.m. **Special comments** Beware if you've got back problems; the ride gets a little bumpy—and wet if you're sitting on the left side of the vehicle. **Authors' rating** Great fun, and you see a host of African wildlife; ★★★★½. **Duration of ride** 8–10 minutes.

DESCRIPTION AND COMMENTS Riders board 17-passenger Land Rovers for a safari and wild river adventure across 16 acres, with one "lucky" guest riding shotgun with the wise-cracking driver. The trip—a "competition" for the world's ultimate off-road trophy—gets off to a mild-but-bumpy start, and everyone has a great view of white rhinoceroses, elephants, Cape buffalo, Nile crocodiles, zebras, antelopes, wildebeests, and other species, with running commentary by the driver.

Before too long, of course, the truck comes to a fork in the road, and the driver must make a choice—taking riders on part two of the trip, a surprising journey that involves splashing through riverbeds, a torrential downpour, and raging white waters, with the Land Rover turning into a floating pontoon with an inflatable underside when a flash flood washes out the bridge. Nothing exceptionally thrilling, but all are laughing as the SUV-cum-boat delivers everyone back from the rushing waters to dry land.

TOURING TIPS The eight- to ten-minute ride can board about 1,600 guests per hour, but because the attraction is popular, make it one of your early rides (either first thing, or after Gwazi and Montu if you're doing Route #1; second to last if you're doing Route #2 or #3). The queue is covered and splits into two lines near the boarding area; pick the shortest line at that point as the split is only to expedite boarding (there is no difference in the experience).

When you board, request a seat on the right side if you want to stay dry. Youngsters under age 6 may be frightened by some of the heavy water effects.

Skyride ★★½

APPEAL BY AGE	PRESCHOOL ★★		GRADE SCHOOL ★★½	TEENS ★★
YOUNG ADULTS ★★		OVER 30 ★★½		SENIORS ★★★

What it is Scenic transportation to Stanleyville. **Scope and scale** Minor attraction. **When to go** In the morning; lines can be long in the afternoon. **Authors' rating** Good way to see the Rhino Rally in action; ★★½. **Duration of ride** 4 minutes.

DESCRIPTION AND COMMENTS This aerial tram travels to Stanleyville. It passes directly over the Rhino Rally attraction and offers views of the Serengeti Plain as well as the roller coasters. You can board here or in Stanleyville, but you cannot stay on for a round trip.

TOURING TIPS If the lines are small, you may use the Skyride as a shortcut from Montu to Kumba and SheiKra. The shortcut may only work early in the morning because if the lines are not small, this ride takes longer than walking; however, it's still faster than the train.

EGYPT

 Clydesdale Hamlet ★★

APPEAL BY AGE	PRESCHOOL ★★½		GRADE SCHOOL ★★½	TEENS ★½
YOUNG ADULTS ★½		OVER 30 ★★		SENIORS ★★½

What it is Horse stable. **Scope and scale** Diversion. **When to go** Anytime. **Authors' rating** Great for kids; ★★.

DESCRIPTION AND COMMENTS This blue-roofed white stable is home to several Clydesdales, huge and beautiful draft horses that are the Anheuser-Busch mascots.

TOURING TIPS These horses are truly amazing to look at, and kids will really enjoy this, but don't waste time here if you're trying to rush through all the coasters and water rides. The horses are sometimes otherwise engaged and the stable may house only one or two horses; sometimes none at all.

King Tut's Tomb ★

APPEAL BY AGE	PRESCHOOL ★	GRADE SCHOOL ★	TEENS ★ ½
YOUNG ADULTS ★ ½		OVER 30 ★★	SENIORS ★★ ½

What it is Walking tour of a re-created tomb. **Scope and scale** Diversion. **When to go** Anytime; don't wait if there's a line. **Authors' rating** Somewhat interesting, but often not worth the time; ★. **Duration of tour** 10 minutes.

DESCRIPTION AND COMMENTS The spirit of King Tut leads you on a tour of this re-creation of his tomb. The narration features information about the tomb's artifacts and his life. Objects on display include replicas of Tut's large throne, chariot, and golden sculpted coffin, as well as urns purportedly containing his internal organs.

TOURING TIPS This air-conditioned attraction provides a break from the heat, but it should be skipped if you're in a hurry. Although a bit dull, it does work as a time-killer for visitors waiting for the rest of their party to ride Montu.

Montu ★★★★★

APPEAL BY AGE	PRESCHOOL †	GRADE SCHOOL ★★★★	TEENS ★★★★★
YOUNG ADULTS ★★★½		OVER 30 ★★★½	SENIORS ★★½

† Preschoolers are generally too short to ride.

What it is Inverted steel super roller coaster. **Scope and scale** Super headliner. **When to go** Before 10 a.m. or after 4 p.m. **Special comments** Riders must be at least 54" tall. **Authors' rating** Incredible; ★★★★★. **Duration of ride** About 3 minutes. **Loading speed** Quick.

DESCRIPTION AND COMMENTS Seats hang below the track and riders' feet dangle on this intense inverted roller coaster, which is among the top five in the country and among the best we've ever ridden. The fast-paced but extremely smooth ride begins with a 13-story drop. Riders are then hurled through a 104-foot inverted vertical loop. Speeds reach 60 miles per hour as riders are accelerated through more dizzying loops and twists, including an Immelman, an inverse loop named after German World War I fighter pilot Max Immelman.

TOURING TIPS Depending on which route you take, try to ride in the morning or later in the afternoon to avoid waits that can be as long as an hour (or even more). If lines are still long, however, don't be discouraged. As many as 32 riders can pile onto each train, so even the longest line will move quickly and steadily.

If you have time, ride twice, first near the back of the train and then in the front row. In the back, you'll glimpse a sea of dangling feet in front of you and be surprised by each twist and turn because you can't see where the track is headed, just legs swooping through the air. Riding in the front gives you a clear, unobstructed view of everything around you, including the huge trees dozens of feet below you on the first drop. If you have to choose one or the other, we definitely recommend the front row. Look for the special front-seat queue once you enter the load station. The wait for the front is usually an extra 20 minutes, but it's worth it for the thrill.

NAIROBI

Animal Nursery ★★★½

APPEAL BY AGE	PRESCHOOL ★★½	GRADE SCHOOL ★★★½	TEENS ★★
YOUNG ADULTS ★★★		OVER 30 ★★½	SENIORS ★★★

What it is Newborns on display. **Scope and scale** Minor attraction. **When to go** Anytime. **Authors' rating** Supercute; ★★★½.

DESCRIPTION AND COMMENTS Busch Gardens is home to more than 2,700 animals, and many of the females often give birth to young. The park also rescues ill or orphaned animal infants, including a sizable amount of endangered species. The animal nursery houses these infants. The large windows at the nursery allow guests to glimpse some of these incredibly cute and cuddly babies, each marked with a small sign to denote species. The quality of the experience depends on which animals have recently been born—during one visit we saw some adorable tiger cubs and scrawny but cute baby birds feeding from an eyedropper—but no matter which animals are on display, you're sure to come down with a small case of the "warm fuzzies."

TOURING TIPS A sign near the entrance usually lists the animals on display. For a tour inside the animal nursery, see the Animal Adventure Tour under the Adventure Tours listing in the Crown Colony section of this book.

Curiosity Caverns ★★½

APPEAL BY AGE	PRESCHOOL ★★½	GRADE SCHOOL ★★★½	TEENS ★★½
YOUNG ADULTS ★★★		OVER 30 ★★★	SENIORS ★★½

What it is Walk-through exhibit of "odd" animals. **Scope and scale** Minor attraction. **When to go** Anytime. **Authors' rating** A cool break; ★★½.

DESCRIPTION AND COMMENTS This seems to be a catchall for types of animals not exhibited elsewhere in the park. You'll see snakes and other reptiles behind glass, including a Burmese python and an anaconda, though there are also a three-toed sloth, bats, and a laughing kookaburra bird (which did not appear to be in the mood for laughter on our last visit).

TOURING TIPS The cooler climate inside Curiosity Caverns makes it an ideal place for reptiles and humans to hide from the heat and the glare outside.

Elephant Habitat ★★

APPEAL BY AGE	PRESCHOOL ★★★	GRADE SCHOOL ★★★	TEENS ★★
YOUNG ADULTS ★★		OVER 30 ★★	SENIORS ★★½

What it is Elephant habitat. **Scope and scale** Minor attraction. **When to go** During interaction times. **Authors' rating** ★★.

DESCRIPTION AND COMMENTS Endangered Asian elephants roam a dry dirt pen. A large pool is deep enough for these huge animals to submerge themselves and escape the Florida heat. The pen is surprisingly small; it's too bad the elephants can't roam the larger Serengeti Plain.

TOURING TIPS Visit during enrichment times, when trainers interact with the animals, sometimes hosing them down. The daily entertainment schedule doesn't list enrichment times for all the animals, so you should ask a keeper. Elephant feeding times are generally at 11:45 a.m., 2:30 p.m., and 5:30 p.m.

Myombe Reserve ★★★

APPEAL BY AGE	PRESCHOOL ★★★	GRADE SCHOOL ★★★	TEENS ★★½
YOUNG ADULTS ★★½		OVER 30 ★★★	SENIORS ★★★

What it is Gorilla and ape habitat. **Scope and scale** Major attraction. **When to go** Anytime before 4 p.m. **Authors' rating** Great theming, informative; ★★★.

DESCRIPTION AND COMMENTS A mist-filled path through lush landscape leads you to this beautiful habitat filled with waterfalls, thick vegetation, and marshland. The first section is home to several chimpanzees that romp through the trees and greenery. The second area features large gorillas. Only one or two of the animals are regularly visible, but at least one can usually be found napping in front of the glass. Two overhead monitors play a video full of interesting information about each animal in the habitat, including how they interact with each other. Chalkboards throughout the exhibit provide facts and figures about the animals.

TOURING TIPS The animals are usually most active before 11 a.m., but check your schedule or the sign in front of the exhibit for guided tour times. After riding Montu, you can snake through this exhibit, which exits into Nairobi, on your way to Kumba. Bronze sculptures of gorillas and chimpanzees placed throughout the exhibit provide some fun photo opportunities. Climb onto the giant gorilla at the entrance or join the train of chimpanzees combing through each other's hair for a unique snapshot.

Serengeti Railway ★★

APPEAL BY AGE	PRESCHOOL ★★½	GRADE SCHOOL ★★½	TEENS ★★
YOUNG ADULTS ★★		OVER 30 ★★★	SENIORS ★★★½

What it is Train tour through Serengeti Plain and around the park. **Scope and scale** Minor attraction. **When to go** Afternoon. **Authors' rating** Relaxing; ★★. **Duration of ride** 12 minutes through animal area exiting at next station; 35 minutes round-trip.

DESCRIPTION AND COMMENTS Riding this train gives your feet a break and provides the best view of the animals along the Serengeti Plain. Because it's quite poky, we don't recommend it as an alternate means of transportation, but the 12-minute trip from the Nairobi station through the Serengeti Plain to the Congo station is worth the time if you're not racing to ride the coasters. On-board guides provide narration from the front of the train, identifying the animals you see and telling a little about their history and habits. The train will take you close to the ostriches, wildebeests, and white rhinos.

TOURING TIPS Since the train runs counter-clockwise, sit on the left-hand side for the best view of the entire plain. If you board at the Nairobi station, get off at the Congo station for Kumba or the Congo River Rapids; get off at Stanleyville for Tanganyika Tidal Wave or the Land of the Dragons children's area.

TIMBUKTU

American Beats ★½

APPEAL BY AGE	PRESCHOOL ★★½		GRADE SCHOOL ★★½		TEENS ★½
YOUNG ADULTS ★★		OVER 30 ★★		SENIORS	★½

What it is Song-and-dance show. **Scope and scale** Minor attraction. **When to go** Check daily entertainment schedule. **Authors' rating** Diversion; ★½. **Duration of show** 25 minutes.

DESCRIPTION AND COMMENTS *American Beats* and *Tropical Nights* both take place at the Desert Grill Restaurant in Timbuktu. The restaurant is a gigantic chow hall, with long tables stretching toward the stage. *American Beats* is the lunchtime show, and if you didn't order cheese on your burger, don't worry, there is plenty in the performance. The performers dress in period clothing and sing pop ballads. Expect the likes of an old Elvis singing young Elvis songs, Olivia Newton John, and Garth Brooks to be on the menu. The show ends with songs about America.

TOURING TIPS The show is more a diversion to diners than an out-and-out show. There is almost no set, and the performers aren't very effective at riling up the crowd. Skip it unless you're eating there when the show begins, and if you don't like the first set, take your food outside.

kids *Cheetah Chase* ★★★

APPEAL BY AGE	PRESCHOOL ★★★		GRADE SCHOOL ★★★½		TEENS ★★
YOUNG ADULTS ★★		OVER 30 ★★★		SENIORS	★★

What it is Kiddie coaster. **Scope and scale** Minor attraction. **When to go** Line is usually relatively short compared with the big coasters, but an early stop would be wise because the line grows as the day goes on. **Special comments** Riders must be at least 6 years old and 46" tall. **Authors' rating** Fun for the little coaster lovers; ★★★. **Duration of ride** Approximately 3 minutes. **Loading speed** Moderate.

DESCRIPTION AND COMMENTS Hairpin turns and mini-drops make this a good choice for thrill seekers who aren't tall enough to take on the big coasters.

TOURING TIPS The line moves quickly here but build in the afternoon due to its proximity to other kiddie rides. This is also a good place to wait for the supercoaster-riders in your party or to burn off some time before *Pirates 4-D*.

Drastic Plastic ★★★

APPEAL BY AGE	PRESCHOOL ★★★		GRADE SCHOOL ★★★½		TEENS ★★★
YOUNG ADULTS ★★★		OVER 30 ★★½		SENIORS	★★½

What it is Percussion show with tubes. **Scope and scale** Minor attraction. **When to go** Check daily entertainment schedule. **Authors' rating** Odd pop; ★★★. **Duration of show** 20 minutes.

DESCRIPTION AND COMMENTS A percussion show utilizing hollow tubes to sound different notes, *Drastic Plastic* is worth a listen if you are in the

Timbuktu area. Five drummers climb around a steel set, playing tunes with a handful of plastic tubes. Think of it as a reverse xylophone. The drummer's choreography matches the music, and with five drummers who have octaves of notes at their disposal, they are able to play many contemporary tunes. We wouldn't buy their record, but the show is unique and energetic.

TOURING TIPS There is no seating, so arrive a little early and set the little ones on the ground next to the stage. Although some climbing about occurs, the bulk of the show is front and center. Don't worry about the car ride home afterward; the tubes are not for sale at the park.

Kiddie Rides ★★½

APPEAL BY AGE	PRESCHOOL ★★★	GRADE SCHOOL †	TEENS †
YOUNG ADULTS †		OVER 30 †	SENIORS †

† Not designed for older kids and adults.

What they are Pint-size, carnival rides. **Scope and scale** Minor attraction. **When to go** Anytime. **Authors' rating** Good diversion for children; ★★½.

DESCRIPTION AND COMMENTS Nothing fancy, but these attractions help kids who aren't old enough to ride the thrillers feel they aren't being left out. Another set of kiddie rides can be found in the Congo.

TOURING TIPS These rides are strategically placed near the adult attractions in this area (Scorpion and Phoenix), so one parent can keep the kids occupied while another rides.

Phoenix ★★

APPEAL BY AGE	PRESCHOOL †	GRADE SCHOOL ★★★	TEENS ★★★
YOUNG ADULTS ★★½		OVER 30 ★★½	SENIORS ★

† Preschoolers are generally too short to ride.

What it is Swinging pendulum ride. **Scope and scale** Minor attraction. **When to go** Anytime. **Special comments** Riders must be at least 48" tall; not for those who get motion sickness. **Authors' rating** Dizzying; ★★. **Duration of ride** 5 minutes.

DESCRIPTION AND COMMENTS A large wooden boat swings back and forth, starting slowly, then gaining speed before making a complete circle with passengers hanging upside down.

TOURING TIPS Remove glasses and anything in your shirt pockets to avoid losing them when the boat is suspended upside down for several seconds.

Sandstorm ★★

APPEAL BY AGE	PRESCHOOL †	GRADE SCHOOL ★★★	TEENS ★★½
YOUNG ADULTS ★★★		OVER 30 ★★½	SENIORS ★★

† Preschoolers are generally too short to ride.

What it is Carnival ride. **Scope and scale** Minor attraction. **When to go** Anytime. **Special comments** Riders must be at least 48" tall. **Authors' rating** Amusing, but not worth a long wait; ★★. **Duration of ride** Approximately 3 minutes. **Loading speed** Slow.

DESCRIPTION AND COMMENTS This is Busch Gardens' version of a midway ride commonly known as the Scrambler. Two to three riders sit in an enclosed car. Four of the cars rotate on one of six arms that circle a central pedestal.

TOURING TIPS Although fun, this ride is nothing special. Skip it if lines are long.

Scorpion ★★★

APPEAL BY AGE	PRESCHOOL †	GRADE SCHOOL ★★★½	TEENS ★★½
YOUNG ADULTS ★★★		OVER 30 ★★★	SENIORS ★★

† Preschoolers are generally too short to ride.

What it is Roller coaster. **Scope and scale** Headliner. **When to go** After 2 p.m. **Special comments** Riders must be at least 42" tall. **Authors' rating** Quick, but exciting; ★★★. **Duration of ride** 1½ minutes.

DESCRIPTION AND COMMENTS This coaster pales in comparison with big sisters Kumba and Montu but has a longer, smoother track than Python. In spite of its small stature, with speeds of 50 miles per hour, a 360-degree vertical loop, and three 360-degree spirals, it's nothing to sneeze at.

TOURING TIPS Lines will be long for this attraction; because it doesn't have the high capacity of Kumba or Montu, they move slowly. Save it for the afternoon, when the wait is almost always shorter.

Timbuktu Theatre/*Pirates 4-D* ★★★½

APPEAL BY AGE	PRESCHOOL ★★½	GRADE SCHOOL ★★★½	TEENS ★★★
YOUNG ADULTS ★★★		OVER 30 ★★½	SENIORS ★★½

What it is 3-D pirate movie packed with extra punch. **Scope and scale** Headliner. **When to go** Early in the morning or after crowds diminish. **Authors' rating** Creative and a lot of fun; ★★★½. **Duration of show** 20 minutes.

DESCRIPTION AND COMMENTS Replacing *R.L. Stine's Haunted Lighthouse 4-D*, *Pirates 4-D* stars Leslie Nielsen as the treacherous Captain Lucky. After abandoning his last crew on a desert island, Captain Lucky returns to retrieve his treasure. Unfortunately for him, his cabin boy is still alive and lying in wait. All ill falls on the captain and his crew of scallywags that includes Eric Idle of Monty Python fame as first mate Pierre.

Although the slapstick antics of the cast are amusing, the 3-D and 4-D effects are underutilized. Unlike *Shrek* at Universal Studios, which was made to explode from the screen and surround the viewer, *Pirates* is more like a 20-minute short film shown in 3-D and highlighted with 4-D effects. You will still have a have a great experience in the 4-D world, but you won't walk out ready to fly your Jolly Roger from the top of Montu.

TOURING TIPS The show times are posted on the back of your park map, spaced around 40 minutes apart. Since the presentation is only 20 minutes, the period between shows seems a little excessive, until you realize that someone has to dry off every seat in this massive theater (yes, that does mean you will get a little wet).

Because of the sparse showings, the lines for the show can be daunting, but the size of the theater should accommodate everyone in line.

Once the ropes are dropped, you will be corralled in front of the doors. Unlike *A Bug's Life* at Disney, which seats from only one side, this theater seats from both, so to get a center seat you should be near the doors when they open.

Tropical Nights   ★½

APPEAL BY AGE	PRESCHOOL ★ ½	GRADE SCHOOL ★★	TEENS ★★½
YOUNG ADULTS ★★½		OVER 30 ★★	SENIORS ★ ½

What it is Song-and-dance show. **Scope and scale** Minor attraction. **When to go** Check daily entertainment schedule. **Authors' rating** Diversion; ★½. **Duration of show** 25 minutes.

DESCRIPTION AND COMMENTS   *Tropical Nights* (as with *American Beats*) takes place at the immense Desert Grill Restaurant in Timbuktu. Neither is particularly good. *Tropical Nights* is the evening show and bears a striking resemblance to *Moroccan Roll*. The set also contains minarets, but this "tribute" is to Latin culture. Songs by Gloria Estefan and Ricky Martin are among the mix of bass-driven Latin pop songs. There is better dancing in this show than in *American Beats,* but the entire show is just as flat.

TOURING TIPS   The show is an attempt to keep crowds around for dinner, and unless the prices and quality of food in the Desert Grill Restaurant are exactly what you are looking for, then you are better off eating somewhere more quiet.

CONGO

Claw Island Tigers   ★★½

APPEAL BY AGE	PRESCHOOL ★★	GRADE SCHOOL ★★★	TEENS ★ ½
YOUNG ADULTS ★★		OVER 30 ★★½	SENIORS ★★½

What it is Tiger habitat. **Scope and scale** Minor attraction. **When to go** Animals are most active in the morning, but they're always visible. **Authors' rating** Beautiful critters, safety-first presentation; ★★½.

DESCRIPTION AND COMMENTS   A lush, sunken island is home to several Bengal tigers, one of which is a rare white tiger. A waterfall-fed lagoon surrounds the island acting as a moat. Visitors can look down on the exhibit from a safe and secure location, but you are rather far away—not that that's a bad thing.

TOURING TIPS   The animals are visible, but they're usually napping in the afternoon. On your morning walk to Kumba, stop by quickly to possibly catch them in action. Check the daily entertainment guide or a listing at the habitat for interaction times.

Congo River Rapids   ★★★

APPEAL BY AGE	PRESCHOOL ★★★½	GRADE SCHOOL ★★★½	TEENS ★★★½
YOUNG ADULTS ★★★		OVER 30 ★★★	SENIORS ★★½

What it is Whitewater raft ride. **Scope and scale** Headliner. **When to go** After 4 p.m. **Special comments** You will get soaked. **Authors' rating** A great time, but

not worth more than a 45-minute wait; ★★★. **Duration of ride** 3 minutes.
Loading speed Slow to moderate; unloading is very slow.

DESCRIPTION AND COMMENTS Whitewater raft rides have become somewhat
of a theme-park standard, and this version is pretty much the status
quo. Twelve riders sit on a circular rubber raft as they float down a jungle river, jostling and spinning in the waves and rapids. Scary signs warn
of dangerous crocodiles in the "river," but no beasts (robotic or otherwise) ever show themselves. It is possible to avoid getting drenched
through the sheer luck of where your boat goes, but in the end, getting
very wet is almost guaranteed due to both water jets operated by mischievous onlookers on a bridge and a final gauntlet of giant water jets
that soaks almost every raft that passes through. There's nothing like
the helpless feeling of watching your boat drift into the path of one of
these megafirehoses.

TOURING TIPS Wear a poncho, either your own or one purchased at nearby
concession huts. Stow as much clothing in the lockers at the dock as you
can take off and remain decent (especially socks—nobody likes squishy
feet). There is no watertight center console on these rafts. Also, know
that long lines are inevitable for this slow-loading and -unloading
attraction. We recommend you ride the roller coasters first, saving this
attraction for later in the afternoon. The cute monkeys on display make
waiting in the first third of the line fairly entertaining.

Kiddie Rides ★★½

APPEAL BY AGE	PRESCHOOL ★★★	GRADE SCHOOL †	TEENS †
YOUNG ADULTS †	OVER 30 †		SENIORS †

† Not designed for older kids and adults.

What they are Pint-sized carnival rides. **Scope and scale** Minor attraction.
When to go Anytime. **Authors' rating** Good diversion for children; ★★½.

DESCRIPTION AND COMMENTS Nothing fancy, but these attractions help kids
who aren't old enough to ride the thrillers feel they aren't being left
out. Similar to the kiddie rides in Timbuktu.

TOURING TIPS These rides are strategically placed near the adult attractions
in this area (Kumba and Python), so one parent can keep the kids occupied while another rides.

Kumba ★★★★

APPEAL BY AGE	PRESCHOOL †	GRADE SCHOOL ★★★★	TEENS ★★★★
YOUNG ADULTS ★★★★	OVER 30 ★★★★		SENIORS ★★

† Preschoolers are generally too short to ride.

What it is Steel super roller coaster. **Scope and scale** Super headliner. **When to go**
Before 11 a.m. or after 2:30 p.m. **Special comments** Riders must be at least 54" tall.
Authors' rating Excellent; ★★★★. **Duration of ride** Approximately 3 minutes.

DESCRIPTION AND COMMENTS Kumba's dramatic loops rise above the tree line in
the Congo area, with a trainload of screaming riders twisting skyward.
Just like sister coaster Montu, Kumba is one of the best in the country.

Unlike Montu's, Kumba's trains sits on top of the track as it roars through 3,900 feet of twists and loops. Reaching speeds of 60 miles per hour, Kumba is certainly fast, but it also offers an incredibly smooth ride. This is a good thing, because the coaster's intense corkscrews will churn your insides something fierce. Thrilling elements include a diving loop, a camelback with a 360-degree spiral, and a 108-foot vertical loop.

TOURING TIPS   Kumba will be the last coaster you ride in the morning taking either route #1, #2, or #3. Following route #1, it will be after Montu; with routes #2 and #3, it will follow SheiKra. Just like Montu and SheiKra, as many as 32 riders can brave Kumba at once, so even if there is a line, the wait shouldn't be unbearable.

Python ★★★

APPEAL BY AGE	PRESCHOOL †	GRADE SCHOOL ★★★½	TEENS ★★★½
YOUNG ADULTS ★★★		OVER 30 ★★★	SENIORS ★★

† *Preschoolers are generally too short to ride.*

What it is Roller coaster. **Scope and scale** Headliner. **When to go** After 3 p.m. **Special comments** Riders must be at least 48" tall. **Authors' rating** A quick adrenaline rush; ★★★. **Duration of ride** under 1 minute.

DESCRIPTION AND COMMENTS   At less than a third the size of Kumba, the bright yellow Python offers a brief thrill. Riders climb six stories before hurling through two vertical loops, exceeding speeds of 40 miles per hour. Be glad the ride is brief since comfort is a secondary concern. The coaster was designed for smaller riders, so for adults it's like stepping into a Ferrari with no legroom. The ride is also rather rough and can slam your head against either the seat or the restraints.

TOURING TIPS   This one's short and doesn't have the large capacity of Kumba and Montu. Save it for the afternoon, when lines should be shorter.

Ubanga-Banga Bumper Cars ★★½

APPEAL BY AGE	PRESCHOOL ★★★	GRADE SCHOOL ★★★	TEENS ★★★
YOUNG ADULTS ★★½		OVER 30 ★★	SENIORS ★

What it is Bumper-car ride. **Scope and scale** Minor attraction. **When to go** Anytime. **Authors' rating** ★★½. **Duration of ride** Approximately 2 minutes, depending on park attendance.

DESCRIPTION AND COMMENTS   Basic carnival bumper-car ride.

TOURING TIPS   Don't waste time waiting in the usually very long line for this attraction if you're on the roller-coaster circuit. However, because this ride is right next to Kumba, it is a perfect place for kids and others in your group to wait for those braving the coaster.

STANLEYVILLE

Dragon's Tale Theatre/*Friends Forever* ★★★

APPEAL BY AGE	PRESCHOOL ★★★★½	GRADE SCHOOL ★★½	TEENS ★
YOUNG ADULTS ★½		OVER 30 ★	SENIORS ★½

What it is Song-and-dance show. **Scope and scale** Minor attraction. **When to go** Check daily entertainment schedule. **Authors' rating** Children's Valium; ★★★. **Duration of show** 15 minutes.

DESCRIPTION AND COMMENTS Dumphrey the Dragon performs at Dragon Tale Theatre, located to the right of the entrance of The Land of the Dragons. The show stars a princess with a supporting cast of singing flowers, an animatronic owl, Sir Robin, a wayward dog, and of course, Dumphrey the Dragon, who "only toasts marshmallows." For a small outdoor stage, the set is well crafted. The songs utilize pop beats and performances are energetic. There is even a semblance of a plot that strings the songs along and should keep your child's attention, at least long enough for you to take a few deep breaths.

TOURING TIPS Sit in the front row of wooden benches and you'll be right next to the princess. If your littlest ones are getting cranky, this should be the cure. With all of the bubbles and frolicking, this may be the happiest place in Tampa.

kids Land of the Dragons ★★★

APPEAL BY AGE	PRESCHOOL ★★★★½	GRADE SCHOOL ★★★	TEENS †
YOUNG ADULTS †		OVER 30 †	SENIORS †

† Not designed for older kids and adults.

What it is Kids' play area. **Scope and scale** Headliner. **When to go** Anytime. **Special comments** Only those less than 56" tall can ride attractions in this area. **Authors' rating** The best theming in Busch Gardens; ★★★.

DESCRIPTION AND COMMENTS With the height limits on its thrill rides, Busch Gardens often banishes children under the magic number of 48 inches tall to the animal exhibits. This enchanting area, however, is reason enough for families with kids to visit the park. The dragon theme is consistent throughout the area, creating some cute attractions, including a mini–Ferris wheel with dragon egg–shaped seats and a tiny dragon water flume. Kids can crawl through a huge net play area and get soaked in a fountain playground. There's also a live show featuring Dumphrey the Dragon entitled *Friends Forever* that plays at the Dragon's Tale Theatre (check the daily entertainment schedule for times).

TOURING TIPS This area is right next to Gwazi and on the same side of the park as Kumba, Python, and Scorpion. Those members of your group who don't do coasters can stay with the kids while others ride.

SheiKra ★★★★★

APPEAL BY AGE	PRESCHOOL †	GRADE SCHOOL ★★★	TEENS ★★★★½
YOUNG ADULTS ★★★★½		OVER 30 ★★★★	SENIORS ★★

† Preschoolers are generally too short to ride.

What it is Quick steel-track dive coaster. **Scope and scale** Super headliner. **When to go** Before 11 a.m. or after 4 p.m. **Special comments** Riders must be at least 54" tall. **Authors' rating** It rides like the commercial; ★★★★★. **Duration of ride** 3 minutes.

DESCRIPTION AND COMMENTS This newest attraction is 200 feet tall, making it the tallest coaster in the state of Florida, as well as the tallest dive coaster in the world and one of only three dive coasters that exist anywhere. (A dive coaster means the ride has a completely vertical drop.) Also incorporated are twists, swooping turns, a second huge plunge, and a tunnel of mist. The drops aren't just steep—riders hurtle down at an average of 70 miles per hour. The cars seat riders eight people across in three rows, so there are no bad seats. Any seat on SheiKra is second only to the front row of Montu.

TOURING TIPS You cannot take anything on this ride and must use a locker ($.50) found across from the entrance. If you are planning on hitting any of the nearby water rides soon after, keep your gear in the locker.

　　If taking route #1, try to head to SheiKra immediately after Gwazi or as late in the day as possible, leaving an hour or so (just in case) to wait in line and ride before the park closes. If you decide to take route #2, hit Gwazi when the park opens, then make SheiKra your second stop. If you opt for route #3, SheiKra will be your third coaster of the morning, after Montu and directly after Gwazi.

Stanley Falls ★★

APPEAL BY AGE	PRESCHOOL ★★★	GRADE SCHOOL ★★★	TEENS ★★
YOUNG ADULTS ★★		OVER 30 ★★½	SENIORS ★★½

What it is Water-flume ride. **Scope and scale** Major attraction. **When to go** After 3 p.m. **Special comments** Children not accompanied by an adult must be at least 46" tall. **Authors' rating** Nothing too exciting; ★★. **Duration of ride** 3 minutes.

DESCRIPTION AND COMMENTS Logs drift along a winding flume before plummeting down a 40-foot drop. There is almost no theming on this ride, but because the little ones can ride with an adult, it's a good way for small children (who are ready for it) to enjoy a moderate thrill. Riders are only slightly splashed on the final big drop.

TOURING TIPS This ride is exciting without being scary or jarring. During peak season, save it for the late afternoon, when lines will be shorter.

Tanganyika Tidal Wave ★★½

APPEAL BY AGE	PRESCHOOL †	GRADE SCHOOL ★★★	TEENS ★★★
YOUNG ADULTS ★★★		OVER 30 ★★★	SENIORS ★★

† Preschoolers are generally too short to ride.

What it is Quick, super water-flume ride. **Scope and scale** Headliner. **When to go** Before 11 a.m. or after 3 p.m. **Special comments** Riders must be at least 48" tall; you will get soaked. **Authors' rating** A long wait for a very short thrill; ★★½. **Duration of ride** 2 minutes.

DESCRIPTION AND COMMENTS The Tanganyika Tidal Wave was king before the Orlando parks realized that a super water-flume ride should entertain you as well as get you wet. Consequently, this ride pales in comparison with Splash Mountain at Walt Disney World or Jurassic Park at Islands of Adventure. It does do a spectacular job of getting you soaked, however. Riders board a 25-passenger boat and slowly float past empty stilt houses and ominous skulls before making the climb to the top of a steep drop. The cars are specifically designed to throw the water onto the passengers, guaranteeing a soggy experience.

TOURING TIPS If you didn't get enough water on the ride, stand on the bridge crossing the splash pool. An enormous wall of water shoots from each dropping car, fully drenching onlookers. If you want the visuals without the bath, there's also a glass wall in the area that blocks the water, one of the most fun diversions in the park.

As you exit the attraction, or if you choose not to ride, visit Orchid Canyon. This gorgeous area features many varieties of orchids growing around waterfalls in artificial rocks.

BIRD GARDENS

Aviary Walk-Thru ★

APPEAL BY AGE	PRESCHOOL ★ ½	GRADE SCHOOL ★	TEENS ★
YOUNG ADULTS ★ ½	OVER 30 ★ ½		SENIORS ★ ★

What it is Small aviary. **Scope and scale** Diversion. **When to go** anytime. **Authors' rating;** ★.

DESCRIPTION AND COMMENTS You may find yourself asking, "Was that it?" Compared with Lory Landing, the Aviary Walk-Thru is hardly an attraction. The path takes you into the aviary, makes a slight turn, and then takes you back out. There are no informational handouts on the birds nor plaques to identify them. The birds are also difficult to spot, but if you look very hard, you might see a Citgo sign.

TOURING TIPS This far corner of the park is quiet, and you may find a bit of solace by the pond near the aviary.

Bird Show Theater/*Wild Wings of Africa* ★★½

APPEAL BY AGE	PRESCHOOL ★ ★	GRADE SCHOOL ★ ★ ½	TEENS · ★
YOUNG ADULTS ★ ★	OVER 30 ★ ★		SENIORS ★ ★ ★

What it is Show featuring exotic birds. **Scope and scale** Minor attraction. **When to go** Check daily entertainment schedule. **Authors' rating** Beautiful birds, but a pretty ho-hum show; ★★½. **Duration of show** 30 minutes.

DESCRIPTION AND COMMENTS Since Disney soared above the bird-show genre with Animal Kingdom's *Flights of Wonder*, this show rubs us as its flightless ancestor. The plodding presentation and poor acoustics do not aid in holding the crowd's interest, although the birds are beautiful. They hold their own with low flights over the crowd and even by singing songs in English. Most of the birds hail from Africa, but a few species from other continents have made their way into the showcase.

TOURING TIPS A few birds may buzz your head as they flit around the theater, a fun effect for adults but sometimes upsetting to the very young. If you're over age 21, you can grab a free beer at the Anheuser-Busch Hospitality

House next door and head to this performance. Watching the gorgeous birds is better than diddling away time at the Hospitality House.

Eagle Canyon   ★★½

APPEAL BY AGE	PRESCHOOL ★★★	GRADE SCHOOL ★★★½	TEENS ★★★
YOUNG ADULTS ★★★½		OVER 30 ★★★½	SENIORS ★★★½

What it is Small area with a few eagles. **Scope and scale** Diversion. **When to go** Anytime. **Authors' rating;** ★★½.

DESCRIPTION AND COMMENTS Hidden behind the Hospitality House, Eagle Canyon is a small display of eagles on loan from the National Fish and Wildlife Service. All the birds have been injured and are being rehabilitated at Busch Gardens. A small moat separates you from the birds, but you are still very close, and the backdrop of rocks makes it a great photo op.

TOURING TIPS You'll have to look twice to find the path to Eagle Canyon, but it is worth a visit. Even on a tether, eagles are majestic creatures.

Gwazi   ★★★½

APPEAL BY AGE	PRESCHOOL †	GRADE SCHOOL ★★★★	TEENS ★★★★
YOUNG ADULTS ★★★★		OVER 30 ★★★★	SENIORS ★★

† Preschoolers are generally too short to ride.

What it is Double wooden roller coaster. **Scope and scale** Super headliner. **When to go** Before 10 a.m. or after 3 p.m. **Special comments** Riders must be at least 48" tall. **Authors' rating** Thrilling, if a little jerky; ★★★½. **Duration of ride** 2½ minutes.

DESCRIPTION AND COMMENTS Those with a nostalgic love for the wooden roller coasters of yore will be pleased with Gwazi. And fans of steel coasters shouldn't be disappointed with the 1.25 million feet of lumber, either. Although it's not as smooth, for a wooden ride, this coaster delivers thrills typically associated with its steel cousins. It's really two roller coasters in one, with two completely different tracks—the Gwazi Lion and the Gwazi Tiger—intertwined to create a frenzied race, including six "fly-by" encounters where riders pass within feet of each other. It's not as intensely confrontational as Dueling Dragons at Islands of Adventure, but it's certainly neat to see a wooden coaster use such an ultramodern gimmick.

TOURING TIPS Head here first thing in the morning to avoid long waits, or with route #3, right after Montu. But if you have time, try the coaster again before leaving the park, as it takes on a new feel after dark. Both of Gwazi's tracks are thrilling; the Tiger is a little wilder on the humps, whereas the Lion is a little faster. Both tracks have separate lines for the front and back cars. The front cars offer the best view, but the back cars whip around more for a little extra thrill. Adults waiting for their party to ride can visit the nearby Hospitality House for free samples of Anheuser-Busch beers. For little ones who don't ride, Land of the Dragons is also nearby.

Lory Landing ★★★

APPEAL BY AGE	PRESCHOOL ★★★	GRADE SCHOOL ★★★	TEENS ★★★
YOUNG ADULTS ★★★	OVER 30 ★★★		SENIORS ★★★½

What it is Interactive aviary. **Scope and scale** Major attraction. **When to go** Birds are hungrier in the morning but don't mind an afternoon snack. **Authors' rating** Cute; ★★★.

DESCRIPTION AND COMMENTS Many area attractions feature aviaries, but this is by far the biggest and the best. Tropical birds from around the world dot the lush landscape, fill the air in free flight, and are displayed in habitats. Purchase a nectar cup for $1, and some of these delightful creatures will be eating right out of your hand. Many will land on your hands, arms, shoulders, or even head, making this attraction a nightmare for those with bird-in-the-hair phobia. The illustrated journal of a fictitious explorer helps differentiate the many species, including lorikeets, hornbills, parrots, and avocets.

TOURING TIPS Try to visit before lunch, because the birds usually get their fill of nectar by early afternoon.

DINING

BUSCH GARDENS OFFERS A SIMILAR SELECTION of food as sister park SeaWorld. Fast food should cost about $7 to $10 per person, including drinks. Carved deli sandwiches on freshly baked bread and fajita wraps are a favorite at **Zagora Café**

For a real treat, try a sit-down meal at **Crown Colony House** restaurant, which offers amazing views of the Serengeti Plain. The menu features salads, sandwiches, pasta, and seafood. For the best deal, go for the family-style dinner of fried chicken or fish, with a vast selection of side dishes; it's $11.95 for adults, $6.95 for kids age 12 and under. Dinner at the restaurant can be combined with an off-road tour of the Serengeti Plain for $56 for adults, $42 for children.

The 1,000-seat, air-conditioned **Desert Grill** restaurant is a nice break from the outside heat. Bare wooden tables surround a stage from which dancers and singers perform shows several times throughout the day, but neither the show nor the food is worth writing home about. Baby-back ribs and Italian entrees like spaghetti and meatballs and fettuccini Alfredo, as well as sandwiches and a full kids' menu, are offered. Keeping in mind that the Desert Grill serves cafeteria-style and feeds thousands daily, the food is not bad and the prices are reasonable, with sandwiches for $7 to $8, desserts for $3, and beer for about $4.

unofficial **TIP**
For those traveling on a budget, McDonald's is within walking distance of the main entrance. Just remember to save your admission ticket and have your hand stamped as you exit.

unofficial **TIP**
The Desert Grill in Timbuktu could almost be considered an attraction because of its grandeur, detail, and authenticity, as well as some great entertainment.

The **Zambia Smokehouse** is the newest indoor-outdoor restaurant, and it's positioned next to the brand-new SheiKra monster coaster, allowing great views of the screaming passengers and the ride's impressive swoops and drops. Entrees like ribs, chicken, and brisket are smoked for several hours and are reasonably priced, ranging from $8 to $12.

SHOPPING

THERE'S PLENTY OF BUSCH GARDENS–LOGO MERCHANDISE, but visitors looking for something more should be happy with the vast selection. Find nature-themed gifts, such as wind chimes and jewelry, at **Nature's Kingdom.** African gifts and crafts, including clothing, brass urns, and leather goods, can be found throughout the park. Most have reasonable prices, although some larger, intricate items can be more expensive. For that hard-to-shop-for adult, try the **Anheuser-Busch Label Stable** or the **West African Trading Company,** which features hand-crafted items from many countries, as well as a walk-in cigar humidor. Like SeaWorld, Busch Gardens offers a vast array of kid-pleasing stuffed animals; kids and parents should be happy with the prices.

PART THREE

CYPRESS GARDENS

CYPRESS GARDENS IS CENTRAL FLORIDA'S oldest theme park. Since its inception in 1936, Cypress Gardens has expanded and now includes a theme park, a water park, a nature park, and a zoo. Each facet is located in a different area of Cypress Gardens: Adventure Grove holds the majority of the park's rides, while Jubilee Junction and Lake Eloise contain the park's shows; Splash Island has all of the wettest attractions; Plantation Gardens, Botanical Gardens, and Topiary Trail round out the horticultural wonders; and Nature's Way hosts the animal exhibits.

Of course, none of the sections of Cypress Gardens would win best in show against any of the major parks in central Florida. How could Nature's Way, host to a mere 300 animals, compete against Busch Gardens' 2,700 animals, or against Disney's giraffes, elephants, rhinos, and lions that roam the savanna at The Animal Kingdom? The key to Cypress Gardens' recent resurgence appears to be offering a taste of everything for one low price. As many tapas fans have found, many small plates of food and no entree can still make for a good meal.

The variety of attractions available under one ticket also makes Cypress Gardens ideal for large groups with a tight budget, or families with a broad age range between members. As with Milton Bradley games, ages 8 to 80 are all able to play. Grandma may wander around the Botanical Gardens while the younger teens swim at the water park, leaving Dad free to take the tykes on the kiddie rides. And everyone should enjoy the classics, such as the water ski show.

Since Cypress Gardens is steeped in heritage, we would be remiss if we did not give a brief history lesson. Julie and Dick Pope founded Cypress Gardens in 1936. Nicknamed Mr. Florida, Dick Pope was a lead advocate for Florida tourism. During his reign, Cypress Gardens became a premiere Florida destination, bringing in such stars as Elvis Presley and Esther Williams with its magnificent gardens and the impromptu creation of performance waterskiing.

cypress gardens

● **ATTRACTIONS**
1. Boardwalk Carousel
2. Citrus Line Railroad
3. *Cypress Belle* Riverboat
4. Cypress Cove Ferry Line
5. Delta Kite Flyer
6. Disk'O
7. Dizzy Dragons
8. *Farm Yard Frolics*
9. Fiesta Express
10. Fire Brigade
11. Fun Slide
12. Galaxy Spin
13. Garden Gondolas
14. Gear Jammers
15. The Inverter
16. Jalopy Junction
17. Junior Rampsters
18. *Mango Bay Water Ski Show*
19. Mega Bounce
20. Nature's Way Zoo
21. *Night Magic* (Seasonal)
22. Okeechobee Rampage

23. Paradise Sky Wheel
24. Pharaoh's Fury
25. Pirate Ship
26. Power Surge
27. Red Baron
28. Rio Grande Train
29. Rockin' Tug
30. Seafari Swings
31. Side Swipers
32. Star Haven Amphitheatre
33. Stars and Stripes
34. Storm Surge
35. Sunshine Sky Adventure
36. Super Truckers
37. Swamp Thing
38. Thunderbolt
39. Tilt-a-Whirl
40. Tiny Trotters
41. Triple Hurricane
42. Upsy-Daisy
43. V-R Gone Wild
44. Wave Runner
45. Yo-Yo Swings

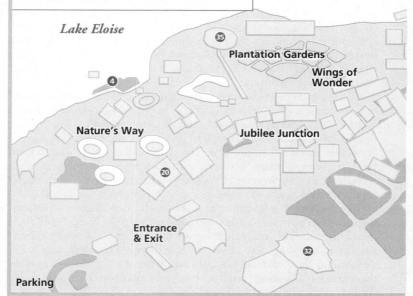

Lake Eloise

Plantation Gardens

Wings of Wonder

Nature's Way

Jubilee Junction

Entrance & Exit

Parking

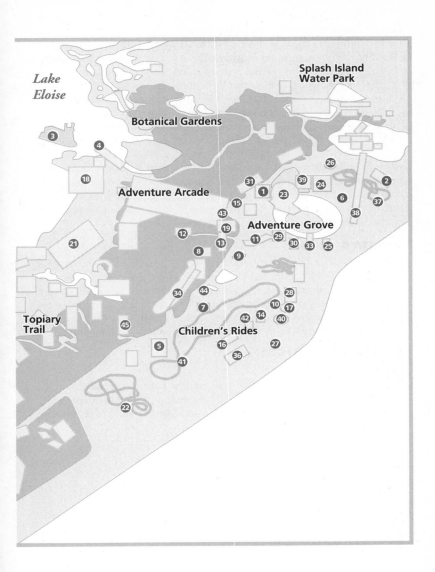

In 1962, Dick Pope turned the park and his penchant for promoting Florida tourism over to his son, Dick Pope Jr., who, as legend has it, was the man who persuaded Walt to move the Mouse to central Florida, proclaiming, "What is good for Florida is good for Cypress Gardens."

unofficial **TIP**
To get the flavor of "pre-Disney" Florida tourist attractions, head to Cypress Gardens.

And as irony dictates, the family sold Cypress Gardens in 1985 to corporate interests. The park plodded on with little direction, changed hands a few times, and finally closed in 2003 due to low attendance. The locals were not pleased with the park's closure, and, with its annual regional impact in the area of $160 million, were elated when Kent Buesher—owner of Wild Adventures in Valdosta, Georgia—purchased Cypress Gardens. After extensive renovations, the park reopened in 2005, drawing a record 1.4 million people. With the addition of new rides, a water park, and a zoo, Cypress Gardens is now one of the 50 most visited parks in the nation.

GETTING THERE

CYPRESS GARDENS IS ROUGHLY 35 MILES and 45 minutes west of Walt Disney World. From the Orlando area, take Interstate 4 west and exit onto US 27 south. Continue on this road about 20 miles. Turn right at FL 540/Cypress Gardens Boulevard. The park is four miles away on the left. Look for green mileage signs that point the way. Parking is $9 for cars and $11 for RVs. A yearlong parking pass is available for $25.

ADMISSION PRICES

Regular Admission

Regular admission is a one-day pass but includes a second day free, within six days of original visit. Tickets include all areas of the park, as well as some concerts or special events. Major concerts require an additional fee.

REGULAR ADMISSION
Adults $39.95 + tax | *Children ages 3–9* $34.95 + tax
Seniors ages 55+ $34.95 + tax

Annual Passports

Passports provide unlimited admission to Cypress Gardens, including all concerts and special events and admission to its sister park, Wild Adventures, in Valdosta, Georgia. The Gold passport includes free parking, 10% off the dinner cruise, 10% off for guests, and 10% off merchandise.

ANNUAL PASSPORT
Adults $69.95 + tax

GOLD PASSPORT
Adults $99.95 + tax

ARRIVING

CYPRESS GARDENS OPENS AT 10 A.M. daily. Closing time is generally 7 p.m. on weekdays and 10 p.m. on weekends, but alters due to seasonal flow and special events.

Begin your day by heading directly to Adventure Grove and hitting the three main coasters: Triple Hurricane, Okeechobee Rampage, and Swamp Thing. With short lines, this should take about 20 minutes including walking. Until Splash Island opens, sample other rides that interest you in Adventure Grove. The majority of the Adventure Grove rides are carnival-type attractions, with the requisite tilt-a-whirl, carousel, and Ferris wheel. Unlike Busch Gardens or Islands of Adventure, this self-dubbed adventure park will *not* hold the interest of kids over age 13.

Splash Island usually opens an hour after the rest of the park. Water-park lines are infamously slow-paced because each rider must clear the slide before the next rider enters. Splash Island is no exception; arrive as soon as it opens, perhaps already wearing your swim gear under your clothes, and head first to the Tonga Tubes, then to the VooDoo Plunge. Enjoy the rest of your time in the water park until things get too crowded, then head off to the shows and exhibits. Show times are printed in your daily entertainment schedule and you may need to alter your touring plans to see every show you are interested in, so review the show schedule on the way to the roller coasters in the morning.

Depending on how much you try to do and see, touring the park may not take an entire day. Plan on four to six hours to experience all of the major attractions. Because the attractions include gardens and wildlife exhibits, the time you spend in these areas depends on your fondness—or patience—for either or both, and these self-paced amusements should be saved until the end of the day.

One final note: Cypress Gardens is not a great destination for teenagers or young adults without children. None of the rides are thrill rides, and there isn't the extra charm of visiting Disney World. When teenagers are at Cypress Gardens, you often find them attempting to make the best of their situation by traveling in packs, a phenomenon we haven't experienced at other parks unless everyone arrived on a school bus. These groups of kids have a tendency to get on the same ride at once, or repeat that ride over and over again, resulting in clogged lines. If you run across a line of 20 to 30 unsupervised teens, go to another ride until the group is through with the attraction and then return. You'll avoid long wait times this way.

unofficial **TIP**
To get your chance to ride the thrill rides, head to the back of the park first.

CONTACTING CYPRESS GARDENS

FOR MORE INFORMATION, call Cypress Gardens at ☎ 863-324-2111 or visit the Web site at **www.cypressgardens.com,** which contains pictures of almost every attraction at the park.

█ ATTRACTIONS

ADVENTURE GROVE

Boardwalk Carousel   ★★★½

APPEAL BY AGE	PRESCHOOL ★★★½	GRADE SCHOOL ★★½	TEENS ★½
YOUNG ADULTS ★½		OVER 30 ★★	SENIORS ★★★½

What it is Carousel. **Scope and scale** Minor attraction. **When to go** Anytime. **Special comments** Children less than 42" tall must ride with an adult. **Authors' rating** ★★★½. **Duration of ride** 3 minutes. **Loading speed** Slow.

DESCRIPTION AND COMMENTS   This double-decker carousel sits next to the Ferris wheel in the center of Adventure Grove. The carousel is the classic archetype. You won't find wild beasts or Dr. Seuss figures to sit on. Instead, beautifully crafted, hand-painted horses gently rise and fall. Even if you don't ride it, stop by to admire the handiwork and attention to detail.

TOURING TIPS   This ride would be better situated in the gardens, away from the hubbub of the bumper cars and the coasters of Adventure Grove. The ride is handicap accessible and has five benches.

Citrus Line Railroad   ★★★

APPEAL BY AGE	PRESCHOOL ★★★½	GRADE SCHOOL ★★	TEENS ★
YOUNG ADULTS ★★		OVER 30 ★★★	SENIORS ★★★½

What it is Train ride. **Scope and scale** Minor attraction. **When to go** Anytime. **Special comments** Must be 42" tall to ride alone. **Authors' rating** ★★★. **Duration of ride** 15 minutes. **Loading speed** Slow.

DESCRIPTION AND COMMENTS   The miniature train chugs along the border of Adventure Grove and has a fully narrated history of the Gardens, slightly different from that found on the Cypress Cove Ferry Line. Although you will see all of the sites the train passes as you walk around Adventure Grove, the little guys will enjoy the 12-miles-per-hour ride, while adults can concentrate on the narration.

TOURING TIPS   You can board the train at either end of Adventure Grove, at Pope Station next to the Triple Hurricane coaster, or at Flagler Station next to the entrance to Splash Island. Walking is faster than riding the train, so if you just miss the train and don't want to wait 20 minutes for its return, walk to the opposite station. The train seats 42 people, so overcrowding is rare.

Disk'O   ★★★

APPEAL BY AGE	PRESCHOOL †	GRADE SCHOOL ★★★½	TEENS ★★★
YOUNG ADULTS ★★★		OVER 30 ★★	SENIORS ½

† Preschoolers are generally too short to ride.

What it is Carnival-type wild ride. **Scope and scale** Major attraction. **When to go** Anytime. **Special comments** Must be 48" tall to ride. **Authors' rating** ★★★. **Duration of ride** 2 minutes. **Loading speed** Fast.

DESCRIPTION AND COMMENTS Riders sit around the edges of a large disc that spins around as it slides up and down a half-pipe. The seats on this ride face outward, so any "projectiles" this ride shakes loose should land clear of the other guests. We can only assume the ride was designed to do this.

TOURING TIPS Fitting into the theme of stomach-stirring rides, this is one of the best, but another one to be wary of if motion sickness is a problem for you or your family members.

Farm Yard Frolics ★★

APPEAL BY AGE	PRESCHOOL ★★½	GRADE SCHOOL ★★★	TEENS ★½
YOUNG ADULTS ★★	OVER 30 ★★★		SENIORS ★★★

What it is Jokes and magic. **Scope and scale** Diversion. **When to go** Check schedule for daily show times. **Authors' rating** Thank goodness it's short; ★★. **Duration of show** 15 minutes.

DESCRIPTION AND COMMENTS Farmer Dan and Billy Bob host a magic show at the farm. Performed on an outdoor stage with wooden benches for seats, the magic show is a compilation of bad jokes and mild illusions. The southern cornball antics are annoying at best, but the use of illusions—as opposed to sleight-of-hand magic—keeps the show entertaining. Children enjoy it and adults can't help but chuckle at the effort put forth for this hokey show.

TOURING TIPS Don't arrive late; it's only 15 minutes.

Galaxy Spin ★★

APPEAL BY AGE	PRESCHOOL ★★½	GRADE SCHOOL ★★★½	TEENS ★★★
YOUNG ADULTS ★★	OVER 30 ★½		SENIORS ★

What it is Mouse coaster. **Scope and scale** Major attraction. **When to go** Early in the day. **Special comments** Must be 42" tall to ride with an adult, 48" tall to ride alone. **Authors' rating** ★★. **Duration of ride** 5 minutes. **Loading speed** Moderate.

DESCRIPTION AND COMMENTS Individual cars, which can spin around 360 degrees, ascend to the top of the track and then wind down through a series of hairpin curves. At each curve, riders are thrust against each other as the car spins around. Not that the quick spin isn't fun once, but the repetition of slamming against each other wears thin by the third turn, and with around 15 turns in all, you'll be happy to get off.

TOURING TIPS Why amusement parks, including parks as big as Disney, continue to punish riders with these mouse coasters is beyond us. Skip this one if you have neck problems, or aren't enthralled by quick stops and starts.

The Inverter ★★½

APPEAL BY AGE	PRESCHOOL †	GRADE SCHOOL ★★½	TEENS ★★★
YOUNG ADULTS ★★★	OVER 30 ★		SENIORS ½

† Preschoolers are generally too short to ride.

What it is Lunch tosser. **Scope and scale** Major attraction. **When to go** Before lunch. **Special comments** Must be 48" tall to ride. **Authors' rating** ★★½. **Duration of ride** 1 minutes, 45 seconds. **Loading speed** Average.

DESCRIPTION AND COMMENTS   Picture a bicycle. The pedal of the bike—that black part you step on—is attached to a crank and can spin freely on its own. The bike's pedal and crank are analogous to this ride in which you, if it were a bike, would be sitting on the pedal as the crank spun around. Although we prefer a nice ride on open trails, many teenagers find The Inverter more amusing.

TOURING TIPS   If you're skipping the Thunderbolt, skip this too as they're closely related on the stomach-tossing scale. Remove anything in shirt pockets so they won't go flying when the car is upside down.

Mega Bounce   ★★½

APPEAL BY AGE	PRESCHOOL ★★½	GRADE SCHOOL ★★★½	TEENS ★★★★
YOUNG ADULTS ★★★		OVER 30 ★½	SENIORS ★

What it is Mouse coaster. **Scope and scale** Minor attraction. **When to go** Early in the day. **Special comments** Must be 42" tall to ride. **Authors' rating** ★★½. **Duration of ride** 4 minutes. **Loading speed** Moderate.

DESCRIPTION AND COMMENTS   If you've ever been attacked by a spinning octopus, then you don't need to ride the Mega Bounce. Arms extend from a central rotating hub and bounce up and down using pneumatic pumps. The quick bursts of compressed air can be heard well before you see the ride. The up-and-down motion is very quick, hence the ride's name.

TOURING TIPS   Add it to the list of tummy tumblers. Ride it before lunch.

Okeechobee Rampage   ★★★

APPEAL BY AGE	PRESCHOOL ★★★½	GRADE SCHOOL ★★★★	TEENS ★★★
YOUNG ADULTS ★★★		OVER 30 ★★	SENIORS ★★

What it is Roller coaster. **Scope and scale** Headliner. **When to go** Before 11 a.m. **Special comments** Must be 36" tall to ride with an adult, 42" to ride alone. **Authors' rating** ★★★. **Duration of ride** 45 seconds. **Loading speed** Fast.

DESCRIPTION AND COMMENTS   This coaster is the shortest in the park, but if the crowds are small (which they often are), the attendants will let riders have a second run. This ride is not comparable to the bigger coasters at Islands of Adventure or Busch Gardens, so don't expect a coaster of the monstrous proportions found in other parks. Taken for what it is—a small-scale, fun-for-the-whole-family kind of adventure—it's pretty darn enjoyable. There are no big hills or steep drops on this one, so even the coaster-shy may enjoy the fast but relatively easy ride.

TOURING TIPS   Again, this is one of the park's major attractions, so the earlier you ride this one, the better. If you are okay with saving the gardens and lake for the end of the day, you can bypass the scenic route and take a left behind the locker station. Walk past the concert stage, and the first thing you'll see is the twisting track.

kids **Paradise Sky Wheel** ★★★

APPEAL BY AGE	PRESCHOOL ★★★★	GRADE SCHOOL ★★★★	TEENS ★★
YOUNG ADULTS ★★		OVER 30 ★★★★	SENIORS ★★★★

What it is Old-fashioned Ferris wheel. **Scope and scale** Minor attraction. **When to go** Anytime. **Special comments** You must be 42" or taller if not accompanied by an adult. **Authors' rating** ★★★. **Duration of ride** 1 minute, 45 seconds; if there's no line, you can ride several times. **Loading speed** Moderate.

DESCRIPTION AND COMMENTS A throwback to the early days of amusement parks, this Ferris wheel might look more in place toward the front of the park, away from its flashy, fast-moving neighbors. But it's a nice break from all the tummy-churning rides, and a fun way to see the whole park, as you probably won't notice much at the top of the Thunderbolt. It might be too subtle for older kids, but preschoolers seem to appreciate its gentleness.

TOURING TIPS Head to the Sky Wheel when your feet are tired or you need a moment to settle your stomach. The line is generally pretty short at any time of day.

Pharaoh's Fury ★½

APPEAL BY AGE	PRESCHOOL †	GRADE SCHOOL ★★★½	TEENS ★★★½
YOUNG ADULTS ★★		OVER 30 ★½	SENIORS ½

† Preschoolers are generally too short to ride.

What it is A sailor's worst nightmare. **Scope and scale** Major attraction. **When to go** Anytime. **Special comments** Must be 48" tall to ride. **Authors' rating** Not for the easily nauseated; ★½. **Duration of ride** 1 minute, 45 seconds. **Loading speed** Slow; the ride can accommodate between 40 and 60 people at a time—if there's no line, you may have to wait as the ride fills up.

DESCRIPTION AND COMMENTS A large Viking ship on a pendulum swings riders to and fro, reaching speeds of close to 80 miles per hour. The boat gains speed throughout the ride, and the last two tick-tocks are a doozy.

TOURING TIPS This is one attraction for which a larger crowd waiting to ride is usually a good thing. The attendants may not run it if there are fewer than 20 people in line, but stop by and check. To get the most out of this ride, sit at either end of the boat. Be aware that people often lose pocket contents. Secure yours in advance.

Power Surge ★★★★

APPEAL BY AGE	PRESCHOOL †	GRADE SCHOOL ★★★½	TEENS ★★★★
YOUNG ADULTS ★★★½		OVER 30 ★★★	SENIORS ½

† Preschoolers are generally too short to ride.

What it is A rotating, spinning ride. **Scope and scale** Major attraction. **When to go** Anytime. **Special comments** Must be 52" tall to ride. **Authors' rating** ★★★★. **Duration of ride** 2 minutes. **Loading speed** Fast.

DESCRIPTION AND COMMENTS This ride seems to defy description, since we've found very few stationary rides that spin you on all three axes. If you took a windmill, placed rotating seats on the end of each blade, and then allowed the windmill to lean to and fro, you might create a cheap knockoff. However you describe it—we will read your letters—the sensation from all the spinning is akin to riding on one of the big steel coasters found at other parks.

TOURING TIPS Although it's not too wild and smoother than it looks, this is another one to try before lunch or a few hours afterward.

Side Swipers ★★★½

APPEAL BY AGE	PRESCHOOL †	GRADE SCHOOL ★★½	TEENS ★★★½
YOUNG ADULTS ★★½		OVER 30 ★★	SENIORS ★★

† Preschoolers are generally too short to ride.

What it is Bumper cars. **Scope and scale** Minor attraction. **When to go** Just before midday. **Special comments** Must be 50" tall and 8 years old to ride with an adult, 75" tall and 13 years old to ride alone. **Authors' rating** ★★★½. **Duration of ride** 8 minutes. **Loading speed** Moderate.

DESCRIPTION AND COMMENTS Next to the Inverter are the bumper cars. Yet another classic, you slam these individual or two-person cars into one another. In a departure from your typical driving vehicle, your brake is controlled with your left foot and your accelerator with your right. There is no reverse, so to get out of a jam turn your wheel all the way to one side and press on the accelerator. While slamming into the other cars is mildly jarring, try to avoid being slammed into the walls—there's not a lot a give.

TOURING TIPS There are 18 cars on the floor, and each round takes eight minutes. Count the heads in line to check the wait time. You will want a few other guests to bump into, but crowds begin to thicken here in the early afternoon.

Storm Surge ★★½

APPEAL BY AGE	PRESCHOOL ★★★½	GRADE SCHOOL ★★★½	TEENS ★★
YOUNG ADULTS ★★		OVER 30 ★★★	SENIORS ★★½

What it is A drier-than-normal waterslide. **Scope and scale** Major attraction. **When to go** Anytime. **Special comments** Must be 42" tall to ride. **Authors' rating** ★★½. **Duration of ride** 2½ minutes. **Loading speed** Fast.

DESCRIPTION AND COMMENTS This ride is an inventive solution for people who want a tube ride but forgot their bathing suits. The high rubber walls of your raft not only protect you from the water, but also catch against the rubber walls of the course, causing you to spin the entire way to the bottom. Up to six people can ride in a raft, so the whole family can ride together, adding to the fun. For the most part, it's a pretty dry experience except for a line of mist machines at the bottom that hit you with a spritz of water—just enough to cool you off, but not enough to soak you through.

TOURING TIPS Younger kids enjoy this raft ride; teens and young adults may find it too slow—and dizzying—to keep them very interested.

Swamp Thing ★★★½

APPEAL BY AGE	PRESCHOOL ★	GRADE SCHOOL ★★★★½	TEENS ★★★½
YOUNG ADULTS ★★★½		OVER 30 ★★	SENIORS ★

What it is An inverted, steel-track roller coaster. **Scope and scale** Headliner. **When to go** Before noon. **Special comments** Must be 44" tall to ride. **Authors' rating** Fast and fun; ★★★½. **Duration of ride** 45 seconds. **Loading speed** Moderate.

DESCRIPTION AND COMMENTS Another of the three coasters at Cypress Gardens, this is the only inverted coaster—that does not mean you go upside-down, but rather, that the track is over your head. Your legs dangle as you zip around the corners and up and down the smooth drops. Some of the turns are sharp and fast. The turns paired with the twists in the track can leave you feeling a little dizzy, and you may bang your cheeks against the restraints.

As with the Okeechobee Rampage, the lift hill is very small, so the coaster pauses when the caboose is at the top of the lift hill. The detaining mechanism then disengages and the train rolls forward. Since the front car of the train is farther down the track, it will be moving slower around the initial bends than the last car. There are not many bends, so we recommend sitting in the last car on both of these coasters although there is some disagreement on the Swamp Thing, since a front seat on the Swamp Thing with nothing around you is similar to flying. Our answer; if the lines are short, try both seats.

TOURING TIPS This orange and blue coaster sits on the opposite end of the park from the two other coasters, which keeps its lines the shortest of the three. Still, because it's one of the more popular attractions, try to head for this one before lunch.

Thunderbolt ★★★½

APPEAL BY AGE	PRESCHOOL ½	GRADE SCHOOL ★★	TEENS ★★★
YOUNG ADULTS ★★★		OVER 30 ★★	SENIORS ½

What it is Tummy tumbler. **Scope and scale** Headliner. **When to go** Before you eat lunch. **Special comments** Must be 42" tall to ride. **Authors' rating** ★★★½. **Duration of ride** 1½ minutes. **Loading speed** Fast.

DESCRIPTION AND COMMENTS A similar but better ride than Universal's Dr. Doom's Fearfall, the Thunderbolt is designed for pure terror. The operator straps you into a jump seat and, with your feet dangling, the tower hoists you 120 feet into the air. To add to the anticipation, your ascent is not only very slow, but a protrusion above your head blocks your view upward so that you have no idea when you've reached the top. Once you are up, it's an exhilarating free fall down, and at 47 miles per hour, not for the faint of stomach.

TOURING TIPS This is another big draw at the park—the line usually isn't very long, but it's worth scoping out after the coasters and before any other rides. Chances are the line will grow as the day goes on. If the entire idea of a blind free fall seems too scary, remember that if you sit on the side where you can see your shadow, you will be able to tell when you've reached the top. And if you don't want to know—*grin*—sit on the other side.

Tilt-a-Whirl ★★★

APPEAL BY AGE	PRESCHOOL ★★★½	GRADE SCHOOL ★★★½	TEENS ★★★
YOUNG ADULTS ★★★		OVER 30 ★★½	SENIORS ★

What it is Spinning cars. **Scope and scale** Minor attraction. **When to go** Anytime. **Special comments** Must be 32–46" tall to ride with an adult, 46" tall to ride alone. **Authors' rating** ★★★. **Duration of ride** 2 minutes. **Loading speed** Fast.

DESCRIPTION AND COMMENTS This carnival classic is located at the far end of Adventure Grove near the Swamp Thing coaster. Two-person carts rotate individually, and spin around a circular track with two raised walls. You've ridden it before, but with its capacity to fit four adults and five children, you might as well introduce your children to it now.

TOURING TIPS The motion sickness is lower on the Tilt-a-Whirl than most of the park's other rides. The ride's ability to move more than 500 people an hour keeps lines at bay.

Triple Hurricane ★★★★

APPEAL BY AGE	PRESCHOOL ★★	GRADE SCHOOL ★★★★	TEENS ★★★½
YOUNG ADULTS ★★★★		OVER 30 ★★★½	SENIORS ★★

What it is Wooden roller coaster. **Scope and scale** Super headliner. **When to go** Before 11 a.m. **Special comments** Must be 36" tall to ride with an adult, 42" to ride alone. **Authors' rating** Quaint, but our choice for the funnest ride in the park; ★★★★. **Duration of ride** 1 minute. **Loading speed** Moderate.

DESCRIPTION AND COMMENTS Even small children may enjoy the dips, four turns (it's an oval), and mini-drops on this old-fashioned "woody." The ride is short for a coaster, lasting about one minute, and the coaster is not very tall, in light of the nearby carnival attractions looming over-head, or most people's expectations. Still, the rattling wooden coaster is fast and one of the main draws in the park.

TOURING TIPS Along with the Okeechobee Rampage and the Swamp Thing, this is one of the park's major rides. Head to these coasters first, as the lines grow as the day goes on. If you enjoy a coaster and the line is still short, loop back around for one more spin before heading to the next ride.

V-R Gone Wild ½

APPEAL BY AGE	PRESCHOOL ★	GRADE SCHOOL ★★	TEENS ★½
YOUNG ADULTS ★½		OVER 30 ½	SENIORS ½

What it is Virtual-reality simulator. **Scope and scale** Minor attraction. **When to go** Never. **Authors' rating** Waste of money; ½. **Duration of ride** 4 minutes. **Loading speed** Slow. **Cost** $3 per person.

DESCRIPTION AND COMMENTS Next to the Mega Bounce is the virtual-reality sim-ulator. After you've donned your goggles, the ride operator instructs you to bounce in your seat, yell, and stomp your feet to calibrate the virtual-reality machine to your weight, loudness, etc. When the simulation begins, you compete against the other riders in an attempt to shoot zombies at a carnival. The plot is frantic and makes absolutely no sense. You shoot with a hand-held controller that is difficult to aim, stomp on the ground to run away from zombies and, as a finale to the confusing rampage, shoot a pro wrestler who bears an uncanny resemblance to The Rock.

TOURING TIPS All 24 seats face out toward the Boardwalk Carousel, so anyone walking by will see you flopping about in your chair. The in-game graphics are terrible, and the sunlight creeps in around your goggles, making it even more difficult to tell what is happening. The only ones who might enjoy the simulator are children, but the violence is so strong that we cannot recommend it. The added $3 charge is just another reason to skip the worst attraction at Cypress Gardens.

Wave Runner ★★

APPEAL BY AGE	PRESCHOOL ★★★½	GRADE SCHOOL ★★★½	TEENS ★★
YOUNG ADULTS ★★		OVER 30 ★★½	SENIORS ★★

What it is Dry water ride. Scope and scale Major attraction. When to go Anytime. Special comments Must be 36" tall to ride with an adult, 42" tall to ride alone. Authors' rating ★★. Duration of ride 2 minutes. Loading speed Moderate.

DESCRIPTION AND COMMENTS Located across from the Storm Surge is another mostly dry water ride. Two enclosed tubes, one dark green and one dark blue, twist down from the top of a 45-foot-tall tower. From the top of the tower, the dark blue tube boards to the right and contains a straightaway, while the dark green tube boards to the left and contains a double corkscrew. The ride allows up to three riders in each raft as long as their combined weight does not exceed 350 pounds.

TOURING TIPS The raft's walls are short, but there is not an excess of water in the tubes. The ride contains a mild catch-22, since the only part of you that will get wet is your feet, yet you're required to wear shoes.

KIDS' RIDES

THE REST OF THE ATTRACTIONS in Adventure Grove are rides meant for children under age 10, and many explicitly for preschoolers. All of the rides are small, and many are miniatures of the larger rides marketed to the older crowd. The rides are located in three adjacent sections of Adventure Grove: along the walkway in front of the Triple Hurricane coaster, in a small area behind the Triple Hurricane coaster, and on the side of the small pond in Adventure Grove closer to the Triple Hurricane but between the Triple Hurricane and the Thunderbolt. Cypress Gardens does not keep enough staff on hand to operate all these rides at once, so if you want to ride one of the rides, ask a nearby attendant when the next operator will be available. Attendants will often fire up any ride you ask to try within a few minutes.

The rides along the walkway in front of the Triple Hurricane are the **Yo-Yo Swings, Delta Kite Flyer, Dizzy Dragons, Fiesta Express, Fun Slide,** and **Garden Gondolas.** The Yo-Yo Swings are a set of individual swings dangling on chains. The chains are attached to a center tower that spins in a circle and hoists riders 25 feet above the ground. On this three-minute ride, riders must be less than 216 pounds and taller than 42 inches. The Delta Kite Flyer also spins around a center tower, but here, you ride on your stomach—like Superman—and are very close to the ground. Each of the six arms holds two places to lie. Riders must be 42 inches tall and the combined weight of the two riders on each arm cannot exceed 275 pounds The Dizzy Dragons is a miniature version of a teacup ride, but instead of teacups, you spin around inside the belly of a dragon. Riders under 36 inches tall must be accompanied by an adult. The Fiesta Express is a very short roller coaster that moves around a small oval track. You must be 36 inches tall to ride. The Fun Slide is a set of three side-by-side slides with bumps all the way down. Riders descend on mats and must be accompanied by an adult if they are less than 42 inches tall. The final ride in this area is the Garden Gondolas. In this ride, made to look like hot air balloons, riders sit in baskets that can swivel around under your power. Each basket is connected to the main tower that spins around and raises riders 35 feet off the ground. Children under 42 inches tall must ride with an adult.

The rides behind the Triple Hurricane coaster are only for preschoolers. They include: **Jalopy Junction, Super Truckers, Red Baron, Upsy-Daisy, Gear Jammers, Tiny Trotters, Fire Brigade, Junior Rampsters,** and the **Rio Grande Train.** Jalopy Junction is a set of pint-sized, 1910s and 1920s cars that run on a small circular track. Children under 36 inches tall must be accompanied by an adult. Super Truckers is exactly the same as Jalopy Junction except that miniature tractor-trailers replace the antique cars. Children must be at least 3 years old to ride; riders 3 to 6 years old must ride with an adult. The Red Baron is a set of red prop planes that spin around a center axis; riders can control the up-and-down movements. Riders need to be between 42 and 52 inches tall to ride. Upsy-Daisy is the same ride as the Red Baron except that riders sit in small seats underneath a hang glider, and you cannot control the up-and-down motion. Again, riders need to be between 42 and 52 inches tall to ride. Another ride for the 42- to 52-inch crowd is Gear Jammers. The ride is a very small carousel, as one might find in front of a shopping center, and contains four trucks to sit in; it does not move up and down. Tiny Trotters is a slightly larger carousel that is also unable to move vertically. Riders sit in a sulky behind a small horse, and riders under 42 inches tall must ride with an adult. The Fire Brigade is the most intricate ride in the kiddie section. Riders stand in the back of a small hook-and-ladder fire engine as it circles a building. Riders then shoot water at the building to attempt to put out the painted flames. You must be 36 inches tall to ride. Junior Rampsters follows the pattern of rides that rotate around a central axis. On this ride, children between the heights of 42 and 56 inches sit in boats that putt around a pond filled with actual water. The last ride in the kiddie area is the Rio Grande Train. The train is a smaller version of the Citrus Line Railroad and runs around a small oval track. Riders under 42 inches tall must be accompanied by an adult.

The third area of kids' rides is located alongside the little pond in Adventure Grove. There are four rides here, and each is a miniature of another ride in the park. They are: **Rockin' Tug, Seafari Swings, Stars and Stripes,** and the **Pirate Ship.** The Rockin' Tug is a small version of the Disk'O, but instead of riding a rotating disc moving along a half-pipe, riders sit in a tugboat. You must be at least 42 inches tall to ride. The Seafari Swings are a small version of the Yo-Yo swings and accommodate riders at least 32 inches tall. Stars and Stripes is the small version of the Thunderbolt, and raises you only about 40 feet in the air. Riders must be at least 42 inches tall. The last miniature version of a major park ride is the Pirate Ship, a smaller version of Pharaoh's Fury. Children under 36 inches tall must be accompanied by a guest over 48 inches tall to ride this pendulum.

SPLASH ISLAND

AFTER YEARS OF CONSTRUCTION, Splash Island opened for the 2006 season. As with the rest of Cypress Gardens' facets, Splash Island is not large, but still contains enough attractions to keep your group entertained for a few hours. Like all the Florida water parks, Splash Island is a seasonal attraction and is closed during winter and during weekdays at the beginning and end of the season. Call ahead to make sure it is open. Although other Florida water parks have ample shady areas, Splash Island contains a substantial lack of locales out of the reach of the sun. Seats along the chain-linked fence provide some shade during the midday heat, but fill up soon after the gate to Splash Island opens at 10 a.m. Even if you snag a shady spot, wear sunscreen anyway. Few things ruin Florida vacations as frequently as red blisters and sun poisoning. Even on cloudy days, waterproof sunblock of SPF 15 or greater is recommended.

Kowabunga Bay   ★★★

| APPEAL BY AGE | PRESCHOOL ★★ | GRADE SCHOOL ★★★★ | TEENS ★★★½ |
| YOUNG ADULTS ★★★ | | OVER 30 ★★★½ | SENIORS ★★★½ |

What it is Wave pool. **Scope and scale** Minor Attraction. **When to go** After the slides. **Special comments** Small but decent. **Authors' rating** ★★★.

DESCRIPTION AND COMMENTS At 20,000 square feet, it's no small pool, but it's not as large as Wet 'n Wild's wave pool and a mere puddle compared to Typhoon Lagoon. Still, with no height requirement and pretty small waves, it's a fine place to splash around.

TOURING TIPS When this area gets too crowded, it probably means that the entire water park is overflowing. Clear tubes can be rented for use in both the Kowabunga Bay wave pool and the Paradise River. Prices for the clear tubes fluctuate between $4 and $9 seasonally. There are free blue tubes in Paradise River, but these tubes cannot be taken to the wave pool.

Paradise River ★★★

APPEAL BY AGE	PRESCHOOL ★★★½	GRADE SCHOOL ★★★	TEENS ★★½
YOUNG ADULTS ★★★½	OVER 30 ★★★★		SENIORS ★★★★

What it is Man-made stream. Scope and scale Minor attraction. When to go Anytime. Special comments Cool and relaxing. Authors' rating Zonk out and float; ★★★.

DESCRIPTION AND COMMENTS What makes these circular brooks interesting is the quality of the theming bordering the water. Paradise River has no theming; it is 10,000 feet of concrete without much shade or imagination. When you close your eyes and drift along it's not too bad, but honestly, how about a palm tree?

TOURING TIPS Wear sunscreen; you may fall asleep. The water is not heated. See the note above in the Kowabunga Bay description about tubes.

Polynesian Adventure ★★★

APPEAL BY AGE	PRESCHOOL ★★★★	GRADE SCHOOL ★★★★	TEENS ★★½
YOUNG ADULTS †	OVER 30 †		SENIORS †

† This attraction is not intended for adults.

What it is Giant wet playground. Scope and scale Minor attraction. When to go Anytime. Special comments Get wet without swimming. Authors' rating ★★★.

DESCRIPTION AND COMMENTS A 42-foot-high jungle gym, the structure contains five small slides, cargo nets, water wheels, water cannons, and a myriad of other contraptions to get you wet. At the top of the playground is an enormous bucket that pours water on the kids inside every few minutes.

TOURING TIPS The structure is built in a shallow wading pool. There are few walls, so most of the structure is visible to adults who want to watch their children but aren't up for getting soaked.

Tonga Tubes ★★★

APPEAL BY AGE	PRESCHOOL †	GRADE SCHOOL ★★★★	TEENS ★★★½
YOUNG ADULTS ★★★	OVER 30 ★★★		SENIORS ★★

† Preschoolers are generally too short to ride.

What it is Waterslide in tubes. Scope and scale Major attraction. When to go First stop in Splash Island. Special comments Must be 48" tall to ride. Authors' rating Standard; ★★★. Duration of ride 30 seconds. Loading speed Very slow.

DESCRIPTION AND COMMENTS There are two slides down from the tower, and there is no great difference between them except that one is yellow and the other is blue. The ride is smooth, if a little short.

TOURING TIPS The lines for this ride grow rapidly as the park fills, so make this your first stop in Splash Island. The slow loading speed creates the biggest lines in all of Cypress Gardens. We've found 30-minute waits for this 30-second ride. Don't assume that since everyone is carrying a tube and thus taking up more space that the line is shorter than it is; it's not.

VooDoo Plunge   ★★★½

APPEAL BY AGE	PRESCHOOL †	GRADE SCHOOL ★★★★½	TEENS ★★★★
YOUNG ADULTS ★★★★		OVER 30 ★★★	SENIORS ★★

† Preschoolers are generally too short to ride.

What it is Body slide. **Scope and scale** Major attraction. **When to go** Second stop in Splash Island. **Special comments** Must be 48" tall to ride. **Authors' rating** Some of the best thrills in the park; ★★★½. **Duration of ride** 20 seconds. **Loading speed** Slow.

DESCRIPTION AND COMMENTS Three slides descend from the top of the 60-foot tower: a green slide, a light blue slide, and a dark blue slide. At the top, the lifeguard will ask which slide you prefer. The green slide is the calmest, an open straight slide with a hump in the middle. The dark blue slide is an enclosed tube that twists downward like a pig's tail. The light blue slide is the scariest and the fastest. After a gradual start, the slide hits a drastic drop that shoots you toward the run-out pool below.

TOURING TIPS Once you've ridden the Tonga Tubes, take a turn on each of the slides. The five stories of stairs you climb for each ride will wear you out long before the excitement wears off. Very little at Cypress Gardens is on par with the competition. These slides are the not the crème of the Florida water parks, but we could see them incorporated into the bigger parks as a minor attraction.

JUBILEE JUNCTION/LAKE ELOISE

Botanical Gardens   ★★★½

APPEAL BY AGE	PRESCHOOL ★★	GRADE SCHOOL ★½	TEENS ★★
YOUNG ADULTS ★★★		OVER 30 ★★★½	SENIORS ★★★★

What it is Large garden. **Scope and scale** Headliner. **When to go** Anytime. **Authors' rating** Relaxing, but could be better; ★★★½.

DESCRIPTION AND COMMENTS Located at the far end of the park, past the Mango Bay Water Ski Show Stadium, are the Botanical Gardens. Although they are filled with live oaks and numerous exotic plants, the gardens have declined over the years due to a lack of upkeep, falling victim to the financial need to expand both Adventure Grove and Splash Island. A stroll through the garden is restful, and every visitor should at least stop in to see the massive banyan tree, whose hanging vines are as thick as tree trunks, making a canopy over a half acre of land.

TOURING TIPS After the three hurricanes rolled over Cypress Gardens during the park's closure in 2004, workers removed all the signage during the cleanup. Cypress Gardens has still not hired a horticulturist to place new signs, or to give the guided tours. As a result, the daily tours are uninformative. We were lucky enough to have an actual horticulturist with us on one of our visits, and his information went well beyond the names of a few random plants as he related to us all of the various species, where they came from, their medical uses, etc. Cypress Gardens is missing out on an opportunity to engage guests and make this attraction more than just a pretty place to visit. Even if Cypress Gardens paid a horticulturist to simply relabel all of the plants and then write a comprehensive fact sheet for the tour guides, the Botanical Gardens would come up to par with the other gardens in central Florida. As it stands now, bring a good field guide on tropical flora.

Cypress Belle Riverboat   ★★★½

| APPEAL BY AGE | PRESCHOOL ★★½ | GRADE SCHOOL ★★★½ | TEENS ★★★ |
| YOUNG ADULTS ★★★★ | OVER 30 ★★★★ | | SENIORS ★★★★ |

What it is Paddleboat tour of the waterfront and beyond. **Scope and scale** Major attraction. **When to go** Daytime tours, Monday–Friday at noon, 2 p.m., and 4 p.m. **Authors' rating** Relaxing but pricey; ★★★½. **Duration of ride** Daytime cruise 60 minutes; dinner cruise 90 minutes. **Cost** Daytime cruise $5.95 + tax per person; dinner cruise $29.99 + tax for adults; $21.95 + tax for children ages 9 and under. Prices do not include park admission.

DESCRIPTION AND COMMENTS   The *Cypress Belle,* the park's paddlewheel riverboat, has been refurbished and is sailing again. The dock for the *Cypress Belle* is located near the Botanical Gardens. There are two cruise options. Daytime cruises run 60 minutes and depart at noon, 2 p.m., and 4 p.m. daily. The cruise takes you along the park's waterfront and out onto Lake Eloise. Expect a full narration similar to those found on the ferry ride and the Citrus Line Railroad. Evening cruises include dinner, and are 90 minutes long. You may choose from prime rib, chicken cordon bleu, and orange roughy. For children ages 9 and under, you have a choice of either hot dogs or chicken fingers. The meal also includes rice pilaf, steamed vegetables, dinner rolls, and your choice of either a slice of pumpkin pie or cheesecake for dessert. Beverages are included in the price, with the exception of alcohol. Beer and wine are available on board for an additional fee. The 4:30 p.m. tour will place you on the lake for dusk and is available on both Saturday and Sunday. The 7 p.m. tour leaves at sunset and is available on both Friday and Saturday.

TOURING TIPS   You should make reservations at ☎ 863-324-2111 before coming to the park. If you decide to go while in the park, tickets are available at the Surf Shop.

Cypress Cove Ferry Line   ★★★

| APPEAL BY AGE | PRESCHOOL ★★½ | GRADE SCHOOL ★★★ | TEENS ★ |
| YOUNG ADULTS ★★★ | OVER 30 ★★★ | | SENIORS ★★★½ |

What it is Boat ride. **Scope and scale** Minor attraction. **When to go** Anytime. **Special comments** Must be 42" tall to ride alone. **Authors' rating** ★★★. **Duration of ride** 10 minutes. **Loading speed** Slow.

DESCRIPTION AND COMMENTS Two modern pontoon boats take guests along the shoreline of Lake Eloise from one end of the park to the other. The short ride is a fully narrated history of the park, focusing on its grandeur in the 1950s. The boats are also a throwback to a calmer Cypress Gardens and fit in well with attractions like the Sky Wheel and the gardens.

TOURING TIPS Each pontoon boats only holds 16 guests each, but the lines are seldom very long since the boats go back and forth continuously. When lines do form, they subside quickly since most guests will choose to walk across the park rather than wait for the next boat. At the moment, the boats run only Friday through Sunday, or during peak visitation days.

Mango Bay Water Ski Show ★★★★

| APPEAL BY AGE | PRESCHOOL ★★★ | GRADE SCHOOL ★★★½ | TEENS ★★★ |
| YOUNG ADULTS ★★★½ | | OVER 30 ★★★★ | SENIORS ★★★½ |

What it is A stunt show on the lake including impressive feats. **Scope and scale** Super headliner. **When to go** Check schedule for performance times. **Authors' rating** ★★★★. **Duration of show** 25 minutes.

DESCRIPTION AND COMMENTS In 1943, Julie Pope began the waterskiing show for a few visiting airmen. The show took off and has grown over the years to include wakeboards, hydrofoils, and launch ramps. The performers are the superstars of Cypress Gardens and are as iconic as the park's southern belles.

The modern show begins with an MC who introduces each of the performers, or group of performers, as they whiz past. A mild comedic plot develops between the MC and a concession worker, but the heart of the show is on the water, where the performers build human pyramids, hold the line with their feet, and even leap over one another. The pacing is a little slow, but builds audience anticipation and appreciation for each stunt.

TOURING TIPS Scope out your seats early; this is a popular attraction. There's not a bad seat in the house, but about halfway up the stadiumlike bleachers is the best vantage point. You may bring in food from the nearby eatery if you're hungry.

Night Magic

| APPEAL BY AGE | NOT OPEN AT PRESS TIME |

What it is Fireworks and laser show. **Scope and scale** Headliner. **When to go** One show nightly during certain seasons and holidays only. **Authors' rating** Not open at press time. **Duration of show** Unknown at press time.

DESCRIPTION AND COMMENTS A combination of lasers and fireworks set to music will illuminate the sky over Mango Bay, the park's central lake.

TOURING TIPS The show is seasonal, staged only during holidays and major events. Come early to grab seats on the grass lawn in front of the lake or inside the water ski show stadium.

Royal Palm Theater/*Figure Skating Show* ★★½

APPEAL BY AGE	PRESCHOOL ★★	GRADE SCHOOL ★★★	TEENS ★½
YOUNG ADULTS ★★	OVER 30 ★★★		SENIORS ★★★

What it is Figure skating show. **Scope and scale** Headliner. **When to go** Anytime; check daily performance schedule. **Authors' rating** Fairly unexciting; ★★½. **Duration of show** 25 minutes.

DESCRIPTION AND COMMENTS Talented skaters and a few impressive moves do little to save the pretty average show; cheesy music and costumes don't help much either. Figure-skating enthusiasts will enjoy it, and it's a cool respite from the heat if you need a break.

TOURING TIPS Save this for the end of the day when feet are tired and everybody's hot and ready for a rest.

Snively Plantation Gardens ★★★

APPEAL BY AGE	PRESCHOOL ★★	GRADE SCHOOL ★★	TEENS ★
YOUNG ADULTS ★★★	OVER 30 ★★★½		SENIORS ★★★½

What it is Manicured grass dotted with beds of beautiful flowers, from azaleas to pansies to roses. **Scope and scale** Major attraction. **When to go** Anytime. **Authors' rating** ★★★.

DESCRIPTION AND COMMENTS At its inception, this was a park about flowers and trees. This, the Topiary Trail, and the Botanical Gardens are the major areas that set this park apart from the rest in Orlando. The plants and trees don't just soften the concrete landscape; they're actually an *attraction*. If you want to get a feel for what Cypress Gardens was originally meant to be, this is a stop worth making.

TOURING TIPS The gardens are rarely crowded, but on very warm days head here as early as possible, as the flowers often droop in the summer heat.

Sunshine Sky Adventure ★★★

APPEAL BY AGE	PRESCHOOL ★	GRADE SCHOOL ★★★	TEENS ★★
YOUNG ADULTS ★★★	OVER 30 ★★★½		SENIORS ★★★★

What it is A platform glides up almost 160 feet and slowly rotates to reveal panoramic views of the area. **Scope and scale** Headliner. **When to go** At the end of your visit. **Special comments** Must be 48" tall to ride without an adult. **Authors' rating** Great view, but not too exciting; ★★★. **Duration of ride** 6 minutes. **Loading speed** Fast.

DESCRIPTION AND COMMENTS The only ride at Cypress Gardens for years, Sunshine Sky Adventure survived the park's renovation. Being 160 feet above the ground in the flattest state in the United States gives you a good view of the surrounding houses, lakes, and orange groves.

TOURING TIPS Stop here on your way out of the park, as it's located near the entrance and everyone will enjoy a slower-paced attraction after the tosses and turns of the other rides. This is definitely not for anyone with a fear of heights.

Topiary Trail ★★★½

APPEAL BY AGE	PRESCHOOL ★★★★	GRADE SCHOOL ★★★½	TEENS ★★
YOUNG ADULTS ★★★		OVER 30 ★★★½	SENIORS ★★★½

What it is Collection of bushes carved into the likenesses of animals, bugs, and other shapes. **Scope and scale** Headliner. **When to go** Anytime. **Authors' rating** Cute and nostalgic; ★★★½.

DESCRIPTION AND COMMENTS Another throwback to the classic Cypress Gardens, this may be hokey, but it's one of our favorite places in the park—take a moment to enjoy the manicured grass lawn and breeze from the lake. And don't forget your cameras: nothing says "wish you were here" like a picture with an octopus-shaped bush.

TOURING TIPS Stop by on your way out of the park; early in the day, as people make their way from the front gates to the rides in the back, many end up stopping here, clogging the walkways and packing the space. Save this stop for the afternoon.

Wings of Wonder Butterfly Arboretum ★★½

APPEAL BY AGE	PRESCHOOL ★★★	GRADE SCHOOL ★★★½	TEENS ★½
YOUNG ADULTS ★★½		OVER 30 ★★★	SENIORS ★★★

What it is Greenhouse that is home to more than 20 species of butterflies. **Scope and scale** Diversion. **When to go** Anytime. **Authors' rating** ★★½.

DESCRIPTION AND COMMENTS This small, humid greenhouse is home to about 20 species of butterflies, although spotting them amid the flowers and greenery poses some difficulties. If you can't spot enough live ones, there is a fine collection of wings pinned in entomology cases as you exit.

TOURING TIPS Swing through here on your way to lunch or out of the park; there's never a line and rarely a crowd, and it takes only about five minutes to see the exhibit fully.

NATURE'S WAY

Nature's Way Zoo ★★★

APPEAL BY AGE	PRESCHOOL ★★★½	GRADE SCHOOL ★★★★½	TEENS ★★
YOUNG ADULTS ★★★½		OVER 30 ★★★★	SENIORS ★★★½

What it is A small zoological exhibit. **Scope and scale** Headliner. **When to go** After all of the other shows or during feeding times. **Authors' rating** Quaint; ★★★.

DESCRIPTION AND COMMENTS It is a small zoo, but there are those who love it. You won't find any elephants or lions at Cypress Gardens (although there is a black panther). What you will see is a small collection of animals from around the world. The more dangerous animals, such as the alligators and crocodiles, are in pits. Birds, monkeys, and other animal cages are at eye level, and you are able to feed the loris and walk through the aviary.

TOURING TIPS Visit after you have experienced all the rides and other attractions. If you have a moment on your way into the park, check with a zookeeper to obtain the day's feeding schedule. Since you can see the entire zoo from its entrance, you should need only about 30 minutes to see it fully.

Pirates of Mango Bay ★★★½

APPEAL BY AGE	PRESCHOOL ★★★	GRADE SCHOOL ★★★★	TEENS ★★★½
YOUNG ADULTS ★★★½	OVER 30 ★★★★		SENIORS ★★★½

What it is Pirates perform comedy. **Scope and scale** Minor attraction. **When to go** Check schedule for performance times. **Authors' rating** Funny; ★★★½. **Duration of show** 20 minutes.

DESCRIPTION AND COMMENTS   Three bumbling pirates searching for the treasure of Blackjack Bonepart would appear to be a trite show, but the script is very well written and littered with puns. The mix of sophomoric humor and rapid-fire witticisms keep both kids and adults entertained. The set is interactive and hosts a few surprises for both the pirates and the audience. The show, tucked in the far corner of the park behind Nature's Way, is itself a hidden treasure.

TOURING TIPS   The first few rows of seats will get wet, and so may the back rows. Loud explosions occur without warning throughout the show and pack enough punch to startle adults and set babies crying.

THE JUNIOR WATER SKI EXPERIENCE AND THE JUNIOR BELLE PROGRAM

THE PARK NOW ALLOWS CHILDREN AGES 10 and under to experience the park's two trademark features, waterskiing and being a southern belle. The **Junior Waterski Experience** brings young kids out onto the lake to attempt barefoot waterskiing. Each child gets into the water and then grabs hold of a poll hoisted out over the side of a boat. As the boat accelerates, the child attempts to hang onto the poll and stand on the surface of the water. Each child is allowed one turn around the lake, or until the turn ends with a sploosh in the water. The program is both free and on a first-come first-served basis, and space is very limited. For your child to participate, you must go to the Surf Shop, located across from the Mango Bay Water Ski Stadium, early in the day. Your child must have his or her own swimsuit, and be fully dressed and ready to go at 1:45 p.m.

For children who enjoy cotillions more than falling in the water, **The Junior Belle Program** lets little girls dress as southern belles for 90 minutes. Stop by Kara's Kastle in Jubilee Junction first thing in the morning to reserve a time slot. Later in the day, stop in to pick up a dress and a hoop skirt. The cost for the costume rental is $24.95 plus tax per child. Don't forget to track down the park's southern belles for a photo op.

STAR HAVEN AMPITHEATRE

CYPRESS GARDENS HOSTS A MYRIAD of big acts at the Star Haven Ampitheatre. Some of the headliners for 2007 include Trace Adkins,

Engelbert Humperdinck, and the Steve Miller Band. Tickets for these shows are not included in the admission price, and you can attend the shows without purchasing park admission. For a full list of the 2007 season, go to Cypress Gardens' Web site at **www.cypressgardens .com/concerts.asp** or call ☎ 863-324-2111 for more information or to purchase tickets over the phone.

DINING

CYPRESS GARDENS OFFERS A FEW MORE CHOICES beyond the standard burger and fries. For the most part, food is not spectacular, but it's less expensive than its theme park counterparts.

For a sit-down meal of traditional southern dishes like chicken and dumplings, macaroni and cheese, biscuits, and cobblers, **Aunt Julie's Country Kitchen** is the place.

Backwater Bill's serves up some second-rate barbecue. The chicken is the only thing worth ordering—the pulled-pork sandwiches are little more than sloppy joes, and the sides were bland and cafeteria-like. We recommend you try another restaurant.

Jubilee Market has an all-American counter with decent hamburgers, hot dogs, and the like, an Italian counter with pizzas and pastas, and a bakery serving pastries and coffee.

Cherry on Top features delicious sundaes, soft-serve, and regular ice cream; **Orange Blossom Confections** has handmade candies, caramel apples, and such.

Dinner cruises are available aboard the *Cypress Belle.* See the *Cypress Belle* listing in the Jubilee Junction/Lake Eloise section for more information.

SHOPPING

SHOPPING IS AN ATTRACTION IN ITSELF in Jubilee Junction. Stores mostly offer country-kitsch merchandise, and it's generally pretty cute. Keep in mind, though, that if you shop first thing in the morning, you'll be toting your purchases throughout the park, so it's best to save these shops for the end of the day.

The **Wood Works Shop** has hand-carved statues, name plaques, and so on, all made of—you guessed it—wood. **Tan Yer Hide** stocks a similarly generic collection of all things leather.

Kara's Kastle features sparkly, frilly, and frou-frou offerings like tiaras, dresses, and tutus. If your little girl loves to shop, you may want to steer clear or you may end up with a bagful of girly goodies.

Christmas fanatics will enjoy **Kringles,** which sells Christmas decorations like nutcrackers, villages, and tree ornaments.

Longwing's Emporium sells garden-related goodies just outside the Wings of Wonder butterfly arboretum.

Crepe Myrtle Candle Company sells candles made in a traditional way, using the berries of the wax myrtle tree, many of which are found on the Cypress Gardens grounds. You can try your hand at candle-making, which is the main draw for this store.

If it has wings or four wheels, chances are you'll find a model of it for sale at **Planes, Trains, and Automobiles.** The best thing to see here is the model railroad—one of the most elaborate we've ever seen.

PART FOUR

GATORLAND

IN THESE DAYS OF GENIAL ZOOKEEPERS, it's hard to imagine a man like Florida showman Owen Godwin, who established Gatorland way back in 1949. More of a reptile-fixated P. T. Barnum than an environmental enthusiast, Godwin traveled the world collecting toothy critters for his zoo collection of gators and "jungle crocs." But the days of aggressive collecting are gone. Most of the alligators are born right in the Gatorland swamp, and Gatorland naturalists will earnestly tell you of their efforts to rehabilitate a variety of injured or displaced animals brought to them from all over Florida.

For more than 50 years, Gatorland has existed as a roadside wonder. Before the days of magic castles and studio back lots, visitors flocked to the Sunshine State for its beaches and wildlife. Sprinkled along the highways that linked the state's natural attractions were tiny outposts of tourism—"must-see" roadside stops meant to break up the monotony of travel. Gatorland fell brilliantly into this category. The park was ripe with tourist appeal—who can resist a park that hawks Florida's most infamous resident, the alligator?

unofficial **TIP** For those who want variety in their sightseeing itinerary, this is the place for a real change of pace.

Today, Gatorland seems to disappear in the clutter of touristy Orlando. But rather than fall victim to its own kitsch or wither in the Disney glare, Gatorland has adapted enough to proudly call itself, "Orlando's best half-day attraction." It doesn't try to be one of the highfalutin theme parks in its backyard. Although the attraction has grown to more than 100 acres, the whole place is barely big enough for a good-sized Walt Disney World parking lot. But nowhere else will you see this many gators and crocs, and nowhere else are they celebrated with such abandon. In short, Gatorland is a hallmark of old Florida made good.

In early November of 2006, Gatorland suffered a fire caused by a malfunctioning heating pad in a snake exhibit. The main offices were

gatorland

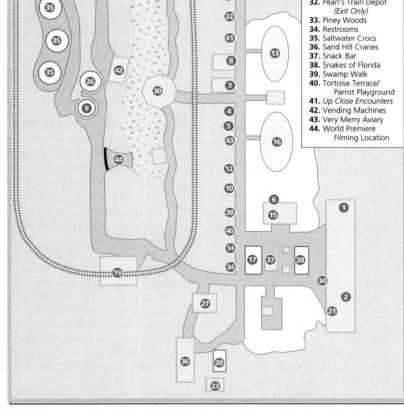

destroyed as well as the gift shop. Two pythons and an alligator were killed, but the rest of the park and its animal inhabitants were spared. The park reopened on November 24, 2006, with a new entrance near the Wrestlin' Arena. Besides this new entrance, nothing major has been altered, according to Gatorland.

GETTING THERE

FROM DISNEY Take FL 192 (or the Osceola Parkway, if you don't mind paying a few bucks in tolls) to FL 441 (Orange Blossom Trail). Turn left. Gatorland is on your right.

FROM ORLANDO Take Interstate 4 to FL 528 (Beeline Highway). Exit at Consulate and turn right. Make a right on FL 441 (Orange Blossom Trail). Gatorland is about seven miles south, between the Osceola Parkway and FL 417 (the Central Florida GreeneWay). Parking is free.

ADMISSION PRICES

FOLLOWING ARE THE FULL ADMISSION PRICES at press time. Coupons are available in Gatorland brochures (found at kiosks throughout Orlando) and at **www.gatorland.com.** The park offers AAA and AARP discounts.

One-day Pass
Adults $19.95 + tax | *Children ages 3–12* $9.95 + tax
Children under age 3 Free

Annual Pass
Adults $32.95 + tax | *Children ages 3–12* $19.98 + tax

ARRIVING

GATORLAND IS OPEN DAILY FROM 9 A.M. TO 5 P.M. Gators don't mind rain (and most observation walkways have canopies), so the attraction is open rain or shine.

unofficial **TIP**
Colder temperatures will make the alligators sluggish and less likely to jump for food.

Gatorland bills itself as a half-day attraction, which makes it the perfect alternative when you don't have a full day to spend at Walt Disney World, SeaWorld, or the Kennedy Space Center Visitor Complex. Plan to spend about three to four hours to see it well. However, the park lends itself to any type of schedule. With nearby parking and the park's manageable size, it is easy to come and go. A small-gauge railroad ride traverses part of the park and passes local flora and fauna in their natural swampy habitat.

Shows and feeding times are scheduled throughout the day, with performances shortly after opening, after lunch, and in midafternoon. Performances are scheduled for easy back-to-back viewing.

Check the show schedule when you arrive. Because the shows are can't-miss attractions, plan your schedule around them. There are

unofficial **TIP**
Plan your visit to this
park around the shows.

plenty of diversions near each show area. The Jungle Crocs of the World feeding "show" is the farthest away, requiring about a 12-minute walk, so keep that in mind when heading for this area of the park.

CONTACTING GATORLAND

FOR MORE INFORMATION, contact Gatorland at ☎ 800-393-JAWS or **www.gatorland.com.**

ATTRACTIONS

Alligator Breeding Marsh and Bird Sanctuary ★★★½

APPEAL BY AGE	PRESCHOOL ★★	GRADE SCHOOL ★★	TEENS ★★
YOUNG ADULTS ★★★	OVER 30 ★★★		SENIORS ★★★

What it is A breeding ground for gators in a picturesque setting. **Scope and scale** Diversion. **When to go** At the warmer part of the day. **Author's rating** The quiet heart of Gatorland; ★★★½.

DESCRIPTION AND COMMENTS The alligator breeding marsh is one of Gatorland's most unexpected attractions. Set in the middle of a park of zoolike cages and enclosures, this large body of water is home to nearly 200 alligators in their natural setting. Once you consider the somewhat grim fact that the park also doubles as an alligator farm selling meat and hides, you realize that you're looking at the real "ranch" behind all the wrestlin' and jumpin'. Despite this eco-unfriendly downer, a flotilla of a couple dozen gators hovering placidly by your feet is enough to make you reconsider leaning over the railing for a better photo. Try out each floor of the three-story observation tower for different (and safely distant) perspectives.

The marsh is also a haven for bird-watchers. Every year, more than 4,000 birds make their home at Gatorland, including green, blue, and tricolored herons, cattle egrets, and cormorants. At feeding time, the trees along the boardwalk marsh fill with waterbirds, including several rare and protected species.

TOURING TIPS For the best view, bring binoculars. It is truly spectacular to feed the gators here (a bag of fish is $5). There is a smaller feeding area elsewhere, but you'll get more of a show if you take the goodies here. On one visit, a family brought several loaves of bread to feed the gators. It was a fascinating sight, and it attracted what seemed like hundreds of creatures. Check the trees on your right as you walk toward the petting farm, with the marsh behind you. During summer visits, they host hundreds of nesting egrets and herons, with the accompanying chirps of their young. Because the second level of the observation tower is above the trees, it provides a rare look at these birds.

Gator Jumparoo Show ★★★★

APPEAL BY AGE PRESCHOOL ★★★   GRADE SCHOOL ★★★★   TEENS ★★★½
YOUNG ADULTS ★★★   OVER 30 ★★★   SENIORS ★★★

What it is It's gators: they jump, you watch—from a distance. **Scope and scale** Super headliner. **When to go** Check entertainment schedule. **Author's rating** Yikes! ★★★★. **Duration of show** 15 minutes.

DESCRIPTION AND COMMENTS This is, as they say, the marrow that has kept visitors circulating through Gatorland for almost 50 years. Visitors gather around a square pond, framed by wooden boardwalks (thankfully with high railings). A trainer ventures out to an all-too-fragile-looking cupola on the water, and then the fun begins. Everyone is encouraged to stamp their feet on the boards, which lets the alligators know that supper's ready. The reptiles come gliding in from adjacent ponds, and the trainer yells and waves to attract them. Plucked chickens are strung up on wires over the water, and them gators commence to jumpin'. Trainers also dangle treats over the water and gators snatch the food right from their hands. After you see a ten-foot-long 300-pounder leap head-high out of the water to crunch some poultry, you'll spend the rest of your time at Gatorland nervously skirting the railings. Visit the nonthreatening lorikeet aviary to calm down if necessary.

TOURING TIPS There's no seating here, so be sure to arrive at least 10 minutes before show time to stake your claim along the railing.

Gator Wrestling Stadium/*Gator Wrestlin' Show* ★★★★

APPEAL BY AGE PRESCHOOL ★★   GRADE SCHOOL ★★★★   TEENS ★★★★
YOUNG ADULTS ★★★   OVER 30 ★★★½   SENIORS ★★★

What it is Where man (especially his head) was not meant to go. **Scope and scale** Super headliner. **When to go** Check entertainment schedule; usually 3 shows daily. **Author's rating** Not to be missed; ★★★★. **Duration of show** 15 minutes.

DESCRIPTION AND COMMENTS There are no bad views in the 800-seat stadium. There is one seat, however, that most audience members would rather not have. That's the perch on the back of an alligator in a sandy pit in the middle of the theater. Here, a wisecracking fool keeps the audience spellbound with his courage—or reckless disregard for bodily integrity—for 15 minutes. The show features two "crackers," the nickname for Florida ranchers who often cracked their whips to get their animals to move. Enlisting their best Foghorn Leghorn impressions, the two play off of each other while one unfortunate soul wrestles the gator, opens its mouth, and even (gulp!) places his chin under its snout.

TOURING TIPS Arrive a bit early to see the "wrestlers" warming up. Although every side offers a good view, the red bleachers typically have the best vantage.

Gatorland Train ★★

APPEAL	BY	AGE	PRESCHOOL ★★★	GRADE SCHOOL ★★★	TEENS ★
YOUNG	ADULTS	★½	OVER 30 ★★	SENIORS ★★½	

What it is A circling train. **Scope and scale** Diversion. **When to go** Anytime for a quick rest of your feet. **Author's rating** Can a gator hijack a train? ★★. **Duration of ride** 6 minutes.

DESCRIPTION AND COMMENTS Given the park's small size, the train isn't really necessary as transportation. But it's good for a break and a different view of the natural areas. Chances are, the nutty guy who narrates your ride will turn up again later in the gator wrestling or *Jumparoo* shows.

TOURING TIPS It costs an extra $2 to ride the train, but you can tack the fee onto your ticket when you arrive. The train is a good way to see the park and rest your feet but skip it if you don't need the break.

Gatorland Zoo ★★

APPEAL	BY	AGE	PRESCHOOL ★★★	GRADE SCHOOL ★★★	TEENS ★★
YOUNG	ADULTS	★★½	OVER 30 ★★	SENIORS ★★	

What it is A collection of animal displays. **Scope and scale** Diversion. **When to go** Between shows. **Author's rating** Fun, but not as cool as gators; ★★.

DESCRIPTION AND COMMENTS Dozens of animal exhibits line the 150-foot main walkway, including a bear, Florida white-tailed deer, emus, llamas, snakes, turtles, tortoises, iguanas, and birds. Allie's Barnyard petting zoo—always a favorite among young children—contains the usual collection of goats and sheep. The walk-through Very Merry Aviary is stocked with lorikeets, tiny multicolored birds that are trained to land on visitors' shoulders in order to drink nectar from a cup (available for $2). Baby alligators are sometimes on display here, and there's a special Snakes of Florida exhibit highlighting local serpents.

TOURING TIPS Zoo exhibits are near both main show areas and are perfect fillers between other shows. Bring a handful of quarters to buy animal food. It's a minimal cost for a big thrill.

Jungle Crocs of the World ★★★

APPEAL	BY	AGE	PRESCHOOL ★★	GRADE SCHOOL ★★★½	TEENS ★★★
YOUNG	ADULTS	★★★	OVER 30 ★★★½	SENIORS ★★★½	

What it is A rare collection of international crocodiles. **Scope and scale** Headliner. **When to go** Around feeding time. **Author's rating** Insidiously catchy theme song; ★★★. **Duration of show** 10 minutes (feeding show).

DESCRIPTION AND COMMENTS As you step onto the boardwalk leading you to Gatorland's newest animal exhibit, you'll soon notice how the park revels in its own cheese factor. Speakers lining the walkway play a song devoted entirely to Owen Godwin and his many adventures to claim this collection of "jungle crocs." This song, a close relative to *The Beverly Hillbillies* theme will not leave your brain for at least an hour after departing Gatorland. But eventually, you come to the crocodile habitats. There are four total, featuring crocodiles from North and South America, Cuba, Asia, and Africa's Nile River. This exhibit features a rare collection of crocodiles, such as the Cuban crocodile. The smallest and most dangerous of breeds, Cuban crocs can leap from the water like dolphins to catch birds in flight. This area includes plenty of sight gags, including downed planes and pup tents that mysteriously lack any human beings.

TOURING TIPS Be sure to stick around for a feeding session, listed on the show schedule. On our latest visit, however, the feeding times were not listed, so you may be forced to ask.

kids Lilly's Pad and Alligator Alley ★★★

| APPEAL BY AGE | PRESCHOOL ★★★ | GRADE SCHOOL ★★★★ | TEENS ★★½ |
| YOUNG ADULTS ★★★ | OVER 30 ★★ | SENIORS ★ | |

What it is A wet and dry playground for kids. Scope and scale Major attraction. When to go When the temperature kicks up a notch. Author's rating A welcome way to cool down; ★★★.

DESCRIPTION AND COMMENTS Small children will go berserk when they see this water playground. Gatorland really shines here, with an area that rivals the children's play fountains at other Orlando parks. You'll find several interactive fountains and other water-soaking games. Nearby, a dry playground is available for those who don't want to get wet.

TOURING TIPS Let the kids loose at Lilly's Pad *after* the shows, so they won't have to walk around wet for the rest of the day.

Swamp Walk ★★★

| APPEAL BY AGE | PRESCHOOL ★ | GRADE SCHOOL ★ | TEENS ★ |
| YOUNG ADULTS ★★½ | OVER 30 ★★★ | SENIORS ★★★ | |

What it is Boardwalk through undisturbed nature. Scope and scale Diversion. When to go When you need some quiet time. Author's rating Natural Florida; ★★★.

DESCRIPTION AND COMMENTS Cross the swinging bridge that leads to a boardwalk trail through a beautiful natural swamp. So far removed from the rest of the attractions that many visitors fail to discover it, the walk is easily one of the most exotic and unusual promenades to be found in all of Florida. The swamp is actually part of the headwaters for the Florida Everglades, the critically important south Florida swampland hundreds of miles away. Winding gracefully with no apparent impact on the environment, the walk, flanked by towering cypress and draped with Spanish moss, disappears deep into the lush, green swamp. Simultaneously tranquil and serene yet bursting with life, the swamp radiates primeval loveliness.

TOURING TIPS Visit the Swamp Walk before sunset, when the mosquitoes come out to feast on unsuspecting Gatorland tourists. There is no fence underneath the railing, so keep an eye on the little ones, although the mere idea that there is a gator in this swamp should be enough to keep them in line.

Up Close Encounters/Snake Show   ★★★

APPEAL BY AGE	PRESCHOOL ★★	GRADE SCHOOL ★★★	TEENS ★★
YOUNG ADULTS ★★★	OVER 30 ★★½	SENIORS ★★	

What it is Educational hands-on animal show. **Scope and scale** Minor attraction. **When to go** When not at the other 3 shows. **Author's rating** Creepy and fun; ★★★.

DESCRIPTION AND COMMENTS This small stadium hosts a show-and-tell of whatever creatures—mostly snakes—the keepers might have in Gatorland's bag of tricks that day. The keepers hold the venomous critters aloft, but visitors can actually handle some of the more passive creatures. Gatorland provides a home for lots of captured or injured wildlife, including animals confiscated from illegal pet traders. One keeper offered to let us hold some friendly snakes and the most recent arrival: a giant emperor scorpion, creepy-crawly as can be. We respectfully declined.

TOURING TIPS Our bad example aside, the best way to enjoy the show is to get close to the creatures and interact. Although the knowledgeable Gatorland naturalists can tell you a lot about the snakes and other animals, the real thrill comes from holding them yourself. If you are not selected to hold the animals during the show, you may hold most of them afterward, including the Burmese python, for a $5 fee.

GATORLAND ADVENTURE TOURS

GATORLAND NOW OFFERS FOUR DIFFERENT up-close encounters with the alligators. Due to the recent fire, we were not able to participate in any of the tours or to update their prices and hours. The four tours are the Rookie Wrestlin' tour, in which guests can "wrestle" a gator (with the gator's mouth taped, of course), the Adventure Hour, which allows guests behind the scenes of the breeding marsh, the Gator Night Shine tour, in which guests look for gators at night, and the Trainer-for-a-Day program, which allows you to shadow a gator wrestler for a day. For times, prices, and more information, contact Gatorland at ☎ 800-393-JAWS.

DINING

DINING AT GATORLAND CAN BE EITHER an adventure or a non-event. It's a letdown if you come to sample its regular menu items. They are nothing spectacular, but then again they are also fairly inexpensive by Orlando theme-park standards. A hamburger is $2.80, and a kids' meal is $4.75. The menu is varied, however, and includes chicken breast and a fish 'n' chips basket.

But who comes to Gatorland to eat a hot dog? No true adventurer can visit without trying at least a bite of gator meat. **Pearl's Smokehouse** features two such items, including gator nuggets and gator ribs.

In humanity's never-ending quest to reduce all animals to nugget form, this is one of the less impressive examples. Yes, the gator nuggets do taste like chicken, but spicier and much tougher. They come with barbecue dipping sauces to mask any unfamiliar tastes. The ribs are a bit more intimidating (large), but quite good. They are also quite small and, consequently, contain small bones, so be careful. Try the sampler platter, which gives you a taste of both treats. If you see a nearby gator eyeing you accusingly, console yourself with the thought that he'd do the same to you—only with less barbecue sauce and a lot more screaming.

unofficial **TIP**
Ever try a gator rib? This could be your chance, and you may be pleasantly surprised.

SHOPPING

IF YOU ARE LOOKING FOR A TACKY FLORIDA SOUVENIR for that prized spot on your mantel, Gatorland is the place. Similar to shops that line US 192, the park hawks everything gator-related you could ever imagine—and even a few things you would, in a sane world, never even consider. There are also several merchandise carts throughout the park and two unique photo locations.

PART FIVE

The HOLY LAND EXPERIENCE

AN ENTIRELY NEW KIND OF THEME PARK opened in Orlando in early 2001. The Holy Land Experience is a re-creation of biblical-era Israel by way of evangelical Christianity. Don't expect a Jehovah Coaster or Red Sea Flume, though—this park is only for thrills of the spiritual kind. The Holy Land Experience has more in common with passive attractions like Gatorland than with places like Walt Disney World or Universal Studios.

> *unofficial* **TIP**
> Not built in a day: you'll notice a similar attention to detail here as in some Disney parks.

At 15 acres, this park is tiny by local standards. It's packed with a half-dozen exhibits and re-creations of structures dating from 1450 BC to the first century AD. Elaborately crafted by the same company that built parts of Walt Disney World and Universal Islands of Adventure, the theming and detail are meticulous and impressive. Costumed performers roam the park and interact with guests, sometimes assembling for performances or impromptu congregations.

Which brings up a big caveat: though the historical re-creations might interest period enthusiasts, straight history is not really the focus here. Some Jewish groups have expressed concern about the appropriation of Jewish history and ritual for a Christian-themed park. Because it's ministry-operated, the park is very open about its evangelical mission. Every exhibit, show, performance, and shop is geared toward the Christian faith—essentially the born-again version. No one will treat you rudely or force you to participate in anything that makes you uncomfortable, but you can no more escape Christianity at the Holy Land Experience than you could escape Mickey Mouse at Walt Disney World. If that's not your cup of tea, then this place is not for you.

> *unofficial* **TIP**
> Goes without saying: come to Holy Land only if you're interested in all things Christian.

If Christian-oriented touring suits you and your family, The Holy Land Experience is a singular

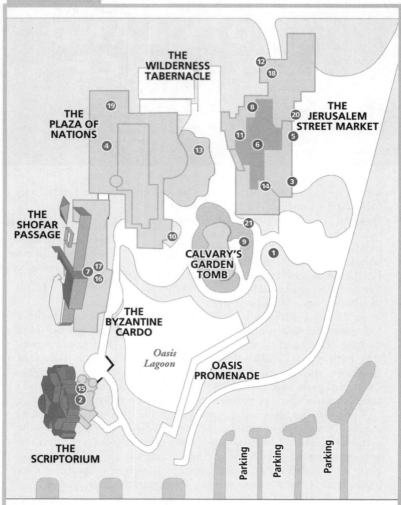

holy land

THE
WILDERNESS
TABERNACLE

THE
PLAZA OF
NATIONS

THE
JERUSALEM
STREET MARKET

THE
SHOFAR
PASSAGE

CALVARY'S
GARDEN
TOMB

THE
BYZANTINE
CARDO

*Oasis
Lagoon*

OASIS
PROMENADE

THE
SCRIPTORIUM

Parking Parking Parking

● **ATTRACTIONS**
1. The Biblical Vegetation
2. ExLibris Book Shoppe
3. Guest Services
4. Herod's Temple
   (The Temple
   of the Great King)
5. Jerusalem City Gate
6. Jerusalem Street Market
7. The Jerusalem Model A.D. 66

8. Methuselah's Mosaics
9. Millstone Garden
10. Oasis Palms Cafe
11. The Old Scroll Shop
12. Qaboo's Outpost
13. The Qumran Caves
14. Restrooms
15. The Scriptorium Center
    for Biblical Antiquities
16. The Shofar Auditorium

17. The Shofar Gift Shop
18. The Sycamore Tree
19. Theatre of Life/The Seed
    of Promise
20. Ticket Center
21. Via Dolorosa Path

attraction. Tremendous press coverage and high initial attendance proved that its creators have hit on something unique. However, a general tourism slump and declining crowds led to a huge increase in ticket prices (not to mention an end to free parking), making the Holy Land Experience less of a deal than it once was. The park's small size makes it a manageable outing, though, and the needs of the elderly, disabled, or foreign tourist get special attention here. In fact, most guests tend to be adults or seniors. Despite the often cutting-edge theming and production values, children are likely to get bored after more than a few hours here (though they may be distracted for a while by the cute baby goats).

GETTING THERE

THE HOLY LAND EXPERIENCE is very easy to find because it's located right off Interstate 4 near Universal Studios Florida. From Disney World or points south, take I-4 east to Exit 78 (just past Universal Studios Florida and the Florida Turnpike). The Holy Land Experience is just off the exit ramp, on the west side of I-4. From Orlando, take I-4 west for five miles to Exit 78.

ADMISSION PRICES

One-day Pass

Adults $35 | *Seniors ages 55+* $30
Children ages 6–12 $23 | *Children under age 6* Free

Multiday and Annual Passes

Jerusalem Gold annual passes cost $70. For groups of 20 or more (six-week advance reservation and three-week advance payment required), admission is $28 for adults and $19 for children ages 6 to 12. Package deals, including a meal inside the park (lunch or dinner), are available for groups of 35 or more (again, advance reservation and payment required). Parking is $5.

ARRIVING

THE HOLY LAND EXPERIENCE IS OPEN DAILY, with special programs during holidays (call ahead for details). Hours are Monday through Thursday, 10 a.m. to 7 p.m.; Friday and Saturday, 10 a.m. to 10 p.m.; and Sunday, noon until 7 p.m. Tickets are purchased at the Ticket Center near the front entrance. If there's a substantial line at the ticket windows, check the Guest Services desk, found through the large double doors to the left of the main entrance; tickets are sometimes sold there as well. Parking for cars, trucks, and RVs is $5. If you or a family member requires transportation within the park, a single baby stroller rents for $5, a double stroller for $7, and motorized scooters are available for $20.

Most of this small park is meant to be enjoyed on a walk-through basis at your own pace, but there are several shows and presentations to see. All but the Scriptorium are less than 30 minutes long, and many repeat throughout the day. A thorough tour of the Holy Land Experience takes just over half a day, assuming you want to experience every single thing. Our advice is to check the daily schedule and make a point of seeing the featured exhibits, using the various live performances and presentations as filler. Since some of the live performances are held only once daily, be sure to arrive a few minutes before 10 a.m. if you want to catch all of the shows.

CONTACTING THE HOLY LAND EXPERIENCE

FOR INFORMATION ABOUT TICKETS, hours, or special presentations, contact the Holy Land Experience at ☎ 866-USA-HOLYLAND or 407-367-2065, or **www.holylandexperience.com.**

ATTRACTIONS

Behold the Lamb ★★★

APPEAL BY AGE	PRESCHOOL ★★½	GRADE SCHOOL ★★★½	TEENS ★★★½
YOUNG ADULTS ★★★½		OVER 30 ★★★★	SENIORS ★★★★

What it is Musical interpretation of Christ's crucifixion. **Scope and scale** Super Headliner. See entertainment schedule for show times, but it is usually the last show of the day. **Authors' rating ★★★. Duration of show** 20 minutes.

DESCRIPTION AND COMMENTS   Located outside the Garden Tomb, this show lets you become witness to Christ's crucifixion and resurrection. Although at the outset of the performance you may believe you'll need to use your imagination to see Christ—Holy Land has a tendency to employ rousing speeches over visual props—an actor does portray the King of Kings. Songs accompany the crucifixion, but all are tempered and reverent. You will not leave singing any of the tunes, but may find yourself uplifted at his sacrifice.

TOURING TIPS   Seating is minimal, so arrive early. A few picnic tables are available, but for the best view along the fence in front of the Tomb, you will have to stand.

Calvary's Garden Tomb ★★

APPEAL BY AGE	PRESCHOOL ★	GRADE SCHOOL ★	TEENS ★
YOUNG ADULTS ★★		OVER 30 ★★	SENIORS ★★½

What it is Re-creation of Christ's empty tomb and setting for dramatic and historical presentations. **Scope and scale** Minor attraction. **When to go** During one of the presentations. **Authors' rating** Not much to see; ★★. **Duration of show** 15–20 minutes; check presentation schedule.

DESCRIPTION AND COMMENTS   Visitors wind their way along a highly attenuated version of the Via Dolorosa ("way of suffering"), which Jesus walked on his way to Calvary to be crucified. Within a few paces, you end up in a garden with Jesus' tomb as its centerpiece, the door stone

rolled away to reveal its emptiness. Regular dramatic and historical presentations of the life of Jesus are held in, around, and above the tomb.

TOURING TIPS   This is an especially similar re-creation of the Garden Tomb in
Israel—serene and poignant. Try to plan your visit during one of the pre-
sentations. The tomb closes to the public about 30 minutes before *The
Lamb of God* show.

The Jerusalem Model AD 66   ★★★½

APPEAL BY AGE	PRESCHOOL ★	GRADE SCHOOL ★★	TEENS ★★★
YOUNG ADULTS ★★★	OVER 30 ★★★½		SENIORS ★★★½

What it is Elaborate replica of ancient Jerusalem. **Scope and scale** Headliner. **When
to go** After experiencing the Scriptorium. **Authors' rating** Very cool; ★★★½.
Duration of show 30 minutes; check daily schedule for presentation times.

DESCRIPTION AND COMMENTS   This is touted as "the world's largest indoor
model of first-century Jerusalem." The 25-foot-wide model is meant to
represent Jerusalem circa AD 66, including the Temple of Jerusalem as
rebuilt by Herod while the Romans ruled the city. You can examine the
model on your own, but a guided lecture is much more informative,
since there are no plaques to reveal what is represented. The lecture
covers what everything in the model is, the history of the era, where
Jesus went during the last week of his life, and more.

TOURING TIPS   Because this is the only headliner attraction with just a few
scheduled openings (as opposed to constant, regular openings on the
half hour or hour), make sure to consult the daily schedule to fit a visit
into your plans. Try to make it to the first opening of the morning to
ensure touring flexibility later on.

The Scriptorium Center for Biblical Antiquities   ★★★

APPEAL BY AGE	PRESCHOOL ★	GRADE SCHOOL ★★½	TEENS ★★½
YOUNG ADULTS ★★★	OVER 30 ★★★		SENIORS ★★★½

What it is Walk-through exhibit detailing the history of the Bible itself. **Scope
and scale** Super headliner. **When to go** Immediately on entering the park.
Authors' rating World-class collection; ★★★. **Duration of show** 55 minutes;
presentations every hour.

DESCRIPTION AND COMMENTS   This museum showcases a fascinating collection of biblical antiquities, some dating from thousands of years ago.
Exhibits include ancient cuneiform, scrolls, Gutenberg and Tyndale
Bibles, manuscripts, and more. Narration guides visitors from room to
room; spotlights shine on particular objects while the narration
explains their historical and religious significance. Theming and attention to detail are the best of anywhere in the park, and the Holy Land
Experience's overriding evangelism is also front and center. The walk-
through ends in a modern home setting that is conspicuously
Bible-free, which is meant to inspire reflection on how we can bring the
Good Book back into our collective lives. (We first thought we'd mis-
takenly wandered into someone's living quarters, until a man in monk's
robes appeared and assured us that it was all part of the program.)

TOURING TIPS Most guests initially visit the attractions near the park entrance. Proceeding immediately to the Scriptorium will get you through it with the first batch of guests (there were only three people in our group) and free you up for other attractions and shows.

Shofar Auditorium/Shows and Lectures ★★★

APPEAL BY AGE	PRESCHOOL ★★½	GRADE SCHOOL ★★★½	TEENS ★★★
YOUNG ADULTS ★★★½		OVER 30 ★★★★	SENIORS ★★★★

What it is Myriad of musicals and lectures. Scope and scale Minor attractions. See entertainment schedule for show times; not all shows are performed each day. Authors' rating ★★★.

DESCRIPTION AND COMMENTS Four different shows and a series of lectures all take place in Shofar Auditorium. The auditorium is located inside the same building as Jerusalem AD 66; the entrance is through the gift shop. The auditorium looks like the inside of many modern churches, with rows of chairs facing the stage, and is decorated in red velvet with Grecian columns. Two large screens can be found at either end of the main stage and are incorporated into all of the shows and presentations.

The four shows that take place in the Shofar Auditorium are *Praise through the Ages, Moses, Centurion,* and *The Ministry of Jesus. Praise through the Ages* is a musical that depicts the evolution of painting and music throughout history, highlighting Western art's direct links to Christianity. To facilitate the lesson, actors dressed in period costumes sing period pieces. The songs range from the chants of Gregorian monks to upbeat modern gospel.

The show *Moses* is also a musical, and relates the account of Moses' mother, Jochebed, and her struggle to save her son from the pharaoh. As told in Exodus, Jochebed places her young child into an ark of bulrushes and sends him down the river. The crux of the story rests on Jochebed's faith that the Lord will protect her child.

Centurion depicts another Biblical story about heavenly protection, that of the centurion and Jesus. The story is of a centurion—a professional Roman officer—who wants to save the life of his servant. The show depicts the Matthew version of events, not the Luke version, and therefore has the centurion asking Jesus for help.

One more show centering on Jesus is *The Ministry of Jesus,* which tells a few of the familiar tales from the New Testament. An actor portrays the Son of God as he heals the blind man, and tells the pharisee and the tax collector, "All who exalt themselves will be humbled and all who humble themselves will be exalted," which is the show's central message.

None of the shows dazzled us or contained significant differences in production elements. We will say that our favorite was *Praise through the Ages* for its range of costumes and toe-tapping songs. In addition to the shows, Shofar Auditorium also hosts a series of lectures that are almost always worth hearing, and usually very insightful. Most of the lecturers have doctoral degrees in theology, or in a corresponding field, and although the lectures change daily, the amount of in-depth history and thorough research is more than most local clergy have time to include in their sermons.

Theater of Life/*The Seed of Promise* ★½

| APPEAL BY AGE | PRESCHOOL ★½ | | GRADE SCHOOL ★★ | | TEENS ★½ |
| YOUNG ADULTS ★★ | | OVER 30 ★★½ | | SENIORS ★★★ | |

What it is Bible high points in movie form. **Scope and scale** Headliner. **When to go** After experiencing the Scriptorium and Jerusalem Model. **Authors' rating** Surprisingly chintzy; ★½. **Duration of show** 25 minutes; shows every half hour.

DESCRIPTION AND COMMENTS The Theater of Life is set in the behemoth Temple of the Great King, a half-scale replica of Herod's temple from first-century Jerusalem. The ornate temple is the gleaming centerpiece of the Holy Land Experience, so you can't miss it. Pass through the Corinthian columns of the Plaza of the Nations to enter the right side of the temple, where the theater is located. *The Seed of Promise* film is a sort of biblical *CliffsNotes,* covering the highlights of both the Old and the New Testament—everything from Genesis all the way to the Second Coming. Shot on location in Jerusalem, the film is projected onto a six-story-high screen. The film aims to be an "emotionally immersive" retelling of these Bible stories, with special effects thrown in for extra punch.

TOURING TIPS *The Seed of Promise* is oddly disjointed and fairly boring, with historical sets and computer-generated effects that already appear dated. A lot of money was poorly spent here. Our advice: rent *The Ten Commandments* when you get home.

The Wilderness Tabernacle ★★½

| APPEAL BY AGE | PRESCHOOL ★★ | | GRADE SCHOOL ★★★ | | TEENS ★★ |
| YOUNG ADULTS ★★ | | OVER 30 ★★★ | | SENIORS ★★★ | |

What it is Historical demonstration of Jewish ritual. **Scope and scale** Headliner. **When to go** Later in the day, when crowds have thinned out. **Authors' rating** Interesting history; ★★½. **Duration of show** 25 minutes; shows every 30 minutes.

DESCRIPTION AND COMMENTS Visitors enter an outside preshow area where they learn about the struggles of the 12 tribes of Israel on their journey to the Promised Land. They then move into an indoor exhibition hall with bleacher seats; the lighting creates the illusion of being outdoors at dusk, and a narrator introduces himself as a Levitical priest and a descendent of Aaron, the brother of Moses. He then reenacts various rituals of the priesthood practiced during the Israelites' 40 years in the desert. Portentous rumbling, fog, and lighting effects accompany prophetic narration broadcast over loudspeakers. The details of ritual are explained plainly enough, even though part of the scenario takes place in an enclosed tent. Even with a few special effects, you are still asked to imagine quite a large amount as the actor mimes many of the rituals taking place, from animal sacrifice to the simple task of taking water from a well.

TOURING TIPS   All seats have good sight lines in this small space. Moving to the far left will guarantee the best vantage to see the final portion of the presentation, as well as allowing for an easy exit.

DINING

THE ONLY RESTAURANT IS an American/Middle Eastern–themed restaurant, the **Oasis Springs Café.** The menu includes fast food suited to the period and geography, such as hummus, falafel, gyros, and entire turkey legs, the latter priced at $5. American choices include the endearingly named Goliath burger. Wandering vendors also sell snacks and drinks throughout the park.

SHOPPING

THE **Jerusalem Street Market** AT THE PARK'S ENTRANCE is the main shopping venue. Various costumed craftspeople hawk their wares, and a cluster of stores sell a variety of souvenirs. Typical gifts like Bibles and crosses are available, but there are also more exotic choices like mosaics, horn shofars, olive-wood crèches, antievolution place mats, or plush-toy camels and lambs. Another small gift shop geared toward books and the history of Bible-making can be found in the Scriptorium, and another can be found outside the Shofar Auditorium.

PART SIX

KENNEDY SPACE CENTER VISITOR COMPLEX

YOU MAY BE OLD ENOUGH to remember the excitement and anticipation of the early days of space exploration. If not, you've probably seen the movies. Regardless, the pioneer spirit of the space program—sparked when President John F. Kennedy promised to land a man on the moon—is contagious.

Kennedy Space Center has been the training area and launch site for most major U.S. space programs, including Project Mercury's manned orbital missions, Project Apollo's voyages to the moon, and the space shuttle program. In addition, weather and communications satellites are regularly put into orbit from here.

After a $100 million expansion in 1999, the Kennedy Space Center Visitor Complex is thoroughly modern and offers all the attractions and amenities of a contemporary theme park. The complex does a wonderful job of capturing the spirit of adventure—and the uncertainty—of the early days of America's space program. It also offers a unique glimpse into the latest NASA advancements and some interesting visions of where the future of space exploration may lead. Aware of the sometimes wide gulf of interests between the average tourist and the hard-core space junkie, the Visitor Complex is much more engaging and kid-friendly than in the past. Serious space cadets can still visit all the authentic installations and buildings they like, and others can marvel at gee-whiz exhibits, IMAX movies, and really giant rockets. Even so, be sensitive to your group's likes and dislikes, especially when it comes to the specialty tours—some of which are hours long and involve lengthy bus rides.

After the terrorist attacks of September 11, 2001, security at Kennedy Space Center increased dramatically. Some of the tours have been drastically altered, with visits to various secure areas reduced or eliminated entirely. If you're considering a tour, we advise you to find out exactly what sights you'll be seeing and from how far away. Check out the individual tour profiles here for guidance, but be

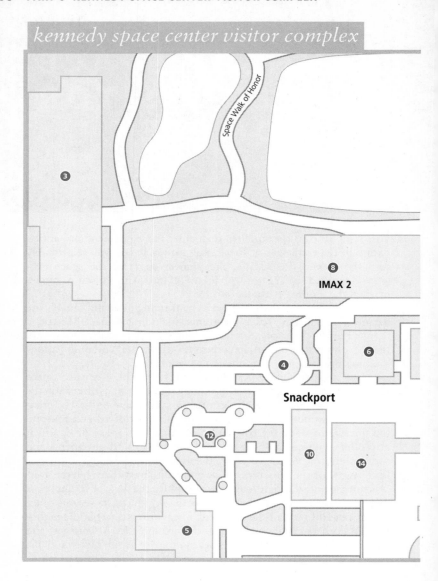

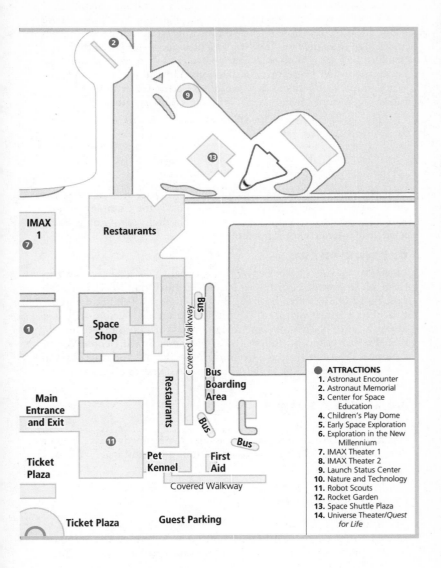

ATTRACTIONS

1. Astronaut Encounter
2. Astronaut Memorial
3. Center for Space Education
4. Children's Play Dome
5. Early Space Exploration
6. Exploration in the New Millennium
7. IMAX Theater 1
8. IMAX Theater 2
9. Launch Status Center
10. Nature and Technology
11. Robot Scouts
12. Rocket Garden
13. Space Shuttle Plaza
14. Universe Theater/*Quest for Life*

advised that all of this can change if security conditions dictate.

We can't stress enough that the tours at Kennedy Space Center are most enjoyable for those with a serious interest in the space program and a high tolerance for "touring at a distance"—and even then, you may not be happy. With stars quite literally in their eyes, visitors can be disappointed by security restrictions and the less than thrilling visual impact of bunker-style buildings seen from a mile away (or more). As a reader from Cherry Hill, New Jersey, writes:

> *The tours are a waste of time (and money). In particular, the NASA Up Close tour is anything but. [Like our tour guide said,] "There's a space shuttle inside that building, over there . . . but you can't see it . . . and there's another shuttle on the launchpad over yonder . . . but you can't see that either."*

If you really want to stay up close with the space stuff, it takes less time, money, and hassle to just explore the Visitor Complex proper. This is especially true for visitors with children, who would likely have little tolerance for a few hours on a bus.

GETTING THERE

KENNEDY SPACE CENTER VISITOR COMPLEX is an easy day trip from most central Florida attractions. From Orlando, visitors can take FL 528 (also called both the Beeline Highway Toll Road and the Beachline Expressway) east. (A round trip on the Beeline will cost about $5 in tolls, so have some cash handy.) Turn onto FL 407 north, then FL 405 east, and follow to the Kennedy Space Center Visitor Complex. You can also take Colonial Drive (FL 50) and travel east to FL 405, but the Beeline is definitely the quickest and easiest route. Parking is free.

ADMISSION PRICES

Standard Admission

The Standard Admission Badge includes the Kennedy Space Center Tour, both IMAX films, and all attractions and exhibits.

STANDARD ADMISSION

Adults $31 + tax | *Children ages 3–11* $21 + tax
Children under age 3 Free

Maximum Access Admission

The Maximum Access Admission includes everything the Standard Admission does plus access to the Astronaut Hall of Fame and interactive spaceflight simulators.

MAXIMUM ACCESS ADMISSION

Adults $38 + tax | *Children ages 3–11* $28 + tax

SPECIAL INTEREST TOURS

Adults $22 + tax | *Children ages 3–11* $16 + tax

ANNUAL PASS

Adults $50 + tax | *Children ages 3–11* $35 + tax

Astronaut Training Experience

If you're really into the astronaut thing, the Astronaut Training Experience (or ATX as it's called) takes visitors ages 8 to 14 and their parent or guardian through two days of the training real astronauts use to get ready for a launch. Zero-gravity simulators; mock mission-control access; a guided, behind-the-scenes tour of Kennedy Space Center; lunch; hotel accommodations; and a final simulated launch and orbit are included in the steep price. This is for true space enthusiasts only. Call ☎ 321-449-4400 for more information or to make reservations. You can also reserve a spot via the Web site: **www.kennedyspacecenter.com.**

unofficial **TIP**
To infinity and beyond: take kids with a real interest in becoming an astronaut on the ATX.

1 ADULT AND 1 CHILD AGES 8–14 $625 + TAX
UP TO 2 ADDITIONAL PARTICIPANTS $275+ TAX EACH

Zero-G Weightless Flight

For the more adventurous and affluent, the Zero-G flight is a new attraction at Kennedy Space Center. An independent group, not the Space Center, takes off from the shuttle landing strip in a Boeing 727. Once airborne, the pilot takes the plane through a series of parabolic maneuvers. After a 45-degree ascent, the plane heads downward, creating a zero-gravity atmosphere for about 30 seconds, then repeats the maneuver over and over again. The price tag for the flight is out of our budget at $3,750 plus tax. Group rates are available, and tickets can be purchased online at **www.gozerog.com** or by phone at ☎ 800-937-6480.

ARRIVING

KENNEDY SPACE CENTER VISITOR COMPLEX is open from 9 a.m. to 5:30 p.m. Unlike other area attractions, the Space Center is closed on Christmas Day and may close for certain shuttle launches. Call ahead before making the drive. Also note that even though the Visitor Complex may be open during shuttle launches, the Launch Complex (LC) 39 Observation Gantry may be closed to tourists when there's "a bird on the pad." Bus tour guides will try to make it up with some other sights around the Space Center, but if you can't see LC 39, you're missing one of the highlights of the tour.

unofficial **TIP**
This facility's tour can take an entire day, so be sure everyone in your group is truly interested in seeing everything there is to see before you board the bus.

Each of the IMAX movies is about 40 minutes long, and the bus tour alone can take more than three hours. If this leaves you feeling overwhelmed, you're right—there's a lot of ground to cover here. The wrong approach is to race from attraction to attraction in one day. Instead, take it slow and soak in some of the better attractions, leaving the others behind.

Most visitors should start their day with some of the exhibits at the hub, which provide an informative background on space history. Then, if you've found one that really meets your interests, head for the bus tour. Buses come frequently (every 15 minutes), but if your timing is off, you can stand a full 15 minutes before boarding, then sit on the bus for a few minutes before taking off. Buses visit LC 39, the Apollo/Saturn V Center, and other locales as the tour's emphasis (or security restrictions) demand. Each of the stops involves movies and displays that are very text-heavy but usually interesting. The movies are wonderful and are of documentary quality, but after a while some may begin to grow tired of the movie-bus-movie-bus shuffle.

After the bus tour, see at least one of the IMAX movies. The five-and-a-half-story screens provide amazing views, and the sound systems are excellent. You can choose from peeking at the moon in 3-D or witnessing the thrilling sensation of spaceflight.

CONTACTING KENNEDY SPACE CENTER

FOR MORE INFORMATION ABOUT Kennedy Space Center, call ☎ 321-449-4444. You can also try ☎ 800-KSC-INFO, but this is a quick, recorded message of basic information that doesn't allow you to transfer to an actual person. The Space Center will mail you a brochure about tours, as well as launch schedule information.

kids You can also visit **www.kennedyspacecenter.com,** which has a page just for kids.

⊞ ATTRACTIONS

VISITOR CENTER COMPLEX HUB

Astronaut Encounter ★½

APPEAL BY AGE	PRESCHOOL ★	GRADE SCHOOL ★ ★ ★	TEENS ★ ½
YOUNG ADULTS ★ ★ ★	OVER 30 ★ ★ ★		SENIORS ★ ★ ★ ½

What it is Talk with a real live astronaut. **Scope and scale** Diversion. **When to go** See daily schedule. **Authors' rating** A bit forced; ★½.

DESCRIPTION AND COMMENTS At scheduled times throughout the day, a NASA astronaut appears in the Universal Theatre for a meet-and-greet. The astronaut's "opening act" is a Visitor Complex MC who warms up the crowd with some fun space facts and nutty science tomfoolery, assisted by a kid volunteer from the audience. The MC then introduces the astronaut, who gives a talk about his or her particular mission in space. A different astronaut will give the lecture on different days. The quality of the lecture varies on each astronaut's mission; a biologist may not excite the children as much as a shuttle pilot.

After the talk, the astronaut will take questions. The Q&A can be dull, so if you want to make it interesting, come with your own questions or have the children come up with questions during the presentation (questions about the dangers of space are good leads to more exciting stories).

Children do seem intrigued, but they don't appear to have the astronaut-hero worship more popular with preceding generations.

For an even more intimate astronaut encounter, sign up for Lunch with an Astronaut. As the name implies, this involves sharing a meal with an astronaut, who first shows a video about life on the space shuttle, then gives a personalized presentation about his or her own space experiences. A Q&A follows, as well as a chance to take photos (a signed souvenir photo is included). The meal (served at 12:30 p.m. daily) consists of rotisserie chicken, salad, sides, dessert, and beverage, with kid-friendly options available. Cost is $60.99 for adults, $43.99 for kids ages 3 to 11, but park admission is included in this price; call ☎ 321-449-4444 for advance reservations or purchase online at **www.kennedyspacecenter.com.** Tickets for Lunch with an Astronaut can also be purchased at the Visitor Complex, but same-day tickets may already be sold out.

unofficial **TIP**
To get up close and personal with an astronaut, have lunch with one—make reservations in advance.

TOURING TIPS Check the daily entertainment schedule for times. If kids get bored, the spread-out seats make it easy to tactfully get up and wander off to another attraction.

Astronaut Memorial ★★★

APPEAL BY AGE	PRESCHOOL ★	GRADE SCHOOL ★	TEENS ★★
YOUNG ADULTS ★★	OVER 30 ★★★		SENIORS ★★★

What it is Memorial to those who died for space exploration. **Scope and scale** Minor attraction. **When to go** At the end of the tour. **Authors' rating** Touching tribute; ★★★.

DESCRIPTION AND COMMENTS The entire memorial tilts and swivels to follow the sun, while mirrors direct the sun's rays onto glass names etched in a black marble slab. You probably won't want to spend a great deal of time here, but it's a poignant thing to see.

TOURING TIPS Visit the kiosk on the side of the Gallery Center Building. There you'll find computers that offer background information on the astronauts on the memorial.

kids Children's Play Dome ★★

APPEAL BY AGE	PRESCHOOL ★★★	GRADE SCHOOL ★★	TEENS †
YOUNG ADULTS †	OVER 30 †		SENIORS †

† This attraction was not designed for older guests.

What it is Kiddie playground. **Scope and scale** Diversion. **When to go** If your older kids are looking at the Rocket Garden, supervise the young ones here. **Authors' rating** Small but cute; ★★.

DESCRIPTION AND COMMENTS This little playground, under cover from the hot sun, is a nice diversion for kids. It's similar to the kids' areas at other attractions, but a space theme prevails.

TOURING TIPS One adult can take the older kids to an IMAX movie or on a stroll through the Rocket Garden, while another supervises the little ones here.

Early Space Exploration ★★★

APPEAL BY AGE	PRESCHOOL ★	GRADE SCHOOL ★½	TEENS ★★
YOUNG ADULTS ★★★	OVER 30 ★★★½		SENIORS ★★★★

What it is Relics from the birth of spaceflight. **Scope and scale** Diversion. **When to go** While waiting for the bus or IMAX films. **Authors' rating** Very informative and nostalgic; ★★★.

DESCRIPTION AND COMMENTS This well-presented series of exhibits documents the birth and maturation of human space exploration. Space suits, lunar landers, and capsules are all on display, highlighting mostly the Mercury and Gemini programs. Newspaper clippings and other ephemera give historical context to the items on display. There's also a good deal of information on how the Russian space program evolved in competition with that of the United States, but the space race is framed as having been ultimately beneficial to both nations.

TOURING TIPS Another pleasant walk-through exhibit. Kids will have less patience with all this "old" stuff, so be prepared for some eye-rolling and heavy sighs if you tarry too long.

Exploration in the New Millennium ★★½

APPEAL BY AGE	PRESCHOOL ★★★	GRADE SCHOOL ★★★½	TEENS ★★
YOUNG ADULTS ★★★	OVER 30 ★★½		SENIORS ★★

What it is Exhibits about the future of space travel. **Scope and scale** Diversion. **When to go** While waiting for the bus or IMAX films. **Authors' rating** Future funky; ★★½.

DESCRIPTION AND COMMENTS A collection of hands-on exhibits that speculate on where our space travelers will go and how they will get there. Some exhibits are educational and straightforward, like many dealing with the various Mars landers and the Pathfinder mission (you can even sign up to send your signature to the Red Planet on the next mission). Other exhibits go on flights of fancy about how futuristic spacecraft will work and about potential colonization of other planets.

TOURING TIPS An easy walk-through, with nothing too surprising. Kids will like the touching-encouraged exhibits. Hit this one as filler when needed.

IMAX Films ★★★½

APPEAL BY AGE	PRESCHOOL ★★★	GRADE SCHOOL ★★★★	TEENS ★★★½
YOUNG ADULTS ★★★★	OVER 30 ★★★½		SENIORS ★★★½

What it is Large-format 3-D films projected onto huge screens with incredible sound systems. **Scope and scale** Headliner. **When to go** Check daily entertainment schedule; perfect during rain. **Authors' rating** Excellent; ★★★½. **Duration of shows** About 40 minutes.

DESCRIPTION AND COMMENTS Kennedy Space Center offers two excellent IMAX films each day:

Magnificent Desolation: Walking on the Moon 3-D. Tom Hanks narrates this 3-D feature of NASA footage mixed with quirky animation. The film focuses on the moon and the Apollo missions, a great supplement to the bus tours.

Space Station 3-D. Narrated by Tom Cruise, this film includes footage shot by 25 astronauts and cosmonauts as they lift off from Earth and visit the International Space Station. Various effects and 3-D models create the illusion that the audience is actually flying in the space shuttle and visiting the station themselves.

TOURING TIPS *Space Station 3-D* is our preference—by a nose—if you are not able to see both films. It offers a complete look at the Space Station, while *Magnificent Desolation* focuses on the moon, which the rest of the Kennedy Space Center covers extensively. Regardless of which movie you choose, we recommend sitting toward the back of the theater for the best view and to fully experience the awesome sound system. You will need to arrive early because these theaters are fairly small. As in most theaters, popcorn, candy, and sodas are available at the concessions stand in the lobby.

Launch Status Center ★★★★

APPEAL BY AGE	PRESCHOOL ★	GRADE SCHOOL ★½	TEENS ★★
YOUNG ADULTS ★★½	OVER 30 ★★★		SENIORS ★★★

What it is Live launch briefings and artifacts on display. **Scope and scale** Major attraction. **When to go** After visiting the Shuttle Plaza. **Authors' rating** Cool to see the real deal; ★★★★.

DESCRIPTION AND COMMENTS The artifacts are neat, but most enjoyable are the live briefings that take place on the hour between 11 a.m. and 5 p.m. Space Center communicators and live footage from throughout the complex give a glimpse into what is happening at the Space Center, or at the International Space Station, the day of your visit.

TOURING TIPS Visit just days before a launch and you'll catch the real action, which could include live video from the shuttle. If you visit when LC 39 is closed for a launch, this will probably be as close as you get.

Mad Mission to Mars: 2025 ★½

APPEAL BY AGE	PRESCHOOL ★★★½	GRADE SCHOOL ★★★	TEENS ★
YOUNG ADULTS ★½	OVER 30 ★½		SENIORS ★

What it is Stage show about science. **Scope and scale** Minor attraction. **When to go** Second or third show of the day. **Authors' rating** Lackluster; ★½.

DESCRIPTION AND COMMENTS *Mad Mission to Mars* is a children's theater piece, and a poor one. The set is a space station but looks more like a high school construct than a theme park attraction. The story involves a trio of actors—a "wacky" astronaut/surfer dude, the straight-laced Professor Prove-It, and a robot—attempting "to school" the audience on a series of science experiments, and perhaps, go to Mars. Having these three with you on your trip to Mars does not make the trip any shorter or the science experiments any more interesting. With minimal special effects to counter the acting, the only bright spot is that a few children are selected to go up on stage.

TOURING TIPS   The *Mad Mission to Mars* appears to be a major miscalculation. Since the theater holds only 92 people, a line builds outside. In Pavlovian fashion, people see a line form and step into it. A simple sign below *Mad Mission to Mars* reading For Preschoolers and the Very Young might solve the problem, but for this skewed vision of the future there is no such sign, so you and your very young party should arrive 45 minutes before show time or go grab lunch instead of attending.

Nature and Technology: Merritt Island National Wildlife Refuge ★½

APPEAL BY AGE	PRESCHOOL ★	GRADE SCHOOL ★½	TEENS ★½
YOUNG ADULTS ★★	OVER 30 ★★		SENIORS ★★

What it is Small exhibit on the coexistence of local wildlife and high technology. **Scope and scale** Diversion. **When to go** Anytime. **Authors' rating** Unremarkable; ★½.

DESCRIPTION AND COMMENTS   Even though it's harmless enough, this walk-through exhibit is largely uninspired, although the pine interior and taxidermic animals make a drastic juxtaposition to the metal shells of the rocket garden. Small displays catalog the lives and habits of various wild animals in the refuge as well as the Cape Canaveral National Seashore including: bald eagles, alligators, otters, sea turtles, manatees, and so on.

TOURING TIPS   Skip this one unless you're killing time while someone else is on the bus or in the movie theater.

Rocket Garden ★★★

APPEAL BY AGE	PRESCHOOL ★	GRADE SCHOOL ★★	TEENS ★
YOUNG ADULTS ★	OVER 30 ★★		SENIORS ★★

What it is Outdoor rocket display. **Scope and scale** Diversion. **When to go** Before you head home. **Authors' rating** Unique; ★★★.

DESCRIPTION AND COMMENTS   Rockets, spacecraft, and antennae dot a vast lawn. The big rockets take center stage and are the perfect backdrop for group photos. If you're wondering what Old Scratch has been up to lately, consult the remnants of SATAN (Satellite Tracking Antenna). The Rocket Garden underwent a massive renovation and refurbishment in 2002, with new landscaping, shade, and fresh coats of paint all around, giving the attraction a much-needed face-lift. Space enthusiasts and grade schoolers may enjoy the climb-in replicas of *Mercury, Gemini,* and *Apollo* capsules.

TOURING TIPS Morning and afternoon guided tours are offered. Check the sign near the garden entrance for times.

Robot Scouts ★★

APPEAL BY AGE	PRESCHOOL ★★		GRADE SCHOOL ★★★	TEENS ★★
YOUNG ADULTS ★★		OVER 30 ★★		SENIORS ★★

What it is Walk-through exhibit featuring robots. **Scope and scale** Minor attraction. **When to go** At the end of the day, if there's time. **Authors' rating** Somewhat hokey; ★★.

DESCRIPTION AND COMMENTS Robot Starquester 2000, an animatronic robot scout, will take you through this exhibition of NASA's past, present, and future robotic space explorers. Starquester 2000 interacts with other space probes, like the Viking Mars Lander and the Hubble Space Telescope, to explain how robotic space exploration aids human exploration.

TOURING TIPS You can hit this exhibit on entering the center, before the bus tours. The tours are continuous and begin about every five minutes. The seating sections are small, so groups of less than ten are preferable.

The Space Shuttle Experience

APPEAL BY AGE	NOT OPEN AT PRESS TIME

What it is Simulation of a space launch. **Scope and scale** Super headliner. **When to go** Make this your first stop.

DESCRIPTION AND COMMENTS Scheduled to open in summer of 2007, the Shuttle Launch Experience purports to simulate "blasting into Earth's orbit." If the ride lives up to the hype, this will be one of the top attractions at the KSC. The ride will be "the most technologically advanced exhibit ever created at NASA's Kennedy Space Center Visitor Complex, using a sophisticated motion-based platform, special-effects seats, and high-fidelity visual and audio."

Riders will enter along a gantry and view all of the preparation for a shuttle launch on large monitors. After the preparations are over, riders will be strapped into the simulator and the countdown will begin. After the launch, you circle the earth and then re-enter her atmosphere via the exit door.

TOURING TIPS The Shuttle Launch Experience is being constructed in the back of the Visitor Complex, near Space Shuttle Plaza and the Launch Status Center. The ride will be a super headliner and should be your first stop when entering the park.

Space Shuttle Plaza ★★★

APPEAL BY AGE	PRESCHOOL ★	GRADE SCHOOL ★★★	TEENS ★★
YOUNG ADULTS ★★	OVER 30 ★★		SENIORS ★★★

What it is View a space shuttle model. **Scope and scale** Minor attraction. **When to go** Immediately before or after bus tour. **Authors' rating** Impressive up close; ★★★.

DESCRIPTION AND COMMENTS The *Explorer,* a full-size replica of the space shuttle, gives you a glimpse of what it's like to be an astronaut working and
living in space. You'll see the flight deck, where astronauts fly the
orbiter during launch and landing, and the cramped mid-deck, where
shuttle crews work on experiments, sleep, and eat.

TOURING TIPS This exhibit is easy to miss if you're racing to the bus tour
because it's off the beaten path. Nevertheless, there may be a long line.
We suggest trying back later in the afternoon rather than waiting for
this interesting but uneventful tour.

U.S. Astronaut Hall of Fame ★★½

| APPEAL BY AGE | PRESCHOOL ★★ | GRADE SCHOOL ★★★ | TEENS ★★½ |
| YOUNG ADULTS ★★½ | | OVER 30 ★★½ | SENIORS ★★★ |

What it is Complex of exhibits and astronaut honor roll. Scope and scale Major
attraction. When to go Anytime. Authors' rating Worth a look if you're
skipping the bus tours; ★★½.

DESCRIPTION AND COMMENTS This building, which is separate from the main
Visitor Complex and set outside the guard gate, houses a collection of
astronaut memorabilia and mementos, including equipment and small
spacecraft, flight patches, and personal items. The Astronaut Hall of
Fame itself takes up one room, listing those honored and inducted so
far. Another room sports an array of simulators that will be of the most
interest to kids, allowing them to land a shuttle, dock with the space
station, walk on the moon, and engage in other spacely pursuits. The
inevitable gift shop rounds out the proceedings.

TOURING TIPS The Hall of Fame is situated down the road from the Visitor
Complex and requires a ten-minute drive to get there. You will have to
use your own vehicle since buses do not run to the Hall of Fame.

You must purchase the Maximum Access Admission to view the Hall
of Fame (simulators and all), or purchase a ticket at the Hall of Fame for
$17 for adults and $13 for children ages 3 to 11. This is a good last stop
before heading to the hotel, as long as you do not want to ride any of
the simulators. The lines at the end of the day are as tedious as any
major theme park's and the rewards are not up to the wait. The Hall of
Fame stays open until 6:30 p.m., an hour past the Visitor Complex but
due to the long lines, a midday excursion, barring any IMAX presentation or bus tour, is a better plan.

Universe Theater/*Quest for Life* ★★½

| APPEAL BY AGE | PRESCHOOL ★ | GRADE SCHOOL ★★ | TEENS ★★½ |
| YOUNG ADULTS ★★ | | OVER 30 ★★ | SENIORS ★★ |

What it is Film about life on other planets. Scope and scale Minor attraction.
When to go Anytime. Authors' rating Amusingly similar to preride film at
Universal's Men in Black: Alien Attack; ★★½. Duration of show 15 minutes.

DESCRIPTION AND COMMENTS Does life exist on other planets? Leading scien-
tists lend evidence that there may have been life on Mars. The film

addresses the likelihood of other planets sustaining life and NASA's plans to determine if life exists in other parts of the universe. It's a bit too earnest in this post–*X-Files* world of ours, but still interesting.

TOURING TIPS Make this your final stop before leaving the Visitor Complex proper.

KENNEDY SPACE CENTER BUS TOUR

BUSES RUN EVERY 15 MINUTES and make three stops around Kennedy Space Center. Tour at your own pace, but the entire trip, making all the stops, should average about three hours. The time spent at each exhibit is up to your discretion. The bus that drops you off will not be the same one that picks you up, so if you buy presents at the gift shops you will have to carry them with you for the remainder of the tour. If you stay on one bus and experience none of the highlights of Kennedy Space Center—not recommended—the bus ride will still take 30 to 45 minutes.

In transit, there's no staring into "space." Television monitors show informative segments on space exploration to prepare you for the next destination. Think of this time as cramming for an exam. If possible, sit near the front of the bus, on the right side, for a better view of buildings in the area. Also, if you're lucky, an alert bus driver will point out signs of wildlife—which include an impressive bald eagle nest—along the way to the following stops:

Apollo/Saturn V Center ★★★★

APPEAL BY AGE	PRESCHOOL ★★★	GRADE SCHOOL ★★★★	TEENS ★★★
YOUNG ADULTS ★★★h	OVER 30 ★★★★		SENIORS ★★★★

What it is Exhibit celebrating the race to the moon. **Scope and scale** Super headliner. **When to go** Anytime. **Authors' rating** Where else can you touch a moon rock?; ★★★★.

DESCRIPTION AND COMMENTS The Apollo/Saturn V Center is a gigantic building (actually constructed around the enormous *Saturn V*!) with several displays. All guests enter a "holding area," where you'll see a nine-minute film on the race to the moon. This film is good, but things only get better.

The next stop is the Firing Room Theater, which catapults you back in time to December 1, 1968, for the launch of the first successful manned mission to the moon. Actual remnants of the original 1960s firing room set the mood, including countdown clocks and launch consoles. Once the show is under way, three large screens take you back to that day with original footage from the Space Center. During this ten-minute presentation, you'll sense the stress of the launch commanders and feel as though you're experiencing the actual launch through some fun special effects.

This is a pride-inducing presentation that prepares you for the real meat and potatoes of the Apollo/Saturn V Center—the actual 363-foot

Saturn V moon rocket. When the doors of the Firing Room Theater open, guests are instantly overwhelmed by the size of the rocket. The amount of power the rocket produced on blastoff (7.5 million pounds of thrust) could light up New York City for an hour and 15 minutes. In addition, this room is filled with space artifacts, including the van used to transport astronauts to the launchpad, a lunar module, and Jim Lovell's *Apollo 13* space suit. But there are more than just dusty relics here. Kennedy Space Center does a great job of telling the history of the era, with storyboards along the walls to document the highlights of each Apollo mission.

Another excellent exhibit at the Apollo/Saturn V Center is the Lunar Theater, where Neil Armstrong narrates a suspenseful documentary about his trip to the moon with *Apollo 11*. Younger generations may be a little shocked at how close the "eagle" came to missing its landing. The set of Lunar Theater enhances the 12-minute film with a few eccentric tricks; the whole production is short, touching, and inspired.

TOURING TIPS If you're traveling with kids, they may well be restless by now. Check out the interactive exhibits or maybe step outside. There is a patio near the dining area where your family can get some fresh air.

LC 39 Observation Gantry ★★★★

APPEAL BY AGE	PRESCHOOL ★★	GRADE SCHOOL ★★★	TEENS ★★
YOUNG ADULTS ★★★	OVER 30 ★★★★		SENIORS ★★★★

What it is Observation area that focuses on the space shuttle. **Scope and scale** Major attraction. **When to go** Anytime. **Authors' rating** Get up close and personal with shuttle launchpads; ★★★★.

DESCRIPTION AND COMMENTS The LC 39 exhibits celebrate the Space Shuttle—the first spacecraft designed to be reusable. A seven-minute film at the LC 39 Theater, narrated by shuttle astronaut Marsha Ivins, explains how NASA engineers and technicians service the shuttle before launch. After the film, the doors open to dump you into a room with model displays. From here, head to the observation gantry, which puts you less than a mile away from Launchpads 39A and 39B, the only sites for launching the space shuttle. These are also the pads from which the *Saturn V* rockets blasted off to the moon during the Apollo program.

TOURING TIPS You'll be tempted to race to the observation gantry, but watching the film first provides for a better appreciation of the views offered there. The intricate launchpad model should be your first stop once the movie doors have opened. The model runs through a launch every few minutes, so to see the pieces move, wait for the countdown.

Once at the observation gantry, look for the Crawlerway path, a road nearly as wide as an eight-lane highway and more than three miles long. It was constructed to bear the weight of the Crawler-Transporter (6 million pounds) that moves the shuttle from the Vehicle Assembly Building to the launchpad.

OTHER TOURS

Cape Canaveral: Then and Now ★★★½

APPEAL BY AGE	PRESCHOOL ★★	GRADE SCHOOL ★★½	TEENS ★★½
YOUNG ADULTS ★★★½	OVER 30 ★★★★		SENIORS ★★★★

What it is Bus tour to Cape Canaveral. **Scope and scale** Headliner. **When to go** Check the daily schedule. **Special comments** Tour is sometimes canceled or altered due to launch activity; photo ID required. **Authors' rating** A piece of NASA history; ★★★½. **Duration of tour** About 2 hours, plus parts of the main bus tour.

DESCRIPTION AND COMMENTS Situated about 15 miles from Kennedy Space Center, Cape Canaveral Air Station is an active launch facility where unmanned rockets are sent into space on NASA, military, and commercial missions. Even more interesting, though, is Cape Canaveral's place in history as the original home of the U.S. space program. It is here that the early Mercury missions, as well as the first Americans, were launched into space. And unlike the main bus excursion, with its faraway viewing, this tour allows you to actually explore these historical locations firsthand. Elements of the main KSC Bus Tour are included in this tour as well.

A highlight of the tour is the Air Force Space and Mission Museum, home of the world's largest outdoor collection of missiles on display.

TOURING TIPS Unfortunately, you are not allowed to tour at your own pace and must depart with the same group on the same bus. This tour costs an extra $22 for adults and $16 extra for children ages 3 to 11 on top of the regular admission and is for true space aficionados only.

NASA Up Close Tour ★½

APPEAL BY AGE	PRESCHOOL ★	GRADE SCHOOL ★	TEENS ★
YOUNG ADULTS ★★	OVER 30 ★★½		SENIORS ★★★

What it is Bus tour of sights not on main tour. **Scope and scale** Headliner. **When to go** Check the daily schedule. **Special comments** Tour is sometimes canceled or altered due to launch activity. **Authors' rating** Fairly tedious; ★½. **Duration of tour** About 2 hours, plus parts of the main tour.

DESCRIPTION AND COMMENTS This tour takes visitors out for photo ops at Launchpads 39A and 39B, the Vehicle Assembly Building (where the shuttle is "stacked" and loaded prior to rolling over to the pads), and likely views of the massive Crawler-Transporter, so-called because it ferries its precious payload to the launchpad at a creeping 1 mile per hour. Various other sundry sites may be visited depending on launches and the whims of your tour guide.

Fair warning: if you are not a down-to-the-bones space program maniac, this tour has the potential to bore you to tears. Despite the tour's name, many buildings are viewed at a distance.

TOURING TIPS Unfortunately, you are not allowed to tour at your own pace and must depart with the same group on the same bus. This tour costs an extra $22 for adults and $16 extra for children ages 3 to 11 on top of the regular admission and is for true space aficionados only.

kids VIEWING A LAUNCH

DOES YOUR CHILD DREAM OF BECOMING AN ASTRONAUT? Maybe you remember the exact day Neil Armstrong set foot on the moon. If so, seeing a live launch is truly awe-inspiring and will leave you with a memory you'll never forget.

Kennedy Space Center offers a bus trip to a viewing site about six miles from the launch area plus Maximum Access Admission to the Visitor Complex, priced at $50 for adults and $40 for children ages 3 to 11. Tickets are generally available up to six weeks in advance of launches and sell out quickly. For more information, call ☎ 321-449-4444.

Launches can also be seen outside of Kennedy Space Center along US 1 in Titusville, Florida, and along US A1A in Cape Canaveral and Cocoa Beach. All of these locations can be reached from FL 528 (Beeline Highway toll road) east. You should arrive early (about three hours in advance), however, as many locals line the streets for launches.

Be aware that some of the attractions at the Kennedy Space Center Visitor Complex may be closed the day of a launch for safety reasons. Also, traffic can be unbearable after a launch, so plan to visit one of the many nearby beaches until roads are clear.

DINING

DON'T PLAN TO GRAB BREAKFAST (or any other meal) in the vicinity of Kennedy Space Center. It is very isolated, and there simply are not any restaurants within 20 miles. There are food locations on site, but they're nothing to cheer about. However, if you must eat, you'll find pizza and such at **Planetary Pizza** and a wider selection in a food court at **Orbit Restaurant. Mila's** offers more of a sit-down, full-service experience. There are also many food stands throughout the entire Kennedy Space Center Visitor Complex for a quick bite.

SHOPPING

THERE ARE GIFT SHOPS AT EACH STOP on the bus tour, and a jumbo gift shop at the Visitor Center hub. Don't be shy—try the freeze-dried ice-cream sandwich or strawberries. You can also find snow globes, space shuttle gummy candy, T-shirts, and more. Prices vary from $2 for candy to $30 for T-shirts.

unofficial **TIP**
Let your kids try astronaut ice cream in the gift shop.

PART SEVEN

SEAWORLD

A WORLD-CLASS MARINE-LIFE THEME PARK, SeaWorld is the odd middle child of central Florida's megaparks—without the allure of Mickey Mouse or the glitz of the movie studio attractions. For years, this park succeeded by appealing to those who appreciated the wonder of sea creatures like killer whales and dolphins. Walt Disney World may have cornered the market on make-believe, but SeaWorld offered the unique opportunity of watching people interact with live animals.

As competition for tourists' time increased and Disney ventured into the wild-animal business with its Animal Kingdom, SeaWorld created new interactive encounters that can't be found at any other area park. SeaWorld also added thrill rides, including a flight simulator, a roller coaster, and a hybrid flume-coaster. Combined with the charm of the animals, these attractions and several entertaining shows have created a whole new SeaWorld that isn't just for the fish-and-whale crowd. Many *Unofficial Guide* readers consider the park to be a favorite part of an Orlando vacation.

> *unofficial* **TIP**
> If you and, yes, even your kids, tire of imitation animals the likes of Minnie and Mickey, try a day at SeaWorld.

A family from England writes:

> *The best organized park [is] SeaWorld. The computer printout we got on arrival had a very useful show schedule, told us which areas were temporarily closed due to construction, and had a readily understandable map. Best of all, there was almost no queuing. We rated this day so highly that it is the park we would most like to visit again.*

A woman from Alberta, Canada, gives her opinion:

> *We chose SeaWorld as our fifth day at "The World." What a pleasant surprise! It was every bit as good (and in some ways better) than WDW itself. Well worth the admission, an excellent entertainment value, educational, well run, and better value for the dollar in food services. Perhaps expand your coverage to give them their due!*

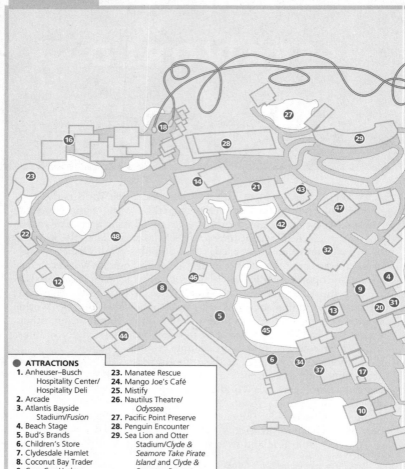

seaworld

● **ATTRACTIONS**

1. Anheuser–Busch
    Hospitality Center/
    Hospitality Deli
2. Arcade
3. Atlantis Bayside
    Stadium/*Fusion*
4. Beach Stage
5. Bud's Brands
6. Children's Store
7. Clydesdale Hamlet
8. Coconut Bay Trader
9. Cruz Cay Harbor
10. Cypress Bakery
11. Dine with Shamu
12. Dolphin Cove
13. Dolphin Nursery
14. Friends of the Wild
15. Games Area
16. Journey to Atlantis
17. Keyhole Photo
18. Kraken
19. The Label Stable
20. Makahiki Luau
21. Mama's Kitchen
22. Manatee Cove

23. Manatee Rescue
24. Mango Joe's Café
25. Mistify
26. Nautilus Theatre/
    Odyssea
27. Pacific Point Preserve
28. Penguin Encounter
29. Sea Lion and Otter
    Stadium/*Clyde &
    Seamore Take Pirate
    Island* and *Clyde &
    Seamore Present
    Sea Lions Tonight*
30. Sea Harbor Pavilions
31. Seafire Inn
32. SeaWorld Theater/
    Pets Ahoy!
33. Shamu Soak Zone!
34. Shamu Souvenir
35. Shamu Stadium/
    Believe!
36. Shamu Underwater
    Viewing
37. Shamu's
    Emporium

38. Shamu's Happy
    Harbor
39. Shark Encounter
40. Sharks Underwater
    Grill
41. Sky Tower
42. Smoky Creek Grill
43. The Spice Mill
44. Stingray Lagoon
45. Tropical Reef
46. Turtle Point
47. Voyager's Wood
    Fired Pizza

48. Whale and Dolphin
    Theatre/
    Blue Horizons
49. Wild Arctic
50. Wild Arctic
    Gift Shop

A father of two from Manitoba, Canada, gives SeaWorld's nighttime laser show top marks, commenting:

> But the absolute topper is the closing laser show, which beats out Illu-miNations at Epcot for extravaganza. The SeaWorld show combines fireworks, lasers, and moving holographic images back-projected on a curtain of water. In the word of our older daughter: awesome! And you watch the whole thing seated in the lakeside arena, instead of jostling for a standing view around the Epcot lagoon.

A reader from Sylvania, Georgia, believes Disney could learn a thing or two from SeaWorld:

> Disney ought to take a look at how well this place is run. I know they don't have the same crowds or the exciting rides, but there is still a lot of entertainment here and never a wait. This allows you to set your pace without worrying about what you'll have to miss. You'll see it all no matter how you do it, you'll come away feeling you got better value for your dollars, you won't feel as tired as a Disney day, and you will probably learn more, too. Only downside is you'll probably be hungry. Food is not one of the park's assets.

unofficial **TIP**
There's more than just marine life at this well-organized park to keep everyone entertained.

On top of its accumulated charms, SeaWorld also boasts its aquatic subpark, Discovery Cove. Here, you can swim with live dolphins—an attraction offered nowhere else in central Florida. All of this makes SeaWorld a great way to shift gears from the Mouse race, while still enjoying the big production values of a major theme-park destination.

GETTING THERE

SEAWORLD IS ABOUT 10 MILES EAST of Walt Disney World. Take Interstate 4 to FL 528 (Beeline Highway east). Exit at the first ramp, which is International Drive. Turn left off the exit ramp. Turn right at Central Florida Parkway. The entrance to SeaWorld is on the right just prior to a large SeaWorld sculpture. Car and motorcycle parking is $9, and preferred parking is available for $14 in a lot closer to the main entrance that fills up quickly. RV and camper parking is $10. Discovery Cove is directly across the Central Florida Parkway from SeaWorld. Parking at the Discovery Cove lot is free.

ADMISSION PRICES

EXCEPT UNDER THE MOST CROWDED CONDITIONS, a typical visitor can see most (if not all) of SeaWorld in one solid day of touring, so a standard One-day Pass makes sense. In fact, SeaWorld has discontinued most of its multiday tickets in favor of package deals and annual passes. However, SeaWorld really wants your business, and there are several options that will get you a lot more time in the park for slightly more money than a one-day ticket. In fact, if you schedule it right, you can use the SeaWorld Fun Card for park admission almost all year long for an extra $5. If you're planning to spend time at other local theme parks, consider the money-saving Orlando FlexTicket. Several deals are also available com-

unofficial **TIP**
It's a major time-saver to pay admission before heading to the park.

bining SeaWorld admission with tickets for Busch Gardens and the water park Adventure Island, both in Tampa (and both also owned by SeaWorld corporate parent Anheuser-Busch). Discounts are available for AAA members, disabled visitors, senior citizens, and military personnel. All tickets, even the FlexTicket, can be purchased on the park's Web site, usually for less (**www.seaworld.com**). Purchasing tickets online, from an authorized vendor, or from any of the authorized ticket agents in Orlando, will save you from the inconvenient logjam at the park ticket kiosks. If you fail to obtain tickets in advance, try the electronic ticket machines located outside SeaWorld's main gate and to the right of the ticket kiosks. To use the machines, bring your credit card and your patience. The touch-screen interface is temperamental at best and the purchase process more complicated than necessary. Select your language choice and then follow the instructions as you would with an ATM. When you are finished—it will take about three to five minutes per purchase—the machine will print out your tickets.

ONE-DAY PASS

Adults $61.95 + tax | *Children ages 3–9* $49.95 + tax
Children under age 3 Free

SeaWorld Fun Card

This pass is by far the best deal for admission to SeaWorld, but there are a few catches. For $5 more than the One-day Pass, you get unlimited admission to SeaWorld for one calendar year, except blackout dates of Easter weekend and December 27th to the 31st. There's also a Fun Card that allows admission to Busch Gardens (with the same restrictions).

FUN CARD

Adults $66.95 + tax | *Children ages 3–9* $54.95 + tax

FUN CARD PLUS BUSCH GARDENS

Adults $119.95 + tax | *Children ages 3–9* $99.95 + tax

Two-park Unlimited Admission Ticket

This pass is a seven-day admission ticket good for both SeaWorld and Busch Gardens and includes a free shuttle between Orlando and Tampa.
All Ages $85 + tax

Annual Passports

These allow unlimited admission to either SeaWorld alone or SeaWorld plus Busch Gardens for one or two years, and includes free general parking and 10% off both merchandise and food purchases in the park(s). The Platinum Passport is only offered for a two-year period and includes free preferred parking, no blackout dates, and ride-again privileges at all Anheuser-Busch parks.

SEAWORLD SILVER PASSPORT (ONE YEAR)

Adults $94.95 + tax | *Children ages 3–9 and seniors* $84.95 + tax

SEAWORLD GOLD PASSPORT (TWO YEARS)

Adults $144.95 + tax | *Children ages 3–9 and seniors* $134.95 + tax

SEAWORLD/BUSCH GARDENS SILVER PASSPORT (ONE YEAR)

Adults $144.95 + tax | *Children ages 3–9 and seniors* $134.95 + tax

SEAWORLD/BUSCH GARDENS GOLD PASSPORT (TWO YEARS)

Adults $219.95 + tax | *Children ages 3–9 and seniors* $209.95 + tax

ANHEUSER-BUSCH PLATINUM PASSPORT (TWO YEARS)

Adults $299.95 + tax | *Children ages 3–9 and seniors* $280.95 + tax

Orlando FlexTicket

This pass is good for up to 14 consecutive days at five parks: Busch Gardens, Universal Studios Florida, Universal Islands of Adventure, SeaWorld, and Wet 'n Wild. There's also a version that excludes Busch Gardens, so be sure to get the one you want.

FLEXTICKET

Adults $251 + tax | *Children ages 3–9 and seniors ages 50+* $214 + tax

FLEXTICKET WITHOUT BUSCH GARDENS

Adults $203 + tax | *Children ages 3–9 and seniors ages 50+* $167 + tax

ARRIVING

SEAWORLD OFFICIALLY OPENS AT 9 A.M. Ropes to a smaller section on the north side drop at 10 a.m., except during the busiest times of the year, when the entire park opens all at once. Closing time fluctuates from 6 or 7 p.m. in late fall and winter to 10 p.m. in the summer and on holidays.

Exploring SeaWorld takes a full day. Because the majority of attractions are shows, it won't be a mad rush to avoid lines like at other theme parks. However, avoiding the rare long wait and large crowds requires getting there early during busy times of the year. Like other area parks, SeaWorld opens its turnstiles at either 8:30 a.m. or 8:45 a.m. depending on the season, which means you can enter the park before the scheduled 9 a.m. opening. You can only wander around a limited area with a bakery and a few shops, however. Nonetheless, during peak season, we suggest you arrive no later than 8:20 a.m., allowing time to park and purchase tickets. At other times, arriving at 8:40 a.m. should give you a jump on the crowds.

While a member of your party purchases tickets, have another track down a SeaWorld map. Map-toting employees are usually positioned in front of the ticket booth. While waiting for the park to open, plan your attack.

During peak season, if you're a fan of water thrill rides, locate the quickest route to Journey to Atlantis, which combines elements of a water ride and dry roller coaster. When the ropes drop, head straight there. You'll be tempted to stop at animal exhibits along the route, but save those for later. The line for Journey to Atlantis will be most manageable early in the day.

unofficial TIP
If you plan on getting wet on the water rides, head for them first.

Right next to Journey to Atlantis is Kraken, SeaWorld's super roller coaster. Lines for this ride will also get longer as the day progresses, so make it an early priority—either right before or right after Journey to Atlantis.

When attendance isn't at its highest, the lines for Journey to Atlantis and Kraken can be quite short. At those times of the year, or if you don't like water rides or coasters, plan to hurry to Dolphin Cove in the Key West area when the park opens. In addition to beating the bulk of the crowd, you'll get to see the animals at their most active time in the morning. You can stand along the edge of this gorgeous two-acre pool teeming with dolphins to get a close-up view. But if the dolphins are one of your main reasons for visiting SeaWorld, use your morning visit to get the feeding schedule for the day, which is posted at the mint-green fish house on the left side of the pool. There is usually a feeding scheduled at 9:15 a.m., and you can get in line to purchase fish right away.

unofficial TIP
Animals at SeaWorld and other parks are most active early in the morning.

Arrange the remainder of your day around the show schedule. Attractions encircle a large lagoon, and the best strategy to see it all is to travel clockwise, especially because the opposite side does not open until 10 a.m. (We've ordered the attractions listings in the clockwise order.) This tactic depends on the entertainment schedule, of course, but at the very least, allow time to see the attractions in the area surrounding each show. You will save time and energy by not roaming aimlessly, and there's not much point in rushing—the entertainment schedule is not designed for immediate back-to-back viewing of shows.

Walt Disney World might be known for its friendly, informative cast members, but they certainly haven't cornered the market. At each animal exhibit in SeaWorld, you can find pleasant and extremely knowledgeable employees who will share interesting information and answer any questions.

SeaWorld also allows visitors to view training sessions that occur at many of the show stadiums. A schedule for these sessions isn't published, but if you're near any of the stadiums between shows, pop in. You can also hang out a bit after a show to possibly catch some unscripted action.

CONTACTING SEAWORLD

FOR MORE INFORMATION, call ☎ 800-327-2424, or visit the SeaWorld Web site at **www.seaworld.com.** If you or your children are interested in learning more about the park's animals before visiting, SeaWorld also maintains a Web site designed for students and teachers at **www.seaworld.org.**

ATTRACTIONS

kids *Believe!*/Shamu Stadium   ★★★★½

APPEAL BY AGE PRESCHOOL ★★★★   GRADE SCHOOL ★★★★½ TEENS ★★★★
YOUNG ADULTS ★★★★½   OVER 30 ★★★★½   SENIORS ★★★★½

What it is Killer whale show. **Scope and scale** Super headliner. **When to go** Check daily entertainment schedule; first show is sometimes more crowded. **Authors' rating** Truly amazing, not to be missed; ★★★★½. **Duration of show** 30 minutes.

DESCRIPTION AND COMMENTS   The new *Believe!* killer whale show has replaced *The Shamu Adventure.* Although many of the stunts are the same, the theatrics surrounding the stunts have increased substantially. A new two-story set capped off with a giant whale's tail, four mammoth rotating LED screens, and a vast sound system that booms an original score by the Czech Philharmonic Orchestra are just the backdrop for the whales and trainers.

Believe!'s theatrics begin with a video clip projected on the four LED video screens about a boy who sets off in a kayak and encounters a whale. The boy's conspicuous fluke-shaped necklace makes it apparent that the trainer, who appears on stage after the video, is a grown-up version of the boy. This theme of the lifelong wonder and inspiration one can find with aquatic wildlife is crystallized when yet another trainer relates her tale about being a young visitor to SeaWorld. Although some adults may find this all bordering on maudlin, young children seem to take the message to heart. To bring the production full circle, the first trainer selects a young child from the audience and hands her his necklace.

The production elements are, of course, only a filler for the real wonder at *Believe!:* the highly trained family of orcas, commonly known as killer whales. Like most celebrities, they're known by stage names—most notably, Shamu and Baby Shamu.

Of course, the trainers and whales work closely and jointly provide the most spectacular sight of the show—a trainer perched on the nose of a whale shooting nearly 30 feet out of the water. The absolute trust and bond of friendship between trainer and whale allow plenty of other maneuvers, including surfing on a whale's back, riding through the water on a whale's nose, or zipping across the water's surface while holding on to a whale's flipper.

If these huge creatures' leaps and arcs are the most spectacular portion of the show, a display of their incredible power is the most stunning. This is when gallons and gallons of 55°F saltwater are flung into the first 14 rows by the flukes of a large whale. The audience is warned, but most folks must not realize how much water will head their way or how cold it really is. Nevertheless, some, especially the under-age-12 set, make it a point to be in the water's path.

Now, this sight is incredible, but the most astonishing scene is yet to come . . . when a five-ton whale, the largest in captivity, makes his splashing rounds. Not only do the folks in the first 14 rows get soaked, but the water actually travels an extra 15 to 20 feet to reach the second tier of this large stadium. If you sit anywhere in the splash zone, Believe! that you will get wet.

TOURING TIPS We're not kidding when we say gallons of chilly salt water. You will get soaked in the first few rows. If you or the kids think you're up for it, you might want to bring some extra clothes to change into after the cold shower. You should leave your cameras with someone out of the range of the corrosive salt water.

Although this is a large stadium, you must arrive early to get a seat. Two CGI penguins will keep you entertained with a video pop quiz. Audience members are amusingly caught off-guard by their image on the screen and must answer a multiple-choice question.

kids *Blue Horizons*/Whale and Dolphin Theatre ★★★

APPEAL BY AGE PRESCHOOL ★★★½   GRADE SCHOOL ★★★★   TEENS ★★½
YOUNG ADULTS ★★★½   OVER 30 ★★★½   SENIORS ★★★½

What it is Killer whale show. **Scope and scale** Headliner. **When to go** Check daily entertainment schedule. **Authors' rating** This remake needs a remake; ★★★. **Duration of show** 30 minutes.

DESCRIPTION AND COMMENTS The *Blue Horizons* show, which includes whales, dolphins, birds, acrobats, spraying water, a huge set with an enormous truss, and a full symphonic score, is one of the premiere attractions at SeaWorld. With all of these elements, the show should succeed. Unfortunately, it contains critical flaws. The plot is incoherent, and the show contains many lulls in action; the only way to grasp the plot is to watch the making-of-*Blue Horizons* video from the SeaWorld Web site (**www.4adventure.com/seaworld/fla/blue_horizons.aspx**). Even after the video, you'll still be a little baffled. The show opens with a young girl named Marina opening a door into a fantasy world, and after that, the plot goes to pot. Without some foreknowledge—and even with it—the appearance of a lady in bird costume with her minions of birdman-acrobats is both disconcerting and confusing. This lady is *supposed* to represent the Spirit of the Sky while her male counterpart in the water is supposed to represent the Spirit of the Sea. Instead, he comes across as the young girl's creepy love interest, partly because of his blue costume that counters the young girl's pink costume, but more because of an inordinate amount of frolicking.

The title of the show—*Blue Horizons*—derives from the horizon line where the sky meets the sea. The young girl wants to be part of the sky and the sea, and so does the set. The set's scale is impressive but the look is less so; the large orbs attached to the backdrop are meant to simultaneously represent clouds and bubbles but play instead as poorly painted globs of glue.

Even with the flaws, the show's animal stunts are impressive. The cetaceans leap in the air and spin underwater while the macaws fly about accompanied by a memorable symphonic score. If a coherent plot can be added, the lulls in action removed, and the human acrobatics integrated with the animal acrobatics, then the show will be spectacular. At the moment, it is only a spectacle whose appeal is for children under age 10.

TOURING TIPS Due to crowd flow into the *Blue Horizons'* stadium, the best entrance to the stadium is located near the Journey to Atlantis attraction. This entrance will place you in front of the stadium, and as long as you arrive 45 minutes to an hour before show time, you should be able to claim a seat upfront.

kids   *Clyde and Seamore Take Pirate Island /*   ★★★½
Sea Lion and Otter Stadium

APPEAL BY AGE PRESCHOOL ★★★★	GRADE SCHOOL ★★★★	TEENS ★★★
YOUNG ADULTS ★★★½	OVER 30 ★★★	SENIORS ★★★

What it is Show featuring sea lions, otters, and a walrus. Scope and scale Headliner. When to go Check daily entertainment schedule. Authors' rating Unabashed cornball comedy; ★★★½. Duration of show 30 minutes.

DESCRIPTION AND COMMENTS One of the three headlining shows at Sea-World, this attraction draws a crowd, so attempt to arrive up to 45 minutes to an hour ahead of show time. Fortunately for early entries, unlike other attractions at SeaWorld, the Clyde and Seamore show has a preshow performer. This pirate-mime warms up the seated audience by mocking the individuals from the incoming crowd. The clown is completely irreverent, so if you are extremely self-conscious, you had better enter from the rear of the stadium.

The irreverence continues onward with the start of the show. The sea lion stars are named Clyde and Seamore; Clyde plays alongside the protagonist Robin Plunder, who has been shipwrecked on the island, while Seamore play the first mate of the pirate ship under the villainous Captain Squid, who is seeking a hidden treasure. The show takes a self-aware and self-deprecating stance as Robin Plunder talks directly to the audience, points out any mistakes made by the sea lions, and even slights Captain Squid on her horrific acting. Due to the great ensemble work between trainers and animals—including the supporting cast members Opie the Otter and Sir Winston Walrus—as well as the coherent plot that showcases the animals talents, this show is the funniest and most well-rounded performance at SeaWorld.

TOURING TIPS Arrive early and from the rear of the stadium to avoid the mime.

Clyde and Seamore Present Sea Lions Tonight / ★★★½ Sea Lion and Otter Stadium

APPEAL BY AGE PRESCHOOL ★★★★ GRADE SCHOOL ★★★★ TEENS ★★★
YOUNG ADULTS ★★★ OVER 30 ★★★ SENIORS ★★★

What it is Animals and trainers spoof SeaWorld attractions. Scope and scale Major attraction. When to go Check daily entertainment schedule; one show nightly but only during peak seasons. Authors' rating Sardonic sea lions; ★★★½. Duration of show 25 minutes.

DESCRIPTION AND COMMENTS Instead of a reprise of the daytime show, *Sea Lions Tonight* is a satirical montage, ribbing all the major shows in the park. *Fusion, Pets Ahoy, Blue Horizons, Believe!,* and even the Budweiser Clydesdales are given the treatment. The satire acts as a self-critique, pointing out a good deal of our own criticisms of the shows, such as the sappiness of *Believe!* and the incomprehensibility of *Fusion.* This new show also involves variations of the "stunts" found in the daytime show, as well as a series of quick costume changes (including a few wardrobe swaps for the animals!). The sharp irreverence and the good-humored jabs at the park's attractions make this as funny as the daytime show and a perfect way to close out your day at SeaWorld.

TOURING TIPS This is a seasonal show, so call ahead to see if your visit coincides with the show's run. Since there is only one performance of this show a day, try to arrive at least 45 minutes early. When you arrive early, you will see the mime from the daytime show again, but he has a difficult time tricking the returning crowd. Still, his antics ease the wait time. The best seating is in the center of the arena, but the only bad seats are behind the pillars.

Clydesdale Hamlet/Hospitality Center ★★

APPEAL BY AGE PRESCHOOL ★★½ GRADE SCHOOL ★★★ TEENS ★½
YOUNG ADULTS ★★½ OVER 30 ★★½ SENIORS ★★½

What it is Stable and free beer. Scope and scale Diversion. When to go Avoid visiting immediately after *Odyssea* or a Shamu show. Authors' rating Most kids will enjoy the horses, most adults will enjoy the beer; ★★.

DESCRIPTION AND COMMENTS An Anheuser-Busch theme park, SeaWorld features a white stable that is home to several Clydesdales, the huge and beautiful draft horses that are the beer company's trademark. Walk through the stable on the way to the Hospitality House. Here, if you're age 21 or older, you can partake in two free samples of Anheuser-Busch beer. You can also sign up for Budweiser Beer School, a free 40-minute class on beer-making, which includes a variety of sample beers and snacks that compliment each beer's flavor. There is a comfortable lounge outside the Beer School, as well as a small area inside with a desk and coloring books for children. Repeating the class to get more beer samples is discouraged.

TOURING TIPS The Clydesdales are incredibly beautiful animals, but skip this area if you're in a hurry. Also, check the entertainment schedule for appearances of the Clydesdales in the park. The Hospitality House also features The Deli. Save time by combining lunch with your free beer sample.

Dolphin Cove ★★★★

APPEAL BY AGE PRESCHOOL ★★★   GRADE SCHOOL ★★★★   TEENS ★★★★
YOUNG ADULTS ★★★★   OVER 30 ★★★★   SENIORS ★★★★

What it is Outdoor dolphin habitat. **Scope and scale** Major attraction. **When to go** In the morning; for scheduled feedings. **Authors' rating** Impressive; ★★★★.

DESCRIPTION AND COMMENTS This sprawling, two-acre habitat is filled with a community of swimming and leaping dolphins. You can stand along one side of the pool and touch or feed the dolphins. A path along the opposite side of the pool leads to an overlook area that provides excellent views and a great photo location. If you can live without touching the dolphins, this area is also much less crowded. Next to the overlook is a walkway to an underwater viewing area that provides the best glimpse of these delightful mammals in action. The interior walkway is air-conditioned and one of the most memorable sights at SeaWorld.

TOURING TIPS Feedings take place at scheduled times throughout the day, usually immediately following the dolphin show at nearby Whale and Dolphin Theatre. Feedings provide the best opportunity to interact with the dolphins, but also generate large crowds. Check the schedule at the fish house to the left of the pool to see if the feeding times fit into your schedule to view the park. A small tray of fish costs $3.

There is a chance to touch the dolphins at other times. SeaWorld employees say the key is simply to keep your hands still under the water and patiently wait for the animals to brush against you. You may see SeaWorld trainers slapping the water to get the dolphins' attention, but this doesn't seem to work for guests. Apparently, the dolphins know and trust the trainers, but they are frightened by strange hands hitting the water.

With the opening of Discovery Cove, SeaWorld's swim-with-the-dolphins subpark, the pool of available dolphins has been stretched a little thin. Some of the park's dolphins might be away at Discovery Cove when you visit, although SeaWorld claims all bases are covered.

Dolphin Nursery ★★

APPEAL BY AGE PRESCHOOL ★   GRADE SCHOOL ★★   TEENS ★
YOUNG ADULTS ★★   OVER 30 ★★   SENIORS ★★

What it is Outdoor pool for expectant dolphins or mothers and calves. **Scope and scale** Diversion. **When to go** Anytime. **Authors' rating** Only worth a quick glimpse unless a baby is present; ★★.

DESCRIPTION AND COMMENTS Seeing this tiny pool that used to be the sole dolphin experience at SeaWorld should make you appreciate Dolphin Cove and Discovery Cove all the more. But the small size is perfect for its current purpose—providing a separate area for pregnant dolphins and new moms and calves. Stop by for a quick glance if it's an expectant dolphin. Stay longer if there's a baby in the pool.

TOURING TIPS This area will be roped off and guests understandably kept away when a dolphin goes into labor. Because it's near the park entrance, swing by on your way out to see if the area has reopened, and you might be able to view mom and baby.

For those who can't get enough of the baby dolphins, SeaWorld offers an interactive experience at the nursery. Guests are allowed to go behind the scenes for a talk with calf caretakers and then are taken poolside to see the little guys nose-to-bottlenose (for obvious reasons, you are not allowed to swim with them). The Dolphin Nursery Close-Up Tour is available to guests ages 10 and older and costs $40 per person; reservations may be made online or by calling ☎ 800-406-2244.

Hiding next to the Dolphin Nursery is one of the most beautiful and secluded areas of SeaWorld. Find the path next to the nursery and enter a lush tropical rain forest. A large banyan tree and 30-foot-tall bamboo trees shade the entire area. Large fish swim in a small pond, and two beautiful macaws perch on a branch.

There is also an aviary featuring blue dacnis and red-legged honey-creepers, both adorably tiny birds. There are no formal benches, but a few stone ledges provide the perfect place to get away from the sun and the theme park hustle and bustle.

Fusion / Atlantis Bayside Stadium ★★★

APPEAL BY AGE	PRESCHOOL ★★★	GRADE SCHOOL ★★★½		TEENS ★★	YOUNG
ADULTS ★★½		OVER 30	★★½	SENIORS	★★★

What it is Water sports stunt show. **Scope and scale** Headliner. **When to go** Check daily entertainment schedule. **Authors' rating** Eclectic; ★★★. **Duration of show** 30 minutes.

DESCRIPTION AND COMMENTS In an attempt to get some use out of the lagoon in the center of the park, SeaWorld has built Atlantis Bayside Stadium. The stadium is currently host to the show *Fusion*, an eclectic—and odd—assortment of things people do next to the water. If *Blue Horizons'* theme is the place where water meets the sky, then *Fusion's* theme is where land meets the water.

The land section of the show consists of an ensemble of very attractive male and female dancers, who gyrate around to pop hits ranging from kiddie-pop to gangster rap. While the dancers clap and spin, just about every conceivable method of transportation whizzes by on the lagoon. Water-skiers, wakeboarders, a hydrofoil-skier, Jet Skis, a sailboat, and even kites are choreographed into the aquatic set. The dancing is a fine distraction while there are no aquatic performers present, and the dancers are adept at shifting your focus to the water when a stunt is about to be performed.

The end result of this mixed production feels like a modern remake of a *Gidget* movie. Albeit incredibly convoluted and incoherent, the aquatic stunts and the enthusiastic dancers in their skimpy outfits are worth a peek.

TOURING TIPS If you have young children, try to arrive 15 to 20 minutes beforehand for the "beach party." Your kids will get to meet with some of the performers, play with hula hoops, and shed a little excess energy prior to the show.

This show is not usually very crowded, so 15 to 20 minutes should be plenty of time to find a seat in the shade before show time.

kids Journey to Atlantis ★★½

APPEAL BY AGE	PRESCHOOL †		GRADE SCHOOL ★★★		TEENS ★★★
YOUNG ADULTS ★★½		OVER 30 ★★			SENIORS ★★

† *Preschoolers are generally too short to ride.*

What it is Water ride and roller coaster combo. **Scope and scale** Headliner. **When to go** Before 10 a.m. or after 4 p.m. during peak season; avoid visiting immediately after a Whale and Dolphin Theatre show. **Special comments** Riders must be 42" tall; pregnant women or people with heart, back, or neck problems should not ride. **Authors' rating** Fun, if not cheesy; ★★½. **Duration of ride** 6 minutes. **Loading speed** Moderate.

DESCRIPTION AND COMMENTS Riders board eight-passenger boats and plunge down a nearly vertical 60-foot waterfall before careening through a mini–roller coaster. Although this ride is housed in a truly impressive edifice that spouts fire and water, the payoff inside is pretty meager. The attraction supposedly takes guests on a voyage through Atlantis as they try to avoid an evil spirit, but even after several trips, we still didn't have a good grasp on this story line (what's up with that goldfish, or sea horse, or whatever it was?). For that reason, and because of an "it's over before you know it" feeling, we have to give the ride lower marks than those of Disney's Splash Mountain. However, Journey to Atlantis definitely provides the bigger thrill.

TOURING TIPS Closer to sunset, the special effects in this attraction are more intense because the darker evening sky helps keep light from leaking into the ride when the boats travel outdoors. However, during peak seasons the wait in line can be an hour or longer, and we don't think Journey to Atlantis is worth that much of your time. For best results, arrive early and dash to this attraction when the park opens at 9 a.m. to minimize the wait. Then stop by in the evening and ride again if the line isn't too long. You can always hit the Kraken roller coaster next door if lines are a problem here; of course, we're prejudiced, because we feel if we must stand in line, it may as well be for a coaster.

Journey to Atlantis will get you wet, especially in the front seats. If you want to minimize the drenching, bring a poncho or purchase one at the gift shop at the attraction. Place any items that you don't want to get soaked, such as cameras, in the pay lockers near the entrance to the queue. Free bins are available at the loading dock, but they are not secured.

kids Kraken ★★★★

APPEAL BY AGE PRESCHOOL †	GRADE SCHOOL ★★★★	TEENS ★★★★
YOUNG ADULTS ★★★½	OVER 30 ★★★	SENIORS ★

† Preschoolers are generally too short to ride.

What it is Roller coaster. **Scope and scale** Super headliner. **When to go** Immediately following a ride on Journey to Atlantis. **Special comments** Riders must be 42" tall; pregnant women or people with heart, back, or neck problems should not ride. **Authors' rating** A real brain rattler; ★★★★. **Duration of ride** 3 minutes. **Loading speed** Moderate.

DESCRIPTION AND COMMENTS The roller coaster war has reached epic proportions in central Florida. SeaWorld enters the battle with Kraken, named after the mythological underwater beast. At a top speed of 65 miles per hour, a length of more than 4,000 feet, and with a first drop of 144 feet, it is Orlando's fastest, longest, and tallest roller coaster. How long will it reign? If history is any indication, it's only a matter of time before Disney or Universal ups the ante yet again.

This "floorless" coaster puts riders in 32 open-sided seats, in eight rows, riding on a pedestal above the track. It's a sort of combination of the newer inverted coasters (where riders dangle in seats, rather than sit in cars) with the open ceiling of a traditional coaster. The net effect is that nothing up, down, or sideways blocks your view, an especially amazing effect on that first big drop—when it seems like you're about to plunge right into a lake.

Despite its overall great fun, be warned that this coaster does not offer the smoothest ride. You will be jerked around a bit, and repeated rides may lead to woozy crab-walking.

TOURING TIPS This extremely popular coaster draws the crowds, but it can move them too. Even large lines will move at a good clip, but you can still cut down your wait by riding before 10 a.m. or after 4 p.m. During peak season, we suggest you arrive when the park opens, ride Journey to Atlantis, and immediately head to Kraken. After getting drenched on Journey, the high-speed coaster trip will help dry you off.

Manatee Rescue ★★★

APPEAL BY AGE PRESCHOOL ★★½	GRADE SCHOOL ★★½	TEENS ★★★
YOUNG ADULTS ★★★	OVER 30 ★★★	SENIORS ★★★

What it is Outdoor manatee habitat and underwater viewing. **Scope and scale** Minor attraction. **When to go** Anytime. **Authors' rating** Remarkable animals in a creative habitat; ★★★.

DESCRIPTION AND COMMENTS Manatees, which are on the endangered species list, are still disappearing at a rapid rate. All of the docile creatures in this exhibit were injured in the wild and have been rescued by SeaWorld. The area resembles an inland canal, a favorite spot of these gentle giants. For most of the rescued animals, this is the last part of their rehabilitation, and many will be returned to their natural environment.

TOURING TIPS Be sure to visit the underwater viewing area. It offers an excellent view of the huge creatures. Along the way, you'll see a short video about the plight of these endangered giants.

On occasion, SeaWorld rescues orphaned baby manatees. Check with an educator in the area to find out if there are any in the exhibit, if they might be bottle-fed, and at what time. It's pure, distilled cuteness.

Mistify ★★★

APPEAL BY AGE PRESCHOOL ★★★   GRADE SCHOOL ★★★   TEENS ★★★
YOUNG ADULTS ★★★   OVER 30 ★★★   SENIORS ★★★

What it is Laser and fireworks show. Scope and scale Major attraction. When to go Check daily entertainment schedule. Special comments Only displayed during peak seasons. Authors' rating Good big booms; ★★★. Duration of show 1 hour.

DESCRIPTION AND COMMENTS Presented over the lagoon in the Waterfront Village. The theme of the show changes frequently, but common elements include fireworks, lasers, and movies projected on a water curtain in the lagoon—all set to music. Although the show might not be quite as spectacular as Disney's *IllumiNations,* it is a great fireworks display and the projections on the water screen are unique.

TOURING TIPS As a pleasant change from Disney's nighttime shows, there's usually no need to stake out a spot hours in advance, although we do recommend arriving about 15 minutes early. In addition, you won't be stuck standing up or with tree-blocked views, because the action is easily seen from the Village's shore. There are a *few* bad spots however, as one reader noted:

We stayed until 10 p.m. to see the Mistify show on the lake at SeaWorld, but unless you are standing in a good position you can't see the film projected on the mist. We had to move to outside the Budweiser shop as there was a good view from there (although there are probably plenty more good vantage points), but that doesn't include the Sand Bar.

Pacific Point Preserve ★★★

APPEAL BY AGE PRESCHOOL ★★★½   GRADE SCHOOL ★★★½   TEENS ★★★
YOUNG ADULTS ★★★   OVER 30 ★★★   SENIORS ★★★

What it is Outdoor sea lion habitat. Scope and scale Major attraction. When to go Feeding times (scattered throughout the day). Authors' rating Fun and startling; ★★★.

DESCRIPTION AND COMMENTS Let the sound of more than 50 barking sea lions and harbor seals lead you to this nifty area tucked behind Sea Lion and

Otter Stadium. An elevated walkway behind a glass partition surrounds the sunken habitat. The animals can be found sunning themselves on the rocky terrain or lounging in the shallow waves. More often, though, they'll be barking impatiently—perhaps very impatiently—for a snack. Although these animals aren't trained, a few of the sea lions will improvise cute antics for food, such as mimicking you sticking out your tongue. Sometimes, they get so excited about a possible meal that their barking reaches amazing, earsplitting levels.

TOURING TIPS If you participate in a feeding, which costs $3 for one tray of fish (or $5 for two), watch out for the large, aggressive birds that lurk in this area. They are poised to steal the fish right out of your hand, snatch one in midair as you toss it to the sea lions, or even land on your head or shoulders to make a grab for the goods (we saw this happen twice).

Look closely at the animals, and you might spot some adorable sea lion or harbor seal pups—especially if you visit during the spring or summer.

kids Penguin Encounter ★★★

APPEAL BY AGE PRESCHOOL ★★★½	GRADE SCHOOL ★★★	TEENS ★★★
YOUNG ADULTS ★★★	OVER 30 ★★★	SENIORS ★★★

What it is Indoor penguin habitat. **Scope and scale** Major attraction. **When to go** Anytime. **Authors' rating** Adorable tuxedo models; ★★★.

DESCRIPTION AND COMMENTS The first section of this exhibit features an icy habitat behind a glass wall, providing an excellent view of the penguins' antics in several feet of water. Step on the people-mover to the right for a close-up view of these critters as they congregate, waddle, and dive into the frigid water. Then circle back behind the people-mover to an elevated section where you can take a longer look at the large emperor penguins. A learning area is just past the habitat, where interactive kiosks provide information about the animals and their environment. The walkway then leads to a smaller exhibit, which is home to puffins and other species that prefer a warmer climate.

TOURING TIPS The pungent penguin odor will hit you before you step through the door, but after a couple minutes you'll get used to it. During summer, SeaWorld darkens the exhibit to simulate the Antarctic environment, where it is actually winter. The birds are still active and visible, but you may need to spend more time on the stationary upper level to get a good look. During this season, you will not be allowed to shoot any photos of the habitat because the flash negates the effect of the darkened room for the animals.

There is a way, albeit astoundingly finicky, to enter the environment via the Penguin Encounter Program. The program is not listed on the park map, so stop by the exhibit to get the daily schedule. Bone up on your penguin facts beforehand; one guest who answers all of the keeper's questions is allowed to enter the environment.

Pets Ahoy!/SeaWorld Theater   ★★★

| APPEAL BY AGE | PRESCHOOL ★★★ | GRADE SCHOOL ★★★ | TEENS ★★½ |
| YOUNG ADULTS ★★★ | | OVER 30 ★★★ | SENIORS ★★★ |

What it is Show featuring trained pets. **Scope and scale** Major attraction. **When to go** Check daily entertainment schedule. **Authors' rating** The truth about cats and dogs?; ★★★. **Duration of show** 25 minutes.

DESCRIPTION AND COMMENTS   Despite its cornball name—SeaWorld's need to uphold its nautical theme seems to exceed its need to reel in a crowd—the show remains a draw due to the elaborate integration of the beach-town set with the animals who inhabit it. The show is a series of skits that each imitate a Rube Goldberg machine: a dog pulls a lever that signals a cat to run across the stage that, in turn, signals a different cat to climb a rope onto a roof, and so on. The skits are accented with sound effects and music, as well as a basic plot that always ends with a humorous, if predictable, twist. The only low points in the show are the appearance of the trainers who demonstrate an animal performing one stunt with neither plot nor set-ploys, and the five-minute shill for the Humane Society, from where most of the animals were rescued. At the end of the show, you can talk to the trainers and get close to the animals; keep your eyes open, kids, you might spot a few creatures Mom has *never even considered* for pets.

TOURING TIPS   The Pets Ahoy Pavilion is located on The Waterfront between the Sky Tower and the southern bridge that leads to Shamu Stadium. The theater is small but, since the show is not a headliner, seats are usually available.

Shamu Express   ★★

| APPEAL BY AGE | PRESCHOOL ★★★ | GRADE SCHOOL ★★★½ | TEENS ★★ |
| YOUNG ADULTS ★½ | | OVER 30 ★★ | SENIORS ★★ |

What it is Children's roller coaster. **Scope and scale** Minor attraction. **When to go** Avoid visiting after a Shamu show. **Special comments** Open from 10 a.m. until an hour before the park closes. **Authors' rating** Thrill ride for kids; ★★.

DESCRIPTION AND COMMENTS   With Kraken towering over the park, riders under 42 inches tall may feel left out of the roller coaster market. SeaWorld consoles its younger riders with the Shamu Express, located in Shamu's Happy Harbor. The coaster is very small, with only 800 feet of track, but the ride is smooth and makes a great starter coaster. Besides, who can resist cars shaped like the park's biggest star?

TOURING TIPS   The roller coaster holds only 28 guests at a time, but the short track keeps the lines from piling up. Still, avoid the Shamu Express, and all of Happy Harbor, directly before and after performances at Shamu Stadium.

Shamu Underwater Viewing   ★★★

| APPEAL BY AGE | PRESCHOOL ★★ | GRADE SCHOOL ★★★ | TEENS ★★½ |
| YOUNG ADULTS ★★★ | | OVER 30 ★★★ | SENIORS ★★★ |

What it is Whale viewing area. **Scope and scale** Minor attraction. **When to go** Avoid visiting immediately before or after a Shamu show. **Authors' rating** Good look at these incredible animals; ★★★.

DESCRIPTION AND COMMENTS Go behind the scenes at Shamu Stadium for a peek at the stars of the show in their 1.5 million-gallon pool. Check the above-water viewing area for a training session or a veterinary visit. When standing "next to" these animals in the underwater viewing area, be prepared to be awestruck by their enormous size.

TOURING TIPS When the animals are not active, or not even present, this area is not worth visiting. Check with the SeaWorld employee usually stationed nearby for the best times to visit on a particular day.

Have your camera ready at the underwater viewing area. The whales usually slowly circle the pool, offering an amazing backdrop for a group photo.

Shamu's Happy Harbor ★★★½

| APPEAL BY AGE | PRESCHOOL ★★★ | GRADE SCHOOL ★★★ | TEENS ★ |
| YOUNG ADULTS ★ | | OVER 30 ★ | SENIORS ★★ |

What it is Children's play area. **Scope and scale** Minor attraction. **When to go** Avoid visiting after a Shamu show. **Special comments** Open from 10 a.m. until an hour before the park closes. **Authors' rating** A nice oversized playground; ★★★½.

DESCRIPTION AND COMMENTS Four stories of net span this three-acre children's play area. Children and brave adults can climb, crawl, and weave through this net jungle. Other activities include an air bubble where kids under 54 inches tall can bounce and play and an interactive submarine with several water cannons and fountains. There is also an area for smaller kids (they must be under 42 inches tall) with a standard ball-filled room and several playground contraptions.

TOURING TIPS Parents can grab a cool drink and relax at Coconut Cove while watching their children play. Most adults should stay clear of the patience-testing, headache-causing steel-drum area, where kids are allowed to bang to their hearts' content.

Shark Encounter ★★★½

| APPEAL BY AGE | PRESCHOOL ★★★ | GRADE SCHOOL ★★★½ | TEENS ★★★★ |
| YOUNG ADULTS ★★★½ | | OVER 30 ★★★½ | SENIORS ★★★½ |

What it is Exhibit of sharks, eels, and other dangerous sea creatures. **Scope and scale** Major attraction. **When to go** Anytime. **Authors' rating** Pleasantly creepy; ★★★½.

DESCRIPTION AND COMMENTS This walk-through exhibit immerses you (almost literally) in the frightening world of dangerous marine life. First, you are surrounded by moray eels as you walk through an acrylic tube at the bottom of a large aquarium. These eels peer out from lairs in an artificial tropical reef or undulate through the water. Next are several large aquariums housing poisonous fish, including the beautiful but lethal scorpion fish and the puffer fish, one of the world's most deadly. Then get ready for the grand finale—a 600,000-gallon tank filled with six species of sharks, including bull sharks, nurse sharks, and lemon sharks, as well as dozens of enormous grouper and other smaller fish. An entire wall of a large room gives a comprehensive view of this beautifully lit tank. Its amazing creatures will glide next to you and directly overhead as you pass through an acrylic tunnel. As you exit the tunnel, you'll learn that it supports 500 tons of salt water, but if necessary, it could handle nearly five times that weight—the equivalent of more than 370 elephants. A reassuring thought.

TOURING TIPS The crowd usually bottlenecks at the eel habitat. If possible, worm your way through the initial backup. The tube is fairly long, and you'll find the same great view with a smaller crowd near the other end.

If you visit SeaWorld on a Tuesday or Thursday, don't miss the feeding frenzy when the sharks in the main habitat feast at 11 a.m. (call beforehand to verify the schedule).

You can get in on the feeding yourself on select days at a small pool at the entrance to the exhibit. Purchase a tray of fish for $3 (two for $5) and toss them cheerfully to small hammerhead and nurse sharks. If that's still not enough all-shark action for you, consider the Sharks Deep Dive, in which guests don scuba or snorkel gear and plunge directly into the shark tank (in a shark cage). Cost is $150 per person including tax; participants must be at least 10 years of age. Call ☎ 800-406-2244 for reservations and information.

Sky Tower ★★

APPEAL BY AGE	PRESCHOOL ★★	GRADE SCHOOL ★★	TEENS ★★
YOUNG ADULTS ★★½		OVER 30 ★★½	SENIORS ★★★

What it is Scenic aerial ride. **Scope and scale** Minor attraction. **When to go** Anytime, although it's quite beautiful at night. **Special comments** Costs $3. **Authors' rating** ★★. **Duration of ride** Nearly 7 minutes. **Loading speed** Slow.

DESCRIPTION AND COMMENTS This attraction forces visitors to make a philosophical decision. Should a theme park charge an additional fee for one of its rides? Although the answer is probably no, a ride to the top of the tower is somewhat calming. The tower has two levels of enclosed seats that rotate as they rise to the top for great views of the park. It's amazing how serene the park looks—and how tiny the killer whales appear—from the top. On a clear day, you can see many other interesting sites, including downtown Orlando, the top of Spaceship Earth at Epcot, and the unmistakable toaster shape of Disney's Contemporary Resort.

TOURING TIPS This attraction closes if lightning or high winds pop up, and both are frequent in central Florida. It also doesn't run during the peak season's nighttime fireworks display. The Sand Bar Lounge at the bottom of the tower serves a variety of refreshments.

Stingray Lagoon ★★★

APPEAL BY AGE	PRESCHOOL ★★		GRADE SCHOOL ★★★½		TEENS ★★★
YOUNG ADULTS ★★★		OVER 30 ★★★		SENIORS ★★½	

What it is Stingray pool. **Scope and scale** Minor attraction. **When to go** Feeding times. **Authors' rating** Ray-riffic; ★★★.

DESCRIPTION AND COMMENTS The shallow water in this waist-high pool is filled with dozens of undulating stingrays. After the death of world-renowned zoologist Steve Irwin (the "Croc Hunter") in 2006 due to a stingray attack, these creatures seem even more menacing than before. However, all of the stingrays at SeaWorld continue to have their barbs removed so they are not a threat to visitors. They may seem ominous, but they are actually quite mellow, and you shouldn't be afraid to stick your fingers into the tank and feel their silky skin.

TOURING TIPS Although a small tray of fish costs $3, don't miss feeding these graceful creatures. (Feedings are scheduled throughout the day.) The fish are slimy, and the tail end must be carefully placed between two fingers, but even the most squeamish in our group enjoyed the stingrays swimming over their hands and lightly sucking the food into their mouths.

Tropical Reef ★★

APPEAL BY AGE	PRESCHOOL ★½		GRADE SCHOOL ★★		TEENS ★
YOUNG ADULTS ★½		OVER 30 ★½		SENIORS ★★	

What it is Indoor aquariums/outdoor tide pool. **Scope and scale** Diversion. **When to go** Anytime; skip if in a hurry. **Authors' rating** Easy to miss; ★★.

DESCRIPTION AND COMMENTS A small outdoor tide pool is home to several sea urchins, sea cucumbers, and spiny lobsters. It's not much to look at, but visitors are encouraged to stick their hands in and touch the urchins—a unique experience. Inside, hundreds of tropical fish swim in numerous aquariums. The aquariums are set into the walls, so the colorful fish are visible only through the front pane of glass. Information and factoids can be found on lighted signs near each aquarium.

TOURING TIPS True fish fanatics only. Others will find their time better spent at the more elaborate exhibits.

Turtle Point ★★

APPEAL BY AGE	PRESCHOOL ★★		GRADE SCHOOL ★★★		TEENS ★★
YOUNG ADULTS ★★		OVER 30 ★★		SENIORS ★★	

What it is Outdoor turtle habitat. **Scope and scale** Diversion. **When to go** Anytime; most informative when an educator is present. **Authors' rating** Just turtles; ★★.

DESCRIPTION AND COMMENTS A white-sand beach and palm trees surround a small pool at this exhibit. Several large turtles can be seen swimming or sunning themselves. Most of them have been rescued by SeaWorld, and many of their injuries are evident, such as missing flippers (caused by discarded fishing line or shark attacks) or cracked shells (from boat propellers).

TOURING TIPS Because the turtles are not terribly active, this attraction is worth only a quick peek. A visit becomes more interesting if an educator is present to talk about the animals and the ways humans can help protect them in the wild.

kids Wild Arctic ★★★½

APPEAL BY AGE	PRESCHOOL ★★★	GRADE SCHOOL ★★★★	TEENS ★★★
YOUNG ADULTS ★★★		OVER 30 ★★½	SENIORS ★★

What it is Simulator ride and animal exhibit. **Scope and scale** Major attraction. **When to go** Avoid going immediately following a Shamu show; wait will be shorter before 11 a.m. and after 4 p.m. **Authors' rating** Animal exhibit is better than the simulator; ★★★½. **Duration of ride** 5 minutes for simulator; at your own pace for exhibit. **Loading speed** Moderate.

DESCRIPTION AND COMMENTS Wild Arctic combines a mediocre simulator ride with a spectacular animal habitat, featuring huge polar bears, blubbery walruses, and sweet-faced beluga whales. The usually long line gives you the option of not riding the simulator—a great idea if you're prone to motion sickness, or have experienced the superior simulators at Disney and Universal. Unfortunately, skipping the simulator will not allow you to enter Wild Artic any sooner; you will still have to watch the simulator's movie before entering.

The simulator provides a bumpy ride aboard a specially designed 59-passenger "helicopter." Once passengers are safely strapped in, the ride ostensibly takes visitors to a remote Arctic research station (the wildlife habitat). On the way, riders fly over polar bears and walruses, but, of course, Things Go Horribly Wrong. A storm blows through, the engine inconveniently fails during an avalanche, and there is much wailing and gnashing of teeth. The loud hullabaloo and dated effects amount to nothing in particular, and in the end you make it to the station unscathed.

As you step off the simulator, or if you bypass it, you'll enter a cavernous, fog-filled room. A walkway on the far side overlooks a large pool that is home to a few beluga whales, and if you're lucky, some cute harbor seals. This room establishes the Arctic theme, but unless it's feeding time, the animals rarely surface here.

Proceed down a wooden ramp and you may come face to face with an enormous polar bear. The most famous inhabitants of this exhibit are twins, Klondike and Snow. The duo received tons of media coverage after they were abandoned by their mother and hand-raised at the Denver Zoo. SeaWorld uses toys and enrichment devices to keep the bears occupied. Variations in their schedule help keep them on their toes, so feeding times change frequently. Next to the bears are the gigantic walruses. These animals are often lounging near the glass or swimming lazily by.

As you descend farther into the exhibit, you'll discover a deep, underwater viewing area. Swarms of fish circle in the polar bear exhibit. If you're lucky, you'll spot a bear diving for fish. In addition, the underwater view gives you a real sense of the walruses' immense size. If it's quiet, you can also hear the deep, reverberating vocalizations of these large beasts. This is also the best location to catch a glimpse of the beluga whales. Looking like puffy, bulbous dolphins, these gentle creatures glide through the water. On occasion, a few playful harbor seals will join them. These crazy critters will come right up to the glass for a staring match with you.

TOURING TIPS   Wild Arctic has two queues: "By Air," which is for the simulator, and "By Land," which still makes you watch the simulator movie, but without all the jarring effects of the ride. Given the so-so quality of the simulator ride, we recommend skipping it if there's a significant line. The animals are definitely worth seeing, though. As in all animal exhibits, several SeaWorld educators are scattered around to answer any questions. Here, they are easy to spot in bright red parkas.

The simulator holds nearly 60 riders, who flood the animal area after each trip. Hang back behind the crowd for a few minutes when the simulator offloads and wait for the masses to clear. Then you can have the area next to the beluga whales mostly to yourself until the ride dumps off the next group.

If this isn't close enough to the whales for you, try the Beluga Interaction Program, where you can swim with, feed, and even attempt to signal to these sub-Arctic mammoths. The price for this program is not cheap, but if you are a beluga enthusiast willing to drop $179, you can make reservations online or by calling ☎ 800-327-2424.

Behind-the-Scenes Tours   ★★★

APPEAL BY AGE PRESCHOOL ★★½	GRADE SCHOOL ★★★½	TEENS ★★½
YOUNG ADULTS ★★★	OVER 30 ★★★½	SENIORS ★★★★

What it is Just what the name implies. **Scope and scale** Major attraction. **When to go** Check education counter for schedule. **Special comments** Cost is $16 for adults, $12 for children ages 3–9 during peak seasons, less in off seasons. **Authors' rating** A great deal; ★★★.

DESCRIPTION AND COMMENTS   Three 60-minute tours are extremely informative and entertaining and well worth the additional charge. A variety of subjects and areas are covered, and the tours and times vary according to the park's (and the animals') schedules. The three different tours include a look at the animal rescue program, the shark tank at Terrors of the Deep, and the penguins at Penguin Encounter at Wild Arctic. A comprehensive six-hour tour including lunch is also offered.

TOURING TIPS   Advance reservations are not accepted for these tours. You must stop by the guided-tour counter at the front of the park on the day of your visit or reserve a spot on the park's Web site (**www.sea world.com**). If you know you'll want to take one of the tours, we recommend making reservations online because the spots fill quickly and reservations are on a first-come, first-served basis.

Taking an hour out of your SeaWorld visit for these tours will require careful planning, but for sea-life enthusiasts, it's a neat experience. Longer tours are also available, and the price increases with each of these tours, but places like the Dolphin Nursery may be worth a few extra dollars.

Marine Mammal Keeper Experience ★★★

APPEAL BY AGE	PRESCHOOL †	GRADE SCHOOL †	TEENS ★★★★
YOUNG ADULTS ★★★★		OVER 30 ★★★	SENIORS ★★½

† Preschoolers and grade-school kids are not old enough.

What it is Chance to shadow a SeaWorld trainer for a day. **Scope and scale** Major attraction. **When to go** Program begins at 7 a.m. **Special comments** Costs $399 (admission is included); participants must be at least 13 years old and 52" tall; passport holders receive a $29 discount. **Authors' rating** Extremely expensive, but worth it for enthusiasts; ★★★.

DESCRIPTION AND COMMENTS   Shadow a genuine SeaWorld trainer during this eight-hour program. Learn through hands-on experience how Sea-World staff members care for and train their animals, from stuffing vitamins into a slimy fish to positive-reinforcement training techniques. The fee includes lunch, a T-shirt, souvenir photo, and a seven-day pass to SeaWorld.

TOURING TIPS   Attendance for this program is limited to four people per day. Calling up to six months ahead is best, but cancellations do occur. For information and reservations, call ☎ 800-423-1178. Participants must be in good physical condition and at least 13 years old.

DINING

SEAWORLD OFFERS MUCH MORE than the usual theme-park fare of burgers and fries. The food for the most part is very good, and prices are a bit lower than at Disney World.

unofficial **TIP**
Cypress Bakery opens early and offers fantastic breakfast breads and pastries.

Your feasting can begin at **Cypress Bakery,** which opens at 8:30 a.m. during the busy season and at 8:45 a.m. otherwise. Choose from a dizzying array of wonderful pastries, cakes, and muffins to enjoy while you plan your day.

Also offered in the morning is a SeaWorld character breakfast, held from 8:45 to 10 a.m. at the **Seafire Inn** in the new Waterfront area. A buffet with classic offerings like scrambled eggs, pancakes, muffins, and fruit is served for $14.95 (adults) and $9.95 (children ages 3 to 9); children under age 3 eat free with reservations. Speaking of reservations, they are recommended, though walk-ups will be seated on availability. Reservations can be made by calling ☎ 800-327-2420. Usually only one character is present, often Shamu.

For a more toothsome experience, try **Sharks Underwater Grill** at the Shark Encounter attraction, which offers "Floribbean" cuisine served next to floor-to-ceiling windows on the shark tank. A typical meal will run $20 per person at this ostensibly upscale eatery.

For quick service, try **Mango Joe's café** for fajitas, salads, and sandwiches; **Mama's Kitchen** for barbecue sandwiches, po'boys, and more; or **Smoky Creek Grill** for barbecue. Another favorite: the hand-carved sandwiches at **The Deli** in the Hospitality House.

Another unique option is the **Backstage at *Believe!*** program (formerly Dine with Shamu), which allows guests to enjoy a buffet-style meal alongside the killer-whale tanks, all the while mingling with trainers and observing behind-the-scenes training exercises. Cost is $37 plus tax for adults and $19 plus tax for kids ages 3 to 9 in addition

unofficial **TIP**
Want to eat alongside Shamu? Try the Backstage at *Believe!* program.

to park admission. During holiday seasons, this experience can sell out months ahead of time. Even during the slower times of year, it's best to call a few weeks in advance to purchase tickets.

Along the Waterfront there are several options, including the **Spice Mill,** a walk-up cafe with selections like jerk chicken, jambalaya, and a saffron chef salad. There's also **Voyager's Wood Fired Pizza,** where the pizza is strangely served on top of a bed of waffle fries. Other dishes include pasta dishes and the tasty Mediterranean foccacia club sandwich.

SHOPPING

UNLIKE AT DISNEY, SHOPPING AT SEAWORLD isn't an attraction in and of itself. There is, of course, a huge selection of SeaWorld merchandise. Some of it is unique, and prices are relatively reasonable. Fans of ocean wildlife can find a vast array of marine merchandise, ranging from high-quality, expensive sculptures to T-shirts, beach towels, and knickknacks. Children will be overwhelmed by the huge selection of stuffed animals, and parents will be pleased by their low prices—many small- to medium-sized toys are priced under $10. Budweiser enthusiasts will enjoy the large selection of Anheuser-Busch merchandise, including beer mugs, caps, and nice golf shirts.

Along the Waterfront area, there are more shopping selections, like the **Tropica Trading Shop** with goods from Africa, Bali, and Indonesia, among other origins, and do-it-yourself shops like a bead store and a doll factory.

DISCOVERY COVE

INSPIRED BY A LARGE NUMBER OF REQUESTS for dolphin swims as well as the success of the original Dolphin Interaction Program, Sea-World created Discovery Cove. This intimate subpark is a welcome departure from the hustle and bustle of other Orlando parks; the relaxed pace here could be the overstimulated family's ticket back to mental health. With a focus on personal service and one-on-one animal encounters, Discovery Cove admits only 1,000 guests per day. The park is also an all-inclusive experience so once you enter, you don't need to open your wallet; provided are: all meals, snacks and beverages plus all animal interactions and swim gear, even parking and a pass to your choice of either SeaWorld or Busch Gardens. The tranquil setting and unobtrusive theming make this park unique for central Florida. Why, there are only two gift shops! And you don't even have to walk through them to get out!

The main draw at Discovery Cove is the chance to swim with a troupe of 30 Atlantic bottlenose dolphins. The 30-minute dolphin swim experience is open to visitors ages 6 and up who are comfortable in the water. The experience begins with an orientation led by trainers and an opportunity for participants to ask questions before entering the dolphin lagoon. Next, small groups wade into shallow water for an introduction to the dolphins in their habitat. The experience culminates with one guest swimming into deeper water to be towed back by holding onto a dolphin's dorsal fin. Afterward, swimmers are invited to discuss their interaction with the trainers, and of course, purchase photographs of themselves with the dolphins. Although this is not an inexpensive endeavor, the singular nature of the experience cannot be overstated. The dolphins are playful, friendly, and frankly amazing to be around. This is as hands-on as it gets. Be aware that you're dealing with a powerful mischievous animal in its element, so don't be surprised if you get splashed, squirted, or even affectionately bonked with a flipper or fluke. The trainers are always in control, though, so there is nothing to fear. Overall, if this is to your taste at all, it's not to be missed. Authors' rating? Five stars.

unofficial **TIP**
Swimming with the fishes: spend a relaxing day at Discovery Cove, surrounded by a pod of dolphins!

Be careful about planning who does what at Discovery Cove. The perils of being left out are illustrated by this letter sent in by a mother of three from Croydon, England:

> *Only two of the five [in our group] swam with the dolphins because that is the only booking we could get. We would recommend that all people in the party swim with the dolphins to avoid the awful, sad feeling of being left out that three of us had. The two children refused to look at their brother, and Dad just wanted to go home. Dad felt guilty, and what was supposed to be the highlight of the trip turned into a downer.*

Not an ideal situation. If you're visiting Discovery Cove as a group, try to time your visit so everyone who wants to swim with the dolphins can.

discovery cove

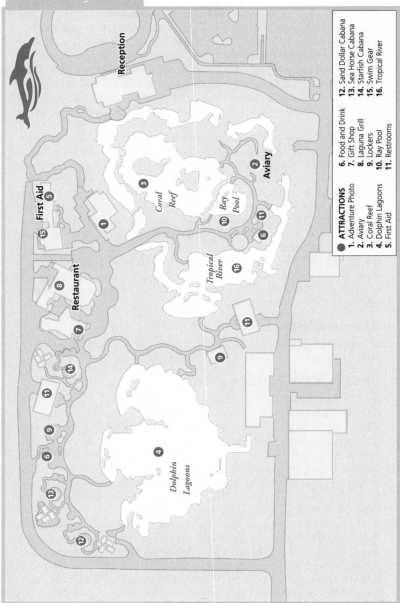

Reception

Coral Reef

Ray Pool

Aviary

Tropical River

First Aid

Restaurant

Dolphin Lagoons

● **ATTRACTIONS**
1. Adventure Photo
2. Aviary
3. Coral Reef
4. Dolphin Lagoons
5. First Aid

6. Food and Drink
7. Gift Shop
8. Laguna Grill
9. Lockers
10. Ray Pool
11. Restrooms

12. Sand Dollar Cabana
13. Sea Horse Cabana
14. Starfish Cabana
15. Swim Gear
16. Tropical River

Other exhibit areas at Discovery Cove include the Coral Reef, the Aviary, the Ray Pool, and the Freshwater Lagoon. You can snorkel or swim in the Coral Reef, which houses thousands of exotic fish and dozens of rays as well as an underwater shipwreck and hidden grottoes. In the Aviary, you can touch and feed gorgeous tropical birds. Stingrays occupy the small Ray Pool next to the Coral Reef; you can wade in among them, under the guidance of a lifeguard. The Freshwater Lagoon is just a salt-free rocky pond, empty of aquatic life. The park is threaded by the freshwater Tropical River, in which you can float or swim to all these areas. Pleasant beaches serve as pathways connecting the attractions.

Guests at Discovery Cove need not be exceptional swimmers—the water is shallow and so heavily salted that it's very difficult not to float. Watchful lifeguards are omnipresent. You'll need to wear your bathing suit and pool shoes as well as a cover-up. On rare days when it's too cold to swim in Orlando, guests are provided with free wetsuits. The park also supplies masks and snorkels, and you get to keep the snorkel (after all, nobody wants to reuse those). Discovery Cove provides "fish"-friendly sunscreen: guests may not use their own sunscreen. You must also remove all watches and jewelry (except wedding bands), as they might end up getting swallowed by the animals if you lose them. Free lockers enable you to stow everything you need to put away, all day. Comfortable, clean, well-appointed bathrooms and showers are also provided.

GETTING THERE

DISCOVERY COVE IS LOCATED DIRECTLY across the Central Florida Parkway from SeaWorld. Parking is free.

PRICES AND RESERVATIONS

DISCOVERY COVE IS OPEN from 9 a.m. until 5:30 p.m. every day of the year. Because admission is limited to 1,000 guests per day, you should purchase tickets well in advance by calling ☎ 877-4-DISCOVERY or visiting **www.discoverycove.com.** There are two admission options. The all-inclusive package is $259 to $279, tax included, (depending on season) per person and includes the dolphin swim, one meal at the Laguna Grill restaurant, unlimited access to the Ray Pool, Coral Reef, Aviary, and Tropical River; use of beach umbrellas, lounge chairs, towels, lockers, and swim and snorkel gear.

If you're not interested in the dolphin swim, the Non-Dolphin Package is $159 to $179 (depending on season) per person for the day and includes everything but the dolphin encounter. Discovery Cove admission includes parking at Discovery Cove as well as a seven-day, unlimited-use pass to either SeaWorld Orlando or Busch Gardens Tampa Bay, making the high price tag a bit easier to swallow. The

Trainer for a Day package includes everything the all-inclusive dolphin package does, along with a second enhanced dolphin experience and backstage tours of the dolphin and shark areas. Admission to participate is $429 to $449, plus tax (depending on season).

ARRIVING

ALTHOUGH THE PARK PROPER doesn't open until 9 a.m., the entrance hall usually opens about 8 a.m., although during peak seasons the park does open at 7:30 a.m. It's not a bad idea to get there a little early, because if you do, you can be among the first guests to register for your dolphin interaction. Guests are assigned time slots for the dolphin swims throughout the day, but you're not assigned your time slot until you show up on the day of your reservation (unless you request it in advance). The later you register, the later in the day your dolphin swim will be. Dolphins are generally more active in the morning, and once you do the interaction, you can spend the rest of your day lazily snorkeling or snoozing on the beach (without worrying about missing your appointment with Flipper).

On registering, you'll be asked to provide a credit card number. You'll then be issued a lanyard card with your picture on it. This card corresponds to the credit card you just gave, so it can be used for purchases anywhere in Discovery Cove. This means you can stow your wallet or purse in a locker for your whole stay. The locker key is also on a lanyard, so it's very easy to keep up with everything.

You'll be assigned one of three cabanas as your meeting place for the dolphin interaction. These are easy to find, because Discovery Cove is really not that large. Show up about five minutes before your assigned time. A trainer will give a short orientation, and then it's off to the dolphin swim. Enjoy.

PART EIGHT

UNIVERSAL ORLANDO

DISNEY-MGM STUDIOS *versus* UNIVERSAL STUDIOS FLORIDA

DISNEY-MGM STUDIOS AND UNIVERSAL STUDIOS FLORIDA are direct competitors. Because both are large and expensive and require at least one day to see, some guests must choose one park over the other. To help you decide, we present a head-to-head comparison of the two parks. In the summer of 1999, Universal launched its second major theme park, Universal's Islands of Adventure, which competes directly with Disney's Magic Kingdom. (Universal Studios Florida theme park, Islands of Adventure theme park, the three Universal hotels, and the CityWalk complex are collectively known as Universal Orlando.)

Both Disney-MGM Studios and Universal Studios Florida draw their theme and inspiration from film and television. Both offer movie- and TV-themed rides and shows, some of which are just for fun, while others provide an educational, behind-the-scenes introduction to the cinematic arts.

Unlike Disney-MGM, Universal Studios Florida's open area includes the entire back lot, where guests can walk at leisure among movie sets. Universal Studios Florida is about twice as large as Disney-MGM, and because almost all of it is open to the public, the crowding and congestion so familiar at Disney-MGM are eliminated. Universal Studios has plenty of elbow room.

unofficial **TIP**
Half of Disney-MGM Studios is off limits to guests—except by guided tour, while most all of Universal Studios Florida is open to exploration.

Both parks include working film and television-production studios. Guests are more likely, however, to see a movie, commercial, or television production in progress at Universal Studios than at Disney-MGM. On any day, production crews will be shooting on the Universal back lot in full view of guests who care to watch.

Attractions are excellent at both parks, though Disney-MGM attractions are on average engineered to move people more efficiently. Each park offers stellar attractions that break new ground, transcending in power, originality, and technology any prior standard for theme-park entertainment. Universal offers Revenge of the Mummy, an indoor roller coaster that combines space-age robotics with live effects and pyrotechnics; *Terminator 2: 3-D*, which we consider the most extraordinary theater attraction in any American theme park; and *Men in Black* Alien Attack, an interactive high-tech ride where guests' actions determine the ending of the story. Disney-MGM Studios features *The Twilight Zone* Tower of Terror, Disney's best attraction to date in our book; Rock 'n' Roller Coaster, an indoor coaster that's launched like a jet off an aircraft carrier; and Jim Henson's *Muppet-Vision 3-D,* a zany theater attraction.

Amazingly, and to the visitor's advantage, each park offers a completely different product mix, so there is little or no redundancy for a person who visits both. Disney-MGM and Universal Studios Florida each provide good exposure to the cinematic arts. Disney-MGM over the years has turned several of its better tours into infomercials for Disney films. At Universal, you can still learn about postproduction, soundstages, set creation, and special effects without being bludgeoned by promotional hype.

We recommend you try one of the studios. If you enjoy one, you probably will enjoy the other. If you have to choose, consider:

I. TOURING TIME If you tour efficiently, it takes about 8 to 10 hours to see Disney-MGM Studios (including a lunch break). Because Universal Studios Florida is larger and contains more rides and shows, touring, including one meal, takes about 9 to 11 hours. One reader laments:

> There is a lot more "standing" at Universal Studios, and it isn't as organized as [Disney-MGM]. Many of the attractions don't open until 10 a.m., and many shows seem to be going at the same time. We were not able to see nearly as many attractions at Universal as we were at [Disney-MGM] during the same amount of time. The one plus [at Universal Studios] is that there seems to be more property, and things are spaced out better so you have more elbow room.

As the reader observes, many Universal Studios attractions do not open until 10 a.m. or later. During one research visit, only a third of the major attractions were up and running when the park opened, and most theater attractions didn't schedule performances until 11 a.m. or after. This means that early in the day all park guests are concentrated among the relatively few attractions in operation. Disney-MGM Studios also has attractions that open late and shows that schedule no performances until late morning. The number of attractions operating at opening time varies according to season, at both parks. As a postscript, you will not have to worry about any of this if you tour either park using our touring plans. We'll keep you one jump ahead of the crowd and make sure that any given attraction is running by the time you get there.

2. CONVENIENCE If you're lodging along International Drive, Interstate 4's northeast corridor, the Orange Blossom Trail (US 441), or in Orlando, Universal Studios Florida is closer. If you're lodging along US 27 or FL 192 or in Kissimmee or Walt Disney World, Disney-MGM Studios is more convenient.

3. ENDURANCE Universal Studios Florida is larger and requires more walking than Disney-MGM, but it is also much less congested, so the walking is easier. Both parks offer wheelchairs and disabled access.

4. COST Both parks cost about the same for one-day admission, food, and incidentals, though Universal admission can be purchased in combo packages that include discounted passes to SeaWorld, Busch Gardens, and/or Wet 'n Wild. When Disney instituted the multiday Magic Your Way admission system in which you pay extra for park-hopping privileges, admissions to the minor parks, and the nonexpiring-pass option, Universal was quick to move in the opposite direction. With Universal multiday passports, all these extras are included free. Also consider that Universal discounts its admission tickets more deeply on its Web site than does Disney.

Universal Studios and Islands of Adventure frequently run admission specials. For two adults and two kids under age 10 who want to visit both Universal parks, Universal offers a free two-day, two-park park-hopping ticket for kids (ages 3 to 9) for every adult two-day, two-park ticket purchased online at **www.universalorlando.com.** Total cost is $212, including tax, for the whole family. It costs a whopping $656, tax included, for the same family to spend two days at Disney parks with park-hopping privileges.

5. BEST DAYS TO GO In order, Tuesdays, Mondays, Thursdays, and Wednesdays are best to visit Universal Studios Florida. For Disney-MGM Studios, see the calendar at **www.touringplans.com.**

6. WHEN TO ARRIVE For Disney-MGM, arrive with your ticket in hand 30 to 40 minutes before official opening time. For Universal Studios, arrive with your admission already purchased about 25 to 35 minutes before official opening time.

7. YOUNG CHILDREN Both Disney-MGM Studios and Universal Studios Florida are relatively adult entertainment offerings. By our reckoning, half the rides and shows at Disney-MGM and about two-thirds at Universal Studios have a significant potential for frightening young children.

8. FOOD For counter-service food, Universal Studios has a decided edge. Disney-MGM full-service restaurants are marginally better.

9. FASTPASS VERSUS UNIVERSAL EXPRESS Until recently, Disney's FASTPASS and Universal Express were roughly comparable. They both offered a system whereby any guest could schedule an appointment to experience an attraction later in the day with little or no waiting. Universal was the first to monkey with the status quo by making unlimited Universal Express passes available to guests in Universal-owned resorts. This meant that resort guests could go right to the front of the line anytime they wished. Next, Universal cooked up an enhanced Express pass, called Universal Express Plus, available to anyone but for an extra charge. Then they got really greedy. In the last installment, Universal terminated Universal Express privileges for all day guests unless they were willing to cough up the extra bucks for Universal Express Plus. This relegates day guests (that is, guests not staying at Universal-owned resorts) without Express Plus to long lines all day. We think that the new Universal system is self-defeating in the long run. The additional cost of Express Plus, combined with visions of endless lines if you don't have one, will keep many day guests away. Meanwhile, the numbers of guests purchasing Express Plus out of self-defense will increase to the point where they create their own long lines, rendering the Express Plus pass largely useless. A privilege isn't a privilege, after all, if everybody has it. Finally, FASTPASS and the old Universal Express system worked because setting appointment times to experience attractions helped to more equally distribute crowds throughout the day. Without appointments, Universal will return to the same recurring bottlenecks as before Universal Express was introduced. Disney, by way of contrast, has maintained an egalitarian philosophy with regard to FASTPASS. Though they're considering some FASTPASS perks for resort guests, the basic program will continue to be available for every Bubba, Bob, and Betty that pass through the turnstiles.

For the moment at least, here is how the current Universal Express program works. Guests at Universal hotels can access the Universal Express lines all day long simply by flashing their hotel keys. This can be especially valuable during peak season. With Universal Express Plus, for an extra $15 or $25 (depending on the season) you can buy a pass that provides line-cutting privileges at each Universal Express attraction at a given park. The Plus feature is good for only one day at one park (no park hopping), and for one ride only on each participating attraction. Speaking of participating attractions, more than 90% of rides and shows are included in the Universal Express program, a much higher percentage than are included in the FASTPASS program at the Disney parks.

UNIVERSAL ORLANDO

UNIVERSAL ORLANDO HAS TRANSFORMED into a complete destination resort, with two theme parks, three hotels, and a shopping, dining, and entertainment complex. The second theme park, Islands of Adventure, opened in 1999 with five themed areas.

A system of roads and two multistory parking facilities are connected by moving sidewalks to **CityWalk,** a shopping, dining, and nighttime-entertainment complex that also serves as a gateway to the Universal Studios Florida and **Islands of Adventure** theme parks. (For more on CityWalk dining, see page 335; for CityWalk entertainment, see page 314.)

LODGING AT UNIVERSAL ORLANDO

UNIVERSAL CURRENTLY HAS three operating resort hotels. The 750-room Portofino Bay Hotel is a gorgeous property set on an artificial bay and themed like an Italian coastal town. The 650-room Hard Rock Hotel is an ultracool "Hotel California" replica, with slick contemporary design and a hip, friendly attitude. The 1,000-room, Polynesian-themed Royal Pacific Resort is sumptuously decorated and richly appointed. All three are excellent hotels; the Portofino and the Hard Rock are on the pricey side, and the Royal Pacific ain't exactly cheap.

Like Disney, Universal offers a number of incentives to stay at their hotels. Perks available that mirror those offered by the Mouse include free parking, delivery to your room of purchases made in the parks, tickets and reservation information from hotel concierges, priority dining reservations at Universal restaurants, and the ability to charge purchases to your room account.

Otherwise, Universal offers complimentary transportation by bus or water taxi to Universal Studios, Islands of Adventure, CityWalk, SeaWorld, and Wet 'n Wild. Hotel guests may use the Universal Express program without limitation all day long (see following pages). Universal lodging guests are also eligible for "next available" table privileges at CityWalk restaurants and similar priority admission to Universal Orlando theme-park shows.

ARRIVING AT UNIVERSAL ORLANDO

THE UNIVERSAL ORLANDO COMPLEX can be accessed directly from Interstate 4. Once on site, you will be directed to park in one of two multi-tiered parking garages. Parking runs $10 for cars and $11 for RVs. Be sure to write down the location of your car before heading for the parks. From the garages, moving sidewalks deliver you to the Universal CityWalk dining, shopping, and entertainment venue described above. From CityWalk, you can access the main entrances of both Universal Studios Florida and Islands of Adventure theme parks. Even with the moving walkways, it takes about 10 to 12 minutes to commute from the garages to the entrances of the theme parks. If you are staying at Walt Disney World and don't have a car, Mears Transportation will shuttle you from your hotel to Universal and back for $13 to $15. Pick-up and return times are at your convenience. To schedule a shuttle call ☎ 407-423-5566 or 800-407-4275.

Universal offers One-day, Two-day, and Annual Passes.

Passes can be obtained in advance on the phone with your credit card at ☎ 800-711-0080. All prices are the same whether you buy your admission at the gate or in advance. Prices shown below include tax.

universal orlando

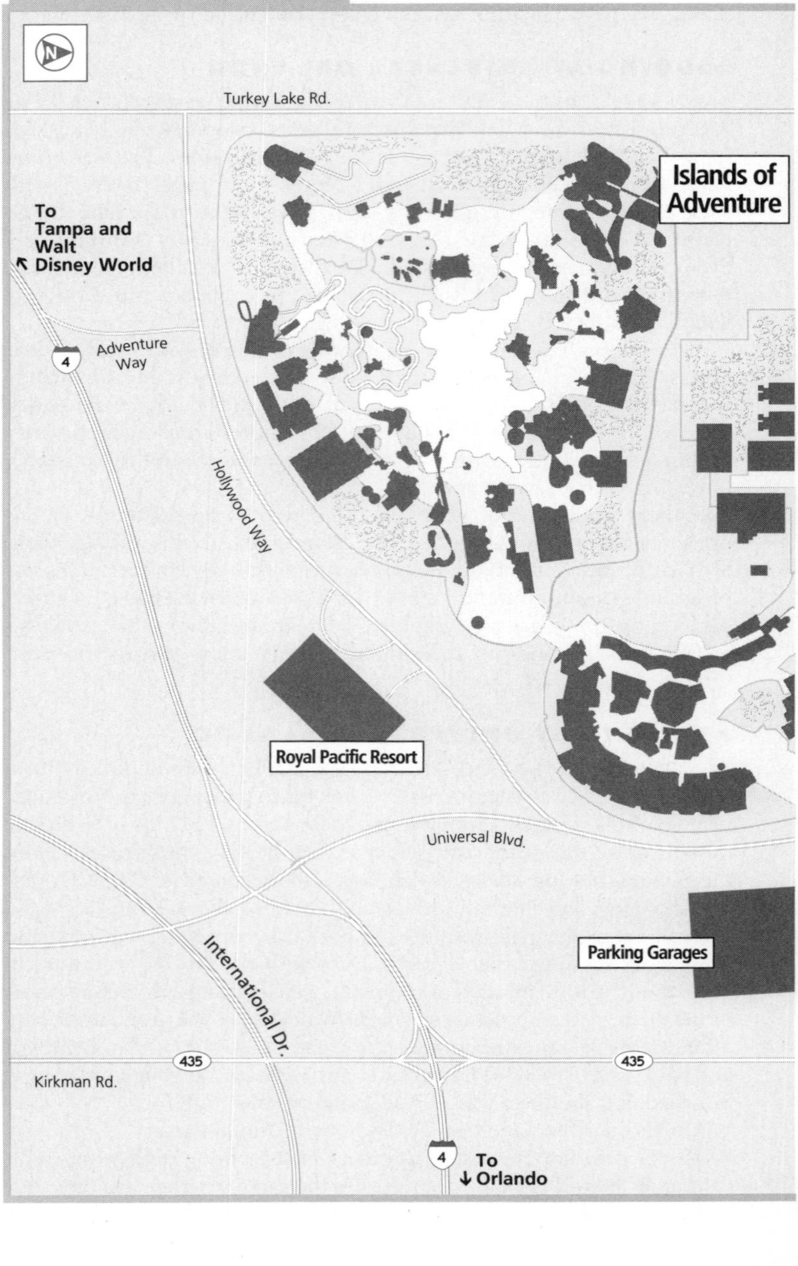

Turkey Lake Rd.

Islands of Adventure

To
Tampa and
Walt
Disney World

Adventure
Way

Hollywood Way

Royal Pacific Resort

Universal Blvd.

Parking Garages

International Dr.

435

435

Kirkman Rd.

To
↓ Orlando

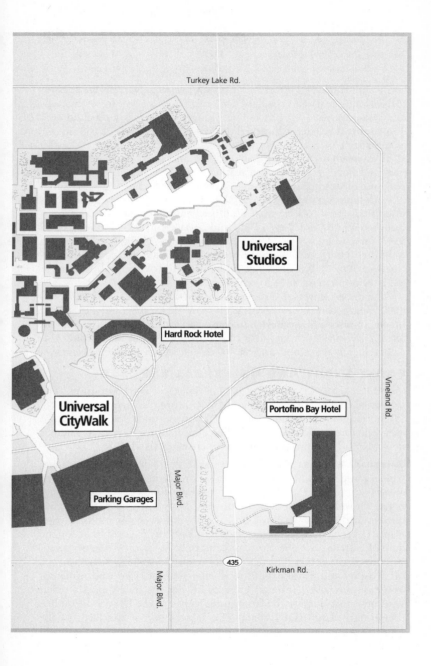

Turkey Lake Rd.

Universal
Studios

Hard Rock Hotel

Universal
CityWalk

Portofino Bay Hotel

Vineland Rd.

Parking Garages

Major Blvd.

435

Kirkman Rd.

Major Blvd.

	Adults	Children (3–9)
One-day, One-park Pass	$64	$51
Two-day, Two-park Pass	$118	All guests
Two-park Annual Power Pass	$129	All guests
Two-park Annual Preferred Pass	$193	All guests

Be sure to check Universal's Web site (**www.universalorlando.com**) for seasonal deals and specials. One recurring special: for every two-day, two-park pass you buy online, you get a free pass for a child ages 3 to 9, plus three free additional days of admission (check the site for availability).

If you want to visit more than one park on a given day, have your park pass and hand stamped when exiting your first park. At your second park, use the readmission turnstile, showing your stamped pass and hand.

Combination passes are available: a four-park, 14-day pass allows unlimited entry to Universal Studios, Universal's Islands of Adventure, SeaWorld, and Wet 'n Wild and costs about $204 for adults and $167 for children (ages 3 to 9). A five-park, 14-day pass provides unlimited entry to Universal Studios, Universal's Islands of Adventure, SeaWorld, Wet 'n Wild, and Busch Gardens and costs about $252 for adults and $214 for children.

The main Universal Orlando information number is ☎ 407-363-8000. Reach Guest Services at ☎ 407-224-4233, schedule a character lunch at **www.universalorlando.com,** and order tickets by mail at ☎ 877-247-5561. The numbers for Lost and Found are ☎ 407-224-4244 (Universal Studios) and ☎ 407-224-4245 (Islands of Adventure).

EARLY ENTRY AND UNIVERSAL EXPRESS

UNIVERSAL NO LONGER OPERATES an early-entry program. The Universal Express program is actually two programs, one for Universal hotel guests, called Universal Express, and one available to everyone for an additional fee, called Universal Express Plus. There is *no longer* a basic program similar to Disney's FASTPASS.

UNIVERSAL EXPRESS PLUS If you're willing to drop the extra cash, you can upgrade your regular ticket to Universal Express Plus, which allows you to use the Express entrance one time only at each designated Universal Express attraction (although we have found that one-time use policy is loose and is only enforced for major attractions on crowded days). Universal Express Plus is good only for the date of purchase *at one park,* and can only be used by one person.

Universal Express Plus prices vary from $15 to $53, cheaper in the off-seasons and more expensive during peak seasons and holidays. You can purchase Universal Express Plus at the theme park's ticket windows, just outside the front gates. Once in the Universal Studios theme park, Universal Express Plus is available at the Back to the Future Store, the Cartoon Store, Shaiken's Souvenirs, and Nickstuff. Inside Islands of Adventure, you can buy Universal Express Plus at

Jurassic Outfitters, Toon Extra, Treasures of Poseidon, the Marvel Alterniverse Store, and at Port Merchants Cart. Universal Express Plus is available on the Internet, but only up to a few months in advance. You must also know what date you plan on using Universal Express Plus, because different dates have different prices.

UNIVERSAL EXPRESS PROGRAM AVAILABLE TO UNIVERSAL RESORT GUESTS The Universal Express program for Universal resort guests allows guests to bypass the regular line anytime and as often as desired by simply showing their room key. This perk far surpasses any perk accorded to guests of Disney resorts.

How Universal Express Impacts Crowd Conditions at the Attractions

This system dramatically affects crowd movement (and touring plans) in the Universal parks. A woman from Yorktown, Virginia, writes:

> *People in the* [Express] *line were let in at a rate of about ten to one over the regular-line folks. This created bottlenecks and long waits for people who didn't have the Express privilege at the very times when it is supposed to be easier to get around!*

SINGLES LINES

AND THERE'S YET ANOTHER OPTION: the singles line. Several attractions have this special line for guests riding alone. As Universal employees will tell you, this line is often even faster than the Express line. We strongly recommend you use the singles line whenever possible, as it will decrease your overall wait and leave more time for repeat rides or just bumming around the parks.

LOCKERS

UNIVERSAL HAS INSTITUTED a mandatory locker system at its big thrill rides. Bags and other items must be placed in lockers outside of the attraction. The lockers are free for the first 1.5 hours. Then, starting at $2 for 2 hours, the price jumps $2 for each additional half-hour, that is, $4 for 2.5 hours, $6 for 3 hours, and so on. If you reach or exceed 5 hours, the price is $14.

The locker banks are easy to find outside of each attraction. Each bank has a small computer in the center. When the sun is bright, the screen is almost impossible to read, so have someone block the sun or use a different computer. After selecting your language, you press your thumb onto the keypad and have your fingerprint scanned. We've seen people walk off cursing at this step, having repeated it over and over with no success. Most patrons press their thumb down too hard. The computer cannot read your thumbprint if it's squished together, so take a deep breathe and just place your thumb on the scanner.

After your thumb scans, you will receive a locker number. Write it down! When you return from your ride, go to the same kiosk machine, enter your locker number, and scan your thumb again. At guest services, family-sized lockers are available for $10 for the entire day, but remember that only the person who used their thumb to get the locker can retrieve anything from the locker.

UNIVERSAL, KIDS, AND SCARY STUFF

ALTHOUGH THERE'S PLENTY FOR YOUNGER CHILDREN to enjoy at the Universal parks, the majority of the major attractions have the potential for wigging out kids under 8 years of age. At Universal Studios Florida, forget Revenge of the Mummy, *Twister, Earthquake, Jaws, Men in Black, Back to the Future*—The Ride, and *Terminator 2: 3-D*. The first part of the E.T. ride is a little intense for a few preschoolers, but the end is all happiness and harmony. Interestingly, very few families report problems with *Beetlejuice's Rock 'n' Roll Graveyard Revue* or *The Universal Horror Make-up Show*. Anything not listed is pretty benign.

unofficial **TIP**
If you have tots ages 7 or younger, consider that many of Universal's attractions can be frightening for little ones.

At Universal's Islands of Adventure, watch out for The Incredible Hulk Coaster, Dr. Doom's Fearfall, The Adventures of Spider-Man, the *Jurassic Park* River Adventure, Dueling Dragons, and *Poseidon's Fury!* Popeye & Bluto's Bilge-Rat Barges is wet and wild, but most younger children handle it well. Dudley Do-Right's Ripsaw Falls is a toss-up, to be considered only if your kids like water-flume rides. The *Sinbad* stunt show includes some explosions and startling special effects, but once again, children tolerate it well. Nothing else should pose a problem.

IVILLAGE LIVE AND BLUE MAN GROUP

IN 2007, UNIVERSAL ORLANDO is adding two theater productions to its list of attractions. *iVillage Live* plays at Islands of Adventure theme park, while Universal Studios theme park is home to *Blue Man Group*. Though the shows are performed inside the theme parks, park admission is not required. *iVillage Live* requires advance reservations but does not charge admission. *Blue Man Group* tickets can be purchased online or at the Universal Box Office.

iVillage Live

iVillage Live is a talk show based on the iVillage Web site, an online community focusing on women's and family issues. Scheduled for noon daily, the show is broadcast live on select NBC stations, Bravo, and on the Internet at **www.ivillagelive.com.** The production includes extensive audience participation, where guests are invited to share stories about issues from pregnancy to shopping. Free tickets for the 300-person audience are available by phone at ☎ 866-448-5360 or via e-mail at **ivillage livetickets@nbcuni.com.** Currently, you must register at least 24 hours before show time, but if the show proves to be a big hit, you may have to apply weeks in advance. After you call or e-mail your ticket request, a Universal agent will get back to you with a ticket confirmation. *iVillage Live* is performed at the former Toon Ampitheatre at Universal's Islands of Adventure. When your reservation is confirmed you will be given instructions concerning when and where to enter the park.

Blue Man Group (opens June 2007)

Blue Man Group gives Orlando its first large-scale introduction to that nebulous genre called "performance art." If the designation "performance art" confuses you, relax—it won't hurt a bit. *Blue Man Group* serves up a stunning show that can be appreciated by all kinds of folks ages 6 to 90.

The three blue men are just that—blue—and bald and mute. Wearing black clothing and skull caps slathered with bright blue grease paint, they deliver a fast-paced show that uses music (mostly percussion) and multimedia effects to make light of contemporary art and life in the information age. The Universal act is just one expression of a franchise that started with three friends in New York's East Village. Now you can catch their zany, wacky, smart stuff in New York, Las Vegas, Boston, Chicago, Berlin, and Toronto, among other places.

Funny, sometimes poignant, and always compelling, *Blue Man Group* pounds out vital, visceral tribal rhythms on complex instruments (made of PVC pipes) that could pass for industrial intestines, and makes seemingly spontaneous eruptions of visual art rendered with marshmallows and a mysterious goo. Their weekly supplies include 25.5 pounds of Cap'n Crunch, 60 Twinkies, 75 gallons of Jell-O, 996 marshmallows, 9.5 gallons of paint, and 185 miles, yes, miles, of rolled recycled paper. If all this sounds silly, it is, but it's also strangely thought-provoking and deals with topics such as the value of modern art, DNA, the persistence of vision, the way rock music moves you, and how we are all connected. (*Hint:* It's not the Internet.)

A live percussion band backs the *Blue Man Group* with a relentless and totally engrossing industrial dance riff. The band resides in long dark alcoves above the stage. At just the right moments, their lofts are lit to reveal a group of neon-colored pulsating skeletons.

Audience participation completes the Blue Man experience. The blue men often move into the audience to bring audience members on stage. At the end of the show, the entire audience is involved in an effort to move a sea of paper across the theater. And a lot of folks can't help standing up to dance—and laugh. Magicians for the creative spirit that resides in us all, the *Blue Man Group* make everyone a co-conspirator in a culminating joyous explosion.

This show is decidedly different and requires an open mind to be appreciated. It also helps to be a little loose, because, like it or not, everybody gets sucked into the production and leaves the theater a little bit lighter in spirit. If you don't want to be pulled onstage to become a part of the improvisation, don't sit in the first half dozen or so rows.

The Universal Box Office is open 9 a.m. to 7 p.m. EST, or you can purchase tickets online at **www.universalorlando.com/bmg_buy_tickets .html#tickets.** Matinee tickets run $45 to $55 for adults and $39 to $45 for children ages 3 through 9. Evening shows are $59 to $69 for adults and $49 to $59 for children. The show is staged in the former Nick Studios Live theater inside Universal Studios. We recommend seats at least 15 rows back from the stage.

∎ UNIVERSAL STUDIOS FLORIDA

UNIVERSAL CITY STUDIOS INC. HAS RUN a studios tour and movie-themed tourist attraction for more than 30 years, predating all Disney parks except Disneyland. In the early 1980s, Universal announced plans to build a new theme-park complex in Florida. But while Universal labored over its new project, Disney jumped into high gear and rushed its own studios and theme park into the market, beating Universal by about two years.

Universal Studios Florida opened in June 1990. At that time, it was almost four times the size of Disney-MGM Studios (Disney-MGM has since expanded somewhat), with much more of the facility accessible to visitors. Like its sister facility in Hollywood, Universal Studios Florida is spacious, beautifully landscaped, meticulously clean, and delightfully varied in its entertainment. Rides are exciting and innovative and, as with many Disney rides, focus on familiar and/or beloved movie characters or situations.

On Universal Studios Florida's *E.T.* ride, you escape the authorities on a flying bike and leave Earth to visit E.T.'s home planet. On the *Jaws* ride, the persistent great white shark makes heart-stopping assaults on your small boat, and in *Earthquake*—The Big One, special effects create one of the most realistic earthquake simulations ever produced. Guests also ride in a DeLorean–cum–time machine in yet another chase, this one based on the film *Back to the Future,* and fight alien bugs with zapper guns on the *Men in Black* ride. New attractions based on the *Jimmy Neutron* and *Shrek* movies raised the entertainment stakes even higher. Universal opened in spring 2004 their most ambitious attraction to date: Revenge of the Mummy. Replacing longtime Universal Studios fixture Kongfrontation and based on *The Mummy* film franchise, it's a combination of roller coaster and dark ride with maglev coaster tracks, robotics technology adapted from the Mars lander, and a pyrotechnic "ceiling of flame."

While these rides incorporate state-of-the-art technology and live up to their billing in terms of excitement, creativity, uniqueness, and special effects, some lack the capacity to handle the number of guests who frequent major Florida tourist destinations. If a ride has great appeal but can accommodate only a small number of guests per ride or per hour, long lines form. It isn't unusual for the wait to exceed an hour and a quarter for the *E.T.* ride.

Not to Be Missed at Universal Studios Florida

Back to the Future—The Ride	Earthquake—The Big One
Jaws	Men in Black Alien Attack
Revenge of the Mummy	Shrek 4-D
Terminator 2: 3-D	Universal 360: A Cinesphere Spectacular

Happily, most shows and theater performances at Universal Studios Florida are in theaters that accommodate large numbers of people. Since many shows run continuously, waits usually don't exceed twice the show's performance time (15 to 30 minutes).

Universal Studios Florida is laid out in an upside-down-L configuration. Beyond the main entrance, a wide boulevard stretches past several shows and rides to Streets of America. Branching off this pedestrian thoroughfare to the right are five streets that access other areas of the studios and intersect a promenade circling a large lake.

The park is divided into six sections: Production Central, New York, Hollywood, San Francisco–Amity, Woody Woodpecker's KidZone, and World Expo. Where one section begins and another ends is blurry, but no matter. Guests orient themselves by the major rides, sets, and landmarks and refer, for instance, to "New York," "the waterfront," "over by *E.T.*," or "by Mel's Diner." The area of Universal Studios Florida open to visitors is about the size of Epcot.

The park offers all standard services and amenities, including stroller and wheelchair rental, lockers, diaper-changing and infant-nursing facilities, car assistance, and foreign-language assistance. Most of the park is accessible to disabled guests, and TDDs are available for the hearing impaired. Almost all services are in the Front Lot, just inside the main entrance.

UNIVERSAL STUDIOS FLORIDA ATTRACTIONS

Animal Actors on Location (Universal Express) ★★★

APPEAL BY AGE	PRESCHOOL ★★★★	GRADE SCHOOL ★★★★	TEENS ★★★
YOUNG ADULTS ★★★	OVER 30 ★★★		SENIORS ★★★★

What it is Animal-tricks and comedy show. **Scope and scale** Major attraction. **When to go** After you have experienced all rides. **Authors' rating** Cute li'l critters; ★★★. **Duration of presentation** 20 minutes. **Probable waiting time** 25 minutes.

DESCRIPTION AND COMMENTS This show integrates video segments with live sketches, jokes, and animal tricks performed onstage. The idea is to create eco-friendly family entertainment. Several of the animal thespians are veterans of television and movies; many were rescued from shelters.

universal studios florida

1. *Animal Actors on Location*
2. *Back to the Future*—The Ride
3. *Beetlejuice's Rock 'n' Roll Graveyard Revue*
4. The Boneyard
5. *A Day in the Park with Barney*
6. *Earthquake*—The Big One
7. *E.T. Adventure*
8. *Fear Factor Live*
9. *Fievel's Playland*
10. *Jaws*
11. Jimmy Neutron's Nicktoon Blast
12. Lucy, A Tribute
13. *Men in Black* Alien Attack
14. Revenge of the Mummy
15. *Shrek 4-D*
16. Sound Stage 54
17. *Terminator 2: 3-D*
18. *Twister*
19. *The Universal Horror Make-up Show*
20. *Universal 360°: A Cinesphere Spectacular*
21. Woody Woodpecker's KidZone

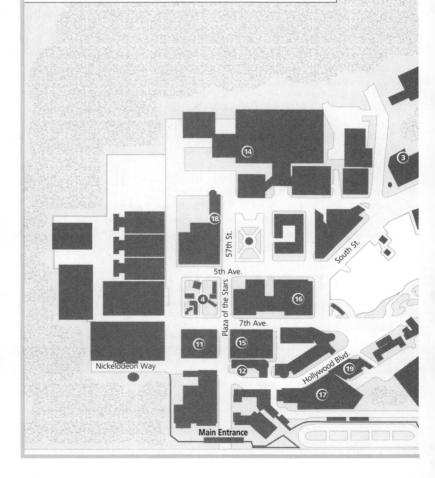

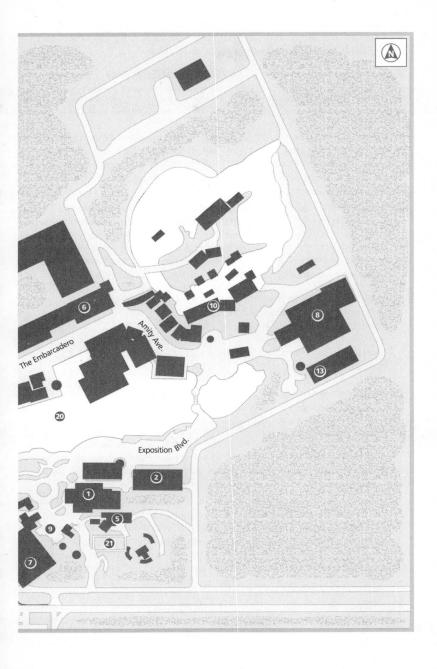

The Embarcadero

Amity Ave.

Exposition Blvd.

Audience members can participate as well—where else will you get the chance to hold an eight-foot albino reticulated python in your lap?

TOURING TIPS Check the daily entertainment schedule for show times. You shouldn't have any trouble getting in to this show.

Back to the Future—The Ride (Universal Express) ★★★★

APPEAL BY AGE	PRESCHOOL †	GRADE SCHOOL ★★★★	TEENS ★★★★
YOUNG ADULTS ★★★★		OVER 30 ★★★★	SENIORS ★★

† Preschoolers are generally too short to ride.

What it is Flight-simulator thrill ride. **Scope and scale** Headliner. **When to go** First thing in the morning after *Mummy* and *Men in Black*. **Special comments** Rough ride; may induce motion sickness. Must be 40" tall to ride. **Authors' rating** Not to be missed, if you have a strong stomach; ★★★★. **Duration of ride** 4½ minutes. **Loading speed** Moderate.

DESCRIPTION AND COMMENTS   Guests in Doc Brown's lab get caught up in a high-speed chase through time that spans a million years. An extremely intense simulator ride, *Back to the Future* is similar to Star Tours and Body Wars at Walt Disney World, but is much rougher and jerkier; the visual effects are wild and powerful. The vehicles (DeLorean time machines) in *Back to the Future* are much smaller than those of Star Tours and Body Wars.

TOURING TIPS   As soon as the park opens, guests stampede to *Mummy, Men in Black,* and *Back to the Future.* Our recommendation: be there at opening and join the rush. If you don't ride before 10:20 a.m., your wait may be exceptionally long. *Note:* Sitting in the rear seat of the car makes the ride more realistic.

Beetlejuice's Rock 'n' Roll Graveyard Revue (Universal Express) ★★★½

APPEAL BY AGE	PRESCHOOL ★★★★	GRADE SCHOOL ★★★★	TEENS ★★★★
YOUNG ADULTS ★★★★		OVER 30 ★★★★	SENIORS ★★★★

What it is Rock-and-roll stage show. **Scope and scale** Almost major attraction. **When to go** At your convenience. **Authors' rating** Outrageous; ★★★½. **Duration of presentation** 18 minutes. **Probable waiting time** None.

DESCRIPTION AND COMMENTS   Revamped in 2006, this high-powered rock-and-roll stage show stars Beetlejuice, Frankenstein, the Bride of Frankenstein, Wolfman, Dracula, and a pair of fly girls called Hip and Hop. The show features contemporary dance and pop songs rather than classic rock. High-energy, silly, bawdy, and generally funnier than it has any right to be, the new version brings this long-running *Revue* back to life (pun intended).

TOURING TIPS   Mercifully, this attraction is under cover.

The Blues Brothers

APPEAL BY AGE	PRESCHOOL ★★★	GRADE SCHOOL ★★★½	TEENS ★★★½
YOUNG ADULTS ★★★½		OVER 30 ★★★★	SENIORS ★★★★

What it is Blues concert. **Scope and scale** Diversion. **When to go** Scheduled show times. **Authors' rating** ★★★. **Special comments** A party in the street. **Duration of presentation** 15 minutes.

DESCRIPTION AND COMMENTS An impromtu concert featuring live impersonators singing and playing saxaphone with a background track. The show takes place on a stoop in the street scene, across from the Revenge of the Mummy. The show is one of the more unconventional diversions we've found. Jake and Elwood pull up in the infamous police cruiser from the Blues Brothers movies, and hop on stage. Interacting with the audience, they begin conga lines in the audience, turning the city set into a scene from a musical—people are literally dancing together in the streets.

TOURING TIPS The concert is a great pick-me-up and the short runtime keeps the energy high. Don't miss this little bit of magic. If you arrive early, you might be able to find a seat on a stoop across the street, but why would you want to sit?

A Day in the Park with Barney (Universal Express) ★★★★

APPEAL BY AGE	PRESCHOOL ★★★★★	GRADE SCHOOL ★★★	TEENS ★★
YOUNG ADULTS ★★★	OVER 30 ★★★		SENIORS ★★★

What it is Live character stage show. **Scope and scale** Major children's attraction. **When to go** Anytime. **Authors' rating** A great hit with preschoolers; ★★★★. **Duration of presentation** 12 minutes plus character greeting. **Probable waiting time** 15 minutes.

DESCRIPTION AND COMMENTS Barney, the purple dinosaur of public-television fame, leads a sing–along with the help of the audience and sidekicks Baby Bop and BJ. A short preshow gets the kids lathered up before they enter Barney's Park (the theater). Interesting theatrical effects include wind, falling leaves, clouds and stars in the simulated sky, and snow. After the show, Barney exits momentarily to allow parents and children to gather along the stage. He then returns and moves from child to child, hugging each and posing for photos.

TOURING TIPS If your child likes Barney, this show is a must. It's happy and upbeat, and the character greeting that follows is the best organized we've seen in any theme park. There's no line and no fighting for Barney's attention. Just relax by the rail and await your hug. There's also a great indoor play area nearby, designed especially for wee tykes.

Earthquake—The Big One (Universal Express) ★★★★

APPEAL BY AGE	PRESCHOOL ★★★	GRADE SCHOOL ★★★★	TEENS ★★★★
YOUNG ADULTS ★★★★	OVER 30 ★★★★		SENIORS ★★★★

What it is Combination theater presentation and adventure ride. **Scope and scale** Major attraction. **When to go** In the morning or late afternoon. **Special comments** May frighten young children. **Authors' rating** Not to be missed; ★★★★. **Duration of presentation** 20 minutes. **Loading speed** Moderate.

DESCRIPTION AND COMMENTS Film shows how miniatures are used to create special effects in earthquake movies, followed by a demonstration of how miniatures, blue screen, and matte painting are integrated with live-action stunt sequences (starring audience volunteers) to create a realistic final product. Afterward, guests board a subway from Oakland to San Francisco and experience an earthquake—the big one. Special effects range from fires and runaway trains to exploding tanker trucks and tidal waves. This is Universal's answer to Disney-MGM's Catastrophe Canyon. The special effects are comparable, but the field of vision is better at Catastrophe Canyon. Nonetheless, *Earthquake* is one of Universal's more compelling efforts.

TOURING TIPS Experience *Earthquake* after tackling the park's other rides.

E.T. Adventure (Universal Express) ★★★½

APPEAL BY AGE	PRESCHOOL ★★★★	GRADE SCHOOL ★★★★	TEENS ★★★
YOUNG ADULTS ★★★	OVER 30 ★★★★		SENIORS ★★★★

What it is Indoor adventure ride based on the *E.T.* movie. Scope and scale Major attraction. When to go Before noon; before 10 a.m. if you have small children. Authors' rating A happy reunion; ★★★½. Duration of ride 4½ minutes. Loading speed Moderate.

DESCRIPTION AND COMMENTS Guests aboard a bicycle-like conveyance escape with E.T. from earthly law enforcement officials and then journey to E.T.'s home planet. The attraction is similar to Peter Pan's Flight at the Magic Kingdom but is longer and has more elaborate special effects and a wilder ride.

TOURING TIPS Most preschoolers and grade-school children love *E.T.* We think it worth a 20- to 30-minute wait, but nothing longer. Lines build quickly after 10 a.m., and waits can be more than two hours on busy days. Ride in the morning or late afternoon. Guests who balk at sitting on the bicycle can ride in a comfortable gondola.

A mother from Columbus, Ohio, writes about horrendous lines at *E.T.*:

The line for E.T. *took two hours! The rest of the family waiting outside thought that we had gone to E.T.'s planet for real.*

A woman from Richmond, Virginia, objects to how Universal represents the waiting time:

We got into E.T. *without much wait, but the line is very deceptive. When you see a lot of people waiting outside and the sign says "ten-minute wait from this point," it means ten minutes until you are inside the building. But there's a very long wait inside [before] you get to the moving vehicles.*

Fear Factor Live ★★★½

APPEAL BY AGE	PRESCHOOL ½	GRADE SCHOOL ★★	TEENS ★★★★
YOUNG ADULTS ★★★	OVER 30 ★★★		SENIORS ★½

What it is Live version of the gross-out-stunt television show on NBC. Scope and scale Headliner. When to go 6 to 8 shows daily; crowds are smallest at the first and second-to-last shows. Authors' rating Great fun if you love the TV show; ★★★½. Duration of presentation 30 minutes.

DESCRIPTION AND COMMENTS *Fear Factor* is a live stage show in which up to six volunteers compete for one prize; this varies but is always a package that contains at least $400 worth of Universal goodies ranging from park tickets to T-shirts. Contestants must be 18 years or older (with a photo ID to prove it) and weigh at least 110 pounds. It is recommended that those demented enough to volunteer arrive at least 75 minutes before show time to sign papers and complete some obligatory training for the specific competitive events. Anyone who does not wish to compete in the stage show itself can sign up for the Critter Challenge or the Food Challenge (described below). With an adult's permission, volunteers as young as 16 can compete in the latter.

The stage show is performed in a covered theater and consists of three different challenges. In the first, all six contestants are suspended two-and-a-half stories in the air and try to hang onto a bar as long as possible. The difficulty is compounded by heavy-duty fans blasting the contestants' faces while they are holding on for dear life (are we having fun yet?). Only four people go on to the next round, and the person who hangs on to the bar the longest gets to choose his or her partner for the next event.

Once the first two contestants are eliminated, it's time for a brief intermission called the Desert Hat Ordeal. This involves the brave audience member–cum–lunatic who has signed up for the Critter Challenge. Prepared with eye goggles and a mouthpiece, the volunteer is put in a chair with a glass case over his or her head. A wheel is spun to determine what will be crawling over the volunteer's head; the creepy-crawly choices include spiders, snakes, roaches, and scorpions. The only incentive to participate is a free photo of the ordeal for contestants to take to their therapist.

In the second challenge, the four remaining contestants are split into two teams to compete in the Eel Tank Relay. This consists of one team member grabbing beanbags out of a tank full of eels and throwing them to his or her partner to catch in a bucket. Audience members drench the contestants with high-powered water guns, further spicing up the event. The team that buckets the most beanbags wins, with the winning team members going on to compete against each other in the final round for the $400 prize package.

As the stage is prepared for the finale, the folks who volunteered for the Food Challenge steel themselves for the Guess What's Crawling to Dinner event. Here four contestants are split into two teams and invited to drink a mixture of sour milk, mystery meat, and various live bugs that are all blended together on stage. The team that drinks the most of the mixture within the time limit wins the glorious prize of a plastic mug that says, "I Ate a Bug," a convenient euphemism for "I have the brain of a nematode." The winners (?) are asked to refrain from upchucking all over the audience as they return to their seats to watch the final challenge.

The last event has the two remaining contestants scramble up a wall to retrieve flags, jump into a car that is lifted in the air, then jump out of the car to retrieve more flags. When the required climbing, jumping, and flag grabbing are accomplished, the first contestant to remove a rocket launcher from the back seat of the car and hit a target on the stage wall wins.

Whether you participate or simply watch, this show will keep your innards in an uproar. But look at the bright side: eating the insect goop in the Food Challenge is the only free lunch available at any Orlando-area theme park.

TOURING TIPS Apparently, the odds are more in your favor for getting into Harvard than being chosen to appear on the TV version of *Fear Factor*, so if you've ever wanted a chance to test your mettle (sanity?), the theme-park show may be your big chance. Participants for the physical stunts are chosen early in the morning outside the theater, so be sure to head there first thing if you want to be a contestant. The victims—er, contestants—for the ick-factor stunts, like the bug-smoothie drinking, are chosen directly from the audience. Sit close to the front and wave your hands like crazy when it comes time for selection. Finally (and seriously), this show is too intense and too gross for children age 8 and under.

Fievel's Playland ★★★★

APPEAL BY AGE	PRESCHOOL ★★★★		GRADE SCHOOL ★★★★
TEENS —	YOUNG ADULTS —	OVER 30 —	SENIORS —

What it is Children's play area with waterslide. Scope and scale Minor attraction. When to go Anytime. Authors' rating A much-needed attraction for preschoolers; ★★★★. Probable waiting time 20–30 minutes for the waterslide; otherwise, no waiting.

DESCRIPTION AND COMMENTS Imaginative playground features ordinary household items reproduced on a giant scale, as a mouse would experience them. Preschoolers and grade-schoolers can climb nets, walk through a huge boot, splash in a sardine-can fountain, seesaw on huge spoons, and climb onto a cow skull. Most of the playground is reserved for preschoolers, but a waterslide–raft ride is open to all ages.

TOURING TIPS Walk into Fievel's Playland without waiting, and stay as long as you want. Younger children love the oversized items, and there's enough to keep teens and adults busy while little ones let off steam. The waterslide–raft ride is open to everyone but is extremely slow to load and carries only 300 riders per hour. With an average wait of 20 to 30 minutes, we don't think the 16-second ride is worth the trouble. Also, you're highly likely to get soaked.

Lack of shade is a major shortcoming of the entire attraction. Don't go during the heat of the day.

Jaws (Universal Express) ★★★★

APPEAL BY AGE	PRESCHOOL ★★★	GRADE SCHOOL ★★★★	TEENS ★★★★
YOUNG ADULTS ★★★★		OVER 30 ★★★★	SENIORS ★★★★

What it is Adventure boat ride. Scope and scale Headliner. When to go Before 11 a.m. or after 5 p.m. Special comments Will frighten young children. Authors' rating Not to be missed; ★★★★. Duration of ride 5 minutes. Loading speed Fast. Probable waiting time per 100 people ahead of you 3 minutes. Assumes All 8 boats are running.

DESCRIPTION AND COMMENTS *Jaws* delivers five minutes of nonstop action, with the huge shark repeatedly attacking. A West Virginia woman, fresh from the Magic Kingdom, told us the shark is "about as pesky as that witch in Snow White." While the story is entirely predictable, the shark is fairly realistic and as big as a boxcar; but what makes the ride unique is its sense of journey. *Jaws* builds an amazing degree of suspense. It isn't just a cruise into the middle of a pond where a rubber fish assaults the boat interminably. Add inventive sets and powerful special effects, and you have a first-rate attraction.

A variable at *Jaws* is the enthusiasm and acting ability of your boat guide. Throughout the ride, the guide must set the tone, elaborate the plot, drive the boat, and fight the shark. Most guides are quite good. They may overact, but you can't fault them for lack of enthusiasm. Consider also that each guide repeats this wrenching ordeal every eight minutes.

TOURING TIPS *Jaws* is well designed to handle crowds. People on the boat's left side tend to get splashed more. If you have young children, consider switching off.

A mother of two from Williamsville, New York, who believes our warning about getting wet should be more strongly emphasized, has this to say:

Your warning about the Jaws attraction . . . is woefully understated. Please warn your readers—we were seated on the first row of the boat. My 9-year-old sat at the end of the boat (first person on the far left), and I was seated next to him. We were wary of these seats as I had read your warning, but I felt prepared. NOT! At "that" moment the water came flooding over the left front side of the boat, thoroughly drenching the two of us and filling our sneakers with water. Unfortunately for us, this was only our third attraction of the day (9:30 a.m.), and we still had a long day ahead of us. It was a rather chilly and windy 62-degree day. We went to the restrooms, removed our shorts, and squeezed out as much water as we could, but we were very cold and uncomfortable all day. This will be our most vivid and lasting memory of our day at Universal Studios!

A dad from Seattle suggests that getting wet takes a backseat to being terrified:

Our 8-year-old was so frightened by Jaws that we scrapped the rest of the Universal tour and went back to E.T. An employee said she wouldn't recommend it to anyone under age 10. Maybe you should change "may frighten small children" to "definitely will scare the pants off most children."

Jimmy Neutron's Nicktoon Blast (Universal Express) ★★★

| APPEAL BY AGE | PRESCHOOL ★★★ | GRADE SCHOOL ★★★★ | TEENS ★★★ |
| YOUNG ADULTS ★★★ | | OVER 30 ★★★ | SENIORS ★★ |

What it is Cartoon science demonstration and simulation ride. **Scope and scale** Major attraction. **When to go** The first hour after park opening or after 5 p.m. **Authors' rating** Incomprehensible but fun; ★★★. **Duration of ride** A little over 4 minutes. **Loading speed** Moderate to slow. **Probable waiting time per 100 people ahead of you** 5 minutes. **Assumes** All 8 simulators in use.

DESCRIPTION AND COMMENTS This ride features motion simulators that move and react in sync with a cartoon projected onto a huge screen. Based on the Nickelodeon movie *Jimmy Neutron: Boy Genius,* this attraction replaced The Funtastic World of Hanna-Barbera. In addition to Jimmy, the attraction features a mob of other characters from Nickelodeon, including SpongeBob SquarePants, the Rugrats, the Fairly OddParents, and the Wild Thornberrys. The story, inasmuch as Universal explains it, takes place in two parts. First, guests are invited to participate in a demonstration of Jimmy's newest invention, which is stolen before the demonstration can proceed. After that, an alien plot is revealed, and guests are strapped into motion-simulator vehicles in order to help Jimmy rescue his invention and defend the Earth. In practice, the plot is incomprehensible (at least to an adult). All we can report after riding about a dozen times is that there is a frenetic high-speed chase punctuated by an abundance of screaming in piercing, very high-pitched, cartoony voices.

TOURING TIPS This attraction draws sizeable crowds primarily because it's just inside the entrance and is next door to the new *Shrek 4-D* attraction. We think Jimmy Neutron is at best a so-so effort, and not much of an improvement over its predecessor. Except for avid *Jimmy Neutron* cartoon fans, in other words, it's expendable. If you can't live without it, ride during the first hour the park is open or after 5 p.m. Be aware that a very small percentage of riders suffer motion sickness. Stationary seating is available and is mandated for persons less than 40 inches tall.

Lucy, A Tribute ★★★

APPEAL BY AGE	PRESCHOOL ★	GRADE SCHOOL ★★	TEENS ★★
YOUNG ADULTS ★★★	OVER 30 ★★★		SENIORS ★★★

What it is Walk-through tribute to Lucille Ball. Scope and scale Diversion. When to go Anytime. Authors' rating A touching remembrance; ★★★. Probable waiting time None.

DESCRIPTION AND COMMENTS The life and career of comedienne Lucille Ball are spotlighted, with emphasis on her role as Lucy Ricardo in the long-running television series *I Love Lucy.* Well designed and informative, the exhibit succeeds admirably in recalling the talent and temperament of the beloved redhead.

TOURING TIPS See Lucy during the hot, crowded midafternoon, or on your way out of the park. Adults could easily stay 15 to 30 minutes. Children, however, get restless after a couple of minutes.

Men in Black Alien Attack (Universal Express) ★★★★½

APPEAL BY AGE	PRESCHOOL †	GRADE SCHOOL ★★★★★	TEENS ★★★★★
YOUNG ADULTS ★★★★★	OVER 30 ★★★★★		SENIORS ★★★★

† Preschoolers generally too short to ride.

What it is Interactive dark thrill ride. Scope and scale Super headliner. When to go In the morning after Revenge of the Mummy. Special comments May induce motion sickness. Must be 42" tall to ride. Authors' rating Buzz Lightyear on steroids; not to be missed; ★★★★½. Duration of ride 2½ minutes. Loading speed Moderate to fast.

DESCRIPTION AND COMMENTS Based on the movie of the same name, *Men in Black* brings together actors Will Smith and Rip Torn (as Agent J and MIB Director Zed) for an interactive sequel to the hit film. The story line has you volunteering as a Men in Black (MIB) trainee. After an introduction warning that aliens "live among us" and articulating MIB's mission to round them up, Zed expands on the finer points of alien-spotting and familiarizes you with your training vehicle and your weapon, an alien "zapper." Following this, you load up and are dispatched on an innocuous training mission that immediately deteriorates into a situation where only you are in a position to prevent aliens from taking over the universe. Now, if you saw the movie, you understand that the aliens are mostly giant exotic bugs and cockroaches and that zapping the aliens involves exploding them into myriad, gooey body parts. Thus, the meat of the ride (no pun intended) consists of careening around Manhattan in your MIB vehicle and shooting aliens. The technology at work is similar to that used in the Spider-Man attraction at Universal's Islands of Adventure, which is to say that it's both a wild ride and one where movies, sets, robotics, and your vehicle are all integrated into a fairly seamless package.

Men in Black is interactive in that your marksmanship and ability to blast yourself out of some tricky situations will determine how the story ends. Also, you are awarded a personal score (like Disney's Buzz Lightyear's Space Ranger Spin) and a score for your car. There are about three dozen possible outcomes and literally thousands of different ride experiences determined by your pluck, performance, and in the final challenge your intestinal fortitude.

TOURING TIPS Each of the 120 or so alien figures has sensors that activate special effects and respond to your zapper. Aim for the eyes and keep shooting until the aliens' eyes turn red. Also, many of the aliens shoot back, causing your vehicle to veer or spin. In the mayhem, you might fail to notice that another vehicle of guests runs along beside you on a dual track. This was included to instill a spirit of competition for anyone who finds blowing up bugs and saving the universe less than stimulating. Note that at a certain point, you can shoot the flashing "vent" on top of this other car and make them spin around. Of course, they can do the same to you.

Although there are many possible endings, the long lines at this headliner attraction will probably dissuade you from experiencing all but one or two. To avoid a long wait, hotfoot it to *MIB* immediately after riding Mummy in the first 30 minutes the park is open.

Revenge of the Mummy (Universal Express) ★★★★½

APPEAL BY AGE	PRESCHOOL ★★	GRADE SCHOOL ★★★★	TEENS ★★★★★
YOUNG ADULTS ★★★★½		OVER 30 ★★★★	SENIORS ★★★½

What it is Combination dark ride and roller coaster. **Scope and scale** Super headliner. **When to go** The first hour the park is open or after 6 p.m. **Special comments** 48" minimum height requirement. **Authors' rating** Killer! ★★★★½. **Duration of ride** 3 minutes. **Probable waiting time per 100 people ahead of you** 7 minutes. **Loading speed** Moderate.

DESCRIPTION AND COMMENTS It's hard to wrap your mind around the attraction, but trust us when we say you're in for a very strange experience. Here, quoting Universal, are some of the things you can look forward to:

- Authentic Egyptian catacombs
- High-velocity show immersion system (something to do with fast baptism?)
- Magnet-propulsion launch wave system
- A "Brain Fire" (!) that hovers [over guests] with temperatures soaring to 2,000°F
- Canoptic jars containing grisly remains.

When you read between the lines, Revenge of the Mummy is an indoor dark ride based on the *Mummy* flicks, where guests fight off "deadly curses and vengeful creatures" while flying through Egyptian tombs and other spooky places on a high-tech roller coaster. The special effects are cutting edge, integrating the best technology from such attractions as *Terminator 2: 3-D*, Spider-Man (the ride), and *Back to the Future*, with groundbreaking visuals. It's way cool.

The queuing area serves to establish the story line: you're in a group touring a set from the *Mummy* films when you enter a tomb where the fantasy world of film gives way to the real thing. Along the way you are warned about a possible curse. The visuals are rich and compelling as the queue makes its way to the loading area where you board a sort of clunky, Jeep-looking vehicle. The ride begins as a slow, very elaborate dark ride, passing through various chambers, including one where flesh-eating scarab beetles descend on you. Suddenly your vehicle stops, then drops backwards and rotates. Here's where the "magnet-propulsion launch wave system" comes in. In more ordinary language, this means you're shot at high speed up the first hill of the roller coaster part of the ride. We don't want to ruin your experience by divulging too much, but the coaster part of the ride offers its own panoply of surprises. We will tell you this, however: there are no barrel rolls or any upside-down stuff. And though it's a wild ride by anyone's definition, the emphasis remains as much on the visuals, robotics, and special effects as on the ride itself.

TOURING TIPS Revenge of the Mummy has a very low riders-per-hour capacity for a super-headliner attraction, and especially for the park's top draw. Waits run longer than an *Academy Awards* show. Your only prayer for a tolerable wait is to be on hand when the park opens and sprint immediately to the Mummy. One fallback is to pay extra for Universal Express, but even with Universal Express expect a sizeable wait after 11 a.m. A second option is to use the singles line. This is often more expedient than Universal Express. Concerning motion sickness, if you can ride Space Mountain without ill effect, you should be fine on Revenge of the Mummy. Switching off is available.

Shrek 4-D (Universal Express) ★★★★½

APPEAL BY AGE	PRESCHOOL ★★★★	GRADE SCHOOL ★★★★★	TEENS ★★★★★
YOUNG ADULTS ★★★★★		OVER 30 ★★★★★	SENIORS ★★★★★

What it is 3-D movie. **Scope and scale** Headliner. **When to go** The first hour the park is open or after 4 p.m. **Authors' rating** Warm, fuzzy mayhem; ★★★★½. **Duration of presentation** 20 minutes.

DESCRIPTION AND COMMENTS Based on characters from the hit movie *Shrek,* the preshow presents the villain from the movie, Lord Farquaad, as he appears on various screens to describe his posthumous plan to reclaim his lost bride, Princess Fiona, who married *Shrek*. The plan is posthumous since Lord Farquaad ostensibly died in the movie, and it's his ghost making the plans, but never mind. Guests then move into the main theater, don their 3-D glasses, and recline in seats equipped with "tactile transducers" and "pneumatic air propulsion and water spray nodules capable of both vertical and horizontal motion." As the 3-D film plays, guests are also subjected to smells relevant to the on-screen action (oh boy).

Technicalities aside, *Shrek 4-D* is a real winner. It's irreverent, frantic, laugh-out-loud funny, and iconoclastic. Concerning the latter, the film takes a good poke at Disney with Pinocchio, the Three Little Pigs, and Tinker Bell (among others) all sucked into the mayhem. The film quality and 3-D effects are great, and like the feature film, it's sweet without being sappy. Plus, in contrast to Disney's *Honey, I Shrunk the Audience* or *It's Tough to Be a Bug!*, *Shrek 4-D* doesn't generally frighten children under age 7.

TOURING TIPS Universal claims they can move 2,400 guests an hour through *Shrek 4-D*. However, its popularity means that Express passes for the day may be gone as early as 10 a.m., and waits in the regular line may exceed an hour. Bear that in mind when scheduling your day.

Street Scenes ★★★★

| APPEAL BY AGE | PRESCHOOL ★★★ | GRADE SCHOOL ★★★★★ | TEENS ★★★★★ |
| YOUNG ADULTS ★★★★★ | | OVER 30 ★★★★★ | SENIORS ★★★★★ |

What it is Elaborate outdoor sets for making films. **Scope and scale** Diversion. **When to go** Anytime. **Special comments** You'll see most sets without special effort as you tour the park. **Authors' rating** One of the park's great assets; ★★★★. **Probable waiting time** No waiting.

DESCRIPTION AND COMMENTS Unlike at Disney-MGM Studios, all Universal Studios Florida's back-lot sets are accessible for guest inspection. They include a New York City street, San Francisco's waterfront, a New England coastal town, Rodeo Drive, and Hollywood Boulevard.

TOURING TIPS You'll see most as you walk through the park.

Terminator 2: 3-D: Battle Across Time ★★★★★

| APPEAL BY AGE | PRESCHOOL ★★★ | GRADE SCHOOL ★★★★ | TEENS ★★★★★ |
| YOUNG ADULTS ★★★★★ | | OVER 30 ★★★★★ | SENIORS ★★★★ |

What it is 3-D thriller mixed-media presentation. **Scope and scale** Super headliner. **When to go** After 3:30 p.m. **Special comments** The nation's best theme-park theater attraction; very intense for some preschoolers and grade-schoolers.

Authors' rating Furiously paced high-tech experience; not to be missed; ★★★★★.
Duration of presentation 20 minutes, including an 8-minute preshow. **Probable waiting time** 20–40 minutes.

DESCRIPTION AND COMMENTS   The evil "cop" from *Terminator 2* morphs to life and battles Arnold Schwarzenegger's T-100 cyborg character. If you missed the *Terminator* flicks, here's the plot: A bad robot arrives from the future to kill a nice boy. Another bad robot (who has been reprogrammed to be good) pops up at the same time to save the boy. The bad robot chases the boy and the rehabilitated robot, menacing the audience in the process.

The attraction, like the films, is all action, and you really don't need to understand much. What's interesting is that it uses 3-D film and a theater full of sophisticated technology to integrate the real with the imaginary. Images seem to move in and out of the film, not only in the manner of traditional 3-D, but also in actuality. Remove your 3-D glasses momentarily and you'll see that the guy on the motorcycle is actually onstage.

We've watched this type of presentation evolve, pioneered by Disney's *Captain EO, Honey, I Shrunk the Audience,* and *Muppet-Vision 3-D. Terminator 2: 3-D,* however, goes way beyond lasers, with moving theater seats, blasts of hot air, and spraying mist. It creates a multidimensional space that blurs the boundary between entertainment and reality. Is it seamless? Not quite, but it's close. We rank *Terminator 2: 3-D* as not to be missed and consider it the absolute best theme-park theater attraction in the United States. If *Terminator 2: 3-D* is the only attraction you see at Universal Studios Florida, you'll have received your money's worth.

TOURING TIPS   The 700-seat theater changes audiences about every 19 minutes. Even so, because the show is popular, expect to wait about 30 to 45 minutes. The attraction, on Hollywood Boulevard near the park's entrance, receives huge traffic during morning and early afternoon. By about 3 p.m., however, lines diminish somewhat. Though you'll still wait, we recommend holding off on *Terminator 2: 3-D* until then. If you can't stay until late afternoon, see the show first thing in the morning. Families with young children should know that the violence characteristic of the *Terminator* movies is largely absent from the attraction. There's suspense and action but not much blood and guts.

Twister (Universal Express)   ★★★½

APPEAL BY AGE	PRESCHOOL ★★	GRADE SCHOOL ★★★★	TEENS ★★★★
YOUNG ADULTS ★★★★		OVER 30 ★★★★	SENIORS ★★★

What it is Theater presentation featuring special effects from the movie *Twister*. **Scope and scale** Major attraction. **When to go** Should be your first show after experiencing all rides. **Special comments** High potential for frightening young children. **Authors' rating** Gusty; ★★★½. **Duration of presentation** 15 minutes. **Probable waiting time** 26 minutes.

DESCRIPTION AND COMMENTS   *Twister* combines an elaborate set and special effects, climaxing with a five-story-tall simulated tornado created by circulating more than 2 million cubic feet of air per minute.

TOURING TIPS   The wind, pounding rain, and freight-train sound of the tornado are deafening, and the entire presentation is exceptionally intense. School children are mightily impressed, while younger children are terrified and overwhelmed. Unless you want the kids hopping in your bed whenever they hear thunder, try this attraction yourself before taking your kids.

Universal 360°: A Cinesphere Spectacular (seasonal) ★★★½

APPEAL BY AGE	PRESCHOOL ★★★	GRADE SCHOOL ★★★★	TEENS ★★★½
YOUNG ADULTS ★★★★		OVER 30 ★★★★	SENIORS ★★★★

What it is Fireworks, lasers, and movies. **Scope and scale** Major attraction. **When to go** 1 show a day, usually 10 minutes before park closes. **Authors' rating** Good effort; ★★★½. **Special comments** Movie trailers galore. **Duration of presentation** 10 minutes.

DESCRIPTION AND COMMENTS For years the Universal theme parks had been without a daily capstone event to compete with Disney's *Fantasmic!* and *IllumiNations*. In July 2006, all that changed with the premiere of *Universal 360°*, a nighttime spectacular presented daily at the Universal Studios lagoon in the middle of the park. The presentation, a celebration of hit movies, is built around four 360-degree projection cinespheres, each 36 feet tall and 30 feet wide. The cinespheres project images relating to the chosen films, augmented by lasers and fireworks. Three hundred speakers positioned around the lagoon broadcast the show's original score. You'll be a little surprised to see the number of films the studio has released over its 95-year existence. The show lacks in water effects (unlike Disney's *IllumiNations*), but to its merit, it is a spectacular closer to a day at the park. *Universal 360°* is presented during the summer and holiday periods with special productions for Halloween and Christmas.

TOURING TIPS The 360-degree projections are split rather awkwardly, since the movies weren't shot to be projected on a sphere. The ends of the lagoon are not recommended for viewing. The best spot is directly across the lagoon from Richter's Burger Co., where the sidewalk makes a small protrusion into the water. This side of the lagoon also offers the best view of the projections on the buildings. Acquiring a place here can be very difficult. We recommend arriving at least 45 minutes ahead of time and taking turns holding the spot while the rest of your crew rides *Jaws* at night.

Before the show begins, realize that not all of the movie clips may be suitable for young viewers. During the horror movie montage that includes scenes from *American Werewolf in Paris,* parents may want to cover some eyes. The action movie montage is also stuffed with gunplay and gore. When the same studio that made movies as diverse as *Psycho* and *Shrek,* or *Hannibal* and *SpongeBob,* wants to make an all-inclusive montage, they are bound to run into some difficulties.

Universal Horror Make-up Show (Universal Express) ★★★½

APPEAL BY AGE	PRESCHOOL ★★★	GRADE SCHOOL ★★★★	TEENS ★★★★
YOUNG ADULTS ★★★★		OVER 30 ★★★★	SENIORS ★★★★

What it is Theater presentation on the art of make-up. **Scope and scale** Major attraction. **When to go** After you have experienced all rides. **Special comments** May frighten young children. **Authors' rating** A gory knee-slapper; ★★★½. **Duration of presentation** 25 minutes. **Probable waiting time** 20 minutes.

DESCRIPTION AND COMMENTS Lively, well-paced look at how make-up artists create film monsters, realistic wounds, severed limbs, and other unmentionables. Funnier and more upbeat than many Universal Studios presentations, the show also presents a wealth of fascinating information. It's excellent and enlightening, if somewhat gory.

TOURING TIPS Exceeding most guests' expectations, the *Horror Make-up Show* is the sleeper attraction at Universal. Its humor and tongue-in-cheek style transcend the gruesome effects, and most folks (including preschoolers) take the blood and guts in stride. It usually isn't too hard to get into.

Woody Woodpecker's Nuthouse Coaster and ★★★
Curious George Goes to Town Playground

| APPEAL BY AGE | PRESCHOOL ★★★★ | GRADE SCHOOL — | TEENS — |
| YOUNG ADULTS — | OVER 30 — | | SENIORS — |

What it is Interactive playground and kid's roller coaster. **Scope and scale** Minor attraction. **When to go** Anytime. **Authors' rating** A good place to let off steam; ★★★.

DESCRIPTION AND COMMENTS Rounding out the selection of other nearby kid-friendly attractions, this KidZone offering consists of Woody Woodpecker's Nuthouse Coaster and an interactive playground called Curious George Goes to Town. The child-sized roller coaster is small enough for kids to enjoy but sturdy enough for adults, though its moderate speed might unnerve some smaller children (the minimum height to ride is 36 inches). The Curious George playground exemplifies the Universal obsession with wet stuff; in addition to innumerable spigots, pipes, and spray guns, two giant roof-mounted buckets periodically dump a thousand gallons of water on unsuspecting visitors below. Kids who want to stay dry can mess around in the foam-ball playground, also equipped with chutes, tubes, and ball-blasters.

TOURING TIPS After its unveiling, Universal employees dubbed this area "Peckerland." Visit after you've experienced all the major attractions.

LIVE ENTERTAINMENT *at*
UNIVERSAL STUDIOS

IN ADDITION TO THE SHOWS PROFILED ABOVE, Universal offers a wide range of street entertainment. Costumed comic-book and cartoon characters (such as Shrek, Donkey, SpongeBob SquarePants, Woody Woodpecker) roam the park for photo ops supplemented by movie star look-alikes, both living and deceased, plus the Frankenstein monster, who can be said to be neither. Musical acts include Blues Brothers impersonators dancing and singing in the New York section of the park and **The Ricky and Lucy Show,** staged on Hollywood Boulevard. Supported by a seven-piece band, the Ricardos do traditional Cuban numbers spiced with trademark *I Love Lucy* comedy.

UNIVERSAL STUDIOS FLORIDA TOURING PLAN

UNIVERSAL STUDIOS FLORIDA ONE-DAY TOURING PLAN

THIS PLAN IS FOR ALL VISITORS. If a ride or show is listed that you don't want to experience, skip that step and proceed to the next. Move quickly from attraction to attraction and, if possible, don't stop for lunch until after Step 9. Minor street shows occur at various times and places throughout the day; check the daily schedule for details.

BUYING ADMISSION TO UNIVERSAL STUDIOS FLORIDA

ONE OF OUR BIG GRIPES ABOUT UNIVERSAL STUDIOS is that there are never enough ticket windows open in the morning to accommodate the crowd. You can arrive 30 minutes before official opening time and still be in line to buy your admission when the park opens. Therefore, we strongly recommend you buy your admission in advance. Passes are available by mail from Universal Studios at ☎ 800-224-3838. They are also sold at the concierge desk or attractions box office of many Orlando-area hotels. If your hotel doesn't offer tickets, try Guest Services at the DoubleTree Hotel ☎ 407-351-1000, at the intersection of Major Boulevard and Kirkman Avenue.

Many hotels that sell Universal admissions don't issue actual passes. Instead, the purchaser gets a voucher that can be redeemed for a pass at the theme park. Fortunately, the voucher-redemption window is separate from the park's ticket sales operation. You can quickly exchange your voucher for a pass and be on your way with little or no wait.

TOURING PLAN

1. Call ☎ 407-363-8000 the day before you visit for the official opening time.

2. On the day of your visit, eat breakfast and arrive at Universal Studios Florida 20 to 25 minutes before opening time with your admission pass or an admission voucher in hand. If you have a voucher, exchange it for a pass at the voucher-redemption window. Pick up a map and the daily entertainment schedule.

3. Line up at the turnstile. Ask any attendant whether any rides or shows are closed that day. Adjust the touring plan accordingly.

4. When the park opens, go straight down the Plaza of the Stars. Pass Rodeo Drive on your right. When you reach Nickelodeon Way on your left, you should be standing by Jimmy Neutron's Nicktoon Blast on your left.

5. Proceed toward the back of the park (past Sound Stage 54) to the New York section and ride Revenge of the Mummy.

6. Now head to *Men in Black* Alien Attack. From Revenge of the Mummy, proceed with the lagoon on your right along the Embarcadero, along Amity Avenue, and over the bridge to get there. If you're leaving from Jimmy Neutron's Nicktoon Blast or *Shrek 4-D,* take a left on Rodeo Drive to Hollywood Boulevard, pass Mel's Diner (on your left), and (keeping the lagoon on your left) go directly to *Men in Black.* Ride.

7. After *Men in Black,* backtrack to *Back to the Future* and ride.

8. Exit left and pass the International Food Bazaar. If crowds are heavy, this might be about time for lunch. If you want to keep going, continue bearing left past *Animal Actors on Location,* and go to the *E.T.* Adventure ride.

9. Retrace your steps toward *Back to the Future.* Keeping the lagoon on your left, cross the bridge to Amity. Ride *Jaws.*

10. Exit and turn left down the Embarcadero. Ride *Earthquake*—The Big One, which is right next door to *Jaws.*

11. Work your way back toward the main entrance and see *Shrek 4-D.*

12. If you're still intact after various alien assaults, a bike ride to another galaxy, a shark attack, an earthquake, and an encounter with an ogre, take on a tornado. Return to Streets of America and see *Twister.* The line will seem long but should move quickly as guests are admitted.

13. If you haven't already eaten, do so now.

14. At this point you have five major attractions yet to see:

    Animal Actors on Location; Beetlejuice's Rock 'n' Roll Graveyard Revue; Fear Factor Live; The Universal Horror Make-up Show; and Terminator 2: 3-D.

    Animal Actors on Location, the *Beetlejuice* show, *Fear Factor Live,* and the *Horror Make-up Show* are performed several times daily, as listed in the entertainment schedule. Plan the remainder of your itinerary according to the next listed shows for these presentations. Try to see *Terminator 2: 3-D* after 3:30 p.m., but whatever you do, don't miss it.

15. Our touring plan doesn't include Woody Woodpecker's KidZone or *A Day in the Park with Barney.* If you're touring with preschoolers, see *Barney* after you ride *E.T.,* and then head for KidZone.

16. If you stay in the park until dark, see *Universal 360°: A Cinesphere Spectacular* (presented seasonally).

17. This concludes the touring plan. Spend the remainder of your day revisiting your favorite attractions or inspecting sets and street scenes you may have missed. Also, check your daily entertainment schedule for live performances that interest you.

UNIVERSAL'S ISLANDS
of ADVENTURE

WHEN UNIVERSAL'S ISLANDS OF ADVENTURE theme park opened in 1999, it provided Universal with enough critical mass to actually compete with Disney. Universal finally has on-site hotels, a shopping and entertainment complex, and two major theme parks. Doubly interesting is that the new Universal park is pretty much just for fun—in other words, a direct competitor to Disney's Magic Kingdom, the most visited theme park in the world. How direct a competitor is it? Check out the box below for a direct comparison.

And though it may take central Florida tourists a while to make the connection, here's what will dawn on them when they finally do: Universal's Islands of Adventure is a state-of-the-art park competing with a Disney park that is more than 35 years old and has not added a new super-headliner attraction for many years.

Of course, that's only how it looks on paper. The Magic Kingdom, after all, is graceful in its maturity and much loved. And then there was the question on everyone's mind: could Universal really pull it off? Recalling the disastrous first year that the Universal Studios Florida park experienced, we held our breath to see if Islands of Adventure's innovative high-tech attractions would work. Well, not only did they work, they were up and running almost two months ahead of schedule. Thus, the clash of the titans is still hot. Universal is coming on strong with the potential of sucking up three days of a tourist's week (more, if you include Universal's strategic relationship with SeaWorld and Busch Gardens). And that's more time than anyone has spent off the Disney campus for a long, long time.

Disney and Universal officially downplay their fierce competition, pointing out that any new theme park or attraction makes central Florida a more marketable destination. Behind closed doors, however, it's a Pepsi-versus-Coke–type rivalry that will keep both companies working hard to gain a competitive edge. The good news, of course, is that all this translates into better and better attractions for you to enjoy.

BEWARE OF THE WET AND WILD

ALTHOUGH WE HAVE DESCRIBED Universal's Islands of Adventure as a direct competitor to the Magic Kingdom, there is one major qualification you should be aware of. Whereas most Magic Kingdom attractions are designed to be enjoyed by guests of any age, attractions at Islands of Adventure are largely created for an under-40 population. The roller coasters at Universal are serious with a capital S, making Space Mountain and Big Thunder Mountain look about as tough as

unofficial **TIP**
Roller coasters at Islands of Adventure are the real deal—not for the faint of heart or for little ones.

unofficial **TIP**
Consider yourself warned: several attractions at Islands of Adventure will drench you to the bone.

Dumbo. In fact, seven out of the nine top attractions at Islands are thrill rides, and of these, there are three that not only scare the bejeezus out of you but also drench you with water.

For families, there are three interactive playgrounds as well as six rides that young children will enjoy. Of the thrill rides, only the two in Toon Lagoon (described later) are marginally appropriate for young children, and even on these rides your child needs to be fairly stalwart.

ISLANDS OF ADVENTURE VERSUS THE MAGIC KINGDOM	
Islands of Adventure	Magic Kingdom
Six Islands (includes Port of Entry)	Seven Lands (includes Main Street)
Two adult roller-coaster attractions	Two adult roller-coaster attractions
A Dumbo-type ride	Dumbo
One flume ride	One flume ride
Toon Lagoon character area	Mickey's Toontown Fair character area

GETTING ORIENTED AT ISLANDS OF ADVENTURE

BOTH UNIVERSAL THEME PARKS are accessed via the Universal CityWalk entertainment complex. Crossing CityWalk from the parking garages, you can bear right to Universal Studios Florida or left to Universal's Islands of Adventure.

Islands of Adventure is arranged much like Epcot's World Showcase, in a large circle surrounding a lake. Unlike Epcot, however, the Islands of Adventure themed areas evidence the sort of thematic continuity pioneered by Disneyland and the Magic Kingdom. Each land, or island in this case, is self-contained and visually consistent in its theme, though you can see parts of the other islands across the lake.

You first encounter the Moroccan-style Port of Entry, where you'll find Guest Services, lockers, stroller and wheelchair rentals, ATM banking, Lost and Found, and shopping. From the Port of Entry, moving clockwise around the lake, you can access Marvel Super Hero Island, Toon Lagoon, *Jurassic Park,* the Lost Continent, and Seuss Landing. You can crisscross the lake on small boats, but there is no in-park transportation.

Not to Be Missed at Islands of Adventure

The Adventures of Spider-Man	Dueling Dragons
The Incredible Hulk Coaster	*Jurassic Park* River Adventure
Poseidon's Fury!	

ISLANDS *of* ADVENTURE ATTRACTIONS

MARVEL SUPER HERO ISLAND

THIS ISLAND, WITH ITS FUTURISTIC AND RETRO-FUTURE design and comic-book signage, offers shopping and attractions based on Marvel Comics characters.

The Amazing Adventures of Spider-Man ★★★★★ (Universal Express)

APPEAL BY AGE	PRESCHOOL ★★★	GRADE SCHOOL ★★★★★	TEENS ★★★★★
YOUNG ADULTS ★★★★★		OVER 30 ★★★★★	SENIORS ★★★★

What it is Indoor adventure simulator ride based on Spider-Man. **Scope and scale** Super headliner. **When to go** Before 10 a.m. **Special comments** Must be 40" tall to ride. **Authors' rating** Our choice for the best attraction in the park; ★★★★★. **Duration of ride** 4½ minutes. **Loading speed** Fast.

DESCRIPTION AND COMMENTS Covering one-and-a-half acres and combining moving ride vehicles, 3-D film, and live action, Spider-Man is frenetic, fluid, and astounding. The visuals are rich, and the ride is wild but not jerky. Although the attractions are not directly comparable, Spider-Man is technologically on a par with Disney-MGM's Tower of Terror, which is to say that it will leave you in awe. As a personal aside, we love both and would be hard-pressed to choose one over the other.

The story line is that you are a reporter for the *Daily Bugle* newspaper (where Peter Parker, aka Spider-Man, works as a mild-mannered photographer), when it's discovered that evil villains have stolen (we promise we're not making this up) the Statue of Liberty. You are drafted on the spot by your cantankerous editor to go get the story. After speeding around and being thrust into "a battle between good and evil," you experience a 400-foot "sensory drop" from a skyscraper roof all the way to the pavement. Because the ride is so wild and the action so continuous, it's hard to understand the plot, but you're so thoroughly entertained that you don't really care. Plus, you'll want to ride again and again. Eventually, with repetition, the story line will begin to make sense.

TOURING TIPS Ride first thing in the morning after The Incredible Hulk Coaster or in the hour before closing.

islands of adventure

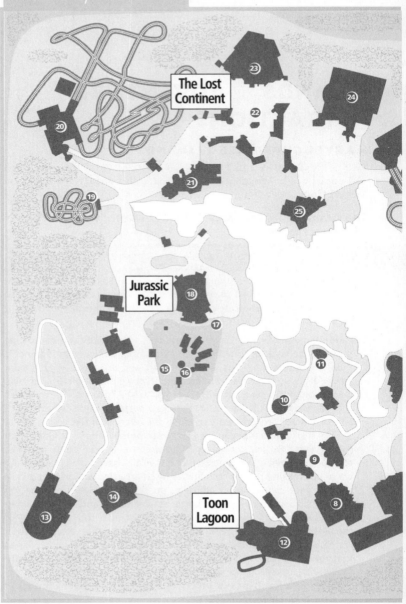

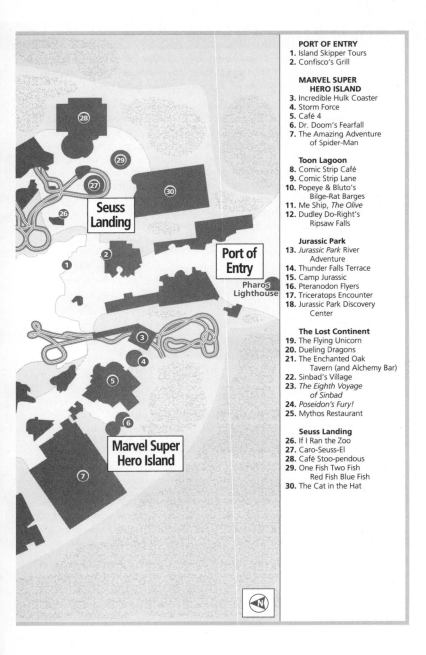

PORT OF ENTRY
1. Island Skipper Tours
2. Confisco's Grill

**MARVEL SUPER
HERO ISLAND**
3. Incredible Hulk Coaster
4. Storm Force
5. Café 4
6. Dr. Doom's Fearfall
7. The Amazing Adventure
   of Spider-Man

Toon Lagoon
8. Comic Strip Café
9. Comic Strip Lane
10. Popeye & Bluto's
    Bilge-Rat Barges
11. Me Ship, *The Olive*
12. Dudley Do-Right's
    Ripsaw Falls

Jurassic Park
13. *Jurassic Park* River
    Adventure
14. Thunder Falls Terrace
15. Camp Jurassic
16. Pteranodon Flyers
17. Triceratops Encounter
18. Jurassic Park Discovery
    Center

The Lost Continent
19. The Flying Unicorn
20. Dueling Dragons
21. The Enchanted Oak
    Tavern (and Alchemy Bar)
22. Sinbad's Village
23. *The Eighth Voyage
    of Sinbad*
24. *Poseidon's Fury!*
25. Mythos Restaurant

Seuss Landing
26. If I Ran the Zoo
27. Caro-Seuss-El
28. Café Stoo-pendous
29. One Fish Two Fish
    Red Fish Blue Fish
30. The Cat in the Hat

Dr. Doom's Fearfall (Universal Express) ★★★

APPEAL BY AGE	PRESCHOOL —	GRADE SCHOOL ★★★	TEENS ★★★★
YOUNG ADULTS ★★★★		OVER 30 ★★★	SENIORS —

What it is Lunch liberator. **Scope and scale** Headliner. **When to go** Before 9:15 a.m. **Special comments** Must be 52" tall to ride. **Authors' rating** More bark than bite; ★★★. **Duration of ride** 40 seconds. **Loading speed** Slow.

DESCRIPTION AND COMMENTS   Here you are (again) strapped into a seat with your feet dangling and blasted 200 feet up in the air and then allowed to partially free-fall back down. If you are having trouble forming a mental image of this attraction, picture the midway game wherein a macho guy swings a sledgehammer, propelling a metal sphere up a vertical shaft. At the top of the shaft is a bell. If the macho man drives the sphere high enough to ring the bell, he wins a prize. Got the idea? OK, on this ride you're the metal sphere.

The good news is this ride looks much worse than it actually is. The scariest part by far is the apprehension that builds as you sit, strapped in, waiting for the thing to launch. The blasting up and free-falling down parts are really very pleasant.

TOURING TIPS   We've seen glaciers that move faster than the line to Dr. Doom. If you want to ride without investing half a day, be one of the first in the park to ride. Fortunately, if you're on hand at opening time, being among the first isn't too difficult (mainly because the nearby Hulk and Spider-Man attractions are bigger draws).

WARNING!
For Bouffants, Rug Wearers, and Elvis Impersonators
This Ride Will Muss Your 'Do

The Incredible Hulk Coaster (Universal Express) ★★★★½

APPEAL BY AGE	PRESCHOOL ★	GRADE SCHOOL ★★★★★	TEENS ★★★★★
YOUNG ADULTS ★★★★		OVER 30 ★★★★	SENIORS ★★★

What it is Roller coaster. **Scope and scale** Super headliner. **When to go** Before 9:30 a.m. **Special comments** Must be 54" tall to ride. **Authors' rating** A coaster-lover's coaster; ★★★★½. **Duration of ride** 1½ minutes. **Loading speed** Moderate.

DESCRIPTION AND COMMENTS   There is, as always, a story line, but for this attraction it's of no importance whatsoever. What you need to know about this attraction is simple. You will be shot like a cannonball from 0 to 40 miles per hour in two seconds, and then you will be flung upside down 100 feet off the ground, which will, of course, induce weightlessness. From there it's a mere seven rollovers punctuated by two plunges into holes in the ground before you're allowed to get out and throw up.

Seriously, the Hulk is a great roller coaster, perhaps the best in Florida, providing a ride comparable to Montu (Busch Gardens) with the added thrill of an accelerated launch (instead of the more typical uphill crank). Plus, like Montu, this coaster has a smooth ride.

TOURING TIPS The Hulk gives Spider-Man a run as the park's most popular attraction. Ride first thing in the morning. Universal provides electronic lockers near the entrance of the Hulk to deposit any items that might depart your person during the Hulk's seven inversions. The locker is free if you only use it for a short time. If you leave things in the locker for a couple of hours, however, you'll have to pay a rental charge. When you reach the boarding area, note that there is a separate line for those who want to ride in the first row.

Storm Force Accelatron (Universal Express) ★★★

APPEAL BY AGE · PRESCHOOL ★★★★   GRADE SCHOOL ★★★   TEENS ★★★
YOUNG ADULTS   ★★★   OVER 30 ★★★   SENIORS   ★★★

What it is Indoor spinning ride. **Scope and scale** Minor attraction. **Special comments** May induce motion sickness. **When to go** Before 10:30 a.m. **Authors' rating** Teacups in the dark; ★★★. **Duration of ride** 1½ minutes. **Loading speed** Slow.

DESCRIPTION AND COMMENTS Storm Force is a spiffed-up indoor version of Disney's nausea-inducing Mad Tea Party. Here you spin to the accompaniment of a simulated thunderstorm and swirling sound and light. There's a story line that loosely ties this midway-type ride to the Marvel Super Hero themed area, but it's largely irrelevant and offers no advice on keeping your lunch down.

TOURING TIPS Ride early or late to avoid long lines. If you're prone to motion sickness, keep your distance.

TOON LAGOON

TOON LAGOON IS CARTOON ART TRANSLATED into real buildings and settings. Whimsical and gaily colored, with rounded and exaggerated lines, Toon Lagoon is Universal's answer to Mickey's Toon-town Fair in the Magic Kingdom. The main difference between the two toon lands is that (as you will see) you have about a 60% chance of drowning at Universal's version.

Comic Strip Lane

What it is Walk-through exhibit and shopping and dining venue. **Scope and scale** Diversion. **When to go** Anytime.

DESCRIPTION AND COMMENTS This is the main street of Toon Lagoon. Here you can visit the domains of Beetle Bailey, Hagar the Horrible, Krazy Kat, the Family Circus, and Blondie and Dagwood, among others. Shops and eateries tie into the cartoon strip theme.

TOURING TIPS This is a great place for photo ops with cartoon characters in their own environment. It's also a great place to drop a few bucks in the diners and shops, but you probably already figured that out.

Dudley Do-Right's Ripsaw Falls (Universal Express) ★★★½

| APPEAL BY AGE | PRESCHOOL ★★★ | GRADE SCHOOL ★★★★ | TEENS ★★★★ |
| YOUNG   ADULTS ★★★ | | OVER   30   ★★★★ | SENIORS   ★★★ |

What it is Flume ride. **Scope and scale** Major attraction. **When to go** Before 11 a.m. **Special comments** Must be 44" tall to ride. **Authors' rating** A minimalist Splash Mountain; ★★★½. **Duration of ride** 5 minutes. **Loading speed** Moderate.

DESCRIPTION AND COMMENTS Inspired by the *Rocky and Bullwinkle* cartoons, this ride features Canadian Mountie Dudley Do-Right as he attempts to save Nell from evil Snidely Whiplash. Story line aside, it's a flume ride, with the inevitable big drop at the end. Universal claims this is the first flume ride to "send riders plummeting 15 feet below the surface of the water." In reality, though, you're just plummeting into a tunnel.

The only problem with this attraction is that everyone inevitably compares it to Splash Mountain at the Magic Kingdom. The flume is as good as Splash Mountain's, and the final drop is a whopper, but the theming and the visuals aren't even in the same league. The art, sets, audio, and jokes at Dudley Do-Right are minimalist at best; it's Dudley Do-Right's two-dimensional approach versus Splash Mountain's three-dimensional presentation. Taken on its own terms, however, Dudley Do-Right is a darn good flume ride.

TOURING TIPS This ride will get you wet, but on average not as wet as you might expect (it looks worse than it is). If you want to stay dry, however, arrive prepared with a poncho or at least a big garbage bag with holes cut out for your head and arms. After riding, take a moment to gauge the timing of the water cannons that go off along the exit walk. This is where you can really get drenched. While younger children are often intimidated by the big drop, those who ride generally enjoy themselves. Ride first thing in the morning after experiencing the Marvel Super Hero rides.

Me Ship, *The Olive* ★★★

| APPEAL BY AGE | PRESCHOOL ★★★★ | GRADE SCHOOL ★★★★ |
| TEENS   ½ | YOUNG ADULTS   ½ | OVER   30   ½ | SENIORS   — |

What it is Interactive playground. **Scope and scale** Minor attraction. **When to go** Anytime. **Authors' rating** Colorful and appealing for kids; ★★★.

DESCRIPTION AND COMMENTS *The Olive* is Popeye's three-story boat come to life as an interactive playground. Younger children can scramble around in Swee'Pea's Playpen, while older sibs shoot water cannons at riders trying to survive the adjacent Bilge-Rat raft ride.

TOURING TIPS If you're into the big rides, save this for later in the day.

Popeye & Bluto's Bilge-Rat Barges ★★★★
(Universal Express)

| APPEAL BY AGE | PRESCHOOL ★★★ | GRADE SCHOOL ★★★★★ | TEENS ★★★★ |
| YOUNG   ADULTS   ★★★★ | | OVER   30   ★★★★ | SENIORS   ★★★ |

What it is White-water raft ride. **Scope and scale** Major attraction. **When to go** Before 10:30 a.m. **Special comments** Must be 42" tall to ride. **Authors'**

rating Bring your own soap; ★★★★. **Duration of ride** 4½ minutes. **Loading speed** Moderate.

DESCRIPTION AND COMMENTS This sweetly named attraction is a white-water raft ride that includes an encounter with an 18-foot-tall octopus. Engineered to ensure that everyone gets drenched, the ride even provides water cannons for highly intelligent nonparticipants ashore to fire at those aboard. The rapids are rougher and more interesting, and the ride longer, than the Animal Kingdom's Kali River Rapids. But nobody surpasses Disney for visuals and theming, though the settings of these two attractions (cartoon set and Asian jungle river, respectively) are hardly comparable.

TOURING TIPS If you didn't drown on Dudley Do-Right, here's a second chance. You'll get a lot wetter from the knees down on this ride, so use your poncho or garbage bag and ride barefoot with your britches rolled up. In terms of beating the crowds, ride the barges in the morning after experiencing the Marvel Super Hero attractions and Dudley Do-Right. If you are lacking foul-weather gear or forgot your trash bag, you might want to put off riding until last thing before leaving the park. Most preschoolers enjoy the raft ride. Those who are frightened react more to the way the rapids look as opposed to the roughness of the ride.

JURASSIC PARK

JURASSIC PARK (FOR ANYONE WHO'S BEEN ASLEEP for 20 years) is a Steven Spielberg film franchise about a fictitious theme park with real dinosaurs. Jurassic Park at Universal's Islands of Adventure is a real theme park (or at least a section of one) with fictitious dinosaurs.

Camp Jurassic   ★★★

| APPEAL BY AGE | PRESCHOOL ★★★ | GRADE SCHOOL ★★★ | TEENS — |
| YOUNG   ADULTS | — | OVER   30 — | SENIORS — |

What it is Interactive play area. **Scope and scale** Minor attraction. **When to go** Anytime. **Authors' rating** Creative playground, confusing layout; ★★★.

DESCRIPTION AND COMMENTS Camp Jurassic is a great place for children to cut loose. Sort of a Jurassic version of Tom Sawyer Island, kids can explore lava pits, caves, mines, and a rain forest.

TOURING TIPS Camp Jurassic will fire the imaginations of the under-13 set. If you don't impose a time limit on the exploration, you could be here a while. The layout of the play area is confusing and intersects the queuing area for Pteranodon Flyers. If your child accidentally lines up for the Pteranodons, he'll be college age before you see him again.

Discovery Center   ★★★

| APPEAL BY AGE | PRESCHOOL ★★★ | GRADE SCHOOL ★★★★ | TEENS ★★★ |
| YOUNG   ADULTS ★★★ | | OVER   30 ★★★ | SENIORS ★★★ |

What it is Interactive natural history exhibit. **Scope and scale** Minor attraction. **When to go** Anytime. **Authors' rating** ★★★.

DESCRIPTION AND COMMENTS The Discovery Center is an interactive, educational exhibit that mixes fiction from the movie *Jurassic Park,* such as using fossil DNA to bring dinosaurs to life, with various skeletal remains and other paleontological displays. One exhibit allows guests to watch an animatronic raptor being hatched. Another allows you to digitally "fuse" your DNA with a dinosaur to see what the resultant creature would look like. Other exhibits include dinosaur egg scanning and identification and a quiz called "You Bet Jurassic."

TOURING TIPS   Cycle back after experiencing all the rides or on a second day. Most folks can digest this exhibit in 10 to 15 minutes.

Jurassic Park River Adventure (Universal Express)   ★★★★

APPEAL BY AGE	PRESCHOOL ★★★	GRADE SCHOOL ★★★★★	TEENS ★★★★★
YOUNG ADULTS ★★★★		OVER 30 ★★★★	SENIORS ★★★★

What it is Indoor-outdoor adventure river-raft ride based on the *Jurassic Park* movies. Scope and scale Super headliner. When to go Before 11 a.m. Special comments Must be 42" tall to ride. Authors' rating Better than its Hollywood cousin; ★★★★. Duration of ride 6½ minutes. Loading speed Fast.

DESCRIPTION AND COMMENTS   Guests board boats for a water tour of Jurassic Park. Everything is tranquil as the tour begins, and the boat floats among large herbivorous dinosaurs such as brontosaurus and stegosaurus. Then, as word is received that some of the carnivores have escaped their enclosure, the tour boat is accidentally diverted into Jurassic Park's maintenance facilities. Here, the boat and its riders are menaced by an assortment of hungry meat-eaters led by the ubiquitous T. rex. At the climactic moment, the boat and its passengers escape by plummeting over an 85-foot drop billed as the "longest, fastest, steepest water descent ever built" (did anyone notice the omission of the word *wettest*?).

TOURING TIPS   Though the boats make a huge splash at the bottom of the 85-foot drop, you don't get all that wet. Unfortunately, before the boat leaves the dock, you must sit in the puddles left by previous riders. Once you're under way there's a little splashing but nothing major until the big drop at the end of the ride. When you hit the bottom, however, enough water will cascade into the air to extinguish a three-alarm fire. Fortunately, not all that much lands in the boat.

   Young children must endure a double whammy on this ride. First, they are stalked by giant, salivating (sometimes spitting) reptiles, and then they're sent catapulting over the falls. Unless your children are fairly stalwart, wait a year or two before you spring the River Adventure on them.

Pteranodon Flyers   ½

APPEAL BY AGE	PRESCHOOL ★★★	GRADE SCHOOL ★★★	TEENS ★
YOUNG ADULTS ★★		OVER 30 ★	SENIORS ★★

What it is Slow as Christmas. Scope and scale Minor attraction. When to go When there's no line. Authors' rating All sizzle, no steak; ½. Duration of ride 1 minute and 25 seconds. Loading speed Slower than a hog in quicksand.

DESCRIPTION AND COMMENTS   This attraction is Islands of Adventure's biggest blunder. Engineered to accommodate only 170 persons per hour (about half the hourly capacity of Dumbo!), the ride swings you along a track that passes over a small part of Jurassic Park. We recommend that you skip this one. Why? Because the Jurassic period will probably end before you reach the front of the line! And your reward for all that waiting? A one-minute-and-fifteen-second ride. Plus, the attraction has a name that nobody over 12 years old can pronounce.

TOURING TIPS Photograph the pteranodon as it flies overhead. You're probably looking at something that will someday be extinct.

THE LOST CONTINENT

THIS AREA IS AN EXOTIC MIX of Silk Road bazaar and ancient ruins, with Greco-Moroccan accents. (And you thought your decorator was nuts.) This is the land of mythical gods, fabled beasts, and expensive souvenirs.

The Lost Continent, however, is also home to one of the better theme-park restaurants you're likely to encounter. Here's what a 30-something man from Fairfield, Connecticut, had to say:

> *Mythos* [restaurant] *was absolutely amazing. I was nervous about such a nice restaurant in the middle of a theme park, but I was proven wrong. A diamond in the rough!*

Dueling Dragons (Universal Express)   ★★★★

APPEAL BY AGE	PRESCHOOL —	GRADE SCHOOL ★★★★	TEENS ★★★★
YOUNG ADULTS ★★★★		OVER 30 ★★★★	SENIORS ★★

What it is Roller coaster. **Scope and scale** Headliner. **When to go** Before 10:30 a.m. **Special comments** Must be 54" tall to ride. **Authors' rating** Almost as good as the Hulk coaster; ★★★★. **Duration of ride** 1 minute and 45 seconds. **Loading speed** Moderate.

DESCRIPTION AND COMMENTS This high-tech coaster launches two trains (Fire and Ice) at the same time on tracks that are closely intertwined. Each track is differently configured so that you get a different experience on each. Several times, a collision with the other train seems imminent, a catastrophe that seems all the more real because the coasters are inverted (that is, suspended from above so that you sit with your feet dangling). At times, the two trains and their passengers are separated by a mere 12 inches.

Because this is an inverted coaster, your view of the action is limited unless you are sitting in the front row. This means that most passengers miss seeing all these near collisions. But don't worry; regardless of where you sit, there's plenty to keep you busy. Dueling Dragons is the highest coaster in the park and also claims the longest drop at 115 feet, not to mention five inversions. And like the Hulk, it's a smooth ride all the way.

Coaster cadets argue about which seat on which train provides the wildest ride. We prefer the front row on either train, but coaster loonies hype the front row of Fire and the last row of Ice.

TOURING TIPS The good news about this ride is that you won't get wet unless you wet yourself. The bad news is that wetting yourself comes pretty naturally. The other bad news is that the queuing area for Dueling Dragons is the longest, most convoluted affair we've ever seen, winding endlessly through a maze of subterranean passages. After what feels like a comprehensive tour of Mammoth Cave, you finally emerge at the loading area where you must choose between riding Fire or Ice. Of course, at this critical juncture, you're as blind as a mole rat from being in the dark for so long. Our advice is to follow the person in front of you until your eyes adjust to the light. Try to ride during the first 90 minutes the park is open. Warn anyone waiting for you that you might be a while. Even if there is no line to speak of, it takes 10 to 12 minutes just to navigate the caverns and not much less time to exit the attraction after riding. However, if lines are low, park employees will open special doors marked "Re-entry to Fire" or "Re-entry to Ice" (depending on what coaster you just rode) that allow you to get right back to the head of the queue and ride again. Finally, if you don't have time to ride both Fire and Ice, be advised that the *Unofficial* crew unanimously prefers Fire to Ice.

The Eighth Voyage of Sinbad (Universal Express) ★★

APPEAL BY AGE	PRESCHOOL ★★★	GRADE SCHOOL ★★★★	TEENS ★★★
YOUNG ADULTS ★★★		OVER 30 ★★★	SENIORS ★★★

What it is Theater stunt show. **Scope and scale** Major attraction. **When to go** Anytime as per the daily entertainment schedule. **Authors' rating** Not inspiring; ★★. **Duration of presentation** 17 minutes. **Probable waiting time** 15 minutes.

DESCRIPTION AND COMMENTS A story about Sinbad the Sailor is the glue that (loosely) binds this stunt show featuring water explosions, ten-foot-tall circles of flame, and various other daunting eruptions and perturbations. The show reminds us of those action movies that substitute a mind-numbing succession of explosions, crashes, and special effects for plot and character development. Concerning *Sinbad,* even if you bear in mind that it's billed as a stunt show, the production is so vacuous and redundant that it's hard to get into the action. Fans of the *Hercules* and *Xena* TV shows might appreciate the humor more than the average showgoer.

TOURING TIPS See *Sinbad* after you've experienced the rides and the better-rated shows. The theater seats 1,700.

The Flying Unicorn (Universal Express) ★★★

APPEAL BY AGE	PRESCHOOL ★★★★★	GRADE SCHOOL ★★★★	TEENS ★★
YOUNG ADULTS ★★		OVER 30 ★	SENIORS ★

What it is Children's roller coaster. **Scope and scale** Minor attraction. **When to go** Before 11 a.m. **Authors' rating** A good beginner's coaster; ★★★. **Duration of ride** 1 minute. **Loading speed** Slow.

DESCRIPTION AND COMMENTS A child-sized roller coaster through a forest setting, the Unicorn provides a nonthreatening way to introduce young children to the genre.

TOURING TIPS This one loads very slowly. Ride before 11 a.m.

Poseidon's Fury! (Universal Express) ★★★★

APPEAL BY AGE	PRESCHOOL ★★	GRADE SCHOOL ★★★★	TEENS ★★★★
YOUNG ADULTS ★★★★		OVER 30 ★★★★	SENIORS ★★★★

What it is High-tech theater attraction. **Scope and scale** Headliner. **When to go** After experiencing all the rides. **Special comments** Audience stands throughout. **Authors' rating** Much improved; ★★★★. **Duration of presentation** 17 minutes including preshow. **Probable waiting time** 25 minutes.

DESCRIPTION AND COMMENTS In the first incarnation of this story, the Greek gods Poseidon and Zeus duked it out, with Poseidon as the heavy. Poseidon fought with water, and Zeus fought with fire, though both sometimes resorted to laser beams and smoke machines. In the new version, the rehabilitated Poseidon now tussles with an evil wizardish guy, and everybody uses fire, water, lasers, smoke machines, and angry lemurs (*Note:* Lemurs are not actually used—just seeing if you're paying attention). As you might have inferred, the new story is somewhat incoherent, but the special effects are still amazing, and the theming of the preshow area is quite imposing. The plot unravels in installments as you pass through a couple of these areas and finally into the main theater. Though the production is a little slow and plodding at first, it wraps up with quite an impressive flourish. There's some great technology at work here. *Poseidon* is by far and away the best of the Islands of Adventure theater attractions.

TOURING TIPS If you are still wet from Dudley Do-Right, the Bilge-Rat Barges, and the *Jurassic Park* River Adventure, you might be tempted to cheer the evil wizard's flame jets in hopes of finally drying out. Our money, however, is on Poseidon. It's legal in Florida for theme parks to get you wet, but setting you on fire is frowned upon.

Frequent explosions and noise may frighten younger children, so exercise caution with preschoolers. Shows run continuously if the technology isn't on the blink. We recommend catching *Poseidon* after experiencing your fill of the rides.

SEUSS LANDING

A TEN-ACRE THEMED AREA BASED ON Dr. Seuss's famous children's books. Like at Mickey's Toontown in the Magic Kingdom, all of the buildings and attractions replicate a whimsical, brightly colored cartoon style with exaggerated features and rounded lines. There are four rides at Seuss Landing (described below) and an interactive play area, **If I Ran the Zoo,** populated by Seuss creatures.

Caro-Seuss-El (Universal Express) ★★★½

APPEAL BY AGE	PRESCHOOL ★★★★	GRADE SCHOOL ★★★★	TEENS —
YOUNG ADULTS —	OVER 30 —		SENIORS —

What it is Merry-go-round. **Scope and scale** Minor attraction. **When to go** Before 10:30 a.m. **Authors' rating** Wonderfully unique; ★★★½. **Duration of ride** 2 minutes. **Loading speed** Slow.

DESCRIPTION AND COMMENTS Totally outrageous, the Caro-Seuss-El is a full-scale, 56-mount merry-go-round made up exclusively of Dr. Seuss characters.

TOURING TIPS Even if you are too old or don't want to ride, this attraction is worth an inspection. Whatever your age, chances are good you'll see some old friends. If you are touring with young children, try to get them on early in the morning.

The Cat in the Hat (Universal Express)　★★★½

APPEAL BY AGE	PRESCHOOL ★★★★	GRADE SCHOOL ★★★★	TEENS ★★★
YOUNG ADULTS ★★★★		OVER 30 ★★★★	SENIORS ★★★★

What it is Indoor adventure ride. **Scope and scale** Major attraction. **When to go** Before 11:30 a.m. **Authors' rating** Seuss would be proud; ★★★½. **Duration of ride** 3½ minutes. **Loading speed** Moderate.

DESCRIPTION AND COMMENTS　Guests ride on "couches" through 18 different sets inhabited by animatronic Seuss characters, including The Cat in the Hat, Thing 1, Thing 2, and the beleaguered goldfish who tries to maintain order in the midst of bedlam. Well done overall, with nothing that should frighten younger children.

TOURING TIPS　This is fun for all ages. Try to ride early.

A father of three from Natick, Massachusetts, thinks we're off base when we say that nothing should frighten younger children:

I think you need to revise the Cat in the Hat Ride review by saying that it has quite the fright potential. My fairly advanced 3½-year-old was terrified on the ride. Besides all the things popping out at you, it whips you around very wildly. My wife took her on the ride, and she was screaming her head off. I did a switch-off and rode it just to see; it was pretty intense, and I nearly got whiplash! Nearly two years later, she still reminds me of the scary Cat in the Hat ride (it hasn't affected her love for the books, though!). Please reconsider your opinion.

The High in the Sky Seuss Trolley Train Ride!　★★★½ (Universal Express)

APPEAL BY AGE	PRESCHOOL ★★★★	GRADE SCHOOL ★★★½	TEENS ★
YOUNG ADULTS ★★½		OVER 30 ★★½	SENIORS ★★★

What it is Elevated train. **Scope and scale** Major attraction. **When to go** Before 11:30 a.m. **Authors' rating** ★★★½. **Special comments** Relaxed look at the park. **Duration of ride** 3½ minutes. **Loading speed** Molasses.

DESCRIPTION AND COMMENTS　Trains putter along elevated tracks, while a voice reads one of four Dr. Seuss stories over the train's speakers. As each train makes its way through Seuss Landing, it passes a series of animatronic characters in scenes that are part of the story being told. Little tunnels and a few mild turns make this a charming ride.

The ride differs depending on the story being told, and that depends on the train you board. There are two tracks at the station. Facing the platform, to your left is the Beech track, which is purple; to your right is the Star track, which is aquamarine. Each track offers two different stories. The Beech track will either recite Dr. Seuss's *ABC's* or a revised version of *And to Think That I Saw It on Mulberry Street*. The Star track offers either *Mr. Brown Can Moo! Can You?* or *The Sneetches*.

TOURING TIPS　The line for this ride is much less charming than the attraction. The trains are small, fitting about 20 people, and the loading speed is glacial. Save High in the Sky for the end of the day or ride first thing in the morning.

One Fish, Two Fish, Red Fish, Blue Fish ★★★½
(Universal Express)

APPEAL BY AGE	PRESCHOOL ★★★★	GRADE SCHOOL ★★★★	TEENS ★★★
YOUNG ADULTS ★★★		OVER 30 ★★★	SENIORS ★★★

What it is Wet version of Dumbo the Flying Elephant. **Scope and scale** Minor attraction. **When to go** Before 10 a.m. **Authors' rating** Who says you can't teach an old ride new tricks?; ★★★½. **Duration of ride** 2 minutes. **Loading speed** Slow.

DESCRIPTION AND COMMENTS Imagine Dumbo with Seuss-style fish instead of elephants and you've got half the story. The other half of the story involves yet another opportunity to drown. Guests steer their fish up or down 15 feet in the air while traveling in circles. At the same time, they try to avoid streams of water projected from "squirt posts." A catchy song provides clues for avoiding the squirting.

Though the ride is ostensibly for kids, the song and the challenge of steering your fish away from the water make this attraction fun for all ages.

TOURING TIPS We don't know what it is about this theme park and water, but you'll get wetter than at a full-immersion baptism.

ISLANDS *of* ADVENTURE TOURING PLAN

ISLANDS OF ADVENTURE ONE-DAY TOURING PLAN

BE AWARE THAT IN THIS PARK there are an inordinate number of attractions that will get you wet. If you want to experience them, come armed with ponchos, large plastic garbage bags, or some other protective covering. Failure to follow this prescription will make for a squishy, sodden day.

This plan is for groups of all sizes and ages and includes thrill rides that may induce motion sickness or get you wet. If the plan calls for you to experience an attraction that does not interest you, simply skip that attraction and proceed to the next step. Be aware that the plan calls for some backtracking. If you have young children in your party, customize the plan to fit their needs and take advantage of switching off at thrill rides.

1. Call ☎ 407-363-8000, the main information number, the day before your visit for the official opening time. Try to purchase your admission sometime prior to the day you intend to tour.
2. On the day of your visit, eat breakfast and arrive at the Islands of Adventure turnstiles 20 to 30 minutes before opening time. Park, buy your admission (if you did not purchase it in advance), and wait at the turnstiles to be admitted.

3. While at the turnstile, ask an attendant whether any rides or shows are closed that day. Adjust the touring plan accordingly.

4. When the park opens, go straight through the Port of Entry and take a left, crossing the bridge into Marvel Super Hero Island. At Super Hero Island, bear left to The Incredible Hulk Coaster.

5. Ride Incredible Hulk.

6. Exiting Hulk, hustle immediately to The Adventures of Spider-Man, also in Marvel Super Hero Island.

7. Dr. Doom's Fearfall, to the left of Spider-Man, is sort of a poor man's Tower of Terror. What's more, it loads about as fast as molasses on a shingle. We suggest you skip it. However, if you're bound and determined to ride, now's the time. *Note:* Steps 8 to 10 involve attractions where you will get wet. If you're not up for a soaking this early in the morning, skip ahead to Step 11, but be advised that you may have a bit of a wait at the Toon Lagoon attractions later in the day.

8. Continuing clockwise around the lake, depart Super Hero Island and cross into Toon Lagoon.

9. In Toon Lagoon, ride Dudley Do-Right's Ripsaw Falls.

10. Also in Toon Lagoon, ride Popeye & Bluto's Bilge-Rat Barges.

11. After the barge ride, keep clockwise around the lake, passing through Jurassic Park without stopping. Continue to the Lost Continent.

12. At the Lost Continent, ride both tracks of Dueling Dragons.

13. While at the Lost Continent, experience *Poseidon's Fury!*

14. Depart the Lost Continent, moving counterclockwise around the lake, and enter Jurassic Park.

15. In Jurassic Park, try the *Jurassic Park* River Adventure.

16. Return to the Lost Continent. Check the daily entertainment schedule for the next performance of *The Eighth Voyage of Sinbad* stunt show. If a show is scheduled to begin within 30 minutes or so, go ahead and check it out. Otherwise, skip ahead to Step 18 and work *Sinbad* in later.

17. From the Lost Continent, move clockwise around the lake to Seuss Landing. Ride The Cat in the Hat.

18. At this point, you will have done all the big stuff. Spend the rest of your day experiencing attractions you bypassed earlier or repeating ones you especially enjoyed.

PART NINE

The WATER PARKS and WATER SPORTS

WET 'N WILD and ADVENTURE ISLAND versus DISNEY WATER PARKS

DISNEY'S WATER PARKS ARE DISTINGUISHED more by their genius for creating an integrated adventure environment than by their slides and individual attractions. At the Disney water parks, both eye and body are deluged with the strange, exotic, humorous, and beautiful. Both Disney water parks are stunningly landscaped. Parking lots, street traffic, and so on are far removed from the swimming areas and out of sight. Also, each park has its own story to tell, a theme that forms the background for your swimming experience. Once you've passed through the turnstile, you're enveloped in a fantasy setting that excludes the outside world.

For many, however, the novelty of the theme is quickly forgotten once they hit the water, and the appreciation of being in an exotic setting gives way to enjoying specific attractions and activities. In other words, your focus narrows from the general atmosphere of the park to the next slide you want to ride. Once this occurs, the most important consideration becomes the quality and number of attractions and activities available and their accessibility relative to crowd conditions. Viewed from this perspective, the non-Disney water parks, especially Universal's Wet 'n Wild, give Disney more than a run for the money. Wet 'n Wild's location in Orlando instead of Adventure Island's location in Tampa doesn't hurt it either. On its own merits, Anheuser-Busch's Adventure Island isn't worth the drive from the Orlando area, where the top-notch water parks like Wet 'n Wild, Blizzard Beach, and Typhoon Lagoon are. But it's a fine way to pass the morning if you've spent the night in Tampa after a visit to Busch Gardens. And there's more to see here than at Tampa's Cypress Gardens' Splash Island, plus the tamer rides and lighter crowds than at the Orlando parks are a nice break for the younger members of your family.

A FLUME-TO-FLUME COMPARISON

THE FOLLOWING CHART PROVIDES a sense of what each water park offers, inside and outside Walt Disney World. In standard theme-park jargon, the water parks refer to their various features, including slides, as attractions. Some individual attractions consist of several slides. If each slide at a specific

SLIDES	BLIZZARD BEACH	TYPHOON LAGOON	WET 'N WILD	ADVENTURE ISLAND
Vertical Speed Body Slide	1	1	2	1
Vertical Speed Tube Slide	1	–	–	–
Twisting Body Slide	–	–	1	4
Camel Hump Body Slide	1	–	1	–
Camel Hump Mat Slide	1	–	–	–
Camel Hump Tube Slide	–	–	1	2
Corkscrew Mat Slide	–	–	1	1
Corkscrew Body Slide	–	3	1	–
Open Corkscrew Tube Slide	3	4	2	3
Dark Corkscrew Tube Slide	1	–	2	1
FLUMES	BLIZZARD BEACH	TYPHOON LAGOON	WET 'N WILD	ADVENTURE ISLAND
1–3-Person Raft Flume	3	2	3	1
4–5-Person Raft Flume	1	1	3	–
Total Slides	12	11	17	13
OTHER ATTRACTIONS				
Interactive Water Ride	1	1	1	1
Wave Pool	1	1	1	1
Surf Pool	–	1	1	1
Snorkeling Pool	–	1	–	–
Lazy River	1	1	1	1
Isolated Children's Area	2	2	2	2
Other Attractions Total	5	7	6	6
Total Slides and Attractions	17	18	23	19

attraction is different, we count them separately. Runoff Rapids at Blizzard Beach, for example, offers three corkscrew slides, each somewhat different. Because most guests want to experience all three, we count each individually. At the Toboggan Racers attraction (also at Blizzard Beach), there are eight identical slides, side by side. There's no reason to ride all eight, so we count the whole attraction as one slide.

Do the numbers tell the story? In the case of Wet 'n Wild, they certainly do. If you can live without the Disney theme setting and story line, Wet 'n Wild offers more attractions and more variety than any of the other parks. Plus, throughout the summer, Wet 'n Wild is open until 11 p.m., offering live bands and dancing nightly. Even if you don't care about the bands or dancing, summer nights are more comfortable, lines for the slides are shorter, and you don't have to worry about sunburn.

unofficial **TIP**
Wet 'n Wild's later summer hours may mean shorter lines for the slides in the evenings.

Did we mention the giant toilet bowl? Wet 'n Wild has an attraction dubbed The Storm. The ride actually looks like a lot of fun, but in all honesty it strongly resembles a huge commode. Riders wash down a chute to gain speed, then circle around a huge bowl before dropping into a pool below. This must be how that goldfish you flushed in third grade felt.

Generally speaking, during the day, you'll find Adventure Island in Tampa the least crowded of the parks, followed by Wet 'n Wild. The Disney parks quite often sell out by about 11 a.m. This is followed by long waits for all the slides.

Although not approaching Disney's standard for aesthetic appeal and landscaping, both Wet 'n Wild and Adventure Island are clean and attractive. In the surf and wave pool department, Disney's Typhoon Lagoon wins hands down. Whereas its surf lagoon produces six-foot waves that you can actually body surf, the wave pools at the other parks offer only "bobbing" action. All of the parks have outstanding water-activity areas for younger children, and each park features at least one unique attraction: Wet 'n Wild has an interactive ride where you control your speed and movements with water blasts; Blizzard Beach has a 1,200-foot water bobsled; Adventure Island has a multistage slide broken up with pools of water; and at Typhoon Lagoon you can snorkel among live fish.

Prices for one-day admission are about the same at Blizzard Beach, Typhoon Lagoon, Wet 'n Wild, and Adventure Island. Discount coupons are often available in free local visitor magazines for Wet 'n Wild.

▌ ■ WET 'N WILD

WET 'N WILD (on International Drive in Orlando, one block east of Interstate 4 at Exit 75A; ☎ 800-992-WILD or 407-351-1800;

www.wetnwildorlando.com) is a non-Disney water-park option. Unlike Typhoon Lagoon and Blizzard Beach, where scenic man-made mountains and integrated themes create a colorful atmosphere, Wet 'n Wild's only theme appears to be concrete, plastic, and water. Fortunately, the thrill, scope, and diversity of its rides make Wet 'n Wild an excellent alternative to the Disney swimming parks. Besides, contrary to what some Disney execs might believe, their water isn't any wetter.

There is no transportation to Wet 'n Wild from Disney property. If you are staying in Walt Disney World, in Lake Buena Vista, or along US 192, you will need a car. If you are staying on International Drive, you can take the International Drive trolley (**www.iridetrolley.com** for schedules and fees). If you drive, there is a large Wet 'n Wild parking lot that charges $7 per day for cars and $8 for vans and RVs. Parking is ample; just be sure to hold the kids' hands when crossing the street.

You can buy your tickets at the main gate. Prices are $38 for adults and $31 for children, and weekday season passes are $47, but call beforehand for special deals and discounts for those in the military, AAA members, Florida residents, and groups. Ticket prices are similar to those of the Disney parks, but if you attend during the summer, the park is open late (9 a.m. to 9 p.m. Monday through Thursday and 9 a.m. to 11 p.m. Friday and Saturday), allowing visitors to hit the slides in the morning, go back to the hotel for lunch and a nap, and then return for a dip at night. Disney water parks typically close by 6 or 7 p.m.

When you get hungry, the main food pavilions are the centrally located **Surf Grill** and **Pizza 'n Subs,** together offering such staples as hamburgers and pizza as well as more-nutritious (and nontraditional) items such as veggie burgers and tabbouleh. Wait times are long, and prices are high but not outrageous. For guests whose budgets and impatience thresholds are less flexible, feel free to bring in a cooler of lunch fixings (remember, glass containers and alcoholic beverages are prohibited, but you can purchase beer inside).

All the slides outside the Kids' Park have a 48-inch height requirement except for multipassenger slides, for which the minimum height is 36 inches if an adult accompanies the short rider; the only exceptions to this are the **Hydra Fighter** and rides at the **Wakezone,** for which the height requirement is 56 inches.

BODY AND MAT SLIDES

SLIDES AT WET 'N WILD INCLUDE **Mach 5, Bomb Bay, Der Stuka, Blue Niagara,** and **The Storm.** The Mach 5 tower, located to the left of the park entrance, consists of three mat slides. The mats increase your speed and eliminate the chafing often experienced on body slides. To go even faster, try to get a newer mat with a smoother bottom. They are easily distinguishable: the new mats have white handles, while the old mats have blue ones.

Among the body slides (those without mats or rafts) are Bomb Bay and Der Stuka, twin speed flumes with pitches up to 79 degrees that descend from the top of a six-story tower. On Bomb Bay you stand on a pair of doors that open, dropping you into the chute. You have to work up the nerve to launch yourself on Der Stuka. The lack of a fully enclosed tube (such as the one on the Humunga Kowabunga speed slide at Typhoon Lagoon) adds the (perhaps justifiable) fear of falling off the 250-foot slides, but their ability to float your stomach somewhere near your teeth is a pretty unforgettable thrill. The Blue Niagara body slides, located on the same tower as the speed flumes, are a pair of slides twisted together like the Karykeion of Hermes, the famous medical seal of two snakes entwined on a staff—an appropriate simile since you might be seeking medical attention for bruising and nausea after riding one of these. The experience in these tubes is rough, dark, and frenzied, more akin to a bad night in Tijuana than a sunny day in Florida.

> *unofficial* **TIP**
> Although the ride attendants say that all three of the Mach 5 slides are equal, the center slide appears to be the zippiest route to the bottom.

The Storm body slide, located near Bomb Bay, Der Stuka, and Blue Niagara, is a hybrid ride: half slide, half toilet bowl. The steep slide creates enough momentum to launch riders into a few laps around the bowl below before they begin slipping toward the hole in the center, eventually falling into a six-foot-deep pool. The ride is exhilarating and disorienting; when the lifeguard at the ending pool begins hollering, just stumble toward his voice and give him a thumbs-up.

RAFT AND TUBE RIDES

THE HEADLINERS AT WET 'N WILD are the raft and tube rides, including **Disco H2O, The Surge, Black Hole, the Bubba Tub, The Flyer,** and **The Blast.** Disco H2O holds up to four people in one raft, ushering them down a long tube into a 1970s-era nightclub complete with lights, music, and a disco ball. The basic design of the ride is similar to that of The Storm (a long tube into a bowl), only not as frantic and disorienting; the disco theme, coupled with the fluidity of the ride, makes it a main draw.

The Surge launches from the same tower as Disco H2O and uses the same four-person rafts. Riders spin down the open-air course, drifting high onto the walls on each banked corner. To reach the top of the walls, try to go with a full raft—as with all raft rides, the more riders squeezed in, the faster you'll all go. Directly across from The Surge's splashdown pool is the entrance for Black Hole. Bring a partner for this one; Black Hole requires two riders on each raft, and honestly, who wants to embark into endless murk without some company? As impressive as the ride seems from afar, the anxiety created by the gaping entrance is the most exciting part of the ride. Yes, it's dark—there is a green piece of track lighting down the entire course—but besides the darkness, the ride lacks the dips and turns found on the other slides. If you're claustrophobic and scared of the dark, this isn't the ride for you; if tight spaces and inky blackness don't give you a rush, then this isn't the ride for you either.

The three gentler raft rides are The Flyer, The Blast, and the Bubba Tub. The first two launch from the same tower as the Mach 5, but their entrance is accessible through the Kids' Park. At the base of the entrance are one- and two-person rafts; these are only for The Blast, so don't carry them up to the tower to the Flyer entrance. The Flyer is a calmer toboggan-style ride in which riders sit one behind the other; it's suitable for families with smaller children. The Blast is a themed ride, like Disco H20, and is the wettest you can get without swimming. The theme of The Blast appears to be a broken water-works, complete with spinning dials and broken pipes, all painted in comic-book red and yellow. From mist to falling water to spraying pipes, this is the best way to cool off at Wet 'n Wild. The Bubba Tub, located across the park from The Flyer and The Blast, is a long, straight track with three hummocks to impede momentum, but with a full tube of four people, you hit the "tub" at a good clip.

OTHER ATTRACTIONS

THE CENTRAL FIXTURE AT WET 'N WILD, the **Surf Lagoon** wave pool, is on par with Blizzard Beach. There is no surfing in this wave pool—unlike the early-morning option at Typhoon Lagoon—but you can rent tubes at the main rental stand or go bobbing with your body. The wave-making machine takes long breaks every day, so when you walk by and see waves, be sure to wade in.

Another any-time-of-day option is the **Lazy River.** Unlike the Lazy River at Typhoon Lagoon, the Lazy River at Wet 'n Wild is a mis-nomer: the circuit is short, the current fast. Don't even bother trying to walk upstream to catch a tube—it's better to swim down the river or wait patiently until one passes within reach.

If you really like waiting patiently, try the **Hydra Fighter** at midday. The ride, which has a 56-inch height requirement, consists of two rotating towers with four arms and four chairs on each. Riders spin around on the towers, firing powerful hoses to both facilitate the spinning and soak the other riders.

Wet 'n Wild's 3,200-square-foot **Kids' Park** is a smaller-scale ver-sion of the adult menu. It's located to the left of the main gate; look for the oversize sandcastle capped off with a big blue bucket. The bucket actually fills with water and tips over, soaking the people in front of the castle, while the castle has two slides that leave from its porticos and one small wet ramp for toddlers located on the castle's left side. There are three longer slides in back of the castle: two body slides and one tube slide. The kids' area also contains a mini–wave pool, a kid-size climbing net, a junior river ride, and two very short zip lines. If keeping your towels in a rented locker is too much of a hassle, the kids' area is a good safe place to keep your towels (but double-check them for boogers before drying off).

WAKEZONE

THE MOST DISTINCTIVE OFFERING AT WET 'N WILD is the Wakezone, situated on a lake that's roughly the same size as the rest of the park and offering three different activities: wakeboarding, kneeboarding, and tubing. The lines can be considerable, especially since the attraction only runs from noon to dusk and is open on weekends only from mid-March to June, daily during the summer, and weekends only from September to mid-October. Be sure to call before going to Wet 'n Wild to see if the area is open that day. To avoid lines, wander over to the Wakezone at least 20 minutes before noon.

At the boarding area, you can choose either a wakeboard or a kneeboard. Helmets and life jackets, provided free at the entrance, are required; there is also a height requirement of 56 inches. The ride is basically a cable with hanging towlines that, like a T-bar at a ski resort, pull riders along the half-mile loop. You board from a slightly submerged dock where you grab the towline as it passes overhead. Brace yourself—towlines have a tendency to jerk. Keep your arms rigid and the nose of the board up. There are no instructors, so watch the other riders and chat up the good ones for tips while you're in line. If you fall down while riding, get out of the cable's path and swim to shore. If you fall where there is no nearby dock, a Jet Ski will come and pick you up.

The name of the tubing ride is **The Wild One.** For an extra fee ($6 per person), a Jet Ski will pull you around the lake while you sit in an inner tube. The ride lasts five minutes, but it's worth the money if you've never been tubing before.

ADVENTURE ISLAND

ADMISSION PRICES

A SINGLE-DAY ADMISSION TO ADVENTURE ISLAND is $34.95 plus tax for adults and $32.95 plus tax for children ages 3 to 9. FunCard admission, good for one calendar year from purchase, is $40.95 plus tax per person, but has some restrictions. From June 3rd until August 6th and during Memorial Day weekend, FunCard holders have to pay $10 per visit. The Silver Passport, good for one year from the date purchased, is $79.95 plus tax and is unrestricted. Discounted tickets are available online, and during slower parts of the year, a $9.95 plus tax second-day add-on is available for use within seven days of the original admission.

ARRIVING

ADVENTURE ISLAND IS OPEN FROM 9:30 A.M. TO 6 P.M., or 10 a.m. to 5 p.m. depending on the day of your visit. The park is closed from November to February, and open only on select days during March and October. Call ahead for park hours the day of your visit. You should arrive at the park at least 30 minutes before it opens, as the parking lot fills quickly and during the peak season reaches capacity before noon. By arriving early, you will be able to park directly in front of the main entrance and should be able to both purchase tickets and visit all of the attractions before any crowds begin to form.

Besides affording quick access to the ticket booth, parking close to the entrance is also helpful if you bring a picnic. Large coolers are permitted in the park but glass containers, alcoholic beverages, and knives are prohibited. Although the theming at Adventure Island is light, there are some wonderful shaded picnic areas. All of the picnic areas are to the left of the park entrance. We recommend the picnic tables under the live oaks between the Everglides and the Riptide. Quieter picnic spots, also in the shade, can be found behind the Riptide, and a gazebo—first come, first served—is located near the run-out pool for the Caribbean Corkscrew.

To purchase food within the park, stop by the **Surfside Café** at the park's entrance, or **Mango Joe's** in the rear of the park near the Volley Ball Spike Zone. Surfside Café offers traditional grill food and pizza, but healthy choices such as a turkey wrap are available. Unfortunately, seating here is all outside without any shade. Mango Joe's has a more diverse menu, including burger platters, PB&Js, and chicken fajitas. The prices at both eateries are $2.69 for standard theme-park fare with fries, $6.39 for a cheeseburger platter, and $2.39 for a small soda (a large is $2.79).

When you want to buy food, you may find your money is soaked. Adventure Island's solution to wet money is a scannable armband. Using a credit card or cash, you may preload an armband with the amount of money you would like to spend. When purchasing food or merchandise, swipe your armband and the money is deducted from your account. The program, available at Guest Services, is free, and any leftover money on the armband is fully refunded. The armband, cash, or credit card can be used at any of the snack bars and at the gift shop where you can purchase sunscreen, swim equipment, or any other forgotten items (for a severe markup).

If you want to store any gear that you have purchased or brought, small lockers are available for $8 each, $3 of which is refunded to you on the return of your key, but only as a gift certificate to the gift shop. The locker keys come with a safety pin to clip to your clothing, and there is no fee for lost keys. Be aware, if you receive a key numbered between 1 and 650, your locker will be on an elevated wooden platform above a small lake. The slats in the platform are far apart, so be very careful about dropping anything as you open and close your locker; there's no way to get it back without persuading an employee to let you go swimming.

Although you may be able to coax an employee to let you into restricted areas, there is no finagling your way onto the rides if you don't meet the height requirements.

For all of the major body slides or raft rides, you must be at least 42 inches tall, although a few require that you be at least 48 inches tall to ride. There are slides and other attractions that have no height requirement. If we do not mention a height requirement for an attraction, you may assume that the height requirement is 42 inches.

GETTING THERE

TO GET TO ADVENTURE ISLAND, follow the directions to Busch Gardens in Tampa in the Busch Gardens chapter. Once you have arrived on East Busch Boulevard, continue to Busch Gardens. Turn left onto McKinley Drive, the first road past Busch Gardens, and you will find Adventure Island on your right. The park is set back from the road, and there is ample parking, costing $5 for both cars and campers.

CONTACTING ADVENTURE ISLAND

FOR MORE INFORMATION, contact Adventure Island at ☎ 888-800-5447 or **www.4adventure.com.**

ATTRACTIONS

Raft Rides

Adventure Island hosts five raft rides, and in clockwise order from the entrance they are: **The Everglides, Calypso Coaster, Aruba Tuba, Key West Rapids,** and the **Wahoo Run.** All of the raft rides are tame, but the Wahoo Run is as good a ride as any found at Wet 'n Wild.

The Everglides is the first ride you come to when you take a left at the entrance. At the bottom of the run-out pool, pick up a yellow sled. The sleds are rather heavy, but even children should have no problem carrying them up to the top of the 72-foot tower. To get down from the top, you can choose either of the two identical slides. Once you're settled in your sled, signal to the lifeguard that you are ready and then hold onto the side handles. A hydraulic ram lifts the back of your sled and pitches you forward down the slide. Although the drop is exhilarating, skipping across a 60-foot run-out pool is the high point of the ride. You can steer your sled by lightly pulling on the handles and leaning in the direction you want to go.

Across from the Everglides is the tower for the Aruba Tuba and the Calypso Coaster. Each ride requires different rafts and tubes, so double-check to make sure you have the transportation you want before you schlep it to the top of the tower (if you get confused as to which tube goes on which slide, pick up your tube from the run-out pool at the base of the slide that you want to ride). The Aruba Tuba is green, and requires either a single-person tube or a two-person raft. The slide has both open and enclosed portions, and as you spin around backward, the pitch-dark patches will take you by surprise. The Aruba Tuba's curves are both plentiful and evenly spaced, creating a more docile and rhythmic run than Calypso Coaster's. The Calypso Coaster tube is white, and you may use either single-person blue tubes or double-person rafts. The slide is faster than the Aruba Tuba and sends you high onto the walls. Regrettably, there are no steep pitches common on other raft rides, just a steady side-to-side motion.

The Adventure Island ride with the greatest lack of pitch is the Key West Rapids, located in the back, left-hand corner of the park. You may ride in single-person tubes or in two-person rafts, but the combined weight of the raft cannot exceed 900 pounds—according to the sign at the base of the ride. Children under 42 inches tall may ride if they wear a life vest, available at stations around the park. From the top of the tower, you can see into Busch Gardens and down toward the Greater Tampa area. Although the height exceeds that of almost all of the other attractions (except for the Wahoo Run), the trip down Key West Rapids, interrupted with three small pools, is equivalent to a green trail on a ski mountain. The pools in the middle of the slide are unique, but there appears to have been a mild miscalculation in the strength of the pools' water jets that are supposed to push you across each pool to the next portion of the slide. Instead of being pushed via jets, you get tugged from one portion to the next by a lifeguard waiting in each pool. Although the ride down is meandering and slow, the final drop is steep, waking you up just in time to make your way to the next attraction.

In the opposite corner of the park from Key West Rapids is Wahoo Run, tucked away behind the Runaway Rapids. Our favorite ride in the park, Wahoo Run seats up to five people with a combined weight of 800 pounds. Children under 42 inches tall may ride as long as they wear a life vest. There is no lap riding, so little guys must be able to sit up on their own. After everyone is on board, the raft is sent spinning as it descends through both open and enclosed sections of slide. Unlike other enclosed slides, Wahoo Run has a wide enough diameter on its enclosed sections to keep claustrophobia at bay. Small waterfalls splash down on you as you enter and exit each of the enclosed sections. Even though these portions are pitch-black, there are no steep drops, so breathe easy. The ride is fast enough to keep thrill junkies entertained, but smooth enough for the entire family to enjoy.

Body and Mat Slides

The body and mat slides at Adventure Island are, for the most part, tamer than those at Wet 'n Wild. The calmer rides are on par with Disney's Typhoon Lagoon, although the slides are generally shorter than

Disney's. These calmer, shorter slides allow younger guests moderate thrills without forcing them to ride through a whitewash of water that may frighten them. There are five attractions at Adventure Island that contain body or mat slides, and only two of them are moderately frantic. The five attractions are, in clockwise order beginning at the park's entrance: the **Gulf Scream,** the **Riptide,** the **Caribbean Corkscrew,** the **Water Moccasin,** and the **Runaway Rapids.**

The Gulf Scream is across from the Everglides and is one of the two body slide attractions built for older kids. Riders must be 48 inches tall to take the plunge from the top of the 210-foot tower. The slide is a straight descent, allowing riders to gain speeds of up to 25 miles per hour before dumping them into the run-out pool. Even though it is a moderately thrilling straight slide, we can't count it as a speed flume since there is no major drop at the beginning, like that found on the Der Stuka slide at Wet 'n Wild. Still, the ride is the fastest your body will go at Adventure Island without the aid of a tube, and it should meet or exceed your expectations.

The Riptide is the newest attraction at Adventure Island, and with all of the media buzz—rampant television advertisements and radio spots—we expected a bit more. The only mat slide in the park, Riptide is not as fast or entertaining as Wet 'n Wild's Mach 5 mat slide, in part because all the mats at Riptide have corrugated bottoms, making them slower. The Riptide slide is also shorter than the Mach 5, and although we would usually just write this off as a ride for younger kids, there is a 48-inch height requirement to ride. The attraction consists of two pink and two blue enclosed tubes that descend from the 55-foot tower. Four riders begin at the same time and race one another to the bottom. To get the most out of these mats, keep your feet off the slide, and move your body weight as far forward as comfortable while keeping your center of gravity pressed low. Take the turns high and stay in the center of the slide for the straightaways. Other than that, the slides nearest the lifeguard stand toward the inside are a bit shorter than the outer slides.

Another enclosed slide is the Caribbean Corkscrew body slide. Eerily similar to the Blue Niagara slide at Wet 'n Wild, these two intertwined cylinders are twisted together like Twizzler™ candy and are just as likely to cause tooth loss. The ride is not as violent as the Blue Niagara, but you will still be unceremoniously ground and mashed about in the dark until you are finally spat out into the run-out pool.

A more amenable attraction is the Water Moccasin, located near the Key West Rapids. The Water Moccasin consists of three slides. The slides are set up like a mouth harp, with two slides curving around to each side of the pool and one flume dropping into the center. All of the slides are short, a benefit since the seams between each section of tubing have mild ridges that may sting your back as you pass over them. The truncated flume has the fewest seams and is also the fastest. There are no height requirements for the Water Moccasin.

If you enjoy mellow, shorter slides, five such slides are located in the Runaway Rapids, located in the rock formation to the right of the park's entrance. None of these slides has a height requirement. The rocks, which each slide weaves through, make up the best theming in the park. As you climb up the path through the rocks, it diverges in two directions. The path to the left takes you to the kiddie slide, numbered and named #1-Corkscrew Canal and #2-Little Squirt. The Corkscrew Canal wraps around a central post, while the Little Squirt takes you straight down. Children may wear life vests if they sit in the laps of adults. The path to the right winds through a crag in the rocks that contains a stream and a bench, and then rises up to the slides, numbered and named #3–Corkscrew Falls, #4–River of No Returns, and #5–Barracuda Run. Although all three slides are very similar, the ride is anything but. Corkscrew Falls is the fastest, River of No Returns is the rowdiest with plenty of sharp turns, and Barracuda Run is the most scenic, with bamboo and palm leaves overhead. Although there is no height requirement, there is no lap riding or life vests allowed on these three slides.

Other Attractions

Adventure Island has a few other attractions that merit note. They are, again in clockwise order: the **Ramblin' Bayou, Splash Attack, Fabian's Funport,** the **Endless Surf Wavepool,** and the **Paradise Lagoon.** Ramblin' Bayou is a stream that encircles the left side of the park. Much larger than Wet 'n Wild's Lazy River, Ramblin' Bayou is more akin to the stream at Typhoon Lagoon. Although the theming isn't Disney grade, palm trees and flower beds line the Ramblin' Bayou, giving you something to look at as you float around on your inner tube. The stream splits at one point; the left-hand channel takes you back around immediately toward the Riptide, while going right extends your ride, taking you through a greenhouse coated in Spanish moss. Be advised that there are sprinklers in the greenhouse and the water is noticeably cooler than that of the stream. There are no height requirements for Ramblin' Bayou, but children under 42 inches tall must wear a life vest. There are no lines here, and when the other attractions are crowded, wade into the stream, grab a tube, and wait till the crowds thin out for lunch.

Ramblin' Bayou will take you next to Splash Attack, a wet jungle gym similar to Polynesian Adventure at Cypress Gardens. Splash Attack has no water underneath, but plenty above. Perched atop the four slides, cargo nets, water cannons, treehouse, and other contraptions is a 1,000-gallon bucket that dumps water onto its victims underneath every seven minutes. Parents who want to watch their kids will be able to see them from a dry vantage point, but there is very little shade available, so it's best to bring an umbrella or a bottle of sunscreen.

Fabian's Funport is another wet jungle gym and is located between the Spike Zone and the Endless Surf Wavepool. Fabian's Funport caters to a 50-inch-tall-and-under crowd, and although its play area is not as large as Wet 'n Wild's kids' zone, Fabian's miniature wave pool, water mushrooms, wet tunnels, and mini-aqueducts serve their purpose of keeping the little ones cool. The maximum water depth is 12 inches and swim diapers are required.

Behind Fabian's Funport and Mango Joe's cafe is the **Spike Zone Volleyball Court.** The area does not see much activity unless a tournament is under way, but volleyballs are available at Mango Joe's for a refundable deposit. Sunbathers who want to savor the illusion of being at the beach should head here to lie out on the secluded sands.

For those interested in regular bathing, the Endless Surf Wavepool is the place to head. Located in the center of the park, it's impossible to miss. The wave pool is about the same size as Wet 'n Wild's wave pool, but at the head of the pool, replacing the big Wet 'n Wild sign, is a countdown clock that clicks off the time until the waves begin again. Unlike other wave pools, the Endless Surf Wavepool makes choppy waves only up to five-feet high.

Paradise Lagoon is another large pool, sans the waves. Although swimming about is fun, the draw here is the three "cliff"-jumping platforms and two small slides, located at the back of the lagoon. Jumpers wait until a lifeguard sets the streetlight signal to green, and then jump the 10 feet—feet first only—into the pool. There are two staging areas, and facing the water from above, the left-hand area contains both slides and one jumping platform. (Be sure to hold your nose when you go through the slides, or you'll come up spitting water.) The right-hand area contains no slides but two cliff-jumping platforms. Although the 10-foot jump into the water is the same from both left and right, many jumpers will wait in line on the left for the platform next to the slides, while the other two platforms go unused. Skip the line and go to the right-hand area, wait for the green light, and jump in.

WATER SPORTS

BUENA VISTA WATERSPORTS

Getting There

FROM DISNEY Take World Center Parkway to FL 535 (also called Kissimmee Vineland Road) and turn left. Just before you cross under Interstate 4, you will see a small sign on your right for Buena Vista WaterSports. If you miss the sign, do not pass under I-4. Instead, take a right onto Vineland Avenue and pull into the parking lot. The parking lot is connected to Lake Bryan Drive. Buena Vista WaterSports is at 13245 Lake Bryan Drive, Orlando.

FROM ORLANDO Take I-4 to Exit 68 and go south on FL 535. You should be able to see the sign for Buena Vista WaterSports on your left almost immediately after you start south.

Admission Prices

Buena Vista WaterSports rents out Seadoo GTI Jet Skis that fit two to three people and pontoon boats that accommodate 12 guests each. The fee for either a **Jet Ski** or a **pontoon boat** is $90 per hour. To drive either, you need to be at least 18 years of age. Young adults between the ages of 18 and 22 will need a boat safety license, a written test that can be taken on-site for a $5 fee, and is good for one year anywhere in Florida.

Buena Vista will also tow you behind their competition ski boats on either a **tube,** a **banana sled,** a **kneeboard, water skis,** or a **wakeboard.** The cost, including equipment rental is $45 for 15 minutes, $75 for 30 minutes, or $130 for a full hour. Although it's not stated, a "tips for tips" gratuity policy for personal instruction is the standard for most vacation activities.

Arriving

Located in an old lakeside mansion, Buena Vista WaterSports is only a ten-minute drive from Walt Disney World. Buena Vista is open year-round, weather permitting, from 10 a.m. to 5 p.m. daily.

Once you've gotten off of the stress-filled freeways and byways of Greater Orlando, you'll welcome the laid-back surfer atmosphere lakeside. The wicker chairs on the antebellum mansion's large wooden deck face the lake, and although we could tide ourselves over with a game of volleyball and a cooler filled with snacks, the action's on the water, so don't forget to bring a swimsuit, sunscreen, and a towel.

Be sure to call ahead before you come to Buena Vista WaterSports. The lakefront site holds many competitions throughout the summer. When these are under way, you will not be able to rent certain vehicles or obtain lessons. The entire facility is also rented out for occasional parties, which also will preclude you from using the site.

Contacting Buena Vista WaterSports

For more information, call ☎ 407-239-6939 or **www.bvwatersports.com.**

ORLANDO WATERSPORTS COMPLEX

Admission Prices

All prices are listed without tax.

1 Hour $21 + tax and equipment rental for adults and $21 for children ages 16 and under

2 Hours $27 + tax and equipment rental for adults and $25 for children ages 16 and under

4 Hours $33 + tax and equipment rental for adults and $30 for children ages 16 and under

All-day Pass $40 + tax and equipment rental for adults and $36 for children ages 16 and under

Weekly Pass $185.50 + tax and daily equipment rental

Basic Equipment Rental $3 for a basic wakeboard, $2 for a life vest, $4 for both; $5 for one-hour helmet or wet-suit rental, $10 for two hours, $15 for one day. Other types of water transportation (skis, kneeboards, and the like) are available at the Pro Shop for $10 to $30.

Lessons

Cable Lessons Children ages 10 and under must take a lesson before being allowed to use the cable. 45-minute cable lessons are $65. Children ages 10 and under receive an additional two-hour pass with the lesson.

Boat Lessons 30 minutes, $50; one hour, $95.

All-you-can-ride Pass includes three sets with the boat and an all-day cable pass: $175.

Getting There

Getting to the Orlando Watersports Complex can be rather difficult, although it is visible off of the Beeline Expressway (also called the Beachline Toll Road or FL 528). From I-4, take Exit 72 east. Take the Beeline east from Orlando toward Kennedy Space Center to Exit 4. (You will have to bring $1.50 for round-trip tolls.) Exit onto Orange Blossom Trail/FL 441/Consulate Drive. Follow the signs to Orange Blossom Trail/441, then take a left on South Orange Blossom Trail. After a half-mile, turn right onto Landstreet Road and follow it for 2 miles to the large yellow sign for the Orlando Watersports Complex at 8615 Florida Rock Road. Follow the road, cross the railroad tracks, and stick to the right. Within a few hundred yards you will be at the blue gates of the complex.

Arriving

Orlando Watersports is open Monday through Friday, 11 a.m. to 9 p.m., and Saturday and Sunday, 10 a.m. to 9 p.m., from March to September. From October to February, it is open daily, 11 a.m. to 8 p.m.

The 50-acre complex features **two tow-cable courses for wakeboarding, water-skiing, kneeboarding,** and **wake-skating** (similar to wakeboarding except that your feet are not attached to the board). The novice park is larger and contains one small jump that you can ride over if you choose, but only if you wear a helmet. The advanced park is smaller and features large ramps, tabletops, and rails to slide on. The advanced park requires a helmet. In order to ride in the advanced park, you must first show your competence by completing at least one lap in the novice park.

The tow-cable system is moderately complex, so here is how it works. A single, thick elevated cable, like those found on ski resort chairlifts, moves around the perimeter of the pond at a constant speed. Permanently attached to the thick cable are a series of evenly spaced cable carriers (for explanation purposes, envision the cable carriers as large hooks). The last components of the system are the thin cables that dangle from the cable carriers. At the dangling end of the thin cables is the handle that the riders hold.

The departure area is a long dock that slopes down to the water. Riders wait their turn in a queue. When their turn is approaching, riders put on their boards and stand in ankle-deep water. Riders then take hold of the handle to a thin cable and stand by for the next cable carrier. As the cable carrier passes overhead, it unhooks the thin cable used by the previous rider and then hooks into the thin cable held by the awaiting rider. Riders, if they hold on while being jerked forward, are now off the dock and skimming around the pond.

The novice pond has nine cable carriers and the advanced pond has four; this means that only nine people can be on the novice pond at one time and only four on the advanced pond at one time. When the park is crowded, each rider is allowed one lap around the pond before he or she has to let go of the handle. To avoid crowds, arrive when the park opens. Within two hours after opening, the lines can become excessive. During the off-season or on slow days, riders are allowed as many as five laps around the pond before they have to let go. When your turn is up, or if you fall, let go of the handle and swim out of the way of other riders. Detach your board and finish swimming to the shoreline, then walk back around to the queue for another go.

Riders under the age of 18 need a release form signed by their parent or guardian for any activity at the Orlando Watersports Complex. Forms can be signed on-site or can be faxed to ☎ 407-816-9070.

Before you get in the water, you can store your gear in lockers on land. Lockers cost $3, but require an additional $5 deposit that is repaid when you return the key. There are also adequate changing facilities on-site (bring your towel, sunscreen, and swimsuit), and food is available at the concession stand. Among other items, a cheeseburger is $4, a slice of cheese pizza is $2.75, and bottled sodas are $1.50.

Contacting Orlando Watersports Complex

For more information about site availability, contact Orlando Watersports Complex at ☎ 407-251-3100 or **www.orlandowatersports.com**.

PART TEN

MINIATURE GOLF

ORLANDO WOULDN'T BE A VACATION TOWN without miniature golf. Almost as abundant as fast-food chains, miniature golf courses dot the landscape on US 192, International Drive, FL 535, and inside Walt Disney World. Orlando has 15 courses, including the two at Disney, but more are springing up all the time. Since courses have different themes, quality of play, costs, and such, the golf course profiles that follow offer comparisons as well as short reviews focusing on what makes each course unique, plus course location and contact information.

Most of the miniature golf in the Greater Orlando area features long greens with few obstacles. You won't find ball-eating clowns or obnoxious windmills on any of the courses in town—the only places offering this ilk of in-course obstacles are the Disney courses. What you will find are 18 holes on clean grounds, trick shots, lots of cascading water, and a myriad of different themes.

The rules for miniature golf do differ from course to course, but the basics are fairly standard. A group consists of a maximum of four to five players. To tee off, all players in a group hit their shot. The player whose shot is farthest from the cup shoots first, then the next player, and so on. The maximum amount of strokes per hole is six. When you hit the ball out of bounds or into a water trap, retrieve the ball and place it back on the course as close to the trap as possible; you will incur a one-stroke penalty. When you lose your ball in the water and you can't recover it, you can get another ball from the main booth, but you will incur a two-stroke penalty. There is no running at any of the courses, and all of the establishments are very wary about injury. By purchasing a ticket, you waive your right to sue if you fall or stumble, or get hit with a club or a ball. If you swing the putter back too far—as if making a slap shot in hockey—you will be asked to leave. The odds of injury are much greater crossing International Drive, so don't let that rule dissuade you from one of the best family games around.

Bonanza Golf   ★★½
7761 West US 192 (Irlo Bronson Memorial Highway), Kissimmee;
☎ 407-396-7536

Hours Daily, 9 a.m.–midnight. **Cost** $7.95 for adults; $6.95 for children ages 3–9; and free for children ages 2 and under.

DESCRIPTION AND COMMENTS At the far end of US 192, you will find Bonanza Golf. There are two courses here, but the play on both is the same. Bonanza Golf has the longest greens of any of the courses (excluding Disney's Fantasia Fairway), but most are flat with a dogleg left or right. The long greens make the holes fairly easy, if not a bit bland.

The theming is supposedly a mining town, but is light at best. We don't expect animatronics, but one prospector or a few pieces of mining equipment would animate this rather dull and uninspired course. Even the waterfall, which should add some charisma to the holes, faces out toward the parking lot. Still, the grounds are very clean and all the greens are in fine condition.

Congo River Kissimmee   ★★★★½
4777 West US 192, Kissimmee; ☎ 407 396-6900; www.congoriver.com

Hours Daily, 10 a.m.–midnight. **Cost** $10.45 + tax for adults; $8.45 + tax for children ages 6–9; and free for children ages 5 and under.

DESCRIPTION AND COMMENTS Another member of the Congo River family, the Kissimmee location is very similar to the other courses in theming and play, but it is by far the largest. There are two courses at the Kissimmee location, dubbed Stanley and Livingston. Stanley is more difficult than Livingston by six shots. Although we prefer the play on the Stanley course, the Livingston course is more scenic with one hole on a boat, and a path that takes you next to the crashed zebra-striped plane. The Kissimmee location is mountainous, filled with thin paths that make backtracking to the entrance difficult and can also make finding the next hole slightly confusing. The entire complex, including the air-conditioned bathrooms, is clean, and the greens are all in great condition. The staff is accommodating and very friendly.

Congo River Orlando   ★★★★
6312 International Drive, Orlando; ☎ 407-352-0042;
www.congoriver.com

Hours Daily, 10 a.m.–midnight. **Cost** $10.45 + tax for adults; $8.45 + tax for children ages 6–9; and free for children ages 5 and under.

DESCRIPTION AND COMMENTS Next to Wet 'n Wild is another of the three Congo River courses. This is the smallest of the courses, but the play is equally as enjoyable as the others. The two courses are the Livingston, with a par of 41, and the Stanley, with a par of 43. The challenges at Congo River Orlando are the long uphill shots, which are plentiful. As with the other Congo Rivers, the grounds are clean, the African-themed course is in great condition, and the staff is friendly. However, due to its location next to Wet 'n Wild on I-Drive, this course is more crowded during the day than the other Congo River courses and can become packed at night. Although we enjoyed this course, you might be better off proceeding up I-Drive a few more blocks until you reach Congo River Universal.

Congo River Universal ★★★★
5901 International Drive, Orlando; ☎ **407-248-9181;**
www.congoriver.com

Hours Monday–Thursday, 10 a.m.–11 p.m.; Saturday and Sunday, 10 a.m.–midnight. **Cost** $10.45 + tax for adults; $8.45 + tax for children ages 5–9; and free for children ages 4 and under.

DESCRIPTION AND COMMENTS Congo River Universal is just a short drive up from Wet 'n Wild. The entire place is new, the grounds are superbly clean, and the lies of the greens put the ball where you aim it. There is only one course and the first nine holes are relatively level, making them handicapped accessible, but not as challenging as holes at the other Congo River locations.

What sets this apart from its kin is the quality of theming. All the Congo River golf courses have African themes, but the execution here surpasses the others. To start with, the course is built both around and within a large red-rock mountain. On the mountain, you will find a Land Rover stuck in a waterfall, a zebra-striped airplane sticking out of a slope, and caverns with skeletons. A great baobab tree caps off this I-Drive landmark. Even some of the holes are themed: hole #7 is played on a dilapidated ship.

Congo River Universal also contains a few nongolf attractions. Like the two other Congo River courses, the Universal course has a baby alligator pit with pieces of meat to feed the gators, available for $3.15, but it also contains a pond filled with koi you can feed for $0.25, a gift shop, a small arcade, and a game called Congo River Hoops that consists of 18 basketball hoops slung in unorthodox ways.

Fantasia Gardens ★★★★½
1205 Epcot Resorts Boulevard, Lake Buena Vista; ☎ **407-560-4870**

Hours Daily, 10 a.m.–11 p.m. **Cost** $11.45 for adults; $9.06 for children ages 3–9; repeat rounds are $5.73 for adults and $4.53 for children ages 3–9, all tax included.

DESCRIPTION AND COMMENTS Disney creativity is uncanny. A short walk from the Dolphin Hotel, Fantasia Gardens has two courses, one called Fantasia Gardens and the other called Fantasia Fairway. Although the greens have been bleached out by the sun and trodden down by tourists, Fantasia Gardens is one of the best courses in Orlando. What Disney excels at is not making difficult holes (they aren't), or making big rocky mountains to play on (none of those either), but instead making each hole unique. Each hole is themed after a different character from the *Fantasia* movies, including Cupid, the flamingos, and the ballerina hippos. From holes that sound trumpets when you sink a putt to fountains on motion sensors that squirt water at you as you walk along, Disney has set the bar for creative design.

The Fantasia Fairway is, literally, a miniature golf course. There are grass greens and sand traps. The holes are long, some in excess of 100 feet. You can't use any irons, but you will have to putt farther than you ever have before. Both of these courses are open to non-Disney guests.

Full Speed Race and Golf ★★
5720 West US 192, Kissimmee (at Old-Town); ☎ 407-397-7455; www.fullspeed.cc

Hours Monday–Friday, 3 p.m.–midnight; Friday and Saturday, noon–midnight. **Cost** $10 for adults; $8 for children; $5 for repeat players; $20 for simulator and minigolf; $50 for all-day simulator and minigolf.

DESCRIPTION AND COMMENTS A lesser minigolf course, its claim to fame is being the only "indoor, black-light, race-car-themed 18-hole minigolf course." With all these qualifiers, we're not surprised to find a mediocre course. The carpeting is black, and under the black lights, both your ball and the obstacles glow. The black carpet makes the small bumps and hills almost impossible to see, so many of your shots may go askew. There are no major hills or wild shots in this humdrum one-story course. The decor consists of airbrushed pictures of flaming cars, and the course obstacles are painted car parts made of hard foam. To complete the effect, 1980s hair metal plays over the sound system. With 14 other minigolf locations in Orlando, there is no need to spend your money here unless you buy a package deal with the NASCAR simulator. Early-bird specials may be available for play before noon, but call ahead to check.

Hawaiian Rumble Adventure Golf, Buena Vista ★★½
13529 South Apopka-Vineland Road, Orlando; ☎ 407-239-8300

Hours Sunday–Thursday, 10 a.m.–11 p.m.; Friday and Saturday, 10 a.m.–midnight. **Cost** $9.95 + tax for adults; $7.95 + tax for children ages 4–10; and free for children ages 3 and under.

DESCRIPTION AND COMMENTS Like the Hawaiian Rumble course on I-Drive, the course on FL 535 in Buena Vista has two courses named the Lani and the Kahuna. Although the Lani is supposed to be the more difficult, we didn't notice a significant difference between them. What is obvious is that Hawaiian Rumble Buena Vista pales next to the I-Drive locale. The greens at Buena Vista are dirty, and the play is relatively flat. There is a large volcano in the middle and a few flowers, but the theming ends there. For some reason, Hawaiian Rumble Buena Vista also has a penchant for hiring grumpy employees. The only bonus here is that Internet access costs $3.25 for 15 minutes and $0.25 for each additional minute.

Hawaiian Rumble Adventure Golf, I-Drive ★★★½
8969 International Drive, Orlando; ☎ 407-351-7733

Hours Sunday–Thursday, 10 a.m.–11 p.m.; Friday and Saturday, 10 a.m.–midnight. **Cost** $9.95 + tax for adults; $7.95 + tax for children ages 4–10; and free for children ages 3 and under.

DESCRIPTION AND COMMENTS Located next to Wonderworks on I-Drive. Parking is available just behind the course, but you will have to walk around the front to enter. One of the busiest courses in Orlando, Hawaiian Rumble features a 40-foot volcano, plenty of flora, fountains, and a series of streams. Unlike the heavily rock-themed Pirate's Cove locales or Congo Rivers, Hawaiian Rumble is a very flat course; you can play through the volcano but not on it.

There are two courses, the Kahuna and the Lani. Kahuna is easier and takes players through the volcano. Lani is very challenging. Hole #5 has a long uphill green ending in a jump over the stream. The 17th hole, where players hit the ball through a series of logs, is one of the more creative, and difficult, holes around.

There is a concession stand at the entrance as well as a Ben & Jerry's ice-cream parlor. Internet access is also available for $3.95 for the first 15 minutes and $0.25 for each additional minute.

Pirate's Cove International Drive ★★★½
8501 International Drive, Orlando; ☎ 407-352-7378;
www.piratescove.net/location/5

Hours Daily, 9 a.m.–11:30 p.m. **Cost** $9.95 + tax for adults; $8.95 + tax for children ages 4–12; and free for children ages 3 and under; 36-Hole Special is $13.95 + tax for adults and $12.50 + tax for children ages 4–12.

DESCRIPTION AND COMMENTS Pirate's Cove on I-Drive is almost impossible to miss: it's located between the Castle Hotel and Titanic: The Experience. Just keep an eye out for the pirate marooned in the middle of a lake. Pirate's Cove has two courses. The Captain's Adventure course is easier, taking players along the front edge of the pond before they climb the hill. Plaques along the way aid the theme as they tell the story of pirate William Kidd. Blackbeard's Challenge is more difficult and offers plenty of opportunities to lose a ball in the water, including a large water gap shot on hole #9. The holes get harder as you proceed, and the fairways contain lots of rolling hills and sloping greens.

Although the course is very clean and the maintenance crew does its best, the course has some worn spots due to the high volume of visitors who spot it from I-Drive. Crowds here can be an issue, especially at night. If you like pirates and don't mind driving, you may want to play one of the other two pirate-themed courses in Orlando, even if their theming is not quite as involved. If you do visit, don't forget to take a photo-op in the stockade.

Pirate's Cove Lake Buena Vista ★★★★
12545 FL 535, Lake Buena Vista; ☎ 407-827-1242;
www.piratescove.net/location/4

Hours Daily, 9 a.m.–11 p.m. **Cost** $9.49 + tax for adults; $8.49 + tax for children ages 4–12; and free for children ages 3 and under; 36-Hole Special is $13.49 + tax for adults and $12.49 + tax for children ages 4–12.

DESCRIPTION AND COMMENTS You will see this course every time you take I-4 through Orlando. Located in the rear of the Crossroads Shopping Center, this Pirate's Cove location is less crowded than its I-Drive sibling, and the Buena Vista locale offers the same high-caliber theming and challenging courses.

The courses' names are, yet again, Captain Kidd's Adventure and Blackbeard's Challenge. Captain Kidd's is the easier course, taking players to the top of the mountain as well as through the caverns under the waterfalls on holes #13 and #14, two of the more scenic holes in Orlando. Blackbeard's Challenge has fine lies, which means the ball goes where you aim it. A few long downhill shots, however, make hitting par difficult. The greens are tidy, and excluding the I-4 traffic, the setting, with the palms and flora adorning the top of the rocky hill, is excellent.

Pirate Island ★★★
4330 West Vine Street, Kissimmee; ☎ 407-396-4660;
www.pirateislandgolf.com

Hours Daily, 9 a.m.–11:30 p.m. **Cost** $9.95 + tax for adults; $8.95 + tax for children ages 4–12; and free for children ages 3 and under; All-Day Play is available for $11.95 + tax per person.

DESCRIPTION AND COMMENTS Located where US 192 meets West Vine. Although it is not part of the Pirate's Cove franchise, Pirate Island has all of the requisite pirate theming, including a half-sunken ship in the pond. There are two courses, Captain Kidd's course and Blackbeard's course, but here Blackbeard's course is easier. Actually, most of the holes here are easier than the holes at its pirate counterparts, and the theming is not quite the same quality. What makes this course enjoyable is the elbow room. Pirate Island has more acreage than the other pirate courses, making its layout open and uncluttered. The entire place is immaculate, without even a leaf on the greens. Less overhead vegetation helps Pirate Island keep both this open feeling and clean grounds, but guests should be sure to wear sunscreen if they come during the day.

The Putting Edge ★★★½
5250 International Drive (inside the Festival Bay Mall), Orlando;
☎ 407-248-8180; www.puttingedge.com

Hours Monday–Thursday, 11 a.m.–9 p.m.; Friday and Saturday, 11 a.m.–11 p.m.; Sunday, 11 a.m.–7:30 p.m. **Cost** $8.50 + tax for adults; $7.50 + tax for children ages 7–12; $6 + tax for children ages 5–6; and free for children ages 4 and under.

DESCRIPTION AND COMMENTS Inside the Festival Bay Mall at the top of I-Drive, next to the Cinemark Theatres, is an underrated course. Although there is only one flat course, it is entirely under backlights. Unlike Full Speed Race and Golf's car extravaganza, the theme here is aquatic. The music is also more tempered, with a mix of current Top 40 tunes. The edges of each course are well-marked, and each shot is moderately interesting. Younger players will enjoy both the easy shots and the charming theme, and the indoor location makes it a perfect rainy-day getaway.

River Adventure Golf ★★
4535 West US 192, Kissimmee; ☎ 407-396-4666

Hours Daily, 9 a.m.–11 p.m. Cost $7.95 + tax per person; free for children ages 4 and under.

DESCRIPTION AND COMMENTS Near Medieval Times, on the other side of US 192, is River Adventure Golf. There is only one 18-hole course here, and it is in a mild state of disrepair. The paint is chipped, the greens are dirty, and some of the lies for the balls are warped. We managed to get a ball stuck on the second hole. The course does not have a large mountain, but there is a slight hill as well as a small stream that runs through the course. Although the whole place is rather grim in comparison with other Orlando area courses, it is still better than the courses most people will find in their hometowns. The greens are short, making the play easier. Par is 49, although most players should be able to shoot under par.

Tiki Island ★★★½
7460 International Drive, Orlando; ☎ 407-248-8180;
www.tikiislandvolcanogolf.com

Hours Daily, 10 a.m.–11:30 p.m. Cost $9.95 + tax for adults; $8.95 + tax for children ages 3–12; and free for children ages 2 and under.

DESCRIPTION AND COMMENTS Tiki Island, located across from Magical Midway on I-Drive, has two courses. The Tiki Falls course has yellow signage and is easier, while the Volcano Voyage course has orange signage and is more difficult. The terrain is mountainous, explicitly clear when you attempt hole #3 on Volcano Voyage, a thin left dogleg uphill. The only way to get the ball clear of the corner is just to whack it. Many of the other holes are equally difficult, and the greens are not very clean and have been patched.

The theme here is hard to understand, falling somewhere between *Land of the Lost* and *Jurassic Park*. We understand Tiki Island's tiki huts, bouncy jungle bridge, and South Pacific flavor including a volcano that erupts every 20 minutes nightly, but who brought all the dinosaurs? Wherever they came from—it appears to be the same creature shop that stocks Dinosaur World, but this isn't verified—they dominate the landscape and occasionally roar (that's right). Tiki Island has gone to some trouble to incorporate them into the landscape, including informative fact plaques in front of each dinosaur.

The dinosaur theme continues with the course's other draw, a set of brontosaurus-shaped paddleboats you can paddle around the tiny out-lying moat for $7.99 a turn. The course also offers a small arcade, and the staff is friendly and helpful.

Winter Summerland   ★★★★
1548 West Buena Vista Drive, Lake Buena Vista; ☎ 407-560-3000

Hours Daily, 10 a.m.–11 p.m. **Cost** $11.45 for adults; $9.06 for children ages 3–9; repeat rounds are $5.73 for adults and $4.53 for children ages 3–9, all tax included; free for children ages 2 and under.

DESCRIPTION AND COMMENTS Inside Disney property, near the entrance to Blizzard Beach, you will find out what happens when the Imagineers set their minds to making an "ordinary" miniature golf course. There are two 18-hole courses, the Winter course and the Summer course. The play on each course is the same, but Winter features a snowy Christmas theme, while Summer features a sandy Christmas theme. Although Winter Summerland is small, the Imagineers have put in the effort to make each of the 36 holes unique. The in-course obstacles, such as sand and snow castles, all have interactive components. Some holes make noise, some blow air, and a few even attempt to block your shot! None of the holes are too difficult for children, making this an ideal family stop. One caveat: Winter Summerland's compactness may have you bumping elbows with other guests. The courses can be a mob scene during the day and unplayable at night.

PART ELEVEN

OLD-TOWN

OLD-TOWN CELEBRATED ITS 20TH ANNIVERSARY in 2006. The longevity of this four-block Main Street relies upon its exclusive mixture of shopping, restaurants, carnival attractions, and thrill rides. Old-Town is fashioned to be like a modern Mayberry with the fair in town. The atmosphere is akin to East Coast beach towns like Ocean City, Maryland, or Myrtle Beach, South Carolina. Although the storefronts are attractive, Old-Town has not undergone the Disney-styled whitewash of magic and charm.

As you walk down the street, you will pass storefronts ranging from trinket shops to spas, tattoo parlors to sunglass huts, and tobacco merchants to marionette dealers. Bars and restaurants are interspersed among the shops, and at either end of Old-Town's Main Street are areas dedicated to carnival and thrill rides. Indeed, two of the more terrifying rides in Orlando—the Human Slingshot and the Sky Coaster—are located just a few blocks apart. There are also plenty of gentler rides for young children.

Old-Town also offers events throughout the year, including its famous weekly automotive shows. Bikers congregate here on Thursday nights, classic cars roll in on Friday nights, and antique autos parade down Main Street on Saturdays. A live band, creating a spirited party atmosphere, accompanies most of these shows.

One of the fine features about Old-Town is that these shows, and admittance in general, are all free. Parking is also gratis. These perks allow potential patrons to peruse the storefronts, restaurants, rides, and other attractions before committing any cash. Since all you have to invest to visit Old-Town is your time, it becomes a hard deal to pass up.

GETTING THERE

OLD-TOWN IS LOCATED ON WEST US 192 (Irlo Bronson Memorial Highway), about five minutes from Walt Disney World. From Interstate

4, take Exit 64 east onto 192. Old-Town will be just over a mile ahead on your right.

ADMISSION PRICES

THE BUSINESS MODEL FOR OLD-TOWN SEPARATES it from any amusement park in the area. Competing companies either lease or own each store and attraction, so one set of tickets or coupons is not valid for every experience. For example, Old-Town gift certificates are not accepted at Sky Coaster, while carnival tickets will not get you into Grimm's Haunted House. The lack of a common currency frees you to spend as you see fit, but also bumps up the prices on all of the rides; it appears there is little profit sharing among companies.

Old-Town tickets cost $1 apiece. The cheapest rides cost two tickets, while the most expensive rides on the ticket system cost five tickets. You can purchase all-day armbands for ticketed rides priced at $25 for adults and $15 for children under 42 inches tall. For other deals, see the Ticket Rides section farther along in this chapter.

One additional caveat: for simplicity, we have conflated Sky Coaster Thrill Park into Old-Town. Although Sky Coaster and its surrounding attractions are owned and operated by a separate company and are not officially located on Old-Town property, the adjacent location with paths leading directly into Old-Town makes it appear to any visitor that they are one and the same, and for the purposes of touring—we are not doing a property audit—we will include these attractions as part of Old-Town.

ARRIVING

OLD-TOWN IS OPEN EVERY DAY OF THE YEAR from 10 a.m. until 11 p.m. Most of the rides are open from noon to 11 p.m. Every Friday and Saturday night, Old-Town hosts a classic car show. The Friday show includes cars made between 1973–1987, begins at 5 p.m. and lasts until 11 p.m., with a parade down Main Street at 9 p.m. On Saturday, cars of a pre-1973 vintage are on hand. The show begins at 1 p.m., and the cars cruise down Main Street at 8:30 p.m. A live band, weather permitting, accompanies the car shows. There is also a motorcycle show on Thursdays. As with parking and admission to Old-Town, the show is free.

CONTACTING OLD-TOWN

FOR MORE INFORMATION, call ☎ 407-396-4888 or visit their Web site, **www.old-town.com**.

RIDES *and* ATTRACTIONS

OLD-TOWN PROPER CONSISTS OF FOUR BLOCKS on Main Street. Located between US 192 and the first block of Old-Town are the

Human Slingshot and an area called the Swing Zone. Adjacent to the Swing Zone—and behind the Burger King—is the Sky Coaster Thrill Zone. At the other end of Old-Town's Main Street, just behind the fourth block, are a myriad of carnival rides and the Windstorm Roller Coaster. The only attractions outside of these three main areas are the Old-Town Bull, Grimm's Haunted House, and the Wax Museum. They are all located between blocks three and four.

Since the admission system at Old-Town is tricky to understand, we have divided the rides and attractions into ones that take cash and credit cards only, and ones that require Old-Town tickets.

NONTICKET RIDES

Basketball Game 1 ★★

APPEAL BY AGE	PRESCHOOL ★	GRADE SCHOOL ★★½	TEENS ★★½
YOUNG ADULTS ★★		OVER 30 ★½	SENIORS ★½

What it is Shoot baskets for prizes. **Scope and scale** Minor attraction. **Authors' rating**; ★★. **Cost** $2.

DESCRIPTION AND COMMENTS A carnival game in which you shoot basketballs through a hoop to win prizes. The more baskets you make, the better your prize.

TOURING TIPS Unless you are a skilled player, you're better off taking your two dollars and going to the gift shops.

Bicycle ★★½

APPEAL BY AGE	PRESCHOOL ★★	GRADE SCHOOL ★★★	TEENS ★★½
YOUNG ADULTS ★★½		OVER 30 ★★	SENIORS ★½

What it is Bicycle swing set. **Scope and scale** Minor attraction. **Special comments** Must be at least 48" tall to ride. **Authors' rating** ★★½. **Duration of ride** 3 minutes. **Cost** $3.

DESCRIPTION AND COMMENTS A pedal-driven cart is suspended between two posts, like the Pharaoh's Fury ride. The faster you pedal, the higher you go, and if you pedal fast enough, you can spin the "bicycle" over the bar.

TOURING TIPS This ride is not crowded and much more work than fun.

Bumper Cars ★★★

APPEAL BY AGE	PRESCHOOL ★★★	GRADE SCHOOL ★★★★	TEENS ★★½
YOUNG ADULTS ★★★		OVER 30 ★★★	SENIORS ★★½

What it is Disco-themed bumper cars. **Scope and scale** Minor attraction. **Special comments** Must be 48" tall to ride. **Authors' rating** No deductibles; ★★★. **Duration of ride** 8–10 minutes. **Cost** $5 for singles; $7 for double cars.

DESCRIPTION AND COMMENTS The carts are in better shape than some of the competition's, but nothing particularly special. Although the interior has a 1970s disco theme, the music is 1980s hair metal—we suppose it's a subtle message about the timelessness of bumper cars.

TOURING TIPS Not crowded, come anytime. Bumper cars do not have a reverse, so if you get stuck, just cock the wheel hard over and press the gas.

G-Force Drag Race ★★★½

APPEAL BY AGE	PRESCHOOL ★★★	GRADE SCHOOL ★★★★	TEENS ★★★½
YOUNG ADULTS ★★★		OVER 30 ★★★½	SENIORS ★★

What it is Fast cars on a track. **Scope and scale** Headliner. **Special comments** Must be at least 52" tall to ride, 48" to be a passenger. **Authors' rating** Too short for the cash; ★★★½. **Duration of ride** 3 minutes. **Loading speed** Slow. **Cost** $30 for the driver; $10 for a passenger.

DESCRIPTION AND COMMENTS Side-by-side dragsters accelerate from 0 to 110 miles per hour in two seconds. Instead of being powered by gas or alcohol, the G-Force dragsters run on compressed air. Once you're strapped into your seat, the compressed air tank powers up. After the lights count down from red to green, you press the accelerator with your foot and blast off down the track. You don't steer the dragster; the wheels on the outside are for show only. Instead, the cars run along a metal beam, much like a roller coaster. Unlike a roller coaster, G-Force doesn't flip or dip, just accelerates, so as long as you have your head pressed against the headrest at the start, there is no jarring. Although the thrill of blasting off is exhilarating, the entire ride, including backing down the track, takes only 15 seconds.

TOURING TIPS For $30, you'll want to experience this ride only if you're an avid racing fan. Most of your time is spent buckling into the car. Your only control over the vehicle is pressing the accelerator to start you down the track, and if someone is in the car next to you, this test of reaction time determines the winner. The lights descend in the order of red, then two yellows, then green. Try to time your foot to hit the pedal right before the light turns green, and the flashing billboard won't broadcast you as being the, and we quote, "LOSER!!!"

Grimm's Haunted House ★★★

APPEAL BY AGE	PRESCHOOL ★★½	GRADE SCHOOL ★★★½	TEENS ★★★½
YOUNG ADULTS ★★★		OVER 30 ★★½	SENIORS ★★

What it is Walk through a haunted house. **Scope and scale** Major attraction. **Authors' rating** ★★★. **Cost** $9.35 + tax for adults; $6.75 + tax for children ages 9 and under.

DESCRIPTION AND COMMENTS Grimm's Haunted House is much less frightening and detailed than Skull Kingdom. As you make your way through the rooms, an actor attempts to scare you at each darkened turn. There is no plot, just moderately scary displays and dioramas. The grotesque has found a home here, and the final exhibit—we won't spoil it—is macabre and a bit tasteless. The designers attempted to lengthen the tour with a series of claustrophobic hallways, but even with the compact design, the house is not large enough to warrant the price tag.

TOURING TIPS The haunting takes place on the second floor, so you must be able to climb stairs to participate. Leading up to Halloween, lines are as gruesome as the house, so try to stop in during the day if you're visiting in October. There is no running or flashlights allowed at Grimm's.

Happy Days Go-Carts ★★★

APPEAL BY AGE	PRESCHOOL —	GRADE SCHOOL ★★★★	TEENS ★★★½
YOUNG ADULTS ★★½		OVER 30 ★★½	SENIORS ★★½

What it is Small go-cart track. **Scope and scale** Major attraction. **Special comments** Must be 58" tall to drive; no height requirement for passengers. **Authors' rating** Small; ★★★. **Duration of ride** 8–10 minutes. **Cost** $6 per person; $2 for passengers in double carts.

DESCRIPTION AND COMMENTS The go-cart track is one of the smallest in Orlando, but they did the best they could with the single oval track, having one of the longer sides bend inward to create two more turns and elevating the straightaway opposite. The simple shape allows you to pass other carts, but after eight minutes, it becomes a bit repetitious.

TOURING TIPS The cars are in rather poor shape compared with other local tracks, but their condition does not affect their speed. Still, FunSpot is the place to go for go-carts. Being the only track at Old-Town, Happy Days Go-Carts becomes very crowded in the evenings, but a full track is more exciting than an empty one. Once you've begun the race, you are forced to continue until it is completely over, since opening the gate to pit row would halt all the other carts.

Human Slingshot ★★★½

APPEAL BY AGE	PRESCHOOL †	GRADE SCHOOL †	TEENS ★★★★½
YOUNG ADULTS ★★★★		OVER 30 ★★★★	SENIORS ★★

† Sample size too small to develop rating.

What it is 180-foot slingshot. **Scope and scale** Major attraction. **Special comments** Must be 52" tall to ride. **Authors' rating** Scarier to watch than to ride; ★★★½. **Duration of ride** 4 minutes. **Loading speed** Slow. **Cost** $25 per person.

DESCRIPTION AND COMMENTS The Slingshot is a massive steel V shape with flashing rainbow lights located near the front of Old-Town. Riders latch into a two-person cart at the base of the V, where a bungee-cord system runs down the legs of the V to the cart, like a slingshot. Once you're latched in, the tethered cart is pulled below the boarding area, then released, flinging riders 365 feet into the air, spinning head over feet the entire time. After the initial launch, the elastic cable makes for a smooth rise and fall. Surprisingly, the ride is almost peaceful, and less frightening than many of the major roller coasters in the area. Being more than 300 feet above the ground silences much surrounding noise, and the nighttime view is even better—for a few seconds at a time as you bob—than the Sky Coaster's. As with most rides, the thrill is in the anticipation, not in the event. For $25 dollars, however, you're better off taking a helicopter for sightseeing or, for thrill junkies, paying out a few more bucks for the Sky Coaster.

TOURING TIPS The cart must have two people in it to keep balanced, but a ride operator will go with you if you can't convince any of your friends or family. Riding at night is more thrilling, but long lines begin after 7 p.m. During high season, the wait can be over one hour long, but watching everyone else is almost better than riding it yourself.

Laser Tag ★★★

| APPEAL BY AGE | PRESCHOOL ★★½ | GRADE SCHOOL ★★★★ | TEENS ★★★ |
| YOUNG ADULTS ★★½ | | OVER 30 ★★★ | SENIORS ★★½ |

What it is Real-life shoot-'em-up. **Scope and scale** Major attraction. **Authors' rating** Good padding; ★★★. Duration 8–10 minutes. **Cost** $5.

DESCRIPTION AND COMMENTS Forgoing the carpeted floor and many solid partitions in Lazerworks at Wonderworks, Laser Tag at Old-Town is fully padded with large air sacks. The room is smaller than at Wonderworks, but the padding allows shooters to dive and roll around to avoid getting hit, and with less cover to hide behind, you'll find yourself fully prone more often than not.

TOURING TIPS Since the course is inflatable, shoes are not permitted inside. All participants must come with clean socks or wear a provided pair. The vests that register the tally are a bit cumbersome and the lasers are hard to aim. Your best bet is to sneak up on people and to keep moving.

MiniGolf/Full Speed Race and Golf ★★

| APPEAL BY AGE | PRESCHOOL ★★★ | GRADE SCHOOL ★★★ | TEENS ★★½ |
| YOUNG ADULTS ★★ | | OVER 30 ★★ | SENIORS ★★ |

What it is Race-car-themed minigolf. **Scope and scale** Minor attraction. **Authors' rating** Boring course; ★★. **Cost** $10 for adults; $8 for children; $5 for repeat players; $20 for both simulator and minigolf; $50 for all-day simulator and minigolf.

DESCRIPTION AND COMMENTS A lesser minigolf course, its claim to fame is being the only "indoor, black-light, race-car-themed 18-hole minigolf course." With all of these qualifiers, we're not surprised to find a mediocre course. The carpeting is black, and under the black light, both your ball and the obstacles glow. The black carpet makes the small bumps and hills almost impossible to see, so many of your shots may go askew. There are no major hills or wild shots in this uninspired one-story course. The decor consists of airbrushed pictures of flaming cars, and the course obstacles are painted car parts made of hard foam. To complete the effect, 1980s hair metal plays over the sound system.

TOURING TIPS With 14 other minigolf courses in Orlando, there is no need to spend your money here, unless you buy a package deal with the NASCAR simulator. Early-bird specials may be available for play before noon, but call ahead to check.

NASCAR Simulators/Full Speed Race and Golf ★★★½

APPEAL BY AGE	PRESCHOOL ★★★	GRADE SCHOOL ★★★★	TEENS ★★★★
YOUNG ADULTS ★★★½		OVER 30 ★★★★	SENIORS ★★★½

What it is Full-motion NASCAR race. **Scope and scale** Headliner. **Authors' rating** ★★★½. **Duration of ride** 6 minutes. **Loading speed** Slow. **Cost** $15 for first time; $7 for each additional turn; $5 for a passenger; $20 for simulator and minigolf; $50 for all-day simulator and minigolf.

DESCRIPTION AND COMMENTS Each simulator is a 4/5-scale representation of an actual racing stock car. You can choose from six cars: Bud, Dodge, DuPont, Home Depot, Miller, or Sony. Your group may also choose from six tracks: Atlanta, Bristol, Charlotte, Daytona, Daytona with no restricted weights, and Richmond. After you select manual or automatic transmission, an attendant furnishes you a brief tutorial on how to drive the car. Once you're inside, you will be immersed in the three screens that wrap around your car, allowing you peripheral vision as you race. The simulators are full-motion, meaning that when you hit another car, your car rattles and shakes. The graphics are Xbox quality, but not exceptional. Winning the race is challenging; we found ourselves skidding out more than passing other cars. Attempting to tell what place you are in is also difficult. The attendant will tell you periodically, but it is hard to hear him over the faux-engine noise.

TOURING TIPS The cars are not complete replicas of the stock cars, but for a simulator, the interior is fairly accurate. You will find the seats stiff and uncomfortable, but you aren't racing a 300-lap circuit. Four to ten laps, depending on the track, is all the six-minute simulator allows. At the end of the race, the attendant hands each rider a sheet with their race statistics, leaving you a bit awed at the skill of real NASCAR drivers.

Old-Town Bull ★★★

APPEAL BY AGE	PRESCHOOL —	GRADE SCHOOL ★★★	TEENS ★★½
YOUNG ADULTS ★★★½		OVER 30 ★★★½	SENIORS ★★

What it is Mechanical bull. **Scope and scale** Minor attraction. **Authors' rating** ★★★. **Cost** $10 for adults; $5 for children.

DESCRIPTION AND COMMENTS As any fan of the 1970s classic movie *Urban Cowboy* already knows, a mechanical bull is a machine with a saddle that bucks riders up, down, and around, attempting to knock the rider off. It's the gear-and-motor approximation of bull riding found in rodeos. Old-Town's bull is one and the same and has enough padding on the ground to minimize injuries, although you must sign a waiver before riding.

TOURING TIPS The ride doesn't open until later in the day when crowds are heavier.

Sky Coaster ★★★★½

APPEAL BY AGE	PRESCHOOL ★★★	GRADE SCHOOL ★★★★	TEENS ★★★★½
YOUNG ADULTS ★★★★½		OVER 30 ★★★★	SENIORS ★★

What it is A 300-foot-tall pendulum. Scope and scale Headliner. Special comments Must be 42" tall to ride. Authors' rating Adrenaline; ★★★★½. Duration of ride 6 minutes. Loading speed Very slow. Cost $40 for single-person flight; $35 per person for double-person flight; $30.75 per person for triple-person flight; coupons available.

DESCRIPTION AND COMMENTS Sky Coaster is one of the most thrilling, and expensive, rides in Orlando. Situated over a pond, Sky Coaster looks like the buttress of a large suspension bridge. At 300 feet, the giant pendulum ride dwarfs many of the area's attractions; from the top, you can see Epcot.

After suiting up in a harness resembling a knee-length apron, you proceed to a wooden platform in the center of the pond. Ride operators then raise you up and attach your harness to two cables, one to pull you aloft and one to swing from. You are attached so your head is toward the ground—you fly on your stomach like Superman—and then pulled backward to the top of the far tower. At the end of a 3-2-1 countdown, you pull your own rip cord (yipe!) and plummet toward the earth. After a 130-foot free fall, the pendulum action takes over and gently swings you across the pond at speeds up to 80 miles per hour, depending on the weight of the passengers. To disembark, you must grab a pole and stop yourself over the wooden platform.

TOURING TIPS Because Sky Coaster can handle only about 20 people an hour, the wait can be excruciating. We recommend coming during the middle of the day when crowds are fewer and the view from the top is better. The price is steep, but the three-person deal is not a bad call, since increasing the mass of a pendulum increases its speed. If the ride were $15, we would ride it twice, but at $40 for a single rider for less than one minute of ride time, you'll need a disposable income. Remember, $40 is more than half the price of an entire day at Disney.

Wax Museum   ★★★

APPEAL BY AGE	PRESCHOOL ★★½	GRADE SCHOOL ★★★½	TEENS ★★★½
YOUNG ADULTS ★★★		OVER 30 ★★½	SENIORS ★★

What it is Wax sculptures of the famous. Scope and scale Major attraction. Authors' rating ★★★. Cost $7 for adults; $5 for children; and free for children ages 5 and under.

DESCRIPTION AND COMMENTS With all of the animatronics in Orlando, wax museums feel like half an attraction. Celebrities and historical figures are set behind glass or velvet ropes. There is no set order to the first few rooms of the exhibit, with Pope John Paul II stationed directly across from singers Boy George and George Michael. Quality varies from sculpture to sculpture, with some looking as if they are ready to talk, and others only recognizable by their signature clothing or by reading their name plaques. The later rooms take on some organization; the Tower of London room holds members of both the House of Windsor and Tudor Dynasty. The very last room, called the dungeon, holds no famous people, but instead sculptures of mutilation. Parents with small children may take a detour to the exit.

TOURING TIPS   You can pose in front of the figures, but cannot put your arms around them for photo ops. Check with the ticket person outside to see if any of the celebrities inside meet your fancy.

TICKET RIDES

ALL OF THE RIDES BELOW ARE on the Old-Town ticket system. Tickets each cost $1; mild discounts are available in the ValuePaks: 22 tickets for $20 and 35 tickets for $30. All-day ride wristbands are also available and make more sense than either of the ValuePaks. Wristbands cost $25 for adults and $15 for children under 42 inches tall. On Sunday, wristbands can be purchased for use from noon until 6 p.m. for $15, regardless of age. Tickets and wristbands may be purchased at the ticket booth in the front of the park.

Rides before the First Block of Old-Town

Old-Town Ferris Wheel   ★★★

APPEAL BY AGE	PRESCHOOL ★★★★	GRADE SCHOOL ★★★★	TEENS ★★
YOUNG ADULTS ★★	OVER 30 ★★★★		SENIORS ★★★★

What it is Old-fashioned Ferris wheel. **Scope and scale** Minor attraction. **When to go** Anytime. **Special comments** You must be at least 42" tall to ride alone, or at least 52" tall to bring a child. **Authors' rating** ★★★. **Duration of ride** 1 minute, 45 seconds; if there's no line, you can ride several times. **Loading speed** Moderate. **Cost** 3 tickets.

DESCRIPTION AND COMMENTS   A throwback to the early days of amusement parks, this Ferris wheel spins over US 192 under the gleam of its flashy, fast-moving neighbors. But it's a nice break from all the tummy-churning rides and a fun way to see the whole park, as you probably won't notice much at the top of the Super Shot. It might be too subtle for older kids, but preschoolers seem to appreciate its gentleness.

TOURING TIPS   Head to the Ferris wheel when your feet are tired or you need a moment to settle your stomach. The line is generally pretty short any time of day.

Pharaoh's Fury   ★½

APPEAL BY AGE	PRESCHOOL ½	GRADE SCHOOL ★★★½	TEENS ★★★½
YOUNG ADULTS ★★	OVER 30 ★½		SENIORS ½

What it is A sailor's worst nightmare. **Scope and scale** Major attraction. **When to go** Anytime. **Special comments** Must be at least 48" tall to ride, and at least 60" tall to ride with a child. **Authors' rating** Not for the easily nauseated; ★½. **Duration of ride** 1 minute, 45 seconds. **Loading speed** Slow; the ride can accommodate between 40 and 60 people at a time—if there's no line, you may have to wait as the ride fills up. **Cost** 3 tickets.

DESCRIPTION AND COMMENTS   A large ship on a pendulum swings riders to and fro, reaching speeds of close to 80 miles per hour. The boat gains speed throughout the ride, and the last two tick-tocks are a doozy.

TOURING TIPS   This is one attraction where a larger crowd waiting to ride is usually a good thing. The attendants may not run it if there are fewer than 20 people in line, but stop by and check. To get the most out of this ride, sit at either end of the boat. Be aware that people often lose pocket contents. Secure yours in advance.

The Super Shot   ★★★½

APPEAL BY AGE	PRESCHOOL †	GRADE SCHOOL ★★★	TEENS ★★★★½
YOUNG ADULTS ★★★		OVER 30 ★★	SENIORS ½

† Preschoolers are generally too short to ride.

What it is Tummy tumbler. **Scope and scale** Headliner. **When to go** Before you eat dinner. **Special comments** Must be at least 42" tall to ride. **Authors' rating** ★★★½. **Duration of ride** 1½ minutes. **Loading speed** Fast. **Cost** 5 tickets.

DESCRIPTION AND COMMENTS   A similar but better ride than Universal's Dr. Doom's Fearfall, the Super Shot is designed for pure terror. The operator straps you into a jump seat and, with your feet dangling, hoists you up a tower to a height of 120 feet. To add to the anticipation, your ascent is not only very slow, but a protrusion above your head blocks your view upward, so you have no idea when you've reached the top. Once you're there, it's an exhilarating free fall down, and at 47 miles per hour, not for the faint of stomach.

TOURING TIPS   This is another big draw at Old-Town, and the lines can get long in the evening. If the entire idea of an unexpected drop seems too scary, remember that if you sit on the side where you can see your shadow (during the day), you will be able to tell when you've reached the top. And if you don't want to know—grin—sit on the other side.

Wave Swinger   ★★½

APPEAL BY AGE	PRESCHOOL ★★★½	GRADE SCHOOL ★★★	TEENS ★½
YOUNG ADULTS ★★		OVER 30 ★½	SENIORS ½

What it is Swings. **Scope and scale** Minor attraction. **When to go** Anytime. **Special comments** Must be at least 42" tall to ride. **Authors' rating** ★★½. **Duration of ride** 3 minutes. **Loading speed** Slow. **Cost** 3 tickets.

DESCRIPTION AND COMMENTS   A set of swings dangles from a central tower. The tower spins around and raises the riders into the air. This version is smaller than the Yo-Yo at Cypress Gardens and doesn't hold much thrill for older kids.

TOURING TIPS   The ride has a high volume and a high turnover rate, although the loading time is slow. Don't expect big lines.

Rides after the Fourth Block at Old-Town

Baja Buggy Merry-Go-Round   ★★

APPEAL BY AGE	PRESCHOOL ★★★½	GRADE SCHOOL ★★★	TEENS ★½
YOUNG ADULTS ★★		OVER 30 ★★½	SENIORS ★★★

What it is A bouncy merry-go-round. **Scope and scale** Minor attraction. **When to go** Anytime. **Special comments** Must be at least 36" tall to ride alone, or must ride with an adult who is at least 60" tall. **Authors' rating** ★★. **Duration of ride** 2 minutes. **Loading speed** Moderate. **Cost** 2 tickets.

DESCRIPTION AND COMMENTS This kiddie ride is a small version of the Mega Bounce found at Cypress Gardens. Riders sit in little carts made to look like dune buggies. The buggies are attached to a small tower that turns, and the buggies bounce up and down.

TOURING TIPS This is only for the little guys.

Dragon Wagon ★★

APPEAL BY AGE	PRESCHOOL ★★★½	GRADE SCHOOL ★★★	TEENS ★½
YOUNG ADULTS ★½		OVER 30 ★★	SENIORS ★★

What it is Even smaller steel coaster. **Scope and scale** Minor attraction. **When to go** Anytime. **Special comments** Must be at least 42" tall to ride alone, or must ride with an adult who is at least 60" tall. **Authors' rating** ★★. **Duration of ride** 2 minutes. **Loading speed** Moderate. **Cost** 2 tickets.

DESCRIPTION AND COMMENTS Smaller even than Windstorm, this attraction is here primarily for children who are just a bit too short for the bigger coaster adjacent. The coaster track is almost identical, but smaller. There are a few ups and downs, but nothing thrilling.

TOURING TIPS Don't worry about lines here. This coaster is around only to placate children too short for Windstorm.

Flying Teacups ★★★

APPEAL BY AGE	PRESCHOOL ★★★½	GRADE SCHOOL ★★★	TEENS ★½
YOUNG ADULTS ★★		OVER 30 ★★½	SENIORS ★★★

What it is Spinning teacups. **Scope and scale** Minor attraction. **When to go** Anytime. **Special comments** Must be at least 42" tall to ride alone, or must ride with an adult who is at least 60" tall. **Authors' rating** ★★★. **Duration of ride** 2½ minutes. **Loading speed** Moderate. **Cost** 2 tickets.

DESCRIPTION AND COMMENTS It's a small teacup ride. Riders sit in teacups that they can spin individually. All of the teacups rotate in a circle. There's little more to say.

TOURING TIPS You will need strong hands to spin the teacups at full speed. Work as a team to keep up your momentum.

The Scrambler ★★★

APPEAL BY AGE	PRESCHOOL ★★½	GRADE SCHOOL ★★★½	TEENS ★★★★
YOUNG ADULTS ★★★		OVER 30 ★★½	SENIORS ★★

What it is Two-person carts attached to a central hub. **Scope and scale** Major attraction. **When to go** Early. **Special comments** Must be at least 48" tall to ride alone, or must ride with an adult who is at least 60" tall. **Authors' rating** ★★★. **Duration of ride** 2 minutes. **Loading speed** Moderate. **Cost** 3 tickets.

DESCRIPTION AND COMMENTS Another carnival classic, The Scrambler has three arms with a set of spinning chairs attached to the end of each arm. The chairs whiz in close to one another as the entire apparatus spins around. Since riders move closer to and farther from the central axis, the experience is like being the ball tethered to a paddle in that childhood toy.

TOURING TIPS The Scrambler is on par with Pharaoh's Fury and Super Shot for the most extreme ticket rides at Old-Town. It may make some riders a bit queasy.

Tilt-a-Whirl ★★★

APPEAL BY AGE	PRESCHOOL ★★★½	GRADE SCHOOL ★★★½	TEENS ★★★
YOUNG ADULTS ★★★		OVER 30 ★★½	SENIORS ★

What it is Spinning cars. **Scope and scale** Major attraction. **When to go** Anytime. **Special comments** Must be at least 46" tall to ride alone, or must ride with an adult who is at least 60" tall. **Authors' rating** ★★★. **Duration of ride** 2 minutes. **Loading speed** Fast. **Cost** 3 tickets.

DESCRIPTION AND COMMENTS This carnival classic consists of cars that rotate individually and spin around a circular track with two raised walls. You've ridden it before, but with its capacity to fit four adults and five children, you might as well introduce your children to it now.

TOURING TIPS The motion sickness is lower on the Tilt-a-Whirl than on most of Old-Town's other rides. The ride's ability to move more than 500 people an hour keeps lines at bay.

Windstorm Roller Coaster ★★

APPEAL BY AGE	PRESCHOOL †	GRADE SCHOOL ★★★½	TEENS ★★½
YOUNG ADULTS ★★½		OVER 30 ★★½	SENIORS ★★

† Preschoolers are generally too short to ride.

What it is Small steel coaster. **Scope and scale** Major attraction. **When to go** Early. **Special comments** Must be at least 48" tall to ride alone, or at least 40" tall to ride with an adult who is at least 60" tall. **Authors' rating** ★★. **Duration of ride** 3 minutes. **Loading speed** Moderate. **Cost** 5 tickets.

DESCRIPTION AND COMMENTS The roller coaster in Old-Town is smaller than the other local coasters. This is no Kraken, but the small steel coaster does hold some thrills for smaller riders. Riders sit in cars on top of the track, and ascend the drop hill. They then descend around the large oval, up and down a series of bumps and rolls. The ride is unimpressive, and any of the equally compact coasters at Cypress Gardens offers a better ride.

TOURING TIPS Since this is the only real coaster at Old-Town, the lines can be lengthy. Head here directly after purchasing tickets.

DINING

OLD-TOWN HAS A WIDE VARIETY OF DINING OPTIONS. There is Chinese food at **Spring Roll Chinese Gourmet,** fast food at **A&W All American Food,** more upscale options at **Fred Marion's Sports Grille.** Even at Fred Marion's, none of the entrées exceed $20. Our pick for the best deal in the park is **Flipper's Pizza** located near the front entrance. Diners can get a nine-inch pizza with one topping and a soda for $5.49 plus tax. For pizza in an amusement park setting, this is an exceptional deal. Burger King and a slew of local restaurants are located just outside of Old-Town.

SHOPPING

NO MAIN STREET WOULD BE COMPLETE without shops, and shops line all four blocks of Old-Town. Although Old-Town contains 75 specialty shops—more than we can mention here—there aren't very many bargains and don't expect flea-market prices. They've hooked you with the carnival rides, and now it's time to unload a barrage of souvenirs, but that's no different from any other Florida park.

On the first block, you'll find **Groovy,** a store packed with 1960s hippie memorabilia, **Old-Town Leather** (a shop for bikers), **House of Ireland,** and the **Wave Surf** shop all on the right side of the street. Across the street is the **Union Jack,** which sells British goods, and a quirky shop called **Pet Palace** where, among other things, you can purchase outfits for your dogs and cats.

On the corner of the second block is **Walkin' Around,** a store filled with 1950s memorabilia, including T-shirts, period recordings on CD, posters, and so on. **Tobacco Works,** a water-pipe store, and **Magic Max's** are also on the second block. At Magic Max's you can buy magic tricks and illusion kits, but you can see how they work only if you purchase them. **Kandlestix,** a candle outlet, is also on the second block.

On the third block, you will find **Time for Pleasure Salon and Spa.** For $100, you can get a one-hour body massage, a one-hour European facial, and 40 minutes of hand and foot treatment. This is a perfect stop for mom while dad takes the kids around to the rides. Across the street is **Sunny and Company Toys,** which sells marionettes. Prices range from $8.50 for a small puppet to $50 for large puppets.

The fourth block hosts a **Hello Kitty** store, and a tattoo parlor that is open late, just in case you thought drinking was a good idea. **Old Town Candy** and **The General Store** are across the street. The General Store is themed to feel like a vintage hometown market, but instead of coffee cans and potatoes you'll find Coca-Cola memorabilia and fake road signs. On the same side of the street is **Black Market Minerals,** an African-themed store with a collection of rocks, sculptures, and wind chimes.

PART TWELVE

INTERNATIONAL DRIVE

AT ITS INCEPTION, INTERNATIONAL DRIVE, also known as I-Drive, was nothing but a small road off Interstate 4 serving local area hotels. After Disney came to town in 1971, developers were soon to follow. Now servicing Universal, SeaWorld, two smaller amusement parks, a host of roadside attractions, multitudes of hotels, eateries, bars, malls, and the Orlando Convention Center, International Drive has become its own attraction.

Of course, many attractions found on International Drive are covered in other parts of this book (SeaWorld, Universal, Water Parks, Miniature Golf, and the like), but there are still more attractions that are worthwhile and noteworthy. The two amusement parks, FunSpot Action Park and Magical Midway, offer thrill rides, go-cart tracks, and top-notch arcades. Wonderworks, Ripley's Believe It or Not!, and Titanic: The Experience not only all have eye-catching edifices, but also can be categorized as museums. Although all three cater to entertainment instead of learning, Wonderworks is ostensibly a science museum, Ripley's a museum of natural history, and Titanic a museum of living history. And both Skull Kingdom and SkyVenture offer thrills that will have you screaming, but for very different reasons.

There are so many options along International Drive that you may want to set aside a day just to explore this strip. Since International Drive contains an amalgamation of sideshow entertainments, each too large to fit into a major theme park but each too small to occupy a full or even half day of touring, picking three to four attractions is both a pleasant and paced way to experience what's roadside.

PLAN AHEAD

IN CONTRAST TO OTHER FAMOUS ROADS, like the Strip in Vegas, you won't want to spend your vacation time cruising up and down this seven-mile drag. Since International Drive is just four lanes wide (only occasionally six), the influx of tourists clogs the road, creating waits that can exceed two hours. Since the wait time, especially from 8 a.m to 10 a.m. and from 4 p.m. to 8 p.m., is excessive, you should plan what sites you want to visit and what times you would like to visit them. Even if you plan your visits to avoid the rush hours, remember that traffic lights, pedestrians, and U-turning vehicles can make International Drive a hectic passage at anytime.

But don't let the traffic dissuade you from visiting the attractions of your choice. If you stay in a hotel in the area, you should be able to become one of those pedestrians slowing down the cars. The I-Drive Trolley is also an option for short hops. The fee is nominal and schedules are available at their Web site at **www.iridetrolley.com.**

Since many of the attractions on International Drive are open late, most until midnight or afterward, visitors can spend their days at the major parks and, with any leftover energy, step out at night. Attractions will be more crowded in the evening than during midday, so you will need to schedule more time at night to experience them.

Most of the attractions along International Drive are enclosed, so when large thunderstorms threaten, many visitors choose to hop around International Drive instead of hoofing around major theme parks in the rain. Since crowds build during rainy days, make sure to arrive at least 30 minutes earlier than normal to any attraction you want to visit. Touring first thing in the morning is also advantageous, and will keep both you and your umbrella dry.

GETTING THERE

INTERNATIONAL DRIVE EXTENDS FROM the Central Florida Parkway to a cul-de-sac at the Prime Outlet Mall. You can reach International Drive from any exit between Exit 71–Exit 75A off I-4.

▌ ATTRACTIONS

FunSpot Action Park   ★★★

| APPEAL BY AGE | PRESCHOOL ★★ | GRADE SCHOOL ★★★ | TEENS ★★★★½ |
| YOUNG   ADULTS   ★★★ | | OVER   30   ★★★ | SENIORS   ★★ |

555 Del Verde Way, Orlando; ☎ 407-363-3867; www.fun-spot.com

Hours Daily (peak season), 10 a.m.–midnight; Monday–Thursday (off season), noon–11 p.m.; Friday, noon–midnight; Saturday, 10 a.m.–midnight; and Sunday, 10 a.m.–11 p.m. **Authors' rating** ★★★.

DESCRIPTION AND COMMENTS Past Skull Kingdom on I-Drive, you'll see Del Verde Way. Snuck in behind a shopping center is FunSpot Action Park, visible from I-Drive by its enormous Ferris wheel. FunSpot is a small amusement park, and like Magical Midway, its appeal rests in its go-cart tracks, carnival rides, and arcades. FunSpot is larger than Magical Midway, and although FunSpot does not contain rides on par with Magical

Midway's Human Slingshot or StarFlyer, FunSpot possesses superior go-cart tracks and better arcades.

Indeed, FunSpot has the best go-cart tracks in Orlando. There is both free parking and free admission, so you can wander through the site and peruse the attractions before you purchase tickets or wristbands, although FunSpot may instate a $4.95 general admission charge for the 2007 season for guests who do not want to use the rides or the go-carts.

ATTRACTION PRICES *Tickets:* $3 apiece; go-carts cost two tickets while all other rides cost one ticket.

FunSpot offers four armbands. Each is good for the entire day and includes the free-play arcade. When selecting armbands, take the height and age of your group into consideration. There is no need to purchase armbands that are out of the height or age range of the rider.

- *Go-cart armband* $34.95 plus tax per person, unlimited go-cart tracks and rides.
- *Commander armband* $29.95 plus tax per person, Commander go-cart track only and unlimited rides.
- *Rides armband* $24.95 plus tax per person, Cadet go-cart track only and unlimited rides.
- *Kid's Spot armband* $14.95 plus tax per person, valid only for the Kid's Spot area.

GO-CARTS The main draw at FunSpot is the go-carts. The go-carts cost two tickets per ride, unless you have an armband. In contrast to Magical Midway's wooden tracks, FunSpot has concrete tracks that allow for both a faster and smoother ride. The concrete tracks also allow FunSpot patrons to operate go-carts rain or shine. There are five tracks here, and collectively, they are better than any of the other local area tracks. Since FunSpot is slightly hidden from the main drag, the tracks are often less crowded.

The four main tracks are the **Quadhelix,** the **Conquest,** the **Commander,** and the **Thrasher.** The fifth is a kiddie attraction called the **Cadet Track,** a short oval located in the back corner of the park that requires kids to be at least 4 years old and 42 inches tall. All the other tracks are color coded to make them easier to distinguish.

The **Quadhelix** is yellow, and the longest track at 1,600 feet. As the name entails, the multistory track comprises four interlaced corkscrews. The lack of long straightaways or very sharp turns makes it difficult to pass other go-carts, but if you're not feeling very competitive, the banked turns and elevated layout are a good use of your ticket. Riders are usually allowed five laps, totaling about nine minutes, and riders must be at least 10 years old and 52 inches tall.

The tallest track at FunSpot is the blue **Conquest** track at 28 feet high, but with underpowered go-carts, height is not an advantage. The dawdling ascent through the long corkscrew is rewarded with a fast but short downhill leg, and the rest of the track winds slowly back to the starting gate. After five laps and eight minutes, you'll be ready for something else. As with the Quadhelix, riders must be at least 10 years old and at least 52 inches tall.

The **Commander** track is green. The compact figure-eight design makes it the shortest of the four major tracks. The track is also flatter, which lends the Commander track toward use as a racetrack, although ride operators frown upon rigorous competition and strictly enforce the "no-bumping" rule. A moderate thrill, however, is still available when you head to the inside of the first corner at top speed, where you should be able to get a little air over the set of rolls. It's a little rough on your tailbone, but should make you grin nonetheless. Riders must be at least 8 years old and 50 inches tall.

The **Thrasher** track is red, and if you're competitive, the best race-track in Orlando. The track is completely flat and packed with hairpin turns and short straightaways. The variety of angles in the course, from slow bends to hairpins, will both test your skill as a driver and allow you the opportunity to pass other carts. Besides the intense ride, the unassuming flat track will have shorter lines, since most guests will be drawn toward the multistoried Quadhelix and Conquest tracks. Riders must be at least 12 years old and 54 inches tall.

OTHER ATTRACTIONS   The handful of rides at FunSpot are quaint and generic, and each costs one ticket per ride. Tickets cost $3 each, but rides are included with the purchase of an armband. There are **bumper cars** in a small arena, **bumper boats** in a small pool, a large **Ferris wheel,** and three common carnival rides. The carnival rides all spin you around a center axis, but do not invert you. They are the **Scrambler,** the **Sky Glider,** and the **Paratrooper** (riding the latter is akin to sitting on the side of a massive wobbly tire).

Also at a cost of one ticket per ride, and also included with armband purchases, are rides for the very young. Located in the **Kid's Spot,** these rides are recommended for kids ages 2 to 5. The tiny area contains a set of **miniature teacups,** a **carousel, kiddie swings,** and a few other minor rides, including a pair of the **oscillating trucks** commonly found outside shopping centers.

Although the ride selection at FunSpot is meager, FunSpot does boast central Florida's largest **arcade.** It's actually two arcades, a token arcade downstairs and a free-play arcade upstairs. Each token for the downstairs arcade costs $0.25, unless you buy the tokens in bulk. The three bulk-token options are: 120 tokens for $25 (a 16% discount), 400 tokens for $75 (a 25% discount), or 1,000 tokens for $175 (a 30% discount). Most of the games cost one token per turn, but a few take as many as four tokens to play.

While the downstairs arcade houses all of the newest arcade games, the upstairs free-play arcade is a collection of vintage games ranging from the more modern, like The Simpsons and Tekken, to the classic games like Pac-man, Defender, and Centipede. The free-play arcade also has pinball machines and a few Xboxes. On its own, the free-play arcade costs $5.95 plus tax, but is included with the purchase of any of the armband deals. Since guests have no time restraint and unlimited replay on all of the games, you may find it difficult to play your favorite old-school games, but with more than 60 machines available, finding a comparable game shouldn't be difficult.

When the video games wear you out, you can pick up some food at the snack bar downstairs. A slice of cheese pizza costs $2.25, and a cheeseburger combo that includes small fries and a soda costs $6.25.

Ripley's Believe It or Not! Orlando Odditorium ★★★

APPEAL BY AGE	PRESCHOOL ★★	GRADE SCHOOL ★★★½	TEENS ★★★½
YOUNG ADULTS ★★★½		OVER 30 ★★★	SENIORS ★★★½

8201 International Drive; ☎ 407-363-4418; www.ripleysorlando.com

Hours Daily, 9 a.m.–1 a.m., with last entry at midnight. **Cost** $18.95 for adults; $11.95 for children ages 4–12; and free for children ages 3 and under. **Authors' rating ★★★**.

DESCRIPTION AND COMMENTS With one side of the building slipping into a sinkhole (on purpose, of course), Ripley's is another of the odder buildings on I-Drive. Located just a few blocks from Wonderworks (the oddest building on I-Drive), Ripley's is open 9 a.m. until 1 a.m., with the last entry available at midnight; parking is free. To tour the exhibits, you should need only about an hour. Even with the quick turnaround of guests, the lines for Ripley's can be monstrous, with wait times outside exceeding an hour. On rainy days, be sure to arrive at least 20 minutes before opening, or come very late in the evening.

Ripley's consists of a series of galleries, each with a different twist. Each gallery hosts a menagerie of odds and ends from around the world that fit with each room's general theme. The collection consists mainly of optical illusions, anthropologic oddities, genetic oddities, and some of the oddest objects built by man.

Once you enter, a hologram of Mr. Ripley greets you, one of the many optical illusions inside. Most of the other optical illusions are simple posters with questions like, "Which line is longer: >—<, or <—>?" Others are on a grander scale, such as the billiards room, a room built to appear flat, but that is actually listing to one side. The Inversion Tunnel is another large-scale illusion, and just like the Wonderworks version, the tunnel can make you believe you are spinning sideways.

The anthropologic and animal oddities may also set your head spinning. They include wax sculptures of deformities, Siamese piglets, ceremonial masks, and a shrunken head. After these galleries, guests can walk through the man-made oddities, from the strange—an authentic vampire-slaying kit—to the stranger—a replica of a Rolls Royce made from 1,016,711 matchsticks, or the portrait of Elvis constructed from 600 smaller portraits.

Since Ripley's is more of an amusement than a museum, many of the descriptive plaques in front of each item contain factoids instead of in-depth accounts. You won't find any lengthy analysis of items to educate you inside the Odditorium. You will, however, be privy to a fine collection of some fringe aspects of nature and humanity.

Magical Midway   ★★½

| APPEAL BY AGE | PRESCHOOL ★★ | GRADE SCHOOL ★★½ | TEENS ★★½ |
| YOUNG   ADULTS ★★ | | OVER   30   ★½ | SENIORS   ★ |

7001 International Drive; ☎ 407-370-5353; www.magicalmidway.com

Hours Vary, but usually daily, 10 a.m.–midnight. **Authors' rating** ★★½.

DESCRIPTION AND COMMENTS   Near the north end of I-Drive, well after Wonderworks but before SkyVenture, are the hard-to-miss signs for Magical Midway. The enormous towers of both the Human Slingshot and StarFlyer shouldn't make finding it very difficult. The parking at the Midway is free but minimal. You can park across the street, but be wary of rubbernecking drivers while crossing I-Drive traffic. The I-Drive Trolley is also a sound option for arriving (**www.iridetrolley.com**).

Magical Midway's location, front and center on International Drive, draws many visitors, and their wear on the facility is apparent. The heavy traffic in the amusement park also makes riding the attractions during evening visits tedious at best.

Fortunately, the park offers free admission, so you can take a look around before you decide to purchase any wristbands or tickets.

ATTRACTION PRICES   Admission never includes the Human Slingshot, and only one ride on the StarFlyer.

- *Play-all-day armband* $27.95 plus tax per person, includes all-day unlimited go-carts and rides and one StarFlyer ride.
- *Three-hour armband* $22.95 plus tax per person, includes three hours of unlimited go-carts and rides, and one StarFlyer ride.
- *Midway armband* $15.95 plus tax per person, includes unlimited rides all day, ten arcade tokens, and one StarFlyer ride.

GO-CARTS   Magical Midway has three go-cart tracks called the **Avalanche,** the **Alpine Jump,** and the **Fast Track.** You must be at least 12 years old and 58 inches tall to drive the single-seat carts, while the two-seat carts require the driver to be at least 16 years old with a valid driver's license and the passenger to be at least 5 years old and 36 inches tall. The two-seat carts are available only on the Avalanche and the Alpine Jump tracks.

On the multistory Avalanche and Alpine Jump tracks, be prepared for a very bumpy ride. Instead of concrete, slats of wood are laid across the tracks. Although the Midway attempts to keep the slats as flat as possible, the design flaw not only slows the carts as they clank over the seams, but the raised ridges of wood will leave your tailbone aching.

The **Avalanche** track is the largest track and the most popular. The track begins with a corkscrew and winds around in a figure eight as it descends. The conservative straightaways and slow bends did not impress us; neither did the long lines that build during the day and are unbearable at night.

The **Alpine Jump** track is a shorter version of the Avalanche and contains all the same construction problems. After driving up a long and tedious corkscrew, you are given a brief burst of speed down a straightaway, but the banked turns quickly cease any major thrills. The track is less crowded than the Avalanche, but the ride is shorter. With a lack of sharp turns and speed, passing other drivers is difficult. Your best bet is to wait till someone slows down to ease the jostling caused by the wooden slats, or to move on to the Fast Track.

The **Fast Track** is the best track for racing. A single concrete oval, the track is small, but large enough to allow you to accelerate your cart to top speed before making the turns. Since you are allowed the same amount of time on this track as on either of the others (about eight minutes), you will have time to practice the turns and pass and re-pass your friends. Since the track is simplistic and small, many patrons will skip it for the long lines and slow, bumpy ride on the other tracks; don't be so hasty.

OTHER ATTRACTIONS As with FunSpot Action Park, Magical Midway includes a small **bumper car arena** with a height requirement of 48 inches and an even smaller **bumper boat pool** with a height requirement of 42 inches. However, Magical Midway's four rides—the **Tornado, Space Blast, StarFlyer,** and **Slingshot**—are all more thrilling than any found at FunSpot.

The **Tornado** is a standard carnival ride with a height requirement of 48 inches. Eight cars that rotate independently and each contain four seats are attached to the arms of a central spinning post. Although it is rather passé, it accomplishes what all centrifuge carnival rides are meant to: it makes you dizzy.

The **Space Blast** has a 48-inch height minimum and is similar to Universal's Dr. Doom FearFall ride, without any of the theming or grandeur. You sit in a seat that is launched 180 feet into the air, and then free falls back to the ground. The ride is short, and the three Gs of force are not dazzling.

The eye-catcher at Magical Midway, and the newest addition, is the **StarFlyer** with a height requirement of 44 inches. Towering over I-Drive, the StarFlyer is a **set of rotating swings** that lifts riders up 230 feet and spins them at up to 54 miles per hour. To facilitate the thrill, the swing chains were built to be about one centimeter thick, forcing patrons to place their trust in Orlando's safety inspectors. Once you've overcome the vision of having your body flung onto I-Drive, you will have to resist the urge of having your stomach follow suit. Although the ride may induce motion sickness and mild terror, the view from the top of the StarFlyer is one of the best in Orlando. One ride on the StarFlyer is included with the purchase of any of the armbands. Without an armband, the ride costs $7 for the first ride, and $5 for each additional ride.

The **Human Slingshot** is not included in any armband admissions and costs $25 per person, and you must be at least 52 inches tall to ride. The Human Slingshot is the same as the one at Old-Town (the one at Magical Midway is actually taller by a foot or so, and only noticeable if you're bragging).

The structure is a massive V shape with flashing rainbow lights. Riders latch into a two-person cart at the base of the V, and a bungee-cord system stretches down the legs of the V to the cart—like a slingshot. Once you're latched in, the cart is pulled below the boarding area, then released, flinging riders 365 feet into the air, spinning head over feet the entire time. Surprisingly, the ride is almost peaceful and less frightening than many of the major roller coasters in the area. After the initial launch, the elastic cable makes for a smooth rise and fall. Being more than 300 feet above the ground silences much surrounding noise, and the nighttime view is even better—for a few seconds at a time as you bob—than even the StarFlyer's. As with most rides, the thrill is in the anticipation, not in the event. For $25 dollars, however, you're better off taking a helicopter for sightseeing or, for thrill junkies, paying out a few more bucks for the Sky Coaster at Old-Town.

SkyVenture ★★★½

APPEAL BY AGE	PRESCHOOL ★★★★	GRADE SCHOOL ★★★★	TEENS ★★★½
YOUNG ADULTS ★★★		OVER 30 ★★★½	SENIORS ★★★

6805 Visitor Circle, Orlando; ☎ 407-903-1150 or 800-SKYFUN1; www.skyventureorlando.com

Hours Daily, 10 a.m.–11 p.m. **Cost:** $39.95 + tax for visitors ages 3 and up. **Authors' rating** ★★★½.

DESCRIPTION AND COMMENTS SkyVenture is a high-velocity vertical wind tunnel that attempts to re-create the thrill of skydiving. While headed north on I-Drive, you will find the tunnel on the left-hand side after Magical Midway but before the Skull Kingdom and directly across the street from Wet 'n Wild. From I-4, just take Exit 75A and turn away from Universal. The tunnel resembles a large spaceship and is painted blue and yellow. The tunnel, when not floating tourists, is used for skydiving team-member training to coordinate stunts before they leap. Unlike jumping out of a plane, "skydiving" in the tunnel works by having five large fans at the top of the tunnel suck air upward. The balanced suction creates a wind tunnel for you to float around in, and although you won't experience the acceleration of free-falling from thousands of feet, you will be able to float around in relative safety. Although the price is steep, at $34.95 plus tax per person for only two minutes of actual flight time, it is still much cheaper than actually skydiving. Children under age 18 will need the signature of a parent or legal guardian on the waiver form in order to fly.

After purchasing your ticket, proceed up the staircase to the waiting room. The waiting room is a series of metal benches on one side of the flight chamber. The flight chamber is enclosed in Plexiglas, so if you arrive a few minutes early or are waiting for a member of your group to fly, you can watch other guests float around, and if you are lucky, you might see an instructor performing a few aerial stunts.

Once your time comes, an instructor will usher you upstairs, where you will be given all of the proper equipment, including a helmet, a flight suit, elbow and knee pads, earplugs, and proper footwear if you forgot it. You will also be allowed access to a locker where you can store the contents of your pockets, jewelry, and any other belongings that may be displaced during flight.

After you are suited up, you proceed to the preflight briefing room and watch a video on basic body positioning and hand signals. After the video, the instructor gives every student a chance to practice the in-flight pose. Remember, once you're in the flight chamber you have only two minutes of flight time, so optimize your flight time by memorizing the hand signals and asking any questions beforehand. The hands signals are necessary because the wind tunnel is too loud for speech.

The hand signals are as follows:

- One finger pointed up—*raise your chin*
- Two fingers pointed straight out—*slowly straighten your legs*
- Two fingers curled in—*slowly bend your legs at the knees*
- Cupped hand facing downward—*arch your back*
- Spreading fingers—*spread your fingers*
- Raising hands—*raise your hands from the shoulder.*

Once your preflight briefing is finished, your instructor will take you down to the flight chamber. After the instructor signals the operator to fire up the wind tunnel, he will gesture you in one by one. When entering the chamber, put your hands by your head—as if you're surrendering—and slowly lean forward until the air catches you.

Your two-minute flight time will be divided into one-minute sections. The end of each session is marked with a loud alarm and a red flashing siren. When this occurs, make your way slowly to the exit door and the instructor will help you out. While you wait for your next turn—wait time depends upon the amount of people in your group—you'll have time to reflect on what adjustments you'll need to make to improve your next flight.

The first thing you are apt to notice is that flying in the wind tunnel is very difficult. Unless your body posture is perfect, you will careen toward the Plexiglas or end up face first in the netting on the bottom. Thankfully, the instructors are very helpful and hands-on, keeping you from running headlong into the Plexiglas. But don't worry; if you can't get the hang of flying in two minutes and fail to find the right position, the instructor can take hold of you and fly you both into the air.

Safety in the wind tunnel is important, so avoid sudden movements. You'll find that very subtle changes in your posture can affect how you are flying. You do not have to worry about flying too high in the tunnel; you will not get sucked up into any massive fan. Go as high as you want to—if you are able—and for the best flight, watch and follow the instructor's hand signals.

After you have completed both of your flights, you will go back upstairs and remove your gear. After you change, you'll receive a certificate with your name on it. Before leaving, consider tipping your instructor. Tipping is not expected, but with an instructor in any sport, whether it is surfing, skating, or skiing, a "tip for tips" policy is generally a good practice.

Skull Kingdom ★★

| APPEAL BY AGE | PRESCHOOL ★ | GRADE SCHOOL ★★★ | TEENS ★★★½ |
| YOUNG ADULTS ★★★½ | | OVER 30 ★★½ | SENIORS ★ |

5933 American Way, Orlando; ☎ 407-354-1564; www.skullkingdom.com

Hours 10 a.m.–midnight. **Cost** $8.99 + tax per person for shows from 10 a.m.–5 p.m.; $14.04 per person for shows after 5 p.m. **Authors' rating** ★★.

DESCRIPTION AND COMMENTS Across the street from Wet 'n Wild on International Drive is Skull Kingdom, a massive haunted house. The fake gray stonework and gigantic skull entrance make this building easy to recognize. Getting there is a bit more difficult. The entrance is off of I-Drive, so if you're headed northbound on I-Drive, be sure to pass Skull Kingdom and then turn left into the parking lot. If you turn too soon, you will cross over I-4 and end up at Universal Studios.

The main entrance for Skull Kingdom is through the mouth of the enormous skull. The daytime show, from 10 a.m. until 5 p.m. is $8.99 per person, while the evening shows, which include live actors, are from 5 p.m. until midnight and cost $14.04 per person. Both are self-guided walking tours and take between 10 and 15 minutes. For information on the Chamber of Magic, see our write-up on it in the After Dark section under Dinner Shows. Read this before purchasing tickets because the show is terrible. The cost for the Skull Kingdom and Chamber of Magic dinner show combo package is $28.25 for adults and $24.45 for children and seniors.

Actors make the evening tours at Skull Kingdom both scarier and more exciting, thus the price difference. We feel that the entire experience is overpriced, but if you do decide to go, splurge for the evening show. We won't spoil the surprises in the Haunted House with an in-depth analysis. We were impressed with the creativity and theming, and there is considerable use of both animatronics and wax sculptures. Everything inside of Skull Kingdom either creaks, groans, leaps, or shakes, keeping all the guests on their toes. Unlike Grimm's Haunted House in Old-Town, Skull Kingdom does not emphasize grotesque displays (although there are a few), but instead attempts to scare via surprise. Older teens and young adults will find the effects amusing, while young children will be terrified and high-strung adults might have a heart attack. Even with the foreknowledge that nothing here can harm you, even we found ourselves quickening our pace.

Titanic: The Experience ★★

| APPEAL BY AGE | PRESCHOOL ★ | GRADE SCHOOL ★★ | TEENS ★½ |
| YOUNG ADULTS ★★ | | OVER 30 ★★½ | SENIORS ★★★ |

8445 International Drive, Orlando; ☎ 407-248-1166 or 407-345-9337; www.titanicshipofdreams.com

Hours Seasonally, 9 a.m.–9 p.m., last tours Monday–Thursday at 8 p.m.; Friday–Sunday at 9 p.m. **Cost** $21.25 for adults (tax included); $13.79 for children (tax included). **Authors' rating** ★★.

DESCRIPTION AND COMMENTS   On I-Drive at the Mercado Plaza and near Ripley's Believe It or Not! you will see an upside-down pyramid jutting out of a building like the prow of a ship, marking the ticket booth for Titanic: The Experience. Titanic is generally open 9 a.m. until 9 p.m. Tickets cost $19.95 plus tax for adults and $12.95 plus tax for children ages 5 to 12; they're free for children ages 4 and under. Tours last one hour and begin on the hour. The entrance for Titanic is not at the ticket booth, but is located a short walk away in the Mercado Plaza.

Titanic is not an amusement park or a show; it is an overpriced museum filled with replicas of structures from the *Titanic* and period pieces from other ships. It is a fine museum, if you have a great interest in the *Titanic,* and comes complete with a guided tour. The tour guides assume the identity of a passenger who was onboard the *Titanic.* Depending on your guide, his or her narration can either save or sink your experience.

Your first tour guide greets you at the entrance and ushers you into the first room, where you watch a video on the building of the *Titanic.* The museum is set up chronologically, so after the video you are taken into rooms featuring ship schematics, details of the launch, and such. Your first tour guide leaves you in a room themed to look like the boarding dock in Southampton, England, complete with period luggage and ambient ship noise. When your second tour guide arrives, in the persona of a person who was on the ship, you enter the *Titanic.* The tour guide walks you through the preceding days' events, and then in a fit of melodrama relates the circumstances of the tragedy.

The theming at Titanic is excellent, and the museum's full-scale replications of living quarters, hallways, and the grand staircase are all well crafted, but can only be seen from behind velvet ropes. The last rooms contain low lighting to create a nighttime atmosphere, and the small replica of the ship's railing, with stars and cold air, is the only time you will truly feel you are on board a ship.

What Titanic lacks are interactive exhibits. Besides the block of ice set to the temperature of the water the night the *Titanic* sank, and the room containing the ship's railing, you will constantly feel that you are in a building, and for children, trapped in a museum. The presence of the guides is meant to transport you back in time, but since you stand on a tiled floor and look at the scenery, the guides' talk about how guests are "on board the ship" is unconvincing. The guides also need to decide whether, as characters, they are still alive and taking guests on a tour of the ship while things begin to go wrong, or if they are talking to us posthumously. The blurred line only adds to our inability to suspend disbelief. We'd prefer if the guides were ghosts, able to answer questions about all aspects of the events at anytime, without having to break character.

With the character breaks and the lack of interactive displays, children will be bored, and the only people the museum will interest are avid *Titanic* enthusiasts.

Wonderworks   ★★★½

APPEAL BY AGE	PRESCHOOL ★★★½	GRADE SCHOOL ★★★★	TEENS ★★★½
YOUNG ADULTS ★★★		OVER 30 ★★★	SENIORS ★★

9067 International Drive, Orlando; ☎ 407-351-8800; www.wonderworksonline.com

Hours Daily, 9 a.m.–midnight. **Cost** $19.95 + tax for adults; $14.95 + tax for seniors and children ages 4–12; and free for children ages 3 and under. **Authors' rating** ★★★½.

DESCRIPTION AND COMMENTS The unmistakable upside-down building is located on I-Drive in Orlando, between the Convention Center and Ripley's Believe it Or Not!. The interior of Wonderworks is stacked with small displays, a cross between a science museum and an arcade. Kids will enjoy this place more than adults, but even the older crowd can find a few exhibits to interest them. When the learning is completed, there is a laser-tag facility upstairs.

To enter Wonderworks, you must first pass through the Inversion Tunnel, a very effective optical illusion that gives you the sensation of spinning upside down. If you begin to get queasy, or fear you'll be hurled over the left-hand railing, simply close your eyes and walk forward. Once you've successfully cleared the tunnel and are fully inverted, you can watch other visitors wobbling their way into the first of the four rooms at Wonderworks.

Room 1 The main attractions in the first room are the **Hurricane Hole,** the **Earthquake Simulators,** the **Anti-Gravity Chamber,** the **Global VR,** and the **Famous Disasters** quiz center. The **Hurricane Hole** is a small box with four metal poles, such as you'd find in a subway car. Before the 65 mile-per-hour winds start blowing, you'll receive safety glasses and a brief tutorial on hurricanes (part of that tutorial stating that the 65 mile-per-hour winds in the Hurricane Hole are not slower than the requisite 75 mile-per-hour winds needed to call it a hurricane). The wind blows for less than a minute and, for its full impact, the best place to stand is directly in front of the fan.

The **Earthquake Simulators** are two small open-sided boxes next to the Hurricane Hole. Each box contains seating for four adults at a booth you would find at a diner. Once you are seated, the "earthquake" begins with a series of tremors and jolts, replicating the effects of an earthquake of 5.3 on the Richter scale. The effect is equivalent to driving on a dirt road.

Next to the Earthquake Simulators is the **Famous Disasters** quiz center where you can play tic-tac-toe on a series of computers. If you get the question right, you get the square. The quiz center is a good place to sit and wait your turn to play the **Global VR,** a virtual reality video game, although the wait time is not worth the experience. There are two yellow helmets, but no time limit on how long each player is allowed to play this first-person shooter. The in-game experience is akin to sitting too close to your television and playing on an out-of-date video system. The graphics are low quality, but the concept of controlling your view by turning your head has potential. A better illusion is located in the **Anti-Gravity Chamber,** where water appears to run toward the ceiling. Take a minute to figure out how the illusion is created before heading upstairs to the second room.

Room 2 The second main room at Wonderworks contains the **Bed of Nails,** the **Bubble Lab, Virtual Hoops, Swim with the Sharks,** the **Velocity Tunnel,** and the **WonderWall.** The **Bed of Nails** sits in the center of the room and contains 3,497 nails. To keep your weight evenly distributed, you lie on a plastic plank and the nails rise from beneath you. Although lying on nails is uncomfortable, it makes a great photo op. Next to the Bed of Nails is the **WonderWall,** a human-sized example of pin art. People press their hands or faces into a screen of flat-tipped pins, raising the pins on the other side to make a cast. The WonderWall is a scaled-up version of most pin art, with 40,000 pins in all.

If using your entire body to play interests you, then both **Virtual Hoops** and **Swim with the Sharks** are worth a try. In both of these exhibits, you stand in front of a blue screen and your image is projected into a virtual world on a video screen in front of you. In Virtual Hoops, you can play basketball or block soccer shots, while in Swim with the Sharks, you collect gold coins and avoid predators. The graphics are bad in both games, and the on-screen play is two-dimensional (as well as difficult), but the technology is something to marvel at.

Another exhibit that highlights technology is the **Velocity Tunnel,** where, after selecting a major league batter—choices include Barry Bonds—you throw actual baseballs at a slitted screen, giving you more respect for the real guys out on the mound.

If all the high-tech attractions are overcrowded or uninteresting to your children, there is always the **Bubble Lab,** an entire corner of the room dedicated to bubbles and bubble making. Just about every conceivable device for blowing bubbles is represented here, including the bubble screen and bubbles that can fit you inside.

Room 3 In the third room at Wonderworks, you will find most of the exhibits on sound, as well as a large collection of print illusions, including some by M. C. Escher. There is an oversized version of the Parker Brothers' game **Simon™** and a giant piano for which you step on the keys to play the notes. The **3-D sound booths** are located in the corner near the entrance to the fourth room. In these booths, you sit in the darkness and listen to the effects of surround sound in a confined space.

Room 4 The fourth and final room in Wonderworks contains a small space exhibit, a selection of computer banks, and the full-motion **Max Flight Simulators.** The space exhibit includes a replica of the *Mercury* capsule with a fake control panel, a large astronaut suit, and a computer terminal where you can attempt to land a space shuttle by lining up the nose with the runway.

The computer banks around the perimeter of the room also hold another flight simulator where you can fly an F-18 fighter jet. The three computer-screen displays that cover your main peripheral vision, coupled with the quality of graphics, make this the best of the simulators, including the full-motion Max Flight Simulators. Other computer bank exhibits include the face-morpher that combines the faces of members of your party, Wonderworks **Tic-Tac-Toe,** where you answer Wonderfacts questions to gain your X or O, and the **Drum Machine,** where kids can smack and bang to their hearts' content and to the annoyance of anyone stuck standing in the Max Flight Simulator line.

The **Max Flight Simulators** are the main attraction in the fourth room. They are the only rides at Wonderworks and, as far as we're concerned, not worth the wait. The simulators have strict requirements for entry: riders must be 48 inches or taller, you must have two riders, and riders' weight must be within 100 pounds of each other with a maximum weight of 500 pounds. If your measurements are within the limits, you can enter the line and prepare to wait. Each ride takes five minutes and fits only two riders, so if only one of the two simulators is running—a distinct possibility—then 12 people ahead of you will mean a wait time of 30 minutes. We've seen lines of more than 40 people during off-days, all listening to the children slamming away on the drum machine. To avoid the line, try to come to Wonderworks early on a weekday morning and head directly to the simulator. Of course, once you've made it to the head of the line, you'll find a very bad simulator. Although you can fully invert and rotate the cockpit of your fighter jet, and can toggle back and forth between who is piloting and who is shooting, the graphics are so terrible that you can barely tell what blips are the enemies. This ride is truly a letdown, and for the most part a drastic waste of time.

Lazerworks   Once you've exited through the turnstile at the far side of the fourth room, the learning aspect of Wonderworks is gone. The last area at Wonderworks is upstairs, where there is a small arcade and a large laser-tag room. The arcade and the Lazerworks area are accessible without paying for Wonderworks (use the elevator in the lobby), a convenient alternative if you decide to return and play.

In laser tag, each player is given a laser gun to shoot other players and a vest that registers each shot, placing your scores on a large screen in the arcade. Once your vest has been activated, you may enter the Lazerworks room, where you can hide behind panels and shoot at other players. Once you've been shot, your gun stops firing and your vest stops accepting hits for a few seconds, and then restarts, allowing you time to run to another area of the room. Besides shooting other players, you can also shoot lights on the partitions for extra points. The key to winning is to keep moving and to aim well.

Tickets

- $4.95 single game ($5.27 with tax); replay is an extra $3 plus tax
- $14.95 for unlimited play from 9 p.m. until midnight, Monday through Thursday

PART THIRTEEN

AIRBOAT TOURS, HORSE RIDES, ZOOS, *and* NATURE TOURS

DISNEY'S ANIMAL KINGDOM, SEAWORLD, and Busch Gardens all have unique and spectacular animal exhibits, yet, the massive scale of each of these parks prohibits some Orlando visitors from experiencing all three—or any—of the major animal attractions of central Florida. Since each of these parks requires an entire day to visit, costs upward of $50 per person, and is ostensibly a man-made re-creation of the natural environment, many visitors will opt for a smaller, cheaper, and more grassroots operation to fulfill their wonder for wild creatures. Orlando offers fulfillment in many forms. Airboat tours of the local lakes, nearby zoos, conservation projects, and horseback tours are all amenable answers to allow for animals in your itinerary. The quality of the attractions does vary drastically, and although none—or very few—are on par with an open-back truck ride on the Serengeti at Busch Gardens or a swim with the dolphins at Discovery Cove, they are all sound additions to a trip laden with animatronic creatures and miles of concrete.

AIRBOATS

AN AIRBOAT IS A FLAT-BOTTOMED BOAT powered by a large fan. The versatile machine, which can travel on both water and flat land, allows vacationers to explore the wetlands of central Florida. All the airboat tours near Orlando operate on lakes, so do not expect much of the swampy terrain common to the Everglades. You will see plenty of wildlife on these tours, and any ornithologists should have a field day. The two animals that awe most visitors are the bald eagle and the American alligator—you have a very good chance of seeing both on these tours, although neither animal is guaranteed. Some, but not all, bald eagles are migratory birds, flying north in the summer and returning in the winter. Migrating eagles do return to the same nest year after year, so clued-in tour guides will show you where their nests are located.

Bald eagles may be the animal icon of the United States, but the alligator is the animal icon of Florida (animated mice coming in a close second). You can see and feed baby alligators at Congo River Universal minigolf, or marvel at the full-sized gators at Gatorland. Wild alligators, on the other hand, are more difficult to spot, and you may see only their eyes and snout above the water. There are a few tricks to help you spot wild alligators. Alligators are exothermic, or cold-blooded, which means they have a minimal amount of inner body temperature regulation and must rely on the outside sources of heat like air and water to stay alive. Alligators are most active between 82°F and 92°F but seem to be easiest to spot when the air temperature outside is less than 84°F. During the winter, alligators stop feeding when the ambient temperature drops below 70°F, and become dormant, lying low in alligator holes, when the temperature drops below 55°F. Watch the weather during your visit and try to pick a day when the water is cool and the air temperature is around 84°F. Even if you follow none of our advice, chances are you will see at least one alligator.

At a distance, telling an alligator from a clump of floating mud can be difficult unless you can see the alligator's eyes, or part of its tail. Some operators offer night tours with "gator shining." Like many nocturnal animals, alligators have a layer of cells below their retinas that reflect light back into their photoreceptors, increasing night vision. When you shine a flashlight into a nocturnal animal's eyes at night, this layer of cells (called *tapetum lucidum*) creates an eerie red glow. You will see more alligators on night tours—but only their eyes, and water fowl are scarce.

A sign at Glades Adventure reads, "If you are seeking hype, sensationalism, or fantasy, there are many fine theme parks available nearby." We couldn't have said it better. Airboat tours are a great way to get out on the water on a hot afternoon, blast around a lake, and see much of the local wildlife. They aren't amusement rides, and you should have at least a hint of curiosity about the natural world before you go. Most tours require reservations, so plan ahead. Many of the airboat tours take coupons that can be printed online or found in any of the free magazines around town.

AIRBOAT TOURS

Airboat Rentals   ★★★½
4266 West Highway 192, Kissimmee; ☎ 407-847-3672; www.airboatrentals.com

---

Hours 9 a.m.–5 p.m. **Cost** Airboat rental, 1 hour: $30 for 1 boat; boats seat either 4 adults or 2 adults and 3 children. Electric boat rental, 1 hour: $25 for 1 boat; boats seat 6 people. Canoe rental, 1 hour: $7 for 1 canoe; canoes seat 2 people. **Authors' rating** ★★★½.

DESCRIPTION AND COMMENTS   You will find Airboat Rentals (that's the name of the company) on US 192, just beyond Medieval Times. As the name states, they do rent airboats, but not the large airboats that are available for tours. These airboats are very small with only 18 horsepower engines, but on the plus side, you get to drive them! They do not offer hearing protection, but these airboats are quieter than their larger counterparts.

Airboats are rented out in one-hour increments. You can go to the top of Shingle Creek and back in about 40 minutes, leaving you time to float around where you see fit. You won't see alligators, but we did spot a few turtles and birds. The area up Shingle Creek is a cypress swamp, but you can still see signs of civilization through the woods, and your peace and quite is disturbed with the noise of other airboats.

The best deal at Airboat Rentals is not the miniature airboats, but instead is the electric boats. With seating for six adults, and only $25 for an hour, these boats can take you down Shingle Creek (the opposite direction of the airboats), to a more secluded and undisturbed area. The electric boats are almost silent and cruise between six and eight knots. With a full boat, you can have a picnic on the water for less than $5 a person, away from the traffic and crowds of Orlando. Fishing-rod rental is available for $5 a rod. During summer months and evenings, be sure to bring bug repellent, or you won't be the only one having a picnic.

Big Toho Airboat Rides   ★★★
In the public parking lot next to 101 Lakeshore Boulevard, Kissimmee;
☎ **888-937-6843; www.orlandoswamptours.com**

Hours By reservation. **Cost** Daytime airboat tour, 45 minutes: $35 per person with coupon; children ages 6 and under are free; minimum of 2 paying guests. Evening airboat tour, around 80 minutes: Prices vary. **Authors' rating** ★★★.

DESCRIPTION AND COMMENTS   Big Toho is the airboat tour closest to Orlando. They do not have a permanent ticket booth location, but launch from a public boat ramp on the north end of Lake Tohopekaliga (Lake Toho for short). The public boat ramp is easy enough to find, but be aware, a separate company called Big Toho Marina does have a permanent dock nearby; make sure to go to the public parking lot in front of the public dock.

The owner and operator, Brent, is a jovial character and happy to demonstrate the handiness of his airboat, popping over the reed beds and skimming through the lotus fields. Although he operates close to TJ's Airboats, his tour contains better scenery (the view, however, is still marred with industrial plants and power lines). The information on the tour is lackluster but the boat's speed and handling should keep you entertained, and makes this the most thrilling airboat ride available. Big Toho specializes in night tours lasting about 80 minutes, and for anyone who felt comfy camping next to Florida lakes, the plethora of red eyes should install just the right amount of fear.

Children ages 6 and under are free with two paying adults, and the airboat holds up to seven guests. However, if you decide to bring five kids and two adults, we strongly suggest leaving a big tip. Coupons and advertisements are available in all the free local magazines and should be brought with you, but if you forget them, you should still be able to receive the stated coupon price.

Boggy Creek Airboat Tours   ★★★
Two locations: 2001 East Southport Road, Kissimmee, and 3702 Big Bass Road, Kissimmee; ☎ 407-344-9550; www.bcairboats.com

Hours 9 a.m.–4:30 p.m. Cost Airboat tours, 30 minutes: $21.95 + tax for adults; $15.95 + tax for children ages 3–12; and free for children ages 2 and under. Private airboat tour, 45 minutes: $45 per person, 2–6 people required. Night airboat tours, 60 minutes: $34.95 + tax for adults; $29.95 + tax for children ages 3-12; and free for gator-bait ages 2 and under; reservations required weeks in advance, 6-person minimum. Wildlife safari tour (Southport only), 40 minutes: $21.95 + tax for adults; $15.95 + tax for children ages 3–12; and free for children ages 2 and under. 30-minute airboat tour and wildlife safari combo (Southport only), 70 minutes: $36.80 for adults; $28.70 for children ages 3–12; and free for children ages 2 and under. Authors' rating ★★★.

DESCRIPTION AND COMMENTS Boggy Creek Airboat Tours operates from two locations: one on Lake Toho and the other, a 45-minute drive from WDW, on West Lake Toho, a separate lake. Both locations offer very similar tours. The airboats each fit 18 people and have bench seating instead of height-staggered seating, so you should attempt to sit in the front row for the best view.

The 30-minute airboat tour leaves every half hour, beginning at 9 a.m., and takes you out onto the lake alongside open cow pastures. Herons and egrets are visible here, as well as a few other birds. The tours do not pass through reeds or much marsh, but stick instead to the open water. Houses dot the landscape at both locations, but the development at both sites is not as pronounced as found on tours that operate from the north end of Lake Toho. The guides provide a moderate amount of information, including how to estimate an alligator's length (the amount of inches between the eyes and the snout is equal to the alligator's length in feet). The ride is stop-and-go, pausing every time someone suspects a gator is present, and at only 30 minutes, seems over before it has begun.

Boggy Creek is one of the most popular tours in the area due to their accessible locations and prolific advertising. They do not require reservations for the 30-minute airboat tours, although we strongly recommend making them. When you do make your reservation, find out if enough other guests have reserved spots for the boat to leave at the appointed time.

At the Southport location, Boggy Creek also offers a Wildlife Tour. The "swamp buggy" tour boards directly behind the cabin. buggy is a short bus on a large lift kit, including 5½-foot-diameter tires. Even with these oversized tires the ride is jarring, so do not bring any coffee or containers without tops. Since the bus is so far off the ground, you board from a ramp onto the back of the buggy. All seating faces inward, so there is minimal obstruction of your line of sight; in order to hear the driver it is better to sit near the front of the buggy.

The tour takes place on an 8,000-acre cattle ranch and nature preserve. The buggy follows a dirt path, past the storage barn and out into the preserve. The route takes you past multiple feeders, designed to disperse food at different times of day. The feeders attract the indigenous wildlife, which includes, among others: Osceola turkeys, sandhill cranes, bald eagles (seasonal), Illinois white-tailed deer, raccoons, and wild boar. Near the end of your Florida safari, the path literally enters the gator pond. With the buggy's tires deep in water, the driver throws cuts of raw chicken to the alligators who shimmy up onto small islands on either side of the buggy. A fence separates the gators from the buggy, so don't worry about becoming a second course.

The Wildlife Safari Tour is a good add-on to the airboat ride and makes the 45-minute drive worthwhile. If you want both to see a large alligator and then watch it feed, this is, next to Gatorland, the best place. However, if you're interested in sundry facts, the drivers are not particularly informative (more of a farmer's perspective than a naturalist's), but in order to hear some small tidbits about the animals, sit near the front of the buggy. There is a tip jar for the driver, and a dollar a person will suffice.

Glades Adventure ★★★½
4715 Kissimmee Park Road, St. Cloud; ☎ 407-891-2222; www.gladesadventures.com

Hours 9 a.m.–5 p.m.; by reservation. **Cost** Daytime airboat tours, 60 minutes: $29.95 + tax for adults; $19.95 + tax for children ages 3–12; and free for children ages 2 and under; bring the coupon found in any of the free local advertising magazines. **Authors' rating ★★★½.**

DESCRIPTION AND COMMENTS You can find Glades Adventure in a campground a few miles from Orlando. In the small office at the campground is a terrarium that is home to a few baby gators, and if you ask nicely, the staff will let you hold the toothy critters. The staff's knowledge of local wildlife, from the receptionists to the tour guides, is above average. When it's time for the tour, you board a six-passenger airboat and meander off onto the southern end of Lake Toho. This end of the lake has fewer developments than the north end, allowing you to encounter a more pristine Florida.

On your tour, your guide may reveal a few eagle nests. The eagle pairs here leave during the summer, but lone immature eagles are found year-round. Other wildlife includes anhingas, spoonbills, and, of course,

guides at Glades Adventure carry a pair of binoculars, so
rve the birds even if they are perched up a distant tree.
re peaceful and can involve a bit of drifting under the
ear sunscreen and sit back with one eye closed and the
look for gators.

Airboat Tours ★★★★½

3301 Lake Cypress Road, Kenansville; ☎ 407-957-2277;
www.ospreyecotours.com

Hours 9 a.m.– 4:30 p.m. with night tours available; all tours by reservation only.
Cost Daytime airboat tour, 60 minutes: $45 + tax for adults; $35 + tax for
children ages 4–12; and free for children ages 3 and under. Night tours, 60
minutes: Same price as daytime tours, minimum of 4 guests; reservations only.
Daytime airboat tour, 30 minutes: $27.50 per person. Eco-tour, 75 minutes: $60
per person. **Authors' rating** Fantastic; ★★★★½.

DESCRIPTION AND COMMENTS If you don't mind a longer drive, and have a bit
more money to spend, Lake Cypress Airboat Tours are the best in the
Kissimmee area. After a one-hour drive from the WDW area, you make
your way down a 2.3-mile dirt road to the edge of Lake Cypress. There
is a small camp set up at the end of the lake, complete with a big deck
to picnic on and plenty of shade under the live oaks (you can pick up
picnic supplies at the Winn-Dixie about ten miles before Lake Cypress).

Depending on the tour you decide on, your group can be as large as 20
people, but the 75-minute Eco-Tour seats a maximum of eight people and
is the best airboat tour in central Florida. The Eco-Tour is aboard brand-
new yellow airboats that are both faster and less deafening than any of
their local counterparts. Guests don headsets complete with micro-
phones, allowing the entire tour to be fully narrated and interactive without having to stop the boat. Each guest is lent a pair of binoculars, and
ponchos, for the brief afternoon showers, are also provided.

Beside the amenities and insightful narration (far and away the most
informative in the area), what makes the tour special is the location. On
Lake Cypress, unlike Lake Toho, there are no developments or any other
houses besides the camp. The wildlife is abundant, and although the
types of birds vary due to the season, kites, roseate spoonbills, a variety
of ducks, and bald eagles are all regular visitors. According to Lake
Cypress Airboats, the Eco-Tour passes through the highest concentra-
tion of bald eagles in Florida. The wildlife is astounding, but the terrain
also sets this tour apart. Instead of sticking to the lake, you may go
down a small canal, into the reed beds, and up and over the wetlands.
The canal, during the cooler months, is a great place to see alligators
basking on the banks.

If the $60 Eco-Tour seems a bit steep (you could nearly spend a day
at SeaWorld for that price), Lake Cypress offers other tours. Rates for
these tours are listed above. The tours are on slightly larger boats, and
don't have the headsets found on the Eco-Tour, but the tours still contain all the same scenery and the same erudite guides.

TJ's Airboats ★★
Richardson's Fish Camp, 1550 Scotty Road, Kissimmee; ☎ 407-846-4287

Hours 9 a.m.–4:30 p.m. **Cost** Daytime airboat rides, 40 minutes: $28 + tax for adults; $23 + tax for children ages 3 and under; $84 minimum charge for each 6-person boat, but you can schedule a ride with others. **Authors' rating ★★.**

DESCRIPTION AND COMMENTS   TJ's Airboats is located at Richardson's Fish Camp, a short drive from Kissimmee. The nearby location is TJ's greatest asset, although the friendly staff doesn't hurt it either. The fish camp is small but does include a store stocked with fishing gear and snacks. Smoking is permitted inside, so waiting at the tables is hazardous to your health.

The welfare of the passengers' hearing is also a secondary concern. TJ's is the only guided airboat tour in the area that does not require hearing protection—one can only wonder why. You cannot hear the driver's comments while the fan is spinning nor will you be able to hear much after the trip is over. We all came away with a mild case of tinnitus. They do offer earplugs, but you have to ask. Do not leave the dock without them.

Even when the guides talk, the tour is not very informative, stating few if any facts on alligators. You have a good chance of spotting alligators and an assortment of birds; however, the Kissimmee skyline dampens the natural wonder.

▌OTHER ANIMAL ATTRACTIONS

THERE IS A FINE ASSORTMENT OF OTHER CREATURES in the Orlando area that do not pose the threat of cleaving an arm. These attractions allow visitors to spend a half day away from the zoo of visitors on US 192 and I-Drive, and to come in contact with a more natural side of central Florida.

Audubon of Florida's Center for Birds of Prey ★★★½
1101 Audubon Way, Maitland; ☎ 407-644-0190;
www.audubonofflorida.org

Hours Tuesday–Sunday, 10 a.m.–4 p.m. **Cost** $5 for adults; $4 for children ages 3–12. **Authors' rating ★★★½.**

DESCRIPTION AND COMMENTS   With a mission to "conserve, protect, and restore Florida's natural resources" the Center for Birds of Prey is an outreach facility for rehabilitating injured or ill birds of prey. Over 12,000 birds have been treated here since its inception in 1979. For such a small center, with barely two-and-a-half acres of land, this is quite a feat. The center is also the leading North American caretaker of bald eagles, with more than 250 birds treated. Forty percent of the birds treated here are released back into the wild. Those that are unable to be rehabilitated are kept here or sent to other care facilities.

The small grounds have quite a number of birds, including peregrine falcons, barred owls, burrowing owls, northern caracaras, red-tailed hawks, kestrels, and kites. You will not be allowed to hold any of the animals, but if you ask a keeper, he or she may give you an up-close look. The keepers are very friendly, so ask plenty of questions. Guided tours are available only to groups larger than ten people, cost $100, and require reservations. The guidebook rental for a self-guided tour is included in the normal admission price.

A great addendum to the nearby Orlando Science Museum or the Central Florida Zoo, the price is right if you can find the place. Since the town of Maitland did not replace the signage it removed for recent roadwork, the Birds of Prey Center is almost impossible to locate. Here are the directions from Interstate 4: take Exit 87 headed east, to Fairbanks Avenue. Take a left on Fairbanks, then a right on Wymore. Cross Lee Road and continue to the next light (Kennedy Boulevard) and turn right. Continue to East Street. Make a left onto East Street. The Center is just ahead at the three-way stop on your left. Even with the directions, we were forced to call multiple times so, here's their number: ☎ 407-644-0190. If that doesn't get you anywhere, just ask the locals; people walking dogs and jogging tend to know where they are going.

The Central Florida Zoo   ★★★½
3755 NW Highway, Sanford (off I-4 at Exit 104 on US 17-92);
☎ **407-323-4450; www.centralfloridazoo.org**

Hours Daily, 9 a.m.–5 p.m.; closed Thanksgiving Day and Christmas Day. **Cost** $8.95 for adults; $6.95 for seniors (ages 60+); $4.95 for children ages 3–12. **Authors' rating ★★★½.**

DESCRIPTION AND COMMENTS   To see the animals at Busch Gardens or at Disney's Animal Kingdom, you have to buy admission to the entire park. If you were not able to spend an entire day of your trip at either of these destinations or found their prices overbearing, the Central Florida Zoo is worth a visit. It may be a slight drive from Orlando, taking about 30 minutes, but it is closer than Busch Gardens and makes a great half-day trip.

The zoo was founded in 1923 as the Sanford Zoo and moved to its current location in 1975 and has been growing ever since. The zoo bills itself as an educational center, and with the wide variety of animals and animal encounters on weekends and holidays, along with a purported 75,000 children visitors a year, it fulfills its purpose.

The variety of species is impressive for such a small zoo. Asian elephants, cheetahs, crocodiles, kangaroos, and zebus are some of the more interesting animals you will see as you traverse the boardwalks, etched with names of prior visitors.

Weekend visitors will be able to partake in the zoo's lectures and animal interactions. The current weekend schedule is as follows, but is subject to change at any time, so call ahead before the day of your visit: Elephant Demonstrations at 11 a.m. and 2 p.m., a Bird Show at 11:30

a.m., Bug Encounters at 1 p.m., Primate Feeding at 2:15 p.m., Feline Feeding at 2:30 p.m., and Reptile Demonstrations at 3 p.m. A member of the zoo staff hosts each 15- to 30-minute exhibition and gives a short fact-laden lecture, then answers any questions. One of the best deals around is the Elephant Encounter at 11:15 a.m. on Saturdays and 2:15 p.m. on Sundays where, for $5 above the admission price, guests can touch and feed the elephants. Albeit a skewed comparison, a tour of the savanna to feed the giraffes and antelope at Busch Gardens costs $30 per person.

Since almost all the zoo's exhibits are outside, except for the Discovery Zone with its ten-centimeter millipedes and goliath tarantulas, you will need good weather. Sunscreen and water are also advisable. There is a snack bar on the premises, but you are better bringing your own food; a comfortable picnic area is located inside.

Forever Florida
Florida Eco-Safaris, 4755 N. Kenansville Road, St. Cloud;
☎ **407-957-9794; www.floridaeco-safaris.com**

Hours Vary; reservations required for horseback rides. Cost Horseback ride, 1 hour: $37.50 + tax per person, must be at least 12 years old; 2 hours: $57+ tax per person, must be at least 12 years old; 3 hours: $73 + tax includes lunch, must be at least 12 years old. Eco-safaris, 2½ hours: $24.95 + tax for adults; $19.95 + tax for children ages 6–12; free for children, ages 5 and under. Departs daily at 10 a.m. and 1 p.m. Authors' rating ★★★½.

DESCRIPTION AND COMMENTS A long drive from WDW at about one-and-a-half hours, Forever Florida may fit into your plans if you are either headed to Miami or have just finished an airboat tour south of Kissimmee. Forever Florida is both a working cattle ranch and a nature conservancy. They offer hiking trails, a small petting zoo with pony rides, horseback safaris, and eco-safaris.

When you arrive, you should report to the main desk, located in the Cypress Lodge. The lodge is clean and modern, and contains the Cypress Restaurant, whose menu consists mostly of deep-fried food from the Deep South, with both okra and alligator gracing the menu. A cow-burger with fries costs $5.95 plus tax.

The horseback safaris vary in length from one-hour to multiday excursions and require reservations, close-toed shoes, and long pants. Trips over two hours require group reservations. Although one hour is all the time we need on a plodding horse, you will not see much on the one-hour tour but scrub, dried-out pine trees, and open fields. Unlike the picture on the brochure, this is not swampland. The two-hour tour is somewhat better, culminating in a stop at Bull Creek, a drastically different ecosystem from the rest of the ride's. A small promenade cuts out into the swamp with overhanging cypress and large live oaks. Unfortunately, the stop is all of ten minutes, then you're back in the open fields and scrub brush.

The Eco-Safari Tours are two-and-a-half hours and comprise a preliminary presentation and then a tour that explores both the cattle ranch and the land conservation project. The tour begins with a narrated slide show depicting the history of Forever Florida. Dr. William Broussard owned and operated the Crescent J Ranch, where his children came to play. His eldest son, Allen, was fond of nature and went on to become a conservationist before his life was cut short due to Hodgkin's disease. The conservation project was Allen's last request, and the family has attempted to fulfill his dream. Thirty percent of all of the proceeds go to help purchase more land.

After the tragic and touching tribute, you are ushered onto a vehicle similar to the swamp buggy at Boggy Creek Airboat rides. This buggy, with its huge wheels, takes you first toward the cattle ranch, then past a small ditch with alligators, and then out into the conservation area. The tour is fully narrated, and although it will bore little kids to tears, it is one of the most educational attractions in central Florida. After a ride through the open fields, you arrive at Bull Creek and walk around the promenade, then return back to the lodge.

We support Forever Florida's commitment to preservation, and think they have a fine product, but we would be remiss if we didn't emphasize the barren and uninspiring landscape. Besides Bull Creek, the open plains and mild woodlands are not very scenic. We would like to see Forever Florida expand its operations to include a wider variety of terrain and ecosystems, and think it has tremendous potential. As it stands now, the drive is too far for us to recommend Forever Florida to guests who are not already passing southward.

Grand Cypress Equestrian Center and ★★★½ Western Trail Rides

1 Equestrian Drive, Orlando; ☎ 800-835-7377 or 407-239-6322; www.grandcypress.com

Hours 9 a.m.–4 p.m. **Cost** Western trail ride, $45 for visitors ages 10 and up, **Authors' rating** ★★★½.

DESCRIPTION AND COMMENTS Located inside Disney property, the Grand Cypress resort offers trail rides that are open to the public, although reservations are required. Long pants and closed-toed shoes are also necessary. The Western Trail Rides are 45 minutes in duration, and cost $45 per person, ages 10 and older. The Western Trail Rides are located not at the Equestrian Center (that is a short drive past the Grand Cypress Resort), but instead, are within the grounds of the Grand Cypress Resort. When arriving, ask the guard at the gate for directions. You will go straight ahead, past the hotel, and then follow the signs until you reach the stables.

In a departure from Horse World, the Western Trail Ride takes you through isolated woods. The pace is still plodding and slow, but the vegetation gives riders something to keep them occupied. The unnarrated ride takes you on a meandering trail that switchbacks through the undergrowth. There is no sound of traffic, only the occasional airplane overhead. The ride is peaceful, but still bumpy and uncomfortable for people who don't ride horses.

The Equestrian Center, a short drive past the Grand Cypress Resort on the right, offers a full-service riding stable. The stables are clean, and the instruction is top-notch. A one-hour lesson, including a horse, is $100, and half-hour lessons are available for $55 for visitors ages 7 and up. The stables offer riding packages for all different ages and skill levels, riding for both Western or English styles, summer camps, pony rides, and such. This is your all-in-one horse stop. Call for more information and reservations.

Horse World Riding Stables ★½
3705 South Poinciana Boulevard, Kissimmee;
☎ **407-847-4343; www.horseworldstables.com**

Hours 9 a.m.–4 p.m. **Cost** Nature trail ride, 60 minutes: $39 + tax for visitors ages 6 and up; $16.95 + tax for children ages 5 and under if they ride with a paying adult. Intermediate trail ride, 60 minutes: $47 + tax for visitors ages 10 and up. Advanced trail ride, 60 minutes: $69 + tax for visitors ages 10 and up. The maximum total weight for all the rides is 250 pounds. Riders must where closed-toed shoes, and long pants are recommended. Reservations are also required. **Authors' rating** ★½.

DESCRIPTION AND COMMENTS Twelve miles south of US 192 on Poinciana Boulevard, you will find Horse World. As romantic as riding a horse sounds, it is not for everyone. Horse World's featured ride is the nature ride, and although they may call it a "guided [ride] through the woods," what they mean to say is a guided ride with limited or no narration alongside the Poinciana Highway. After you've mounted the horse and headed off around the pond, the trail follows the side of the road, leaving its sight—but not the sound of its traffic—for very brief intervals. The walking pace, although suitable for very small children, is arduous for anyone older than 6 years of age. Sitting on top of a plodding horse in an uncomfortable saddle, with cars whizzing past is not our idea of entertainment. As for the nature, this quote from our guide during one visit sums it up, "See those sticks on the top of that cell phone tower? That's an eagle's nest." The Intermediate Tour takes a similar path to the Nature Ride but goes slightly quicker and a bit farther. Poinciana Boulevard did not have the current high traffic flow it has now when Horse World opened. Horse World is attempting to build trails that head back into the woods, but it is not worth a visit until these trails are completed, so call ahead to see if these trails have opened.

Petting Farm at Green Meadows ★★½/★★★★
1368 South Poinciana Boulevard, Kissimmee;
☎ **407-846-0770; www.greenmeadowsfarm.com**

Hours Tours operate continuously between 9:30 a.m. and 4 p.m. **Duration of visit** 2–4 hours. **Cost** $19 + tax for adults; free for children ages 2 and under. **Authors' rating** ★★★★ (for preschoolers and grade schoolers); ★★½ for anyone older.

DESCRIPTION AND COMMENTS Six miles down Poinciana Boulevard off US 192, you will find the Petting Farm at Green Meadows on the right-hand side. The 40-acre "farm" features animal interactions. The animals include the standard barnyard fare of chickens and goats, but also more exotic animals like llamas and zorses. After you buy your tickets, the attendant at the booth will show you where you can meet up with the rest of the tour. The tours are continuous, so once you've returned to the same site, you've seen the entire farm. Each station features a different animal, and takes 5 to 15 minutes to visit depending on the size of your tour group.

The farm is clean and well maintained. Although only a fence separates you from the highway, the traffic noise is slight, for the most part, and most of the attractions are set back from the road. Scattered tractors and other farm equipment add to the farm theme (no sharp equipment), and besides the smell of animals, the place is charming.

The animal interactions are as up-close as you can imagine. At the chickens, geese, and duck stations, you are allowed inside the pens and can pick up the animals. Watching guests attempt to catch geese (think of the aphorism about herding cats) may alone be worth the price of admission. You can pet and feed most of the other animals, including the sheep, goats, pigs, and donkeys, and everyone gets a turn to milk the cow and ride the pony. All of the animal feed is free, and there are hand-sanitizer locations at every station. There are some larger animals here, and although you cannot pet all of them, they are worth seeing. These include ostriches, bison, llamas, a zebu, a zorse (a horse-and-zebra offspring), water buffalo, and the like.

Besides the animal exhibits, there is a small train that takes guests around the perimeter of the park, and a hayride. For in-park personal transportation, you can rent a small red wagon for $3 to pull diapers and tired children. Most children will love all of the animal interactions, although the geese can scare the very young. Children will find this place much more interesting than adults will, and you may get a bit restless. Prying them away from the petting zoo, even if they've already seen everything, almost always results in tears, but these can be mended with the bribe of ice cream.

PART FOURTEEN

MUSEUMS *and* CULTURAL ATTRACTIONS

MANY VISITORS TO ORLANDO LIMIT their visits to a few major theme parks, bypassing the local community. There is often no time allotted for days outside the major parks, and with a "run-till-you-drop" vacation mentality, many vacationers will find themselves worn out, in need of the proverbial vacation from their vacation.

Since the ride-to-ride shuffle of the major parks becomes monotonous after a few days, and that distinguishing line between individual attractions begins to blur, it becomes important to spark your brain before atrophy sets in. The museums and cultural attractions of central Florida all offer a convenient way to reactivate your mind, and surprisingly enough, most are very interesting. From Fantasy of Flight's exhibits on pre-jet aircraft, to the Morse Museum's collections of Tiffany glassware, central Florida contains museums and cultural attractions for all ages and tastes. The prices for many of the exhibits are also more affordable than their touristy competition, and crowds and lines are almost always less.

KIDS AND MUSEUMS

MENTION TO A CHILD THAT YOU ARE PLANNING a visit to a museum and you will receive the requisite groans of disgust. Mention that you plan on taking him with you, and you've got a good chance at instigating a full-scale tantrum. Children's negative reactions to museums, gardens, and other cultural attractions are only heightened in Orlando, where the glitz of the major theme parks, with their cartoon-character mascots and patina of utter happiness, emblazons a glazed look in a child's eyes. And, don't forget, your children are on vacation as well, so instilling them with knowledge on their days away from school will be difficult.

Our best advice is to take note of the names of the Orlando Science Center and Fantasy of Flight and to avoid calling the attraction you are going to a museum. Another tactic is balancing your days'

e Historic Bok Sanctuary is on your list, contemplate leav-
ildren with your spouse and sending them to nearby
rdens. Since attractions like the Cornell Museum and the
u Gardens are within blocks of the Orlando Science Cen-
balance your group's day by spending the morning playing
at the Science Center and the afternoon viewing the gardens.

However you plan your itinerary, stay attuned to the likes and dis-
likes of your group. Most of the ticket prices are low, so don't be afraid
to leave early if necessary. Dragging around bawling children is not only
a hassle for you, but disobliges everyone else at an attraction.

ATTRACTIONS

Cornell Fine Arts Museum ★★★★

APPEAL BY AGE	PRESCHOOL ★★	GRADE SCHOOL ★½	TEENS ★★½
YOUNG ADULTS ★★★		OVER 30 ★★★½	SENIORS ★★★

100 Holt Avenue, Winter Park; ☎ 407-646-2526; www.rollins.edu/cfam

Hours Tuesday–Saturday, 10 a.m.–5 p.m.; Sunday, 1–5 p.m. Closed Mondays.
Cost $5 for adults, free for students and children. **Author's rating** ★★★★.

DESCRIPTION AND COMMENTS A recent $7.5-million renovation of the
museum, located on the Rollins College campus, has allowed this six-
gallery museum to show more of its permanent collection. Unlike many
small museums, the Cornell owns paintings by very substantial artists,
including Winslow Homer, Gilbert Stuart, and followers of Peter Paul
Rubens. Although many of the older works are excellent period pieces,
the modern collection is what hooked our fancy. David Hockney, Chuck
Close, Robert Motherwell, Roy Lichtenstein, Willem de Kooning, and
Pablo Picasso are a few of the most prominent artists of the 20th century, and each has works in the museum. The low entrance fee, free
parking, and lakeside location aren't bad visitor bait either.

TOURING TIPS Although the new 9,000-square-foot facility is a major
expansion, the museum still cannot display all 5,000 of its works at
once. The collection rotates every few months, and two of the galleries
regularly feature traveling exhibits. The Cornell is the best fine arts
museum in central Florida, and even though it is small, the permanent
collection dwarfs that of the Orlando Museum of Art.

kids Fantasy of Flight ★★★½

APPEAL BY AGE	PRESCHOOL ★★	GRADE SCHOOL ★★★½	TEENS ★★★½
YOUNG ADULTS ★★★½		OVER 30 ★★★★	SENIORS ★★★★

1400 Broadway Boulevard SE, Polk City; ☎ 863-984-3500;
www.fantasyofflight.com

Hours Daily, 10 a.m.–5 p.m. **Cost** $26.95 + tax for adults; $24.95 + tax for seniors; $13.95 + tax for children ages 6–15; and free for children ages 5 and under. **Authors' rating** ★★★½.

DESCRIPTION AND COMMENTS A 40-minute drive from WDW, Fantasy of Flight is dedicated to its namesake. The museum has two parts, the immersion environments and the hangars. We were a bit startled at the high-quality theming in the immersion environments. Guests walk through an exhibit on the birth of flight, flight in World War I, and then aerial warfare in World War II. Full sound and lighting are used to create atmosphere for each historic period. The birth of flight and World War I exhibits are both small, but the World War II exhibit houses an actual B-17 bomber amid the backdrop of an airfield. The immersion technique is very successful in the World War II exhibit, and the life-sized figures only aid the effect.

Once you've finished the immersion environments, you enter the hangars where aircraft of pre-jet vintage have found a home. Most of the aircraft are set behind ropes, but a few are open to public inspection. Guided tours are available and meet regularly in the corners of the hangars under signs marked Guided Tours. Besides the aircraft, the two hangars also contain a kids' area called Fun with Flight and flight simulators in Fighter Town. In the kids' area you can attempt to land a hang glider—a video simulation—or create paper airplanes to test for distance. The flight simulators in Fighter Town are World War II–era Corsair cockpits with screens inside. The graphics are not amazing, but on par with any of the flight simulators in Orlando.

Activities at Fantasy for Flight are printed out daily, so call ahead to check the schedule for the day you are visiting, since many tours are offered only once a day. Tours include a Tram Tour of the restricted areas, an Engine and Machine Shop Tour, a Woodshop Tour, and a Sheet Metal and Aircraft Assembly Tour. Daily aerial demonstrations are also a huge draw, and usually include some aerobatics in vintage aircraft.

TOURING TIPS There is a direct corollary between your level of interest in aircraft and engineering and the amount of fun you will have here. Although the immersion environments are outstanding, they will take up only about 30 minutes of your visit. Fantasy of Flight makes a good half-day attraction, but children may get bored rather quickly, even with the kids' zone and flight simulators, so try to arrive for the aerial demonstration to give them a perspective on the aircraft at hand. The Rose Compass Diner is also located inside the complex and contains typical diner food at standard prices, a hamburger platter costing $5.95 plus tax.

Harry P. Leu Gardens ★★★½

APPEAL BY AGE	PRESCHOOL ★★	GRADE SCHOOL ★½	TEENS ½
YOUNG ADULTS ★★★½	OVER 30 ★★★★	SENIORS ★★★★	

1920 North Forest Avenue, Orlando; ☎ **407-246-2620;**
www.leugardens.org

Hours Daily except Christmas, 9 a.m.–5 p.m., **Cost** $5 for adults; $1 for children attending K–12th grade; children in preschool and under are free. **Authors' rating ★★★½.**

DESCRIPTION AND COMMENTS Less isolated than the Historic Bok Sanctuary, the Harry P. Leu Gardens are situated in downtown Orlando, only a few blocks from the Science Center and the Orlando Museum of Art. Besides the location, the gardens' free parking and low admission prices are also appealing to visitors.

There are 50 acres' worth of smaller gardens situated within the Harry P. Leu Gardens. You enter through the Tropical Stream Garden, home to a variety of exotic equatorial plants. Continuing clockwise, you'll pass through the Home Demonstration Gardens, where you may pick up tips for landscaping your own yard. Next you will reach the Vegetable Garden and then the Butterfly Gardens, which both contain their respective namesakes.

In the bottom corner of the gardens is the Arid Garden (cactus, and the like) and multitudes of camellias. Indeed, Harry P. Leu Gardens boast the largest camellia collection in the South. As you continue along the paths, you will pass more flowers at the Rose Garden, Daylilies Garden, and Floral Clock, before reaching the forest area. Here, you will find bamboo, pines, live oaks, cycads, and an array of deciduous and coniferous trees. The forest area also borders Lake Rowena, and there is a small overlook to stop at before you make your way back to the entrance.

The Leu Museum House is located at the Gardens, and belonged to the benefactor Harry P. Leu before he donated the land to the City of Orlando in 1961. Tours of this refurbished house are available daily, at 10 a.m. and at 3:30 p.m., but please note, the house is generally closed in July.

TOURING TIPS Children will be bored here, but adults over age 30 and seniors with a green thumb should find more than a few good ideas for their gardens at home. The palm trees and bamboo groves in the back of the Gardens make a great place for a picnic, as does the outcropping deck on the lakefront.

Historic Bok Sanctuary ★★½

| APPEAL BY AGE | PRESCHOOL ★★ | GRADE SCHOOL ★½ | TEENS ½ |
| YOUNG ADULTS ★★★ | OVER 30 ★★★½ | SENIORS ★★★★ | |

1151 Tower Boulevard, Lake Wales; ☎ 863-676-1408; www.boksanctuary.org

Hours Daily, 8 a.m.–6 p.m., with last entrance at 5 p.m. **Cost** $10 for adults; $3 for children ages 3–12; and free for children ages 2 and under. **Authors' rating ★★½.**

DESCRIPTION AND COMMENTS A long, 55-mile drive away from the maelstrom of Orlando entertainment, the Historic Bok Sanctuary is a stately place for those seeking solace. Built on the top of Iron Mountain, the sanctuary offers some spectacular views of the plains 298 feet below—quite an altitude shift in central Florida. The chief attractions are the gardens, the tower, and the Pinewood Estate—although it is quite a trek on the hiking trails. The video at the visitors center and the Window by the Pond (a small cabin with a view of a pond) are mildly interesting.

The gardens were designed by the world-famous landscape architect Frederick Law Olmsted Jr., who, among other achievements, also designed the Rose Garden at the White House. The gardens sprawl over the entire hilltop, and a mixture of concrete and wood-chip walking paths allow you to see most of the landscaping. The design of the gardens is exceptional, but many of the flowers are seasonal, so plan your visit accordingly. There are few plaques to tell you what the plants are, so you will have to bring your keen personal knowledge, or a book.

In the center of the gardens, the Tower at Bok Sanctuary is the centerpiece of the estate. Built on the top of the mountain, this Neo-Gothic colossus dominates the landscape, made even more virile by the reflecting pool at its base. You cannot enter the tower or even cross the moat that surrounds it, so do not plan on getting the view from the top. Daily carillon concerts are played from the bells at the top of the tower, and although some prolonged tones can be discordant, many patrons seem to enjoy the music.

Away from the tower, the Pinewood Estate, on the far side of the hill from the visitors center, joined the Historic Bok Sanctuary in 1970. Tours of this Mediterranean Revivalist mansion get under way at 12 p.m. and 2 p.m. for the additional fee of $6 for adults and $3 for children ages 3 to 12.

TOURING TIPS Do not take kids to the Bok Sanctuary unless they need to be punished or enjoy studying botany in their free time. You will only disturb the other visitors and hand your children more retaliatory fodder for their teenage years.

The Historic Bok Sanctuary is a silent place, and time passes very slowly on the mountain. Self-reflection and boredom are the two chief results of a visit, so prepare your head before you come. Much of the serenity propagated at the visitors center seems forced, but if you are ready for a bit of solitude and don't want to shell out for a mud spa, this is a quality alternative.

Mennello Museum ★★½

APPEAL BY AGE	PRESCHOOL ★	GRADE SCHOOL ★½	TEENS ½
YOUNG ADULTS ★★	OVER 30 ★★★		SENIORS ★★★

900 East Princeton Street; ☎ 407-246-4278; www.mennellomuseum.org

Hours Tuesday–Saturday, 10:30 a.m.–4:30 p.m. Cost $8 for adults; $7 for seniors; $5 for students with ID; and free for children under age 12. Authors' rating ★★½.

DESCRIPTION AND COMMENTS When you walk in, your first question will be, "Where is the rest of the museum?" We're not sure, but the four rooms do hold a fine, if minor, collection of local Florida art. Most of the paintings are by Earl Cunningham, a St. Augustine resident and folk artist. The majority of his works are oil paintings on Masonite. Most depict

...es dotted with ships and houses, images ingrained from his ...ng in Edgecomb, Maine, and his travels up and down the East ...s use of vivid colors is unique and his ability to flatten three-...nal shape is reminiscent of Cubism.

TOURING TIPS Check out an Earl Cunningham painting before arriving to see if it suits your taste. Some works may be found online at **www.mennello museum.org**. Behind the museum is a large grassy area on the side of Lake Formosa, a good place for a picnic.

Morse Museum of American Art ★★★★

APPEAL BY AGE	PRESCHOOL ★	GRADE SCHOOL ★★	TEENS ★★★
YOUNG ADULTS ★★★½	OVER 30 ★★★★		SENIORS ★★★★

44 Park Avenue, Winter Park; ☎ 407-645-5311; www.morsemuseum.org

Hours Tuesday–Saturday, 9:30 a.m.–4 p.m.; Sunday, 1–4 p.m. Closed Mondays. **Cost** $3 for adults; $1 for students; and free for children under age 12. **Authors' rating** ★★★★.

DESCRIPTION AND COMMENTS After watching the introductory video, make your way through one of the world's most extensive and astounding collections of Louis Comfort Tiffany. The collection includes his jewelry, but the real gems—pun intended—are found in his glasswork. Vases, jars, lamps, and stained-glass windows are all testament to his skill as a craftsman.

Also included at the Morse Museum is the Tiffany Chapel. Built in 1893 for the World's Exposition in Chicago, the chapel was almost destroyed multiple times before arriving in Florida in the mid-20th century. The porticos and stained-glass are remarkable, but the chandelier, in the shape of a hypercube cross, will drop your jaw.

TOURING TIPS The one-story museum contains 19 small galleries. The layout is clean and every item is well marked. After walking through the galleries, stop by the gift shop. It does not contain any authentic Tiffany but does hawk some fine glasswork.

Orange County Regional History Center ★★★

APPEAL BY AGE	PRESCHOOL ★★	GRADE SCHOOL ★★★½	TEENS ★★
YOUNG ADULTS ★★★	OVER 30 ★★★½		SENIORS ★★★½

65 East Central Boulevard, Orlando; ☎ 407-836-8500 or 800-965-2030; www.thehistorycenter.org

Hours Monday–Saturday, 10 a.m.–5 p.m., Sunday, noon–5 p.m. **Cost** $7 for adults; $6.50 for seniors and students; $3.50 for children ages 3–12; and free for children ages 2 and under. **Author's rating** ★★★.

DESCRIPTION AND COMMENTS With an apropos location in the heart of downtown Orlando, the history center documents the growth of the Orlando area. Besides the myriad of facts and artifacts, the museum's layout and theming rival those found in other major metro areas. Instead of placing each artifact in a glass case with a small explanatory plaque, the museum has integrated many of them into re-creations, or placed them in unorthodox positions, such as hanging from the ceiling.

Visitors start their chronological tour on the fourth floor with the Timucuan Native American exhibit and the pioneer exhibit. The Timucuan were the original inhabitants of the area, and the museum goes a long way to bring them back to life by displaying original canoes, wax sculptures of the people, and the remains of a massive shell pile. Skipping across the hall transports you a few hundred years into the future to a room dedicated to the first homesteaders. Re-creations of their lives and documents of their hardships fill this room. A replica of a cabin, complete with period tools, is the centerpiece of the exhibit.

Descending to the third floor, visitors will find a restored 1927 criminal court, which is worth a peek if meetings are not being held. Across from this is the exhibit on aviation, where a replica of a B-17 bomber and other flight memorabilia are housed.

The second floor is home to modern regional history, ranging from the civil rights movement to the influence of Disney on the community. The positive economic impact of Disney is balanced against the displays highlighting the rise in crime and expansion of urban sprawl.

TOURING TIPS Although the theming is top-notch, the history lessons of Orange County are not very compelling. Florida residents and locals will find this museum much more entertaining than guests from other states.

For a chronological tour, begin on the top floor and work your way down. Street parking is difficult to find, although there are plenty of parking garages in the neighborhood. If you do find street parking, the two-hour time restraint should allow you enough time to peruse the museum and make it back to your car before you receive a ticket.

Orlando Museum of Art ★★

APPEAL BY AGE	PRESCHOOL ★★½	GRADE SCHOOL ★½	TEENS ★
YOUNG ADULTS ★★½	OVER 30 ★★★		SENIORS ★★

2416 North Mills Avenue, Orlando; ☎ 407-896-4231; www.omart.org

Hours Tuesday–Friday, 10 a.m.–4 p.m.; Saturday and Sunday, noon–4 p.m. Closed Mondays. Cost $8 for adults; $7 for seniors; $5 for students ages 6–18; and free for children ages 5 and under. Authors' rating ★★.

DESCRIPTION AND COMMENTS We expected more from the permanent collection of the largest art museum in the area with the most expensive admission. Two exhibits, one on African art and the other on art of the ancient Americas, along with a few paintings—including a few works by Andy Warhol—are the primary extent of the permanent collection. The museum's small permanent collection is understandable when taking into account its dedication to traveling exhibits, such as the 2006 look at the history of the motorcycle. The museum's size and donor-based fund-raising allow it to display these traveling works, and many of these exhibits are first-rate. Yet, if you are not interested in the main traveling exhibit, the admission price is too high to make the rest of the museum worthwhile.

TOURING TIPS Call ahead to see what exhibit the museum is hosting. Free parking is available in front of the impressive building, and the museum is located within walking distance of both the Mennello Museum and the Orlando Science Center.

kids Orlando Science Center ★★★★½

APPEAL BY AGE	PRESCHOOL ★★★	GRADE SCHOOL ★★★★½	TEENS ★★★½
YOUNG ADULTS ★★★		OVER 30 ★★★½	SENIORS ★★★½

777 East Princeton Street, Orlando; ☎ 407-514-2000 or 888-OSC-4FUN; www.osc.org

Hours Sunday–Tuesday, 10 a.m.–6 p.m.; Wednesday and Thursday, 10 a.m.– 9 p.m.; Friday and Saturday, 10 a.m.–11 p.m. Authors' rating ★★★★½.

DESCRIPTION AND COMMENTS When the thrill rides and shows have pounded your frontal lobe into slack-jawed submission, you may be ready for something more educational. In this case, a trip to the Science Center is a good idea, and not as boring as it might seem. Like Wonderworks, the Science Center contains a menagerie of scientific exhibits geared toward kids, a mixture of playtime and learning. Unlike Wonderworks, the Science Center provides more than a series of factoids that give a gist of the mechanics on hand. Almost every exhibit at the center contains an in-depth analysis of the history and physics behind the items on display. Most of the attractions found at Wonderworks are found at the Orlando Science Center, but with exponentially more attractions, a much larger complex, state funding, an IMAX theater, shorter lines, and cheaper tickets, the Orlando Science Center is the superior choice.

GETTING THERE From Walt Disney World, take I-4 north until you reach Exit 85. As soon as you get off the ramp, turn east and the Science Center will be on your left and parking will be on your right.

ADMISSION Tickets include all Cinedrome (IMAX) presentations, but not all visiting exhibits.

- *Adults* $14.95 + tax
- *Seniors (ages 55+)* $13.95 + tax
- *Students (with ID)* $13.95 + tax
- *Children ages 3–11* $9.95 + tax
- *Children ages 2 and under* Free

ARRIVING The center is open daily from 10 a.m. until 6 p.m., and on Friday and Saturday until 9 p.m. It is closed on Easter, Thanksgiving, Christmas Eve, and Christmas Day.

Parking is located across the street for $3.50 a vehicle. You can also park for free down the block at the Orlando Museum of Art and then walk back. Yet, the parking structure across the street from the center is convenient and contains a footbridge over to the ticket window on the second story of the Science Center.

The building is laid out, like the Guggenheim in New York, around an open and circular center, with a glass elevator in the middle. There are four floors in the Science Center, and since it is rarely crowded, you may see them in any order, although starting on the second floor and working up, saving the first floor for last, is our preferred method. Maps are available at the front desk/ticket window.

CONTACTING THE ORLANDO SCIENCE CENTER You may reach the OSC on the Web at **www.osc.org**, by phone at ☎ 407-514-2000 or toll-free at ☎ 800-OSC-4FUN or by e-mail at info@osc.org.

FIRST FLOOR The first floor, located below the main entrance, contains the cafeteria, the **Nature Hole, Gator Hole, Kid's Zone,** and **Cinedrome**— better known as the IMAX theater. The **Nature Hole** is a room at the base of the stairs with bins of shells and also a few live animals, such as the stripe-kneed tarantula. More animals can be found at the **Gator Hole** that surrounds all but the entrance to the Nature Hole. The Gator Hole is home to baby alligators, sea turtles, and fish. Check the daily schedule for feeding times.

Next to these natural exhibits is the **Kid's Zone,** which takes up most of the first floor. You must be less than 48 inches tall to enter, or accompanying your child. Some high points of the Kid's Zone are the tree house, the orange-picking simulator (we couldn't make that up), and the construction area, where kids can build with blocks.

The real draw on the first floor is not the Kid's Zone, but the **Cinedrome.** The eight-story screen acts as both an IMAX theater and a planetarium. Tickets are included in your entrance fee; however, you will need to stop by the main ticket counter on the second floor before each show—we recommend 45 minutes before—to claim a seat. The quality of the movies varies, but the towering screen makes even the dullest documentary tolerable, and the interesting shows spellbinding. Remember, with any theater attractions, adults with babies and children given to crying should sit in the back of the theater near the aisle. Bawling infants ruin more productions than cell phones ever could, and they don't, no matter how much you shush them, contain an off switch.

SECOND FLOOR The rooms on the second floor include an exhibit on modern inventions, a room dedicated to flight, and an auditorium. The exhibit on modern inventions, entitled **Invention at Play,** contains an assortment of—what else?—modern inventions ranging from the Kevlar vest to the telephone to the Windsurfer. Each display contains a history and fact plaque that will keep most high school physics students on their toes. The depth and quality of information is where the Science Center shines. The displays are also interactive, to use the prior examples: the Kevlar vest contains pieces of fabric to touch, the telephone exhibit displays sound waves on a monitor, and the windsurfing exhibit has a wooden replica of a Windsurfer for you to try to balance on.

Next door, the flight room also has a series of simulators, including one so large it projects the image on the wall. The room has a wind tunnel where kids can don wings and see how lift affects their bodies—not nearly enough breeze to get them airborne. Other highpoints include a kiosk on air-speed indicators, a full-sized replica flying boat, and a paper airplane course where kids can test-fly designs for distance and accuracy.

The auditorium on this floor hosts many science-based shows, with full-time actors. Check your daily schedule for show times.

THIRD FLOOR The **Family Resource Center** and **Cosmic Town** are enticements on the third floor. The **Family Resource Center** is a small room that contains leather couches, magazines, and an HDTV, making it a great hangout for a tired parent. Next door, energetic kids can study kinetics at **Cosmic Town,** a large exhibit devoted to the universe and Earth's natural wonders. Exhibits on the universe include a 360-degree view of Mars, a scale to measure your weight on different planets, info on the Hubble Space Telescope, and such. Perhaps the most interesting Earth exhibits are a small platform where you build a structure out of blocks and then knock it down with a 5.5-level earthquake, and a vortex machine where you can make your own tornado.

FOURTH FLOOR Three major exhibits are located on the top story: **Tech Works, Dinosaurs,** and **The Body Zone. Tech Works** focuses on optics and electricity. You can make a microscope, run water under a strobe light to create the illusion that the drops are standing still, refract lasers around a course using prisms, and measure your body temperature with infrared cameras. For some reason, this area also contains an exhibit on mask making and special effects, but we suppose that is technical as well.

Around the corner, visitors move from modern technology to antediluvian nature. At the **Dinosaurs** exhibit, there are 18 full-sized casts of the skeletons of these ancient beasts, including those of triceratops and T. rex. Actual fossils and other artifacts are housed in glass cases in the center of the room.

In the next room is **The Body Zone.** This exhibit panders to our narcissism, fixating on the human body. Yet, after passing through here, you might not feel so good about yourself. Stair climbers, cut-away models of muscles, and interactive displays on healthy eating can create a mild sense of self-loathing, but not to worry, there is plenty of Astronaut ice cream at the gift shop.

DINING The cafeteria, located on the first floor, has better deals than many Orlando restaurants, not to mention theme parks. A hamburger with fries is $4.50, a slice of cheese pizza is $1.75, and a large soda is $2. The cafeteria also has a great selection of healthy alternatives such as lean sandwiches, milk, juice, yogurt, and salads. Use the food pyramid on the wall and your experience in The Body Zone to make your selections.

SHOPPING The gift shop is also cheaper than many Florida attractions. Most of the items are educational toys. Puzzles, space-shuttle models, books (one conspicuously titled "How to Go to the Bathroom in Space"), dayglow stars to decorate your ceiling, and construction helmets with lanterns are all on sale here. The gift shop is located on the second floor across from the front desk.

Winter Park Boat Tours   ★★★

APPEAL BY AGE   PRESCHOOL ★★   GRADE SCHOOL ★★½   TEENS ★½
YOUNG ADULTS ★★★   OVER 30 ★★★½   SENIORS ★★★★

**312 East Morse Boulevard, Winter Park; ☎ 407-644-4056;
www.scenicboattours.com**

Hours Daily, 10 a.m.–4 p.m. Closed Christmas; tours depart on the hour. **Cost** $10 for adults; $5 for children ages 3–11; and free for children ages 2 and under; no credit cards accepted. **Duration of tour** 1 hour. **Authors' rating ★★★**.

DESCRIPTION AND COMMENTS Winter Park Boat Tours is located on Lake Osceola in Maitland, north of Orlando, a few miles away from the Orlando Science Center and the Orlando Museum of Art, and near the Rollins College campus. The one-hour tours begin on Lake Osceola.

The fully narrated tours take place on 16-passenger pontoon boats and review the history of Maitland County. After passing the summer house of oil tycoon Harry Sinclair, you squeeze through a thin canal into 223-acre Lake Virginia. Modern mansions adorn the east side of the lake, while Rollins College, and the home of the late Mr. Rogers of children's television fame, are to the west. Passing back through the canal and to the other side of Lake Osceola, you head through a longer and thinner canal into Lake Maitland. Here you will see more mansions, including one previously owned by basketball star Horace Grant. The tour is similar to being in the backyard of the very affluent.

TOURING TIPS The boat is a fine way to break up your day while touring museums, and the narration is very informative, although the tour guides are hesitant about revealing the names of the present owners of any of the houses. The boats have no bathrooms and are open to the sun, so be sure to use the facilities dockside and bring sunscreen and, if you own them, polarized sunglasses.

Zora Neale Hurston National Museum of Art   ½
227 East Kennedy Boulevard, Eatonville; ☎ 407-647-3307

Hours Monday–Friday, 9 a.m.–4 p.m. **Cost** Free. **Authors' rating ½**.

DESCRIPTION AND COMMENTS We were very disappointed with this one-room museum, although the price is right. Funded by a foundation in her name, the Zora Neale Hurston Museum exhibits focus on African culture and change frequently, but the one-room space is too small to house much of interest.

TOURING TIPS Unfortunately—doubly so for literary buffs—there is nothing here about the life and times of author Zora Neale Hurston. We are fans of Hurston's writings, but this museum does not do justice to her love of the creative arts. A self-guided walking tour of Eatonville is more substantial. You can find walking-tour brochures at the museum or at many of the businesses in town.

PART FIFTEEN

AFTER DARK

DINNER SHOWS

CENTRAL FLORIDA PROBABLY HAS MORE dinner attractions than anywhere else on earth. The name "dinner attraction" is something of a misnomer, because dinner is rarely the attraction. These are audience-participation shows or events with food served along the way. They range from extravagant productions where guests sit in arenas at long tables to intimate settings at individual tables. Don't expect terrific food, but if you're looking for something entertaining outside of Walt Disney World, consider one of these.

If you decide to try a non-Disney dinner show, scavenge local tourist magazines from brochure racks and hotel desks outside Disney World. These free publications usually have discount coupons for area shows.

THE SHOWS
Arabian Nights

APPEAL BY AGE	PRESCHOOL ★★★½	GRADE SCHOOL ★★★★½	TEENS ★★½
YOUNG ADULTS ★★★½	OVER 30 ★★★		SENIORS ★★★½

6225 US 192 (West Irlo Bronson Highway), Kissimmee; ☎ 407-239-9223

Show times Sunday–Tuesday, Thursday, 6 p.m.; Wednesday, Friday, and Saturday, 8:30 p.m.; only 1 show nightly. **Reservations** Can usually be made through the day of the show. **Cost** $56.60; $31.03 for children ages 3–11. **Discounts** Coupons in local magazines, AAA, seniors, military. **Type of seating** Long rows of benches at tables flanking each side of a large riding arena. All seats face the action. **Menu** Salad, prime rib or chicken breast, mixed vegetables, garlic mashed potatoes, and sheet cake. Children's alternative is chicken fingers with mashed potatoes. **Vegetarian alternative** Lasagna. **Beverages** Unlimited Busch beer, blush wine, tea, coffee, and cola.

DESCRIPTION AND COMMENTS Horses and riders present equestrian skills and trick riding with costumes, music, and theatrical lighting. The loose story line involves a princess who spots a handsome prince, who then disappears. A pair of genies, named Shararazad and Abra-Kadabra, grant her three wishes that, understandably, she uses to try to find the stud on the steed. For the sake of a plot, she doesn't just tell the genie to produce the guy front and center, so instead, they travel the world over—and back in time—to look for him. The search takes them anywhere they might find horses: the circus, the Wild West, the set of *Ben Hur,* and so on. In all, horses perform to musical accompaniment.

If you are an unbridled horse fan, or a little girl (we know of very few who don't like horses and magic-laden princess stories), you're going to think you've died and gone to heaven. Fifty horses, including Lipizzans, palominos, quarter horses, and Arabians, perform 22 acts. The stunts are impressive, and a great deal of skill and timing is employed to pull them off. All of the horse tricks found during an entire performance at Medieval Times, excluding jousting, are performed in just the opening of Arabian Nights. Yet after a while, the tricks start to look the same, and only the costumes and the music are different. However, the short run time of a little over an hour and a half keeps the tedium from setting in. The ending of the show has been changed from a pandering patriotic ploy to a beautiful snowy scene where the horses gambol about the arena. It's truly a lovely sight.

The prime rib is edible, and the lasagna alternative is fine. The salad is unappealing, as is the dessert. In a departure from other dinner theaters, the food here is served in the dark, making each bite a bit of a surprise.

If you decide to purchase any gifts after the show, be wary of the prices. Some of the children's outfits cost around $100.

Capone's Dinner & Show

APPEAL BY AGE	PRESCHOOL ★½	GRADE SCHOOL ★★★★	TEENS ★★★½
YOUNG ADULTS ★★★		OVER 30 ★★★	SENIORS ★★★½

4740 West US 192, Kissimmee; ☎ 407-397-2378

Show times 8 p.m. nightly; changes seasonally. **Reservations** Need to make reservations several days in advance. **Cost** $45.99 + tax; $27.99 + tax for children ages 4–12 (does not include tax or tip). **Discounts** Florida residents, AAA, seniors, military, hospitality workers. **Type of seating** Long tables with large groupings facing an elevated stage; some smaller tables for parties of 2 to 6, balcony seating available. **Menu** Buffet with lasagna, baked ziti, spaghetti, baked chicken, baked ham, boiled potatoes, tossed salad, and brownies. **Vegetarian alternative** Spaghetti, ziti, pasta salad. **Beverages** Unlimited beer, wine, soft drinks, coffee, and tea.

DESCRIPTION AND COMMENTS The audience, attending a celebration for mobster Al Capone at a 1930s speakeasy in Chicago, enters through a secret door using a password. The show is a musical of sorts, with most songs from other sources sung by cast members to recorded accompaniment. The story revolves around two female leads. There is Miss Jewel—the speakeasy's hostess, who is enamored of Detective Marvel, the only cop in Chicago that Capone can't buy—and one of the show's floozies and her gambling boyfriend. (Can you say *Guys and Dolls*)?

The audience parades through the buffet line before the show; seconds are invited. The food, which had been passable in the past, should now just be passed up. During a recent visit, the plastic flowers above the buffet were in dire need of dusting.

For a musical, this show employs a lot of nonsingers. Even the dancing is second-rate. The waiters—who speak with tough-guy accents and kid around with guests—did more to entertain the children than at any other show. Still, the theme is a bit too adult for families.

Two lines form before the show. You must go to the line on the left, directly into the box office to pick up or purchase your tickets before joining the long line of guests leaning against the building. If you don't want to loiter outside, you can buy one drink per person and sit in the "office," which is a lounge upstairs.

Chamber of Magic at Skull Kingdom

APPEAL BY AGE	PRESCHOOL ★★★	GRADE SCHOOL ★★½	TEENS ★
YOUNG ADULTS ★½	OVER 30 ★½		SENIORS ★★

5933 American Way, Orlando; ☎ 407-354-1564

Show times Nightly, 6 p.m. and 8 p.m. **Reservations** Can be made the day of the show. **Cost** $19.75 for adults; $15.97 for seniors and children ages 6 and under; with Skull Kingdom admission, $28.25 for adults; $24.45 for seniors and children ages 6 and under (does not include tax or tip). **Discounts** None. **Type of seating** Communal tables. **Menu** Popcorn, unlimited cheese or pepperoni pizza **Vegetarian alternative** Cheese pizza. **Beverages** Unlimited beer, wine, and soft drinks.

DESCRIPTION AND COMMENTS The scariest thing at Skull Kingdom is the quality of this show. The small room in the back of Skull Kingdom is not set up for magic tricks. The audience is too close to the stage for illusions, and guests seated at tables too far to either side can see the secrets of the sleight-of-hand tricks.

The Chamber of Magic hosts a rotation of magicians, each with different styles and ability to involve the audience. No matter who performs, the magic is all standard sleight-of-hand tricks (ropes, cards, missing foam balls) and unlike The Outta Control Magic Show at Wonderworks, where these tricks are interspersed with wry humor and sound effects, The Chamber of Magic reminds us of a performance at a geriatric home. Very few of the magicians can overcome the small room, smaller stage, and poor lighting. The Chamber of Magic would do well to either pay more money for illusionists and expand the room to accommodate them, or hire on one or two permanent magicians who could integrate the great theming of Skull Kingdom into their sets, making a different sort of horrific magic show than is there now.

Dolly Parton's Dixie Stampede

| APPEAL BY AGE | PRESCHOOL ★★★½ | GRADE SCHOOL ★★★½ | TEENS ★★★ |
| YOUNG ADULTS ★★★½ | | OVER 30 ★★★★ | SENIORS ★★★★ |

8251 Vineland Avenue, Orlando; ☎ 866-443-4943

Show times Sunday–Friday, 6:30 and 8:30 p.m.; Saturdays, seasonal. **Reservations** Can generally be made up to the day of the show. **Cost** $48.99 + tax; $21.99 + tax for children ages 4–11. **Discounts** AAA, military, and seasonal. **Type of seating** Long rows of chairs at tables surrounding a large riding arena. All seats face the show. **Menu** Rotisserie chicken, pork loin, creamy vegetable soup, corn on the cob, half a baked potato, biscuit, and apple-filled pastry. **Vegetarian alternative** Side platter of vegetables (the soup is not vegetarian). **Beverages** Unlimited soft drinks, 2 alcoholic beverages per guest (beer or wine).

DESCRIPTION AND COMMENTS Fifty minutes before the show begins, there's an opening act that changes nightly. Possible acts include a husband-and-wife juggling team, a kooky cowboy, and beautiful horses. The preshow, however, can be painfully corny; if you do arrive early, stroll through the outdoor stables to see the horses before the show.

The Stampede is set in the Civil War–era Deep South, where Union and Confederate soldiers compete against each other in a series of riding competitions. The competitions are intermingled with song and dance numbers that, thanks to Dolly Parton, are better than the other dinner theater's musical numbers—remnants of the songs are still stuck in our heads. There are also periods of audience participation, including the finale where the north section and the south section pass balls down the rows in a race to determine the victor of the evening's events.

The animals are striking and the handlers are quite entertaining. The acting is about average and the set is cute but versatile; the gazebo that lowers for one of the song-and-dance numbers is the highlight of the stadium effects.

The food is very ordinary, though the portions are generous and nothing is bad (unless you are vegetarian); the specialty fruit drink is exceedingly sweet, and we do not recommend it. However, the boot-shaped novelty glasses are a kitschy and fun souvenir.

Makahiki Luau

| APPEAL BY AGE | PRESCHOOL ★★½ | GRADE SCHOOL ★★½ | TEENS ★★ |
| YOUNG ADULTS ★★★ | | OVER 30 ★★★ | SENIORS ★★★½ |

SeaWorld, 7007 SeaWorld Drive, Orlando; ☎ 800-327-2420

Show times Nightly, 6:30 p.m. **Reservations** Need to make reservations at least 3 days in advance; reservations can be made online; payment is due at time of booking. **Cost** $45.95; $29.95 for children ages 3–9; free for children under age 3 with a reservation. **Discounts** seasonally. **Type of seating** Long tables; no separation from other parties. **Menu** Fruit "pu pu" platter, salad, mahi mahi in piña colada sauce, Hawaiian chicken, sweet-and-sour pork, fried rice, vegetables, and a seasonal dessert. **Vegetarian alternative** Mixed vegetables, sticky rice.

Beverages 1 complimentary mai tai; full cash bar. This is the only show to offer just one cocktail, an odd thing, considering the park is owned by Anheuser-Busch, which makes practically all the beer in the world.

DESCRIPTION AND COMMENTS The Makahiki Luau has the appearance of a touring lounge act that might play the Ramada Inn circuit in the Midwest. Even the venue, a large, dark room with a very low ceiling, looks like a motel lounge. In this musical revue featuring singers, dancers, and fire twirlers, a Don Ho–esque singer is given way too much time. The dancers perform well, and the fire twirler who ends the show is impressive, but there is otherwise little excitement.

The food is more varied than at many shows. The mahi mahi is good, but the fruit platter is fairly uninteresting. The food is served family-style, and you may share a platter with another family.

The service is not very attentive. Audience participation is minimal, and children probably will be bored.

kids Medieval Times Dinner and Tournament

APPEAL BY AGE	PRESCHOOL ★ ★ ★ ½	GRADE SCHOOL ★ ★ ★ ½	TEENS ★ ★ ★
YOUNG ADULTS ★ ★ ½	OVER 30 ★ ★ ½		SENIORS ★ ★

4510 East US 192, Kissimmee; ☎ 800-229-8300

Show times Vary according to season and nights. **Reservations** Best to make reservations a week ahead. **Cost** $49.95 + tax; $33.95 + tax for children ages 3–12 (does not include tax or tip). **Discounts** Seniors, military, AAA, hotel employees, travel agents. You get free admission on your birthday with 2 full-paying adults; valid ID required for proof. **Type of seating** Arena style, in rows that face the riding floor. **Menu** Garlic bread, vegetable soup, whole roasted chicken, spare ribs, herb-basted potatoes, and strudel. Everything is eaten by hand. **Vegetarian alternative** Lasagna, or raw veggies with dip plate. **Beverages** 2 rounds of beer, sangria, or soft drinks; cash bar available.

DESCRIPTION AND COMMENTS A tournament set 900 years in the past pits six knights against one another. Audience members are seated in areas corresponding to the color of the knights' pennants and are encouraged to cheer for their knight and boo his opponents. Part of the tournament is actual competition. The knights perform stunts, including hitting a target with a lance or collecting rings on a lance while riding on horseback. After each event, successful knights receive carnations from the queen to toss to young ladies in their sections.

After a while, the tournament takes on a choreographed feel—and with good reason. It comes down to a fight to the finish until only one knight is left standing. There are cheating knights who pull others off their horses and hand-to-hand combat with maces, battle-axes, and swords. The winning knight selects a fair maiden from the audience to be his princess.

In all, the show is mediocre, but the knights give 100% (the bruises they must get!). The sword fights are so realistic that sparks fly off the metal blades, but the kicking and punching choreography is worse than that found in professional wrestling. Even so, audience participation reaches a fevered pitch, with each section cheering for its knight and calling for the death of the dastardly opponents. It's amazing how bloodthirsty people can be after they've ripped a chicken apart with their bare hands.

With all the horses, jousting, and fighting, children shouldn't be bored (although it does get repetitive), and parents of very young children might be concerned about the violence.

The food is remarkable only in that you eat it with your hands, including a whole chicken you must pull apart. The chicken is good, the ribs a little tough.

Outta Control Magic Show at Wonderworks

APPEAL BY AGE	PRESCHOOL ★★★½	GRADE SCHOOL ★★★★	TEENS ★★
YOUNG ADULTS ★★★½		OVER 30 ★★★½	SENIORS ★★★

9067 International Drive, Orlando; ☎ 407-351-8800

Show times Nightly, 6 p.m. and 8 p.m. Reservations Can be made up to the day of the show. Cost $21.95; $14.90 for children ages 4–12 (does not include tax or tip). Discounts Florida residents, AAA, AARP, military. Type of seating Communal tables. Menu Popcorn, unlimited cheese or pepperoni pizza. Vegetarian alternative Cheese pizza. Beverages Unlimited beer, wine, and soft drinks.

DESCRIPTION AND COMMENTS　For younger children, this is the funniest dinner show in Orlando. Two magicians and one assistant perform sleight-of-hand magic tricks, all the while keeping up a constant barrage of puns and sophomoric humor. A sound effects board with a series of push buttons allows the magicians to add a version of morning radio show humor to their repertoire of jokes, all the while keeping the audience guessing, "What's in the box?!"

Although legerdemain, and a few illusions, will awe young children, adults will find the tricks rather ordinary and will be unimpressed with the magicians' ability to make a sponge ball disappear. However, the magicians' repartee with the audience keeps the show alive and entertaining. Both magicians are gifted at improvising and toying with audience members. Almost every group of people that attends will have a member hauled up onto the stage. If you're brought up, the safest thing to do is just play along. You may get teased and hassled by the magicians, but only a fraction as much as you will be for refusing to come on stage. Besides, it's not good manners to laugh at everyone else without taking a turn.

The show is enjoyable and the food service is good, although the pizza is terrible and you may have to share the popcorn bowls with other people's children. Make sure yours wash theirs before the show.

Pirate's Dinner Adventure

APPEAL BY AGE	PRESCHOOL ★★★½	GRADE SCHOOL ★★★½	TEENS ★★
YOUNG ADULTS ★★½	OVER 30 ★★½		SENIORS ★★★

6400 Carrier Drive, Orlando; ☎ 407-248-0590

Show times Nightly, seasonal, 7:45 p.m. **Reservations** Can be made up to the day of the show. **Cost** $51.95 + tax; $31.95 + tax for children ages 3–11 (does not include tax or tip). **Discounts** Florida residents, AAA, AARP, military, travel agents, Dollar rental car employees, police, firefighters, Girl Scouts. **Type of seating** Arena style. **Menu** Salad, beef and roasted chicken, fresh vegetables, ice cream, and apple cobbler; children's alternative is chicken fingers. **Vegetarian alternative** Lasagna. **Beverages** Unlimited beer, wine, and soft drinks.

DESCRIPTION AND COMMENTS Audience members are told to arrive long before the doors are open to the auditorium. In the meantime, guests mill about and look over maritime memorabilia and nosh on assorted appetizers. The pirate museum, at the far end of the hall, is worth a visit and contains lengthy tales of pirates and their dastardly deeds. As show time approaches, a "host pirate" leads the audience members in song and dance, and a man demonstrates his fire-eating skills. Audience members will later recall that this man had the best meal of the evening. After a bit more preshow, guests are ushered into the dining area, which features a life-sized pirate ship surrounded by water.

The set is impressive, and throughout the evening pirates swoop from overhead, race around the ship in boats powered by electric motors, toss balls into nets with the help of audience volunteers, and bounce on a trampoline that's part of the ship. What's mystifying is that there doesn't seem to be a reason for any of this. The sound system is poor, and it was difficult to tell what is going on and why. Audience members sit in color-coded sections and are encouraged to cheer for pirates wearing their colors as they compete against each other. There's plenty to interest kids. Adults might be interested too, if the story were easier to follow.

Sleuths Mystery Dinner Shows

APPEAL BY AGE	PRESCHOOL ★½	GRADE SCHOOL ★★★	TEENS ★★★½
YOUNG ADULTS ★★★★	OVER 30 ★★★★		SENIORS ★★★★

8267 International Drive, Orlando; ☎ 407-363-1985

Show times Vary nightly; 6 p.m., 7:30 p.m., or 9 p.m. **Reservations** Can be made up to the day of the show. **Cost** $47.95 + tax; $23.95 for children ages 3–11 (does not include tax or tip). **Discounts** Florida residents, AAA, seniors, students, Disney employees, travel agents, military, hospitality employees. **Type of seating** Large round tables that seat 8–10; some smaller tables. **Menu** fruit platter and smoked salmon; assorted hot and cold hors d'oeuvres; tossed salad; choice of

Cornish hen, prime rib (at an extra $3 charge), or lasagna; veggies and a baked potato; mystery dessert. **Vegetarian alternative** Cheese lasagna. **Beverages** Unlimited beer, wine, or soft drinks.

DESCRIPTION AND COMMENTS Sleuths enact a repertory of murder mysteries that the audience must solve. Audience participation is key to the enjoyment. Guests are part of the show from the moment they enter the theater. Actors in character direct seating and try to drop clues as to who and what their parts are in the play. Although they work from a script, much of the show is ad-libbed. Fortunately, the cast tends to be very talented and capable of ad-libbing well. After the audience is seated, the first act occurs, and someone is murdered. During intermission, each table must choose a spokesman and prepare a question for the second act, where the collective audience interrogates the actors in an attempt (foolhardy as it seems due to the actor's elusive responses) to solve the murder. Know that unless you come with a group of eight people, you will probably find yourself interacting with the strangers at your table.

You'll probably have more fun if you go with a large group and occupy your own table. Older children might find the show interesting, but younger ones will be bored and may disturb the other guests who are trying to follow the show.

The food has improved drastically from the old cheese spread and crackers. Guests who arrive early will be able to nibble on a platter of fresh fruit and smoked salmon. The prime rib was tough during our visit, but the Cornish hen was excellent.

FAMILY-FRIENDLY COMEDY SHOWS

MANY OF THE COMEDY CLUBS IN ORLANDO, like Bonkerz at City-Walk, feature performers whose language and subject matter are not acceptable for families, or even most adults. The following comedy shows attempt to run on a PG-13 level, with no cursing and only moderately racy subject matter.

THE SHOWS
Dottie's Comedy Club

APPEAL BY AGE	PRESCHOOL †	GRADE SCHOOL †	TEENS ★★★½
YOUNG ADULTS ★★★½		OVER 30 ★★★½	SENIORS ★★★

† This show is not recommended for younger children.

7052 International Drive, Orlando; ☎ 407-226-3680; www.dottiesorlando.com

Show times *All-Star Comedy & Variety Show* at 7:30 p.m. daily; *I Love Your, Now Please Shut Up!* at 9 p.m. daily. **Cost** $15 per person; 2 free drinks included and attendees should be at least 12 years old for the *All-Star* show and 18 years or older for the 9 p.m. show.

DESCRIPTION AND COMMENTS Dottie's Comedy Club is located on I-Drive, directly across the street from the Magical Midway. Dottie's offers 2 shows daily, the *All-Star Comedy & Variety Show* at 7:30 p.m. and *I Love You, Now Please Shut Up!* featuring Tommy Blaze at 9 p.m. The *All-Star* comedy show lasts 90 minutes, and features three comedians nightly who perform 25-minute sets. Although the cast does rotate, the regulars are Tom Drake, Tommy Blaze, John Ferrentino, and Rich Natoley. All of the comedians, and Dottie herself, have had long careers aboard cruise ships, working on developing clean sets that can be funny without "going blue." Even so, the *All-Star Comedy & Variety Show* is for guests 12 years of age and older and costs $15 per person. (The 9 p.m. show featuring Tommy Blaze is 75 minutes and for mature audiences only, 18 years or older, and is also $15 per person.)

The *All-Star Comedy & Variety Show* usually opens with Tom Drake, Dottie's husband, whose 25-minute set features the standard light fare: airplane jokes, mild ethnic jokes, and observational humor about the Orlando area. His set has long lulls as he warms up the audience, but is spiked with a few humorous observations. Tommy Blaze pushes the boundaries of clean humor with his "observations about the sexes." His lists of truisms about relationships are not new, but many are very funny. Tommy does measure the receptiveness of his audience, so when there are no children present his humor may turn PG-13 and comes closer to the genre of guys' locker-room talk than some families may be comfortable with, but he is tempered when children are present (his 9 p.m. show is very bawdy). Another regular performer is John Ferrentino, whose jokes rely on magic tricks and prop comedy. An accomplished magician, John's set gets laughs by showing how easily magicians fool their audience. His stage presence is magnetic as he reveals some basic secrets of the magic industry. The last regular performer is Rich Natoley, an impressionist, known as the Man of 1,000 voices. His impressions include presidents, SpongeBob, Bill Cosby, and Johnny Cash, to name a few. His satirical set will make you chuckle, and most of his voices are disturbingly real. Remember, laughter begets laughter—that's why there are laugh tracks for sitcoms, so a crowded house almost always makes for a better show than a near empty one. Make reservations for crowded nights. Come expecting a few light laughs and you will be pleasantly surprised.

The comedy club is brand new and features a lounge atmosphere, with small candle-lit tables that seat four guests with a total capacity of 180 guests. Concessions are available outside (popcorn, candy, and the like), and each guest is allowed two free drinks of soda, beer, or wine.

SAK Improv Comedy

| APPEAL BY AGE | PRESCHOOL ★★½ | GRADE SCHOOL ★★★½ | TEENS ★★★★½ |
| YOUNG ADULTS ★★★★ | | OVER 30 ★★★★ | SENIORS ★★★½ |

**398 West Amelia Street, Orlando (downtown, off Exit 83 from I-4);
☎ 407-648-0001; www.sak.com**

Show times Vary for different shows; *Duel of Fools,* Thursday–Saturday at 8 p.m. with periodic performances at 10 p.m. **Cost** $15 per person; $12 for seniors, students, and military.

DESCRIPTION AND COMMENTS   SAK is an improv comedy troupe whose graduates include daytime talk show host Wayne Brady, and writers for shows such as *SNL, Mad TV,* and *Everybody Loves Raymond.*

SAK offers a variety of shows, currently including an improv opera, but their baseline show is the long running *Duel of Fools.* The show features two teams competing in a series of improv sketches, very much like the television show *Whose Line Is It Anyway?* (that also featured Wayne Brady). Since shows besides the *Duel of Fools* change frequently, call or check the Web site for a list of other available shows.

The *Duel of Fools* is a clean show with no cursing, and the humor relies on absurd situations. The types of improv sketches vary throughout the evening from on-the-spot songs based on audience suggestion to raw pantomime. Each sketch is about five minutes, so any that are mundane are over quickly, while the funnier ones continue until the scenario becomes too absurd to comprehend. Since there is no script, the performance varies each show, but the quality of actors remain the same, and their ability to integrate any suggestions into a humorous scene is outstanding.

Parking for SAK is $5 in the parking garage that connects into SAK's rear entrance. A small concession stand offering popcorn, candy, and soda, is across from the ticket booth. The oddly shaped theater is located through a door next to the ticket booth. The theater is wide but only a few rows deep, so when the actors appear on stage, you are only a few feet from the madness.

UNIVERSAL ORLANDO CITYWALK

CITYWALK IS A SHOPPING, DINING, AND entertainment venue that doubles as the entrance plaza for the Universal Studios and Islands of Adventure theme parks. Situated between the parking complex and the theme parks, CityWalk is heavily trafficked all day but truly comes alive at night.

In the evening, CityWalk is Universal's answer to Walt Disney World's Pleasure Island. Like its rival, CityWalk offers a number of nightclubs to sample, but where Disney and Church Street tend to create their own clubs, many of CityWalk's entertainment and restaurant venues depend on well-known brand names. At CityWalk you'll find a Hard Rock Cafe and concert hall; Jimmy Buffett's Margaritaville; a Motown Cafe; NBA City, a sports bar; a NASCAR Sports Grille; a branch of New Orleans' famous Pat O'Brien's club; and a reggae club that celebrates the life and music of Bob Marley. The Red Coconut Club, a new lounge and nightclub, the groove, a high-tech disco, CityJazz, a jazz club that turns into Bonkerz Comedy Club Thursday through Saturday nights, and the Latin Quarter, a space dedicated to food, music, and culture of all 21 Latin nations, all operate without big-name tie-ins.

Another CityWalk distinction is that most of the clubs are also restaurants, or alternatively, most of the restaurants are also clubs. Although there's a lot of culinary variety, restaurants and nightclubs are different animals. Sight lines, room configuration, acoustics, intimacy, and atmosphere—important considerations in a nightclub—are not at all the same in a venue designed to serve meals. Although it's nice to have all that good food available, the club experience is somewhat dulled. Working through the lineup, Pat O'Brien's, the groove, and CityJazz/Bonkerz Comedy Club are more nightclub than restaurant, whereas Margaritaville is more restaurant than club. Bob Marley's and the Latin Quarter are about half and half. The Hard Rock Cafe, NASCAR Sports Grille, NBA City, Emeril's, and Pastamore are restaurants.

GETTING THERE

THE UNIVERSAL FLORIDA COMPLEX can be accessed via Kirkman Road from Interstate 4, Exit 75B. Driving from the Walt Disney World area, take I-4 Exit 74A onto Sand Lake Road heading north (away from International Drive) and turn right onto Turkey Lake Road. Follow the signs to the Turkey Lake Road entrance.

ADMISSION PRICES

CITYWALK'S PARTY PASS ALL-CLUB ACCESS IS $11.99, which gets you into all the clubs (you can also pay $15.40 and add a movie). The Party Pass is complimentary with the purchase of any multiday theme-park admission. Otherwise, you can pay individual cover charges at each club; these tend to run $4 to $8 apiece. Given this price range, getting the all-access pass makes the most sense unless you intend to visit just one club. Not into the club scene? The Meal and Movie Deal is $21.95 and includes—what else?—dinner at one of the CityWalk restaurants (you choose from a special menu) and a movie.

ARRIVING

ONCE WITHIN THE UNIVERSAL COMPLEX, you'll be directed to park in one of two multitiered parking garages. Parking runs $11 for cars and $12 for RVs. Be sure to write down the location of your car before

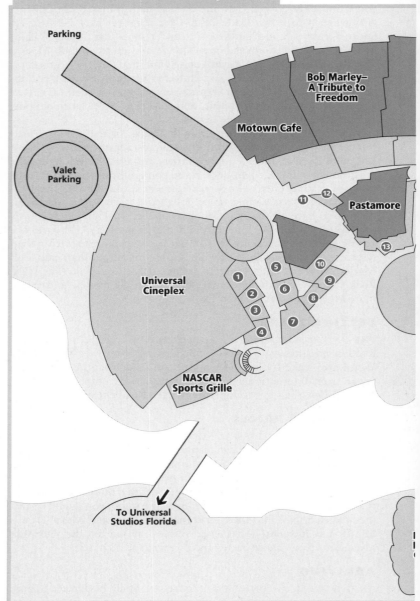

universal orlando—city walk

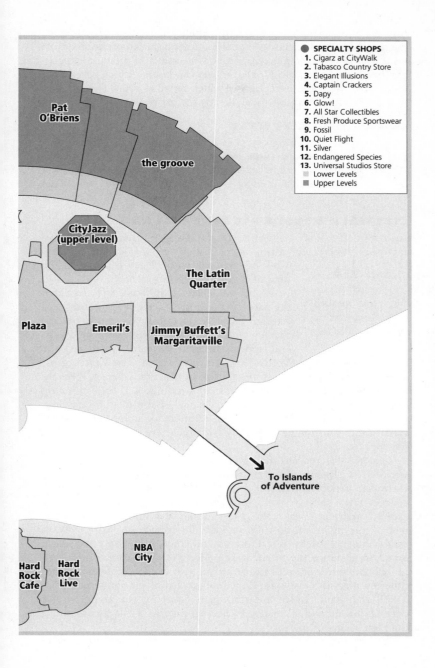

heading out of the garages—the evening will end on a considerably brighter note if you avoid wandering about the garages searching for the rental car. An alternative: if you're out for a special occasion or just want to have everything taken care of, Universal also offers valet parking (two hours) for about $7; $14 for over two hours. After 6 p.m., parking is free, with the exception of valet services. From the garages, moving sidewalks transport you directly to CityWalk.

CONTACTING CITYWALK

CONTACT CITYWALK GUEST SERVICES AT ☎ 407-224-2691, or visit their Web site at **www.citywalk.com.** Keep in mind, though, that City-Walk personnel may not be up on individual club doings, so your best bet may be to contact specific clubs directly when you reach the Orlando area.

CITYWALK VERSUS PLEASURE ISLAND

JUST AS UNIVERSAL'S ISLANDS OF ADVENTURE theme park allows for more direct competition with Disney's Magic Kingdom, City-Walk squares off with Pleasure Island in the field of nightlife entertainment.

unofficial **TIP**
If you're into club-hopping, or just not sure which place you want to spend your wild night out at, head to CityWalk.

As the underdog, CityWalk tries to catch the wave of the hottest fads in nightclubs and dining. Pleasure Island tends more toward themes and trends with long-established general appeal. Because Pleasure Island has the vast pool of Disney World guests to draw from, CityWalk aggressively tries to attract locals in addition to tourists. Overall, Pleasure Island caters to guests who might like to indulge in a little clubbing on their vacation but normally don't make a habit of pub-crawling. CityWalk presents a flashy buffet of premiere nightclubs and restaurants that you might normally find scattered around a large metropolis.

One key difference is that the larger CityWalk is not as physically enclosed as Pleasure Island because it serves as an open portal to the Universal parks. In addition, the CityWalk clubs don't have cover charges until about 9 p.m. So if you're not interested in jumping around, arrive early, pick the club you like best, and settle in for the rest of the night. More than at Pleasure Island, several CityWalk establishments are both restaurants and clubs, allowing you to have dinner and dance the night away under the same roof. Both complexes have outdoor areas featuring frequent live music, festivals, and other events; both also have large multiscreen movie show times.

All that said, which entertainment complex you might prefer depends on individual tastes. Hence we provide a chart comparing the high points of each.

In addition to the clubs and restaurants, there are (of course) shops and a Universal Cineplex multiscreen movie theater. In regard

HOW CITYWALK AND PLEASURE ISLAND COMPARE	
CITYWALK	**PLEASURE ISLAND**
Next to Universal's theme parks	Next to Downtown Disney
Parking decks free after 6 p.m.	Parking is hectic
About $10 (all clubs included)	About $21
Half-local/half-tourist; mostly ages 20–30	Mostly older teens or curious older adults
Nine restaurants	Four restaurants
Three dance clubs	Seven dance clubs
Five live music venues	Three live music venues
Upscale mall fare shopping	Disney memorabilia; hipster clothing

to the clubs, you can pay a cover in each one you visit or opt for a more expensive passport to all the clubs. Because the all-access pass is only $12—less than half the admission to Disney's Pleasure Island—we recommend going with that option rather than fooling with individual cover charges.

CITYWALK CLUBS

Bob Marley—A Tribute to Freedom

What it is Reggae restaurant and club. **Hours** Monday–Friday, 4 p.m.–2 a.m.; Saturday and Sunday, 2 p.m.–2 a.m. **Cuisine** Jamaican-influenced appetizers and main courses. **Entertainment** Reggae bands in the outdoor gazebo after 8 p.m. **Cover** $7 after 7 p.m. nightly (more for special acts).

COMMENTS This club is a re-creation of Marley's home in Kingston, Jamaica, and contains a lot of interesting Marley memorabilia. The courtyard is the center of action. Must be age 21 or over after 10 p.m.

CityJazz

What it is Jazz club and themed restaurant/comedy club. **Hours** Sunday–Thursday, 8 p.m.–1 a.m.; Friday and Saturday, 7 p.m.–2 a.m. **Cuisine** No food. **Entertainment** Live jazz. National stand-up comics appear onstage Thursday–Sunday nights. **Cover** $7; some ticketed events higher.

COMMENTS Jazz club that's also home to *Down Beat* magazine's Jazz Hall of Fame museum (open 3 to 6 p.m.).

the groove

What it is High-tech disco. **Hours** 9 p.m.–2 a.m. **Cuisine** No food. **Entertainment** DJ plays dance tunes. Sometimes there are live bands. **Cover** $5.

COMMENTS Guests must be age 21 or older to enter this très-chic club designed to look like an old theater in the midst of restoration. There are seven bars and several themed cubbyholes for getting away from the thundering sound system. Dancers are barraged with strobes, lasers, and heaven knows what else.

Hard Rock Live

What it is Live music concert hall and club. Hours 7 p.m. until closing. Cuisine Limited menu. Entertainment House band performs weekdays with big-name groups taking over on weekends. Cover $10 for house band. Cover varies for name acts.

COMMENTS Great acoustics, comfortable seating, and good sight lines make this the best concert venue in town. House band is excellent. By the by, the Hard Rock Live concert hall and the Hard Rock Cafe restaurant are separate facilities.

Jimmy Buffett's Margaritaville

What it is Key West–themed restaurant and club. Hours Daily, 11 a.m.–2 a.m. Cuisine Caribbean, Florida fusion, and American. Entertainment Live rock and island-style music after 10 p.m. Cover $7 after 10 p.m.

COMMENTS Jimmy's is a big place with three bars that turns into a nightclub after 10 p.m. If you eat dinner here, you'll probably want to find another vantage point when the band cranks up.

Latin Quarter

What it is Latin salsa-themed restaurant and live music hall. Hours Monday–Friday, 11:30 a.m.–10 p.m.; Saturday and Sunday, noon–2 a.m. Cuisine Latin American. Entertainment Live salsa band nightly. Cover $7 after 10 p.m.

COMMENTS Primarily a restaurant with entertainment on the side. Live salsa music (and often dancing) is performed in sets throughout the night.

Pat O'Brien's Orlando

What it is Dueling pianos sing-along club and restaurant. Hours 4 p.m.–2 a.m. Cuisine Cajun. Entertainment Dueling pianos and sing-alongs. Cover $7 after 6 p.m. for piano bar only.

COMMENTS A clone of the famous New Orleans club of the same name. You can dine in the courtyard or on the terrace without paying a cover. You must be age 21 or over to hang out here.

The Red Coconut Club

What it is Modern lounge and nightclub. Hours Monday–Wednesday, 7 p.m.–2 a.m; Thursday–Sunday, 6 p.m.–2 a.m. Cuisine Expensive appetizers. Entertainment Lounging and dancing. Cover $7 after 9 p.m.

COMMENTS This new nightspot is billed as a nightclub and "ultra-lounge," although what that means is anyone's guess. There is a lounge and a dance floor, and the bar features signature martinis. The first two hours after opening is happy hour and the signature drinks are half-priced.

METROPOLIS AND MATRIX

ALTHOUGH NOT A REAL THREAT TO EITHER Pleasure Island or CityWalk, and certainly not on the scale of Church Street Station, this new pair of conjoined nightclubs does offer an upscale double venue that's convenient to shopping and lodging and yet has no affiliation with the theme parks. The clubs are located on an upper level of the Pointe Orlando shopping complex at 9101 International Drive; parking is available in the adjacent deck. A single cover charge (usually about $10) gets you admission to both clubs, and you can walk back and forth freely. Metropolis is the more chic of the two, with fancy pool tables and several conversation pits bulging with overstuffed sofas and chairs. A small dance floor borders the expansive bar for those who wish to bust a move. Patrons are a little more laid-back than those at the neighboring club. Across the way, Matrix is a straight-ahead dance factory, with a much larger floor, fewer seats, and a generally flashier vibe (not to mention a high-tech lighting rig and pounding sound). Locals, club kids, and other nightlife denizens gravitate here first, then wander over to Metropolis to chill out and relax for a bit.

unofficial **TIP**
If you're looking for non-Disneyesque nightlife, head to Metropolis and/or Matrix.

Both clubs host rotating theme nights, with college night and Latin night being especially popular. Hours are typically Wednesday to Sunday, 9 p.m. until 2 a.m. (Matrix), and Thursday to Sunday, 9 p.m. until 2 a.m. (Metropolis), with occasional extra open nights seasonally. Call ☎ 407-370-3700 for more details, or check out **www.metropolis matrix.com.**

DOWNTOWN ORLANDO/ CHURCH STREET STATION AREA

VISITORS IN THEIR 20S AND EARLY 30S may find the experiences at both CityWalk and Pleasure Island a bit contrived. Indeed, any nighttime entertainment that attempts to bring in families and individuals between the ages of 18 and 80 will have a hard time indulging the "hip" demographic. When you attempt to offer a select amount of evening entertainment over large age and taste ranges, you compromise your selections of music, theming, and prices, usually settling for the most generic solutions possible. For people in their 20s, downtown Orlando makes no compromises in taste. This is a hip urban center, and although it is not New York or Miami, the nearby University of Central Florida provides plenty of other young people to party with over a whole swath of different bars and dance clubs.

Once you're there, remember that bars in the Orlando area close at 2 a.m. The bars below represent a cross section of what is available, but there are many more bars on and around Church Street for you to find and explore. You must be age 21 and over to enter any of the bars and have a valid photo ID, although some nightclubs, like Tabu, may let you in if you are between 18 and 21 years old, but you will not be allowed to drink. Call ahead for details.

GETTING THERE

TAKE INTERSTATE 4 TO EAST ANDERSON STREET, Exit 82C. Turn right onto West Anderson and go a few blocks until you reach South Rosalind Avenue. Turn left on South Rosalind and look for parking. All of the bars are located only a few blocks apart, so if you drive, you can park as long as you want in the garages along Pine Street, just north of Church Street for $5. If you do not have a designated driver, you must take a taxi. A cab ride one-way to Universal costs around $25 while a trip to Disney will cost around $55. There are no good reasons to drive drunk, and Orlando police set up frequent sobriety checkpoints to catch inebriated drivers (if you think we are just being cautious, take a sober drive around Downtown or along I-4 at night). When taking a cab, try to go with a group of people—if you're not with one, check your hotel lobby—to spread the cost.

BARS AND CLUBS

Antiquas

What it is Dance club. **Hours** 8 p.m.–2 a.m. **Entertainment** Latin-flavored music and Miami vibe. **Cover** $5–$8. **Location** 46 West Church Street.

COMMENTS Antiquas attempts to replicate a stereotypical slice of Miami's South Beach district inside a bar. The bar is set up around an enclosed courtyard complete with fake rocks, waterfalls, pinkish lighting, and just like every street in Miami, window ledges with cages for dancers. There is a large dance floor in the center, but it may be difficult to spot with all of the machine-made fog. The music is mostly rap and dance music, with salsa music on Sundays.

Chillers

What it is Nightclub. **Hours** 7 p.m.–2 a.m. **Entertainment** Small dance floor. **Cover** $5–$8 on Friday and Saturday. **Location** 33 West Church Street.

COMMENTS Chillers is a frat boy's fantasy. This compact bar is rather dirty, with the unmistakable scent of stale beer. Young adults in collared shirts make use of the myriad of frozen daiquiri machines that line the wall behind the bar. Upstairs is a small balcony with booth seating. College students will appreciate the $1 well drinks on Wednesday.

Cleo's Lounge

What it is Lounge with pool tables. **Hours** 5 p.m.–2 a.m. **Entertainment** Pool tables, great atmosphere. **Cover** None. **Location** 11 Court Street.

COMMENTS Cleo's is near the Wall Street bars at the corner of 11 Court Street and Pine Street. Recent expansions have made this one of our favorite hangouts. Live DJs often spin underground records, but the music is not so loud as to drown out conversation. The place is cozy and home to "the most inconvenient bathrooms" in Orlando, not that they are terribly hard to get to. Domestic bottles cost $3.50, and they have a large collection of wines. Cleo's is not to be confused with the other Cleo's, a "gentlemen's club" on Orange Blossom Drive.

The Dragon Room

What it is VIP Lounge. **Hours** 7 p.m.–2 a.m. **Entertainment** Other VIPs. **Cover** $20. **Location** 25 West Church Street. **Contact** ☎ 407-843-8600.

COMMENTS When you go out in black shoes and a collared shirt with a large fold of cash, you might be able to get into this chic nightspot, but odds are you're not on the guest list. The crowd here is older, in their early 30s, and don't be surprised when you receive a $12 tab for a vodka and soda. The music is mostly electronic.

The Lodge

What it is Bar made to feel like a ski lodge. **Hours** 5 p.m.–2 a.m. **Entertainment** Beer and talk. **Cover** None. **Location** 49 North Orange Avenue.

COMMENTS Located a short walk up Orange Avenue, The Lodge is where people in their late 20s and early 30s congregate. The bar has a ski-lodge vibe, and for the whole month of July, it celebrates "Christmas in July," decorating the interior with snowmen, Christmas lights, and candy canes. The music is generally 1980s rock ballads, creating a sing-along atmosphere for the moderately older clientele.

Tabu Night Club

What it is Dance club. **Hours** 5 p.m.–2 a.m. **Entertainment** Dancing. **Cover** $5–$10. **Location** 46 North Orange Street. **Contact** ☎ 407-839-1VIP; **www.tabunightclub.com.**

COMMENTS Tabu is a large dance club, and one of the more popular in downtown Orlando. It is more upscale than Antiquas, but less so than the Dragon Room. A VIP section upstairs offers a series of lounges for guests to lie on, but you must reserve a lounge beforehand by calling ☎ 407-839-1VIP. For those of us who aren't VIPs, downstairs gets crowded around 11:30 p.m., and even though it has the largest dance floor in downtown Orlando, the club fills quickly, so try to arrive shortly before the crowd. The club is one of the best places to dance in Orlando, and in the past, has featured performers like 50 Cent, Busta Rhymes, and Paul Oakenfold.

Wall Street Plaza Bars

What it is 8 bars together, 1 cover on weekends. **Hours** Vary. **Entertainment** Some dancing, normal bar activities. **Cover** $6 for entry to area with all bars on Friday and Saturday after 9 p.m. **Location** 18 Wall Street Plaza. **Contact** ☎ 407-849-0471; **www.wallstreetplaza.net**.

COMMENTS These eight bars are the hub of weekend nightlife in downtown Orlando. The bars that put on the weekly block party are the Globe, the Wall Street Cantina, Waitiki, Slingapour's, the Tuk Tuk Room, the Loaded Hog, One-Eyed Jack's, and the Monkey Bar. Almost all the bars have outside seating, and guests can carry drinks from one bar to another. Some serve food into the evening, and the Tuk Tuk Room even offers sushi. Slingapour's has a dance floor, but there are better dance clubs to visit on Church Street after you begin here. This area really takes off around 10:30 p.m., and if you are young and in Orlando, this is our pick for the place to go on the weekends.

PART SIXTEEN

DINING

DINING *outside*
WALT DISNEY WORLD

UNOFFICIAL GUIDE RESEARCHERS LOVE GOOD FOOD and invest a fair amount of time scouting new places to eat. And, because food at Walt Disney World is so expensive, we (like you) have an economic incentive for finding palatable meals outside the World. Unfortunately, the south Orlando tourist area is not exactly a culinary nirvana. If you thrive on fast food and the fare at chain restaurants (Denny's, T.G.I. Friday's, Olive Garden, and the like), you'll be as happy as an alligator on a chicken farm. If, however, you'd like a superlative dining experience, you'll find the pickings limited though less expensive.

Among specialty restaurants location and price will determine your choice. There are, for example, decent Italian restaurants in Walt Disney World and adjoining tourist areas. Which one you select depends on how much you want to spend and how convenient the place is.

Better restaurants outside Walt Disney World cater primarily to adults and aren't as well equipped to deal with children. If, however, you are looking to escape children or want to eat in peace and quiet, you're more likely to find such an environment outside the World.

TAKE OUT EXPRESS

IF YOU'RE STAYING IN A HOTEL OUTSIDE Disney World, **Take Out Express** (7111 Grand National Drive; ☎ 407-352-1170; **takeoutexpress0 .tripod.com**) will deliver a meal from your choice among 20 restaurants, including **T.G.I. Friday's, Toojay's Deli, Passage to India, Sweet Basil, Bella Roma, Taste of Hong Kong, Ocean Grill, Houlihan's,** and **Sizzler.** The delivery charge is $4.99 per restaurant, with a minimum $15 order. Gratuity is added to the bill. Cash, traveler's checks,

Where to Eat outside Walt Disney World

AMERICAN

Boheme* 325 South Orange Avenue, downtown Orlando; ☎ 407-581-4700; **www.grandbohemianhotel.com;** expensive. Elegant, upscale setting, eclectic menu featuring seafood, steaks, and game.

Chatham's Place* 7575 Dr. Phillips Boulevard, Orlando; ☎ 407-345-2992; **www.chathamsplace.com;** moderate to expensive; New American cuisine. The dining room is small and unappealing, but the food and service are some of the best in Orlando.

Hue* 629 E. Central Boulevard, Orlando; ☎ 407-849-1800; **www.hue restaurant.com;** moderate. Chic hot spot in trendy Thornton Park, but the food is still star of the show—try the sea bass.

Luma on Park 290 Park Avenue South, Winter Park; ☎ 407-599-4111; **www.lumaonpark.com;** moderate to expensive. New American cuisine in a cool dining room on Winter Park's trendy Park Avenue.

Pebbles 12551 FL 535, Crossroads Shopping Center, Lake Buena Vista; ☎ 407-827-1111; **www.pebblesworldwide.com;** moderate to expensive. A casual homegrown chain featuring a Florida version of California cuisine.

Seasons 52 7700 West Sand Lake Road, Orlando; ☎ 407-354-5212; **www.seasons52.com;** moderate. Delicious, creative New American food (and low in fat and calories). Solid wine list.

BARBECUE

Bubbalou's Bodacious B-B-Q 5818 Conroy Road, Orlando (near Universal Orlando); ☎ 407-295-1212; **www.bubbalous.com;** inexpensive. Tender, smoky barbecue; tomato-based "killer" sauce.

CARIBBEAN

Bahama Breeze 8849 International Drive, Orlando; ☎ 407-248-2499; **www.bahamabreeze.com;** moderate. A creative and tasty version of Caribbean cuisine from the owners of the Olive Garden and Red Lobster chains.

CHINESE

Ming Court 9188 International Drive, Orlando; ☎ 407-351-9988; **www.mingcourt.com;** expensive. Ask to see the dim sum menu.

CUBAN

Numero Uno* 2499 South Orange Avenue, Orlando; ☎ 407-841-3840; inexpensive. No trip to Florida is complete without a sampling of Cuban food.

Rolando's Cuban Restaurant* 870 East Altamonte Drive, Altamonte Springs; ☎ 407-767-9677; inexpensive. Some of the best Cuban food, served by some of the friendliest folks.

EASTERN EUROPEAN

Chef Henry's Café* 3716 Howell Branch Road, Winter Park; ☎ 407-657-2230; **www.chefhenryscafe.com;** moderate. Family-run cafe with authentic and delicious dishes. Don't leave without having a slice (or five) of the apple strudel.

FRENCH

Le Coq au Vin* 4800 South Orange Avenue, Orlando; ☎ 407-851-6980;
moderate. A perennial local favorite featuring country French cuisine in
a relaxed atmosphere. Reservations required.

INDIAN

Memories of India 7625 Turkey Lake Road, Orlando; ☎ 407-370-3277;
moderate. A quiet atmosphere with some of the best Indian cuisine in the
area. A bit more reasonable than some other I-Drive–area Indian restaurants.

Passage to India 5532 International Drive, Orlando; ☎ 407-351-3456;
www.passagetoindiarestaurant-orlando.com; moderate. A lot of locals
brave International Drive just to dine here.

Shamiana 7040 International Drive, Orlando; ☎ 407-354-1160;
inexpensive. Also serves Pakistani cuisine.

ITALIAN

Antonio's Sand Lake 7559 West Sand Lake Road, Orlando; ☎ 407-363-9191;
www.antoniosonline.com; moderate to expensive. Upscale Italian that's a
popular choice among locals.

Bice Portofino Bay Hotel, Universal Orlando Resort, 5601 Universal Boulevard,
Orlando; ☎ 407-503-3463; expensive. Authentic Italian, great wines.

JAPANESE/SUSHI

Amura 7786 West Sand Lake Road, Orlando; ☎ 407-370-0007; moderate.
A favorite sushi bar for locals. The tempura is popular, too.

Hanamizuki 8255 International Drive, Orlando; ☎ 407-363-7200;
moderate to expensive. Usually filled with Japanese visitors; pricey but
very authentic.

Seito 671 Front Street, Celebration; ☎ 407-566-1889; moderate. Sushi bar,
fusion dishes.

MEXICAN

Chevy's 2809 West Vine Street, Kissimmee; ☎ 407-847-2244; inexpensive
to moderate. Mexican food conveniently located across from the FL 535
entrance to WDW.

Don Pablo's 8717 International Drive, Orlando; ☎ 407-354-1345; inexpensive.
A pretty good chain that uses fresh ingredients. Can be a bit noisy.

Moe's Southwest Grill 19 Blake Boulevard, Celebration; ☎ 321-939-2455;
inexpensive. Tasty southwestern specialties in an attractive setting.

MIDDLE EASTERN

Cedars 7732 West Sand Lake Road, Orlando; ☎ 407-351-6000; **www.cedars
oforlando.com;** inexpensive. Traditional favorites from baba ghanouj to
tabbouleh and lentil soup.

*20 minutes or more from the tourist areas

Where to Eat outside WDW (continued)

NEW WORLD

Norman's 4000 Central Florida Parkway, in the Ritz-Carlton; ☎ 407-393-4333; **www.ritzcarlton.com;** expensive. Norman Van Aken, patron of New World cuisine, offers a menu that changes daily—but you'll always find his sinfully delicious conch chowder. World-class wine menu.

SEAFOOD

Bonefish Grill 7830 West Sand Lake Road, Orlando; ☎ 407-355-7707; **www.bonefishgrill.com;** moderate. Casual setting along busy Restaurant Row on Sand Lake Road. Choose your fish, then choose a favorite sauce to accompany. Also steaks and chicken.

McCormick & Schmick's 4200 Conroy Road, Mall at Millenia, Orlando; ☎ 407-226-6515; **www.mccormickandschmicks.com;** expensive. Menu changes often based on freshness. Raw oysters are a big hit.

STEAK/PRIME RIB

Charlie's Steak House 6107 South Orange Blossom Trail, Orlando; ☎ 407-851-7130; moderate. There are other locations for this small chain, including one just south of the Interstate 4 interchange on US 192.

Del Frisco's* 729 Lee Road, Orlando (quarter mile west of I-4); ☎ 407-645-4443; **www.delfriscosorlando.com;** expensive. A little pricey, but if you're in the mood for a great steak, it's worth it.

Texas de Brazil 5259 International Drive, Orlando; ☎ 407-355-0355; expensive. All-you-care-to-eat in an upscale, Brazilian-style churrascuria. Filet mignon, sausage, pork ribs, chicken, lamb, and more. Kids under age 6 free, ages 7 to 12 half price. Salad bar with more than 40 options.

Vito's Chop House 8633 International Drive, Orlando; ☎ 407-354-2467; **www.vitoschophouse.com;** moderate. Surprisingly upscale meat house with a taste of Tuscany.

THAI

Red Bamboo 6803 South Kirkman Road at International Drive, Orlando; ☎ 407-226-8997; moderate. Housed in an unassuming strip-mall location and acclaimed by Orlando dining critics for its authentic Thai dishes. Impressive wine list.

Thai House* 2117 East Colonial Drive, Orlando; ☎ 407-898-0820; inexpensive. Locals love the "Thai hot" specials at this little diner near downtown.

*20 minutes or more from the tourist areas

MasterCard, VISA, American Express, and Discover are accepted. Hours are 4:30 until 11 p.m.

DINING AT UNIVERSAL CITYWALK

UNIVERSAL ROLLED OUT ITS ANSWER to Downtown Disney with a vengeance in 1999. Like Downtown Disney, CityWalk is a combination of entertainment and dining with a focus on adults. Restaurant tastes run the gamut, from the elegant (**Emeril's Orlando**) to the basic (**NASCAR Sports Grille**), or, if you prefer, from the sublime to the ridiculous. All the restaurants share one common trait: they are loud. But there is good food to be found inside some of them. Most of the restaurants are partners with Universal's culinary team.

BOB MARLEY—A TRIBUTE TO FREEDOM ☎ 407-224-FOOD A medium-sized (and moderately loud) tribute to the reggae superstar.

BUBBA GUMP SHRIMP COMPANY ☎ 407-224-2691 This seafood eatery is part of an international chain inspired by the popular film *Forrest Gump*. As its name suggests, the restaurant specializes in shrimp dishes.

EMERIL'S ORLANDO ☎ 407-224-2424 Chief among dining options here, Emeril's Orlando is Emeril Lagasse's Florida version of his New Orleans restaurant. Lagasse is on hand from time to time, though he tends to stay in the kitchen. But even when he's not there, you're in for some good eating. The food is Louisiana-style with a creative flair.

HARD ROCK CAFE ☎ 407-224-FOOD Serves up so-so burgers, ribs, and other American fare. More remarkable is the extensive collection of music memorabilia, including a pink 1959 Cadillac revolving over the bar. It's the biggest such collection on display anywhere in the Hard Rock chain.

JIMMY BUFFETT'S MARGARITAVILLE ☎ 407-224-2155 A large and noisy tribute to the head Parrothead. None of the food, including the cheeseburger, will make you think you're in paradise, but fans don't seem to care. The focal point is a volcano that erupts occasionally, spewing margarita mix instead of lava.

LATIN QUARTER ☎ 407-224-FOOD Simple Latin cuisine is served here—beans and rice, plantains, flan. Most of the patrons come to dance and drink.

NASCAR SPORTS GRILLE ☎ 407-224-FOOD A large and noisy tribute to all things motorized. You may find yourself sitting under a full-sized race car that from time to time starts up and roars at a too-realistic sound level. The food? See all the logos for oil companies on the walls?

NBA CITY ☎ 407-363-5919 Serves decent theme-restaurant eats. The dining area looks like a miniature basketball arena, and TVs through-out play videos of famous basketball players and key moments in roundball history.

PASTAMORÉ ☎ 407-224-FOOD This is the requisite Italian restaurant. The decor is modern and stylish, and the food—with portions big enough to share—is better than average.

PAT O'BRIEN'S, ☎ 407-224-2106, and **CityJazz** are mostly music venues that serve some food. Pat O'Brien's, behind a facade that looks remarkably similar to the New Orleans original, has the best bites (try the jambalaya).

ONE MAN'S TREASURE

A MAN FROM RICHLAND, Washington, urges:

> I think that you should in future editions promote the Crossroads of
> Buena Vista [Shopping Center] a little stronger. There are plenty
> of non-WDW restaurants at non-WDW prices. The Crossroads is
> nothing less than a small city that can service all of your needs.

CROSSROADS SHOPPING CENTER is on FL 535 directly across from the
entrance to Walt Disney World Village and the Downtown Disney
Resort Area. As the reader suggests, it offers about everything you
might need. Fast food is sold at **McDonald's** and **Taco Bell.** Up a notch
are **Chevy's, T.G.I. Friday's, Jungle Jim's, Pizzeria Uno,** and **Red Lobster.**
(Jungle Jim's arguably whips up some of the best burgers in the Walt
Disney World area.) For a more upscale meal, pick **Pebbles,** featuring
fresh Florida seafood. When you finish eating, shop for sportswear,
swimwear, and athletic shoes.

BUFFETS AND MEAL DEALS
OUTSIDE WALT DISNEY WORLD

BUFFETS, RESTAURANT SPECIALS, AND discount dining abound in the
tourist areas, especially on US 192 (locally known as the Irlo Bronson
Highway) and along International Drive. The local visitor magazines,
distributed free at non-Disney hotels among other places, are packed
with advertisements and discount coupons for seafood feasts, Chinese
buffets, Indian buffets, breakfast buffets, and a host of combination specials for everything from lobster to barbecue. For a family trying to econ-
omize on meals, some of the come-ons are mighty appealing. But are
these places any good? Is the food fresh, tasty, and appealing? Are the
restaurants clean and inviting? Armed with little more than a roll of
Tums, the *Unofficial* research team tried all the eateries that advertise
heavily in the free tourist magazines. Here's what we discovered.

CHINESE SUPER BUFFETS Whoa! Talk about an oxymoron. If you've
ever tried preparing Chinese food, especially a stir-fry, you know that
split-second timing is required to avoid overcooking. So it should
come as no big surprise that Chinese dishes languishing on a buffet
lose their freshness, texture, and flavor in a hurry.

A notable exception is **Asian Harbor Chinese and Japanese Super Buffet** (in Lake Buena Vista at the intersection of FL 535 and FL 536 next to
the CVS drugstore; ☎ 407-238-9998). The restaurant features Chinese
dishes, Japanese seafood, and an Oriental grill bar. Items on the buffet
are replenished frequently to ensure freshness. The best Chinese buffet
in the International Drive area is **Mei Asian Bistro** (8255 International
Drive, in the shopping center just north of Mercado; ☎ 407-352-0867).

INDIAN BUFFETS Indian food works much better on a buffet than Chinese food. The mainstay of Indian buffets is curries. *Curry,* you may
be surprised to know, is essentially the Indian word for "stew." Curry

powder, as sold in the United States, is nothing more than a blend of spices prepackaged to flavor a stew. In India, each curry is prepared with a different combination of spices, and no self-respecting cook would dream of using an off-the-shelf mix. The salient point about Indian buffets is that stews, unlike stir-frys, actually improve with a little aging. If you've ever heated a leftover stew at home and commented that it tasted better than when originally served, it's because the flavors and ingredients continued to marry during the storage period, making it richer and tastier.

In the tourist areas, most Indian restaurants offer a buffet at lunch only—not too convenient if you plan on spending your day at the theme parks. If you're out shopping or taking a day off, here are some Indian buffets worth trying:

Aashirwad 5748 International Drive, at the corner of International Drive and Kirkman Road; ☎ 407-370-9830

Punjab Indian Restaurant 7451 International Drive; ☎ 407-352-7887

Spice Cafe 7536 Dr. Phillips Boulevard, in the Market Place complex at Sand Lake Road and Dr. Phillips Boulevard; ☎ 407-264-0205

BRAZILIAN BUFFETS A number of Brazilian buffets have sprung up along International Drive. The best of these is **Vittorio's** (5159 International Drive, near the outlet malls at the northern end of International Drive; ☎ 407-352-1255).

GENERAL BUFFETS Two buffets, the **Las Vegas Buffet** (5269 West US 192; ☎ 407-397-1288) and **Bill Wong's** (5668 International Drive; ☎ 407-352-5373), offer fair value. The Las Vegas Buffet, the better of the two, features a carving station with prime rib, ham, turkey, and sometimes lamb. Bill Wong's represents itself as a Chinese buffet but shores up its Chinese selections with peel-and-eat shrimp, prime rib, and a nice selection of hot and cold vegetables.

SEAFOOD AND LOBSTER BUFFETS These affairs do not exactly fall under the category of inexpensive dining. Prices range from $20 to $27.95 for early birds (4 p.m. until 6 p.m.) and $29.95 to $32.95 after 6 p.m. The main draw (no pun intended) is all the lobster you can eat. The problem is that lobsters, like Chinese food, don't wear well on a steam table. After a few minutes on the buffet line, they make better tennis balls than dinner. If, however, you have someone in the kitchen who knows how to steam a lobster, and if you grab your lobster immediately after a fresh batch has been brought out, it will probably be fine. There are three lobster buffets on US 192 and another two on International Drive. Although all five do a reasonable job, we prefer **Boston Lobster Feast** (6071 West Irlo Bronson [US 192]; ☎ 407-396-2606; and 8731 International Drive, five blocks north of the Convention Center; ☎ 407-248-8606; **www.bostonlobsterfeast.com**). Both locations are distinguished by a vast variety of seafood in addition to the lobster. The International Drive location is cavernous and insanely noisy, so we prefer the Irlo

Bronson location, where you can actually have a conversation over dinner. There's ample parking at the International Drive location, while parking places are in short supply at the Irlo Bronson restaurant. At about $33 after 6 p.m., dining is expensive at both locations.

BREAKFAST BUFFETS AND ENTREE BUFFETS Entree buffets are offered by most of the area chain steak houses such as **Ponderosa, Sizzler, Western Steer,** and **Golden Corral.** Among them, there are 18 locations in the Walt Disney World area. All serve breakfast, lunch, and dinner. At lunch and dinner, you get the buffet when you buy an entree, usually a steak. Generally speaking, the buffets are less elaborate than a stand-alone buffet and considerably more varied than a salad bar. Breakfast service is a straightforward buffet (that is, there is no obligation to buy an entree). Concerning the food, it's chain-restaurant quality but pretty decent all the same. Prices are a bargain, and you can get in and out at lightning speed—important at breakfast when you're trying to get to the theme parks early. Some locations offer lunch and dinner buffets at a set price without buying an entree.

Though you can argue about which chain serves the best steak, Golden Corral wins the buffet contest hands down, with at least twice as many offerings as its three competitors. Where buffets at Golden Corral, Western Steer, and Ponderosa are pretty consistent from location to location, the buffets at the various Sizzlers vary a good deal. The pick of the Sizzlers is the 4006 West US 192 location. In addition to the steak houses, area **Shoney's** also offer breakfast, lunch, and dinner buffets. Local freebie visitor magazines are full of discount coupons for all of the above.

MEAL DEALS Discount coupons are available for a wide range of restaurants, including some wonderful upscale ethnic places like **Ming's** (Chinese). For those who crave both beef and a bargain, try **JT's Prime Time Restaurant & Bar** (16299 W. Irlo Bronson; ☎ 407-239-6555). JT's serves all-you-can-eat prime rib on Wednesday nights for $18.99. They slice it a little thin but are very attentive in regard to bringing you additional helpings. Other prime rib specials can be found at **Cattleman's Steakhouse,** with locations at 8801 International Drive a quarter of a mile north of the convention center (☎ 407-354-9888) and on US 192 at FL 535 (2948 Vineland Road; ☎ 407-397-1888). Our favorite prime-rib option is **Wild Jack's Steaks & BBQ** (7364 International Drive; ☎ 407-352-4407). The decor is strictly cowboy modern, but the beef is some of the best in town, and the price is right. The best steak deal in the Disney World area is the $9.99, ten-ounce New York strip at the **Black Angus Steak House.** The beef is served with salad, choice of vegetables or potato, and bread, and is available at both locations convenient to Disney: 7516 West Irlo Bronson (US 192), ☎ 407-390-4548; and 6231 International Drive, ☎ 407-354-3333. Another meat eater's delight is the Feast for Four at **Sonny's Real Pit Bar-B-Q,** a Florida chain that turns out good barbecue. For $34 per family of four, you get sliced pork or beef, plus chicken, ribs, beans, slaw, fries, garlic bread, and soft drinks or tea, all served family-style. Locations include: 3189 South John Young Parkway, ☎ 407-847-8889; and on US 192 at 4475 13th Street, ☎ 407-892-2285. No coupons are needed or available for JT's or Sonny's, but coupons are available for the other "meateries."

FAST FOOD IN THE THEME PARKS

BECAUSE MOST MEALS DURING vacation are consumed on the run while touring, we'll tackle counter-service and vendor foods first. Plentiful in all theme parks are hot dogs, hamburgers, chicken sandwiches, green salads, and pizza. They're augmented by special items that relate to the park's theme or the part of the park you're touring. Counter-service prices are fairly consistent from park to park. Expect to pay the same for your coffee or hot dog at Cypress Gardens as at SeaWorld.

Getting your act together in regard to counter-service restaurants in the parks is more a matter of courtesy than necessity. Rude guests rank fifth among reader complaints. A mother from Fort Wayne, Indiana, points out that indecision can be as maddening as outright discourtesy, especially when you're hungry:

> *Every fast-food restaurant has menu signs the size of billboards, but do you think anybody reads them? People waiting in line spend enough time in front of these signs to memorize them, and still don't have a clue what they want when they finally get to the order taker. If by some miracle they've managed to choose between the hot dog and the hamburger, they then fiddle around another ten minutes deciding what size coke to order. Tell your readers PULEEEZ get their orders together ahead of time!*

Cutting Your Dining Time at the Theme Parks

Even if you confine your meals to vendor and counter-service fast food, you lose a lot of time getting food in the theme parks. When it comes to fast food, "fast" may apply to the time you spend eating it, not the time invested in obtaining it.

Here are suggestions for minimizing the time you spend hunting and gathering food:

1. Eat breakfast before arriving. Don't waste touring time eating breakfast at the parks. Besides, many restaurants offer some outstanding breakfast specials. Some hotels furnish small refrigerators in their guest rooms, or rent them. If you can get by on cold cereal, rolls, fruit, and juice, having a fridge in your room will save a ton of time. If you can't get a fridge, bring a cooler.

2. After a good breakfast, buy snacks from vendors in the parks as you tour, or stuff some snacks in a fanny pack. This is very important if you're on a tight schedule and can't spend a lot of time waiting in line for food.

3. All theme-park restaurants are busiest between 11:30 a.m. and 2:15 p.m. for lunch and 6 p.m. and 9 p.m. for dinner. For shorter lines and faster service, don't eat during these hours, especially 12:30 p.m. to 1:30 p.m.

4. Many counter-service restaurants sell cold sandwiches. Buy a cold lunch (except for drinks) before 11:30 a.m. and carry it until you're ready to eat. Ditto for dinner. Bring small plastic bags in which to pack the food. Purchase drinks at the appropriate time from any convenient vendor.

5. Most fast-food eateries have more than one service window. Regardless of time of day, check the lines at all windows before queuing. Sometimes a window that's manned but out of the way will have a much shorter line or none at all. Note, however, that some windows may offer only certain items.

6. If you're short on time and the park closes early, stay until closing and eat dinner later. If the park stays open late, eat dinner about 4 or 4:30 p.m. at the restaurant of your choice. You should miss the last wave of lunchers and sneak in just ahead of the dinner crowd.

Beyond Counter Service: Tips for Saving Money on Food

Though buying food from counter-service restaurants and vendors will save time and money (compared with full-service dining), additional strategies can bolster your budget and maintain your waistline. Here are some suggestions our readers have made over the years:

1. Go on vacation during a period of fasting and abstinence. You can save a fortune and save your soul at the same time!

2. Wear clothes that are slightly too small and make you feel like dieting (no spandex allowed!).

3. Whenever you're feeling hungry, ride attractions that induce motion sickness.

4. Leave your cash and credit cards at your hotel. Buy food only with money your children fish out of fountains and wishing wells.

A Missouri mom writes:

I have shared our very successful meal plan with many families. We stayed six nights and arrived after some days on the beach south of Sarasota. We shopped there and arrived with our steel Coleman cooler well stocked with milk and sandwich fixings. I froze a block of ice in a milk bottle, and we replenished it daily with ice from the resort ice machine. I also froze small packages of deli-type meats for later in the week. We ate cereal, milk, and fruit each morning, with boxed juices. I also had a hot pot to boil water for instant coffee, oatmeal, and soup.

Each child had a belt bag of his own, which he filled from a special box of "goodies" each day. I made a great mystery of filling that box in the weeks before the trip. Some things were actual food, like packages of crackers and cheese, packets of peanuts and raisins. Some were worthless junk, like candy and gum. They grazed from their belt bags at will throughout the day, with no interference from

Mom and Dad. Each also had a small, rectangular plastic water bottle that could hang on the belt. We filled these at water fountains before getting into lines and were the envy of many.

We left the park before noon, ate sandwiches, chips, and soda in the room, and napped. We purchased our evening meal in the park, at a counter-service eatery. We budgeted for both morning and evening snacks from a vendor but often did not need them. It made the occasional treat all the more special. Our cooler had been pretty much emptied by the end of the week, but the block of ice was still there.

We interviewed one woman who brought a huge picnic for her family of five packed in a large diaper/baby paraphernalia bag. She stowed the bag in a locker (offered by all theme parks and swimming parks) and retrieved it when the family was hungry. A Pennsylvania family adds:

Despite the warning against bringing food into the park, we packed a double picnic lunch in a backpack and a small shoulder bag. Even with a small discount, it cost $195 for the seven of us to tour the park for a day, and I felt that spending another $150 or so on two meals was not in the cards. We froze juice boxes to keep the meat sandwiches cool (it worked fine) and had an extra round of juice boxes and peanut-butter sandwiches for a late-afternoon snack. We took raisins and a pack of fig bars for sweets, but didn't carry any other cookies or candy to avoid a "sugar low" during the day. Fruit would have been nice, but it would have been squashed.

Note: Disney has a rule against bringing your own food and drink into the park. Although after 9/11 all packs, purses, diaper bags, and such are searched, security usually does not enforce this ban.

Finally, a mom from Whiteland, Indiana, who purchases drinks in the parks, offers this suggestion:

One "must-take" item if you're traveling with younger kids is a supply of small paper or plastic cups to split drinks, which are both huge and expensive.

DINING *at* UNIVERSAL ORLANDO

ONE OF OUR CONSTANT GRIPES about theme parks is the food. To many guests hustling through the parks, dining is a low priority—they don't mind the typically substandard fare and high prices because their first objective is to see the sights and ride the rides. This is certainly understandable, but the *Unofficial Guide* team is made up of big fans of big eating.

unofficial **TIP**
You may be pleasantly surprised by the quality of the food at Universal Studios Orlando.

UNIVERSAL ORLANDO RESTAURANTS

NAME	CUISINE	OVERALL RATING	COST	QUALITY RATING	VALUE RATING
CITYWALK					
Pastamore	Italian	★★★½	Mod	★★★★	★★★★
Emeril's Orlando	American	★★★½	Exp	★★★	★★★
Hard Rock Cafe	American	★★★	Mod	★★★½	★★★★
Pat O'Brien's	Cajun	★★★	Inexp	★★★½	★★★★
Jimmy Buffett's Margaritaville	Caribbean/American	★★★	Mod	★★★½	★★★
NBA City	American	★★★	Mod	★★★	★★★
Bob Marley	Jamaican/Caribbean	★★½	Mod	★★★½	★★★
NASCAR Sports Grille	American	★★	Mod	★★★	★★
PORTOFINO BAY HOTEL					
Bice	Italian	★★★★½	Exp	★★★★	★★★★
Mama Della's	Italian	★★★	Exp	★★★	★★★
Trattoria del Porto	Italian	★★★	Mod	★★★	★★
ROYAL PACIFIC HOTEL					
Emeril's Tchoup Chop	Pacific Rim	★★★★	Exp	★★★★	★★★
Wantilan Luau	Hawaiian	★★★★	Mod	★★★	★★★
Islands Dining Room	Caribbean	★★★	Mod	★★★	★★★
Jake's American Bar	American	★★	Mod	★★	★★
ISLANDS OF ADVENTURE					
Mythos	Steak/Seafood	★★★	Mod/Exp	★★★★	★★★
Confisco Grille	American	★★½	Mod	★★★½	★★★
HARD ROCK					
The Kitchen	American	★★★★	Mod	★★★	★★★
STUDIOS					
Lombard's Seafood Grille	Seafood	★★½	Mod	★★★½	★★★
Finnegan's	Irish	★★	Mod	★★★	★★

It's our opinion that there's no reason not to expect quality food and service when theme parks invest so much elsewhere in design, production, and development.

The good news is that food in Universal is almost always a cut above and a step ahead of what you can find at Walt Disney World and other parks. More variety, better preparations, and more current trends are generally the rule at Universal. Counter-service and fast-food offerings are comparable to Disney. To help you make choices for sit-down meals at breakfast, lunch, or dinner, we've provided profiles of Universal's full-service places, most of which are located in the CityWalk complex. For information about CityWalk's nightclub scene, see the Universal Orlando CityWalk section in Part Fifteen, After Dark.

In addition to these restaurants, the three Loews hotels on Universal's property offer various full-service dining opportunities. At the Portofino Bay resort, you'll find Mama Della's, with Italian comfort food served in a casual dining space where Mama is in charge. Trattoria del Porto offers many of the same types of dishes but without Mama's interference. For more upscale dining, there's Bice, serving Italian specialties in a romantic atmosphere that includes a strolling guitarist. Across the way is the Hard Rock Hotel's The Palm, a link in the chain of steak houses based on the original in New York and its characteristic wall caricatures. The Hard Rock also hosts Beach Club, a casual bar and grill.

The Royal Pacific brings the second Orlando restaurant from Emeril Lagasse, this one called Emeril's Tchoup Chop. The name is pronounced "chop chop" ("Tchoup" is short for Tchoupitoulas, the street that Lagasse's main New Orleans restaurant is on), and the cuisine is a stylized version of Hawaiian dishes. The food gets mixed reviews, but most people love the decor. Royal Pacific also has good light bites at Jake's American Bar, as well as in the Islands Dining Room, the hotel's version of a coffee shop.

Counter-service fast food is available throughout Universal Studios Orlando. The food compares in quality to McDonald's, Arby's, or Taco Bell, but is more expensive, though often served in larger portions.

UNIVERSAL ORLANDO RESTAURANT PROFILES

BELOW ARE PROFILES for full-service restaurants found in Universal Studios Florida, Islands of Adventure, and the CityWalk complex.

Bice ★★★★½

ITALIAN	EXPENSIVE	QUALITY ★★★★	VALUE ★★★★

Portofino Bay; ☎ 407-503-1415

Customers Locals and tourists. **Reservations** Recommended. **When to go** Dinner. **Entree range** $18–$44. **Payment** AE, D, DC, MC, V. **Service rating** ★★★★★. **Friendliness rating** ★★★★. **Parking** Valet or self-parking; $5 charge for valet. **Bar** Full service. **Wine selection** Very good. **Dress** Resort dressy. **Disabled access** Good. **Hours** Sunday–Thursday, 5:30–10:30 p.m., Friday and Saturday, 5:30–11:30 p.m.

SETTING AND ATMOSPHERE Wood and marble floors, crisp white linens, opulent flower arrangements and waiters in black suits give Bice ("beach-ay") the feeling of a formal restaurant, but there is nothing stiff or fussy about the space or the staff. It is immaculately clean, beautifully lit, and relatively quiet even when it's crowded.

HOUSE SPECIALTIES Menu changes seasonally; selections may include prosciutto with fresh melon and baby greens; homemade braised beef sparerib ravioli with spinach in mushroom-marsala sauce; veal Milanese with cherry tomatoes and arugula; pistachio semifreddo.

ENTERTAINMENT AND AMENITIES Piano in bar.

SUMMARY AND COMMENTS This is part of a chain of very upscale and quite impressive restaurants found in New York, Tokyo, and Las Vegas and other international locales. The food is incredibly fresh, well prepared, and elegant, and the service is top-notch. But be prepared: even a modest meal will put a dent in your wallet, and even though the food and service are definitely worth it, it may be too expensive for many vacationers. If you want to try a variety of things on the menu, split a salad, appetizer, or pasta dish (traditionally eaten before the entree) between two people for a starter; portions are large enough for sharing and the staff is more than happy to accommodate.

Bob Marley—A Tribute to Freedom ★★½

JAMAICAN/CARIBBEAN	MODERATE	QUALITY ★★★½	VALUE ★★★

CityWalk; ☎ 407-224-2262

Customers Locals and tourists. **Reservations** Not accepted. **When to go** Early evening. **Entree range** $8–$17. **Payment** AE, D, MC, V. **Service rating** ★★. **Friendliness rating** ★★★. **Parking** Universal Orlando garage. **Bar** Full service. **Wine selection** Poor. **Dress** Casual; dreadlocks if you have them. **Disabled access** Good. **Hours** Monday–Friday, 4 p.m.–2 a.m.; Saturday and Sunday, 2 p.m.–2 a.m.

SETTING AND ATMOSPHERE The space, said to be fashioned after Bob Marley's island home, gives one the feeling of sitting on a porch or verandah and watching entertainment on a backyard stage. Most of the area is open to the elements, although there are shelters from the occasional rainstorm.

HOUSE SPECIALTIES Jerk-marinated chicken breast; smoky white-cheddar cheese fondue; Jamaican vegetable patties; beef patties.

ENTERTAINMENT AND AMENITIES Live reggae; cover charge after 8 p.m.

SUMMARY AND COMMENTS There is much more emphasis put on the music than the food here, although you can manage a palatable bite to eat while listening to some good tunes. Sure, you're allowed to get up and dance.

Confisco Grille ★★½

AMERICAN	MODERATE	QUALITY ★★★½	VALUE ★★★

Islands of Adventure/Port of Entry; ☎ 407-363-8000

Customers Park guests. **Reservations** Accepted. **When to go** Anytime. **Entree range** $9–$18. **Payment** AE, D, DC, MC, V. **Service rating** ★★. **Friendliness rating** ★★. **Parking** Universal Orlando garage. **Bar** Full service. **Wine selection** Moderate. **Dress** Casual. **Disabled access** Good. **Hours** 11:30 a.m. until park closing; also hosts a character breakfast featuring Spider-Man several mornings throughout the year. Call for details.

SETTING AND ATMOSPHERE   A way station on the road to Morocco, perhaps? Actually, it's meant to look like a customs house.

HOUSE SPECIALTIES   Pad thai; selection of salads; beef and chicken fajitas; grilled sandwiches.

SUMMARY AND COMMENTS   It's clear that the Universal food gurus put all their efforts into the counter-service eateries located throughout the park. Confisco is fine for those times when you just can't stand in another line, even if it is just to get food.

Emeril's Orlando ★★★½

| AMERICAN | EXPENSIVE | QUALITY ★★★ | VALUE ★★★ |

CityWalk; ☎ 407-224-2424

Customers Locals and park guests. **Reservations** Required. **When to go** Early or late evening. **Entree range** $19–$75. **Payment** AE, D, DC, MC, V. **Service rating** ★★★★. **Friendliness rating** ★★★★. **Parking** Universal Orlando garage; valet parking available, check with restaurant about validation. **Bar** Full service. **Wine selection** Very good. **Dress** Casual to dressy. **Disabled access** Good. **Hours** Sunday–Thursday, 11:30 a.m.–2:30 p.m. and 5:30–10 p.m.; Friday and Saturday, 11:30 a.m.–2:30 p.m. and 5:30–11 p.m.

SETTING AND ATMOSPHERE   The main dining room is two stories high and features hardwood floors, wooden beams, and stone walls, all of which act as sounding boards for the noisy dining room. Sliding glass doors lead to the kitchen, where Emeril may or may not be cooking (probably not). Part of the kitchen is open, and there are eight seats at a food bar. These are some of the best seats in the house and shouldn't be turned down, if offered.

HOUSE SPECIALTIES   The menu changes frequently. Signature items that might be available include oyster stew; farm-raised quail; "a study of duck"; and lobster cheesecake.

SUMMARY AND COMMENTS   Owner Emeril Lagasse gained popularity from his show on Food Network, and his restaurants were instant hits. But the food proves he's more than a flash in the proverbial pan. Lagasse also has restaurants in New Orleans and Las Vegas, so it's unlikely he will be on the premises, though he does visit sometimes. *Note:* Reservations can be hard to come by unless booked weeks in advance. To get a table on the same day as your visit, call the restaurant at 3:15 p.m. Reservations that have not been confirmed by that time are canceled and made available to callers.

Emeril's Tchoup Chop ★★★★

| PACIFIC RIM | EXPENSIVE | QUALITY ★★★★ | VALUE ★★★ |

Royal Pacific; ☎ 407-503-CHOP

Customers Locals and park guests. **Reservations** Recommended. **When to go** Dinner. **Entree range** Lunch, $13–$20; dinner, $23–$34. **Payment** AE, D, DC, MC, V.

Service rating ★★★. Friendliness rating ★★★★. Parking Valet or self-parking; $5 charge. Bar Full service. Wine selection Good. Dress Resort dressy. Disabled access Good. Hours Lunch: Monday–Sunday, 11:30 a.m.–2 p.m.; dinner: Sunday–Thursday, 5:30–10 p.m.; Friday and Saturday. 5:30–11 p.m.

SETTING AND ATMOSPHERE It's a cool, attractive, Polynesian-themed room reminiscent of a giant tiki bar, complete with bamboo, waterfalls, sculpted gardens, and giant woks in full view.

HOUSE SPECIALTIES Wok-seared orange sake glazed duck; Thai-style Caesar salad; braised Kobe beef short ribs; banana-cream pie; banana cheesecake.

SUMMARY AND COMMENTS This beautiful room serves up Far-East specialties with some flair, although service can sometimes be a bit slow. The food is tasty, but again, quite pricey. To stick to a tighter budget, go at lunchtime and try the lighter options like the entree-sized soups and salads, and skip dessert.

Finnegan's ★★

IRISH	MODERATE	QUALITY ★★★	VALUE ★★

Universal Studios/New York; ☎ 407-363-8000

Customers Park guests. Reservations Priority seating. When to go Anytime. Entree range $11–$22. Payment AE, D, DC, MC, V. Service rating ★★. Friendliness rating ★★. Parking Universal Orlando garage. Bar Full service. Wine selection Ireland is not really known for its wines; good beer selection, though. Dress Casual. Disabled access Good. Hours Daily, 11 a.m. until park closing.

SETTING AND ATMOSPHERE Fashioned after an Irish pub, albeit one built as a movie set. Along with the requisite pub-like accoutrements—tin ceiling, belt-driven paddle fans—are movie lights and half walls that suggest the back of scenery flats.

HOUSE SPECIALTIES Shepherd's pie; fish and chips; Irish stew; bangers and mash; shrimp Scargo; Irish coffee.

ENTERTAINMENT AND AMENITIES Singer.

SUMMARY AND COMMENTS The fare is modest, but the entertainment is fun and the beer is cold. Add to that the fact that this is only one of two spots in Universal Studios park where you can get a waiter to bring food to you, and the pub fare starts to look a bit more attractive.

Hard Rock Cafe ★★★

AMERICAN	MODERATE	QUALITY ★★★½	VALUE ★★★★

CityWalk; ☎ 407-351-7625

Customers Locals and tourists. Reservations Not accepted. When to go Afternoon or evening. Entree range $10–$22. Payment AE, D, DC, MC, V. Service rating ★★★. Friendliness rating ★★. Parking Universal Orlando garage. Bar Full service. Wine selection Moderate. Dress Casual. Disabled access Good. Hours Daily, 11 a.m.–2 a.m.

SETTING AND ATMOSPHERE This is the biggest HRC in the world (or in the Universe, as they like to say in this part of town). Shaped like the Coliseum, the two-story dining room is a massive museum of rock art memorabilia. The circular center bar features a full-size Cadillac spinning overhead. If you need to be told this is a noisy restaurant, you've never been to a Hard Rock Cafe before. Everyone, however, should visit a Hard Rock at least once.

HOUSE SPECIALTIES Pig sandwich; charbroiled burgers; barbecued ribs; rock-and-roll pot roast; grilled fajitas; T-bone steak.

OTHER RECOMMENDATIONS Hot fudge brownie; chocolate-chip cookie pie.

ENTERTAINMENT AND AMENITIES Rock 'n' roll records and memorabilia.

SUMMARY AND COMMENTS Most people complain about a burger that costs $10. But this is a good burger—half a pound—and it comes with fries. And all the rest of the food is equally as good, which is why Hard Rock Cafe remains the theme restaurant that everyone else wants to imitate.

Jake's American Bar ★★

AMERICAN	MODERATE	QUALITY ★★	VALUE ★★

Royal Pacific Hotel; ☎ 407-503-DINE

Customers Hotel guests. Reservations Not accepted. When to go Early evening. Entree range $10–$20. Payment AE, D, DC, MC, V. Service rating ★★. Friendliness rating ★★★. Parking Valet or self-park; $5 charge for valet. Bar Full service. Wine selection Average. Dress resort casual. Disabled access Good. Hours Daily, 2–11 p.m.; bar, 2 p.m.–2 a.m.

SETTING AND ATMOSPHERE Run-of-the-mill hotel bar and restaurant.

HOUSE SPECIALTIES Pu Pu platter; Brandi's BBQ baby back ribs; steak sandwich; Fly Away Roaster.

ENTERTAINMENT AND AMENITIES Thursday and Sunday, karaoke from 8:30 p.m.–12:30 a.m.; Friday and Saturday, live music from 8:30–11:30 p.m.

SUMMARY AND COMMENTS This is a viable option if you're staying in the hotel, but as far as special meals go, this place doesn't deliver—and really isn't meant to. For a quick meal, this spot is convenient but doesn't merit a visit if you're not already in the area.

Jimmy Buffett's Magaritaville ★★★

CARIBBEAN/AMERICAN	MODERATE	QUALITY ★★★½	VALUE ★★★

CityWalk; ☎ 407-224-2155

Customers Local and tourist parrotheads. Reservations Not accepted. When to go Early evening. Entree range $9–$22. Payment AE, D, DC, MC, V. Service rating ★★★. Friendliness rating ★★★. Parking Universal Orlando garage. Bar Full service. Wine selection Minimal. Dress Flowered shirts, flip-flops. Disabled access Good. Hours Daily, 11 a.m.–2 a.m.

SETTING AND ATMOSPHERE Two-story dining space with many large-screen TVs playing Jimmy Buffett music videos and scenes from his live performances. A volcano above one of the bars occasionally erupts to spew margaritas down the slope into a giant blender.

HOUSE SPECIALTIES Cheeseburgers, of course; conch fritters; Yucatán quesadillas with whole-wheat tortillas; New Orleans nachos; key-lime pie.

ENTERTAINMENT AND AMENITIES Live music on the porch early; band on inside stage late evening.

SUMMARY AND COMMENTS This is a relaxing, festive place but it's not always worth the wait (especially if it's two hours, which it has been known to be). The atmosphere, though, is like a taste of the beach without having to travel to the coast. If the line for a table is outrageous, see if you can sidle up to the bar for a margarita and appetizers, which is just as much—if not more—fun than actually having a full meal. This place is wildly popular with Jimmy Buffett fans standing in line just to get a beeper so they can stand in line some more and wait for a table.

The Kitchen ★★★★

| AMERICAN | MODERATE | QUALITY ★★★ | VALUE ★★★ |

Hard Rock Hotel; ☎ 407-503-DINE

Customers Tourists. Reservations Recommended. When to go Dinner. Entree range $10–$32. Payment AE, D, DC, MC, V. Service rating ★★½. Friendliness rating ★★★★. Parking Valet or self-parking; $5 charge. Bar Full service. Wine selection Good. Dress Casual. Disabled access Good. Hours Daily, 7 a.m.–11 p.m.

SETTING AND ATMOSPHERE Taking on the appearance of the spacious kitchen in a rock megastar's mansion, The Kitchen's walls are adorned with culinary-themed memorabilia from the Hard Rock Hotel's many celebrity guests.

HOUSE SPECIALTIES Seared ahi tuna; chicken chorizo quesadillas; Kobe beef burger; maple-glazed cedar-plank salmon; meatloaf; key-lime tart.

ENTERTAINMENT AND AMENITIES Rock stars occasionally visit to cook their specialties; signed aprons and rock memorabilia on the walls.

SUMMARY AND COMMENTS Though we must admit our expectations weren't too high for this Hard Rock venture, we were pleasantly surprised with the food and service here. Though expensive, the food is actually quite good and the setting is pretty fun. The Kobe beef burger will set you back about $18 but the regular version is just as tasty and much less expensive. Visiting rock stars often perform cooking demonstrations of their favorite dishes at the Chef's Table, so call ahead to see if any rock stars will be in the kitchen—you may find yourself having dinner with Joan Jett or Bob Seger. If dinner is a little out of your price range but you still want the experience, go for the $15.95 breakfast buffet, which includes a host of fresh, yummy selections and an omelet station.

Islands Dining Room ★★★

| CARIBBEAN | MODERATE | QUALITY ★★★ | VALUE ★★★ |

Royal Pacific Hotel; ☎ 407-503-DINE

Customers Hotel guests. **Reservations** Suggested for character dining and during holiday weekends. **When to go** Breakfast, character dinners. **Entree range** breakfast, $8–$19.50; lunch, $12–$17; dinner, $10–$33. **Payment** AE, D, DC, MC, V. **Service rating** ★★★. **Friendliness rating** ★★★. **Parking** Valet or self-park; $5 charge for valet. **Bar** Full service. **Wine selection** Average. **Dress** Casual. **Disabled access** Good. **Hours** Daily, 7 a.m.–10 p.m.

SETTING AND ATMOSPHERE Pretty standard hotel dining room; big and open, and always spotless.

HOUSE SPECIALTIES Guava-barbecue shredded pork on goat-cheese grits; roasted almond and mixed-berry pancakes; Tahitian French toast à l'orange; herb-crusted ahi tuna; panko-crusted chicken breast; Islands sushi sampler for two.

ENTERTAINMENT AND AMENITIES Character dining available on Monday, Tuesday, and Saturday evenings. Other entertainment such as face painters and hula dancers appear other nights; call ahead to confirm.

SUMMARY AND COMMENTS Breakfast here is a treat—the specialties are all tasty and (surprisingly) moderately priced. Lunch and dinner are good, too, but with all the other restaurants around, especially if you're spending the day in the parks, we suggest having a hearty breakfast here and a lighter lunch elsewhere.

Lombard's Seafood Grille   ★★½

SEAFOOD	MODERATE	QUALITY ★★★½	VALUE ★★★

Universal Studios/San Francisco; ☎ 407-363-8000

Customers Park guests. **Reservations** Accepted. **When to go** Anytime. **Entree range** $11–$20. **Payment** AE, D, DC, MC, V. **Service rating** ★★★. **Friendliness rating** ★★. **Parking** Universal Orlando garage. **Bar** Full service. **Wine selection** Good. **Dress** Casual. **Disabled access** Good. **Hours** Daily, 11:30 a.m. until 2 hours before park closes or until park closing, depending on park attendance. Call to verify hours, as there is no set schedule.

SETTING AND ATMOSPHERE Situated on the park's main lagoon, Lombard's looks like a converted wharf-side warehouse. The centerpiece of the brick-walled room is a huge aquarium with bubble-glass windows. A fish-sculpture fountain greets guests.

HOUSE SPECIALTIES Shrimp cioppino ratatouille; ravioli with five cheeses; fried shrimp; fresh fish selections.

SUMMARY AND COMMENTS Lombard's Seafood Grille is now more casually focused. Unfortunately, so is the kitchen. There are arguably better food options in the park, but as one of only two full-service restaurants in Universal Studios park, the place can be crowded.

Mama Della's   ★★★

ITALIAN	EXPENSIVE	QUALITY ★★★	VALUE ★★★

Portofino Bay Hotel; ☎ 407-503-DINE

Customers Hotel guests. **Reservations** Suggested during high season. **When to go** Dinner. **Entree range** $17–$32. **Payment** AE, D, DC, MC, V. **Service rating** ★★★. **Friendliness rating** ★★★★. **Parking** Valet or self-park; $5 charge for valet. **Bar** Full service. **Wine selection** Good. **Dress** Nice casual. **Disabled access** Good. **Hours** Daily, 5–10 p.m.

SETTING AND ATMOSPHERE Just like being in the dining room of a home in Tuscany, with hardwood floors, provincial printed wallpaper, and wooden furniture.

HOUSE SPECIALTIES Baked clams with garlic and oregano; gnochetti with Bolognese sauce; grilled shrimp, scallops, and grouper on cappellini; seared rib-eye steak; chocolate praline crunch cake; lemon cheesecake; and panna cotta.

ENTERTAINMENT AND AMENITIES Strolling musicians on select nights.

SUMMARY AND COMMENTS This falls on the fancy scale somewhere in between Bice and Trattoria del Porto. Traditional Italian food is served in a comfortable atmosphere conducive of a special meal, but not quite as extravagant as its lavish neighbor, Bice. If you want food (almost) as tasty but for (a bit) less dough, Mama Della's is a great choice.

Mythos ★★★

STEAK/SEAFOOD	MOD/EXP	QUALITY ★★★★	VALUE ★★★

Islands of Adventure/The Lost Continent; ☎ 407-224-4533

Customers Park guests. **Reservations** Accepted. **When to go** Early evening. **Entree range** $10–$19. **Payment** AE, D, DC, MC, V. **Service rating** ★★. **Friendliness rating** ★★★. **Parking** Universal Orlando garage. **Bar** Full service. **Wine selection** Good. **Dress** Casual. **Disabled access** Good. **Hours** Daily, 11:30 a.m.–3 p.m. or until park closing; call ahead for closing time.

SETTING AND ATMOSPHERE A grotto-like atmosphere to suggest you're eating in a cave. Large picture windows look out over the central lagoon to the Incredible Hulk roller coaster. You can time your meal by coaster launchings.

HOUSE SPECIALTIES Tempura shrimp sushi; coq au vin; cedar-plank salmon; beef filet; risotto of the day.

SUMMARY AND COMMENTS This was originally the park's one stab at fine dining, but few guests seem to be looking for this sort of dining experience, especially after getting soaked on one of the water-based rides. Things are now more casual, but there is still an emphasis on quality. The food is above-average theme-park eats, and the setting provides a pleasant retreat. Make your reservation early if you want to dine here.

NASCAR Sports Grille ★★

AMERICAN	MODERATE	QUALITY ★★★	VALUE ★★

CityWalk; ☎ 407-224-7223

Customers Racing fans. **Reservations** Not accepted. **When to go** Anytime. **Entree range** $10–$28. **Payment** AE, D, DC, MC, V. **Service rating** ★★. **Friendliness rating** ★★. **Parking** Universal Orlando garage. **Bar** Full service. **Wine selection** Modest. **Dress** Casual; grease-stained jumpsuits okay. **Disabled access** Good. **Hours** Daily, 10 a.m.–11 p.m.

SETTING AND ATMOSPHERE The dining area is on the second level of this two-story building. As you might expect, the room is decorated with a myriad of memorabilia from the world of NASCAR. A full-sized replica of a race car hangs overhead and occasionally revs up, its wheels spinning, and speakers roar with realistic trackside noise.

HOUSE SPECIALTIES Bill France pork chop; filet; rib eye; Smoky Mountain barbecue ribs.

SUMMARY AND COMMENTS This is strictly for serious NASCAR fans who can't get enough of it. And the food? With all those signs for motor oil hanging all over the place, do you have to ask?

NBA City ★★★

AMERICAN	MODERATE	QUALITY ★★★	VALUE ★★★

CityWalk; ☎ 407-363-5919

Customers Basketball fans. **Reservations** Not accepted. **When to go** Anytime. **Entree range** $10–$20. **Payment** AE, D, DC, MC, V. **Service rating** ★★★. **Friendliness rating** ★★★. **Parking** Universal Orlando garage. **Bar** Full service. **Wine selection** Modest. **Dress** Casual. **Disabled access** Good. **Hours** Daily, 11 a.m.–11 p.m.

SETTING AND ATMOSPHERE A giant statue of Logoman, the official NBA figure, guards the entrance to the restaurant. The building is designed to resemble an older arena, complete with an overhead track that circles the main dining floor. Booths line the walls, and each has a TV that plays scenes from great basketball games.

HOUSE SPECIALTIES Grilled salmon; double-thick pork chops; chicken stuffed with mozzarella and spinach; New York strip steak.

SUMMARY AND COMMENTS This was originally another concept from the next-door neighbor, Hard Rock Cafe, but the two entities split soon after this prototype opened. But some of HRC's theme-restaurant quality rubbed off. As themes go, this one is done well. Basketball fans will enjoy the videos and the arcade games in the outer lobby.

Pastamore ★★★½

ITALIAN	MODERATE	QUALITY ★★★★	VALUE ★★★★

CityWalk; ☎ 407-224-2244

Customers Park guests. **Reservations** Priority seating. **When to go** Anytime. **Entree range** $15–$28. **Payment** AE, D, MC, V. **Service rating** ★★. **Friendliness rating** ★★★. **Parking** Universal Orlando garage. **Bar** Full service. **Wine selection** Good Italian wines. **Dress** Casual. **Disabled access** Good. **Hours** Daily, 5 p.m.–midnight.

SETTING AND ATMOSPHERE A very hip sort of neoclassic design with high walls of green, purple, and yellow. The ceiling is tiered and features angles and curves that flow through the large space. Romanesque statues and artistic depictions of Italian landscapes dot the room. An open kitchen is at the rear of the restaurant. Outdoor seating is available.

HOUSE SPECIALTIES Veal parmigiana; chicken piccata; veal Marsala; fettuccine Alfredo; mussels marinara; calamari.

SUMMARY AND COMMENTS The kitchen puts forth a decent effort, even though the food is not quite authentic Italian. Family-style dinners, including antipasti, soup, salad, two entrees, and dessert, are available for $20 per person. Not a bad deal if you're really hungry. For an even better deal, book the chef's table, which is actually a counter overlooking the open kitchen. For a relatively modest fee, you'll have your own personal chef who will create a special menu.

Pat O'Brien's ★★★

CAJUN	INEXPENSIVE	QUALITY ★★★½	VALUE ★★★★

CityWalk; ☎ 407-224-2106

Customers Tourists. **Reservations** Not accepted. **When to go** Anytime. **Entree range** $8–$17. **Payment** AE, D, DC, MC, V. **Service rating** ★★. **Friendliness rating** ★★★. **Parking** Universal Orlando garage. **Bar** Full service. **Wine selection** Modest. **Dress** Casual. **Disabled access** Good. **Hours** Daily, 4 p.m.–1 a.m.

SETTING AND ATMOSPHERE A fairly faithful rendition of the original Pat O'Brien's in New Orleans, right down to the fire-and-water fountain in the courtyard. The outdoor dining area is the most pleasant place to eat; inside areas feature a noisy bar and another room with dueling pianos.

HOUSE SPECIALTIES Shrimp gumbo; jambalaya; muffuletta; red beans and rice.

SUMMARY AND COMMENTS The food is surprisingly good, and surprisingly affordable. Be careful about ordering a Hurricane, the restaurant's signature drink. You are automatically charged for the souvenir glass, and if you don't want it, you must turn it in at the bar for a refund.

Trattoria del Porto ★★★

ITALIAN MODERATE	QUALITY ★★★	VALUE ★★

Portofino Bay Hotel; ☎ 407-503-DINE

Customers Hotel guests. **Reservations** Suggested for dinner. **When to go** Lunch. **Entree range** Lunch, $10–$17; dinner, $15–$30. **Payment** AE, D, DC, MC, V. **Service rating** ★★★. **Friendliness rating** ★★★. **Parking** Valet or self-park; $5 charge for valet. **Bar** Full service. **Wine selection** Average. **Dress** Resort casual. **Disabled access** Good. **Hours** Daily, 7 a.m.–11 p.m., but closed for dinner Tuesday and Wednesday.

SETTING AND ATMOSPHERE Like a boisterous down-home Italian kitchen.

HOUSE SPECIALTIES gnocchi verdi; grouper Milanese; filet mignon; open-faced ravioli with gulf shrimp; pizza Bianca; meatball sandwich.

ENTERTAINMENT AND AMENITIES Character dining available on select evenings; call ahead to confirm.

SUMMARY AND COMMENTS Where Mama Della's succeeds in not feeling like a hotel restaurant, Trattoria del Porto does not. The food is perfectly fine and moderately priced (relatively speaking) but lunch is your best option here. Omelettes at breakfast can set you back more than $10, and dinner options are limited. If the poolside snack bar isn't your thing, or if you must try a meal here, lunch is your best bet.

Wantilan Luau ★★★★

HAWAIIAN	MODERATE	QUALITY ★★★	VALUE ★★★

Royal Pacific Hotel; ☎ 407-503-DINE

Customers Tourists. Reservations Accepted. When to go Dinner only. Buffet $49.50 adults; $29 children ages 3–11. (Prices include tax, gratuity for everyone, and mai tais, wine, and beer for guests ages 21 and older.) Payment AE, D, DC, MC, V. Service rating ★★★. Friendliness rating ★★★★. Parking Valet or self-park; $5 charge for valet. Bar Mai tais, wine, and beer available. Dress Flowered shirts, beachy casual. Disabled access Average. Hours Every Saturday night year-round; an additional Friday night show runs from May through early September.

SETTING AND ATMOSPHERE A typical luau setting with tiki torches and wooden tables.

HOUSE SPECIALTIES Buffet includes pit-roasted suckling pig with spiced rum-soaked pineapple purée; guava-barbecued short ribs; whole roasted South Pacific wahoo; lomi lomi chicken with Maui onions; tropical fruits.

ENTERTAINMENT AND AMENITIES Polynesian dancing, storytelling, hula dancers, live music.

SUMMARY AND COMMENTS This is a fun diversion and a change of scenery from the other restaurants offered on Universal property. Though dinner is a bit expensive, the entertainment is worth it. A separate children's buffet keeps kids happy with offerings like chicken fingers, macaroni, and pizza.

ACCOMMODATIONS INDEX

RESTAURANT INDEX

SUBJECT INDEX

Unofficial Guide Reader Survey

If you'd like to express your opinion about traveling in Central Florida or this guidebook, complete the following survey and mail it to:

Unofficial Guide Reader Survey
P.O. Box 43673
Birmingham, AL 35243

Inclusive dates of your visit:_____

Members of your party:

	Person 1	Person 2	Person 3	Person 4	Person 5
Gender:	M F	M F	M F	M F	M F
Age:					

How many times have you been to Central Florida?_____
On your most recent trip, where did you stay?_____

Concerning your accommodations, on a scale of 100 as best and 0 as worst, how would you rate:

The quality of your room?   The value of your room?
The quietness of your room?   Check-in/checkout efficiency?
Shuttle service to the airport?   Swimming-pool facilities?

Did you rent a car?_____   From whom?_____

Concerning your rental car, on a scale of 100 as best and 0 as worst, how would you rate:

Pickup-processing efficiency?____   Return-processing efficiency?____
Condition of the car?____   Cleanliness of the car?____
Airport-shuttle efficiency?____

Concerning your dining experiences:
Estimate your meals in restaurants per day?_____
Approximately how much did your party spend on meals per day?____
_____

Favorite restaurants in Central Florida: _____
_____

Did you buy this guide before leaving? _____ While on your trip?_____

How did you hear about this guide? (check all that apply)

Loaned or recommended by a friend ☐   Radio or TV ☐
Newspaper or magazine ☐   Bookstore salesperson ☐
Just picked it out on my own ☐   Library ☐
Internet ☐

What other guidebooks did you use on this trip? _____

_____

_____

On a scale of 100 as best and 0 as worst, how would you rate them?

_____

_____

Using the same scale, how would you rate the *Unofficial Guide*(s)?

_____

Are *Unofficial Guides* readily available at bookstores in your area? _____

Have you used other *Unofficial Guides*? _____

Which one(s)? _____

_____

Comments about your Central Florida trip or the *Unofficial Guide*(s):

_____

_____

_____

_____

_____

_____

_____

_____

_____

_____

_____

_____

_____

_____

_____